ENCOUNTERS
WITH DARKNESS

ENCOUNTERS WITH DARKNESS

French and German Writers on World War II

Frederick J. Harris

New York   Oxford
OXFORD UNIVERSITY PRESS
1983

Copyright © 1983 by Frederick J. Harris

Library of Congress Cataloging in Publication Data

Harris, Frederick John, 1943–
Encounters with darkness, French and German
writers on World War II.

Bibliography: p.
Includes index.
1. French literature—20th century—History and
criticism.   2. German literature—20th century—
History and criticism.   3. World War, 1939–1945—
Literature and the war.   I. Title.
PQ307.W4H3   1983   840′.9′358   82-12576
ISBN 0-19-503246-2

Printing (last digit):   9 8 7 6 5 4 3 2 1

Printed in the United States of America

Permission to reprint from material in copyright is gratefully acknowl-
edged.

HEINRICH BÖLL: From GROUP PORTRAIT WITH LADY, En-
glish translation, copyright © 1973 by Heinrich Böll and Leila Vennewitz, reprinted by permission of Joan Daves, Verlag Kiepenheuer
& Witsch GmbH, and Martin Secher & Warburg Limited.

BERTOLT BRECHT: From "The Visions of Simone Machard," written in collaboration with Lion Feuchtwanger, translated by Ralph
Manheim, from COLLECTED PLAYS, copyright © 1957 by Suhrkamp Verlag, reprinted by permission of Random House, Inc.

LOTHAR-GÜNTHER BUCHHEIM: From THE BOAT, translated
by Denver and Helen Lindley, copyright © 1975 by Alfred A. Knopf,
Inc., reprinted by permission of Alfred A. Knopf, Inc.

LOUIS-FERDINAND CELINE: From FEERIE POUR UNE AUTRE
FOIS, II. NORMANCE, copyright 1954 by Editions Gallimard, re-

In memory of my father who was killed
August 2, 1944, fighting in the
American army in the liberation of France.

Preface

This book is a study of World War II in France and Germany as French and German fiction and drama have portrayed it. For purposes of analysis I have chosen to retain the distinction that earlier war literature traditionally maintained between the battlefront and the homefront. This distinction is, however, no longer entirely valid in a war in which the homefront so rapidly became the battlefront and in which "every soldier who pulled a trigger found a child in his line of fire."[1] World War II was different from any other war that had ever been fought. The Spanish Civil War was only a kind of dress rehearsal for the major production. Both in terms of the technology available and of the atrocities committed against civilian populations, either as a direct result of the fighting or more cruelly still, because they were the specifically designated victims of Nazi ideology, World War II was an experience without precedent. The writings of Barbusse, the early Remarque, or Kafka, Picasso's painting *Guernica,* and films like Jean Renoir's *La Grande Illusion* had not prepared mankind for the ordeal that befell it. To evoke and re-create the events, settings, and situations of this war those who wrote about it have made ample use of the literary techniques of the past. Some, however, reached beyond these techniques to seek out new stylistic and structural devices, for the old styles and structures no longer always adequately translated the experience.

This book has two aims: first, to examine what kind of war it was that Sartre, Saint-Exupéry, Céline, Remarque, Grass, Böll, and others have portrayed in fiction, drama, and some diary excerpts and other autobiographical notations that I have selected for consideration because I believe them to be among the most interesting, representative, and revealing of the texts dealing with World War II; and second, to show just how and by what literary means they described the war. I have limited myself to the war as it was fought between France and Germany and as it was experienced on the homefront by the French and German people.

On the whole the number of French books chosen exceeds that of the German books. Aside from those who left metropolitan France for a kind of self-imposed exile in North Africa or America and those who fled to England to help carry on the fight, the war and the Occupation placed the vast majority of the French in frequent if not daily contact with the Germans. For France, World War II was almost exclusively a war against Germany, and French literature appropriately reflects that fixation. But even though the Occupation of France lasted over four years, the war in France was over much too quickly to excite Germany's imagination or challenge her stamina. For the average German these challenges came in Russia, at Stalingrad or thereafter, or on the homefront as the Allied bombings of Germany increased in momentum after 1942. To study German literature as it evolved out of the experiences on the Russian front would be of very certain interest. But it would be of little relevance in a book whose primary focus is on the war in France and the aftermath of the French defeat; namely, the German Occupation, the French Résistance, and the transfer of numerous French in one capacity or another to Germany. On the other hand, the German experience on the homefront is of crucial importance. In 1940 virtually the whole French army was made prisoner of war and taken off to Germany; later, French laborers volunteered or were conscripted to work on German farms and in German factories, French detainees were earmarked for German concentration camps either because they were involved in anti-German activities like those of the Résistance or simply because they were Jews, and finally, as the war drew to a close, French collaborators hoping to escape their country's vengeance looked to Germany for refuge and

won at least temporary asylum there. One cannot understand
the war in France, it seems to me, and the aftermath of her
defeat without knowing something about the Germans and the
society from which they came. For they were the ones who
waged the war, administered the Occupation, and received,
primarily because of the obligations they themselves imposed
on France, a whole variety of French people onto their soil.
World War II effected drastic movements among the populations of Europe, and from the beginning of the war in 1939 to
its end in 1945 French and Germans found themselves willingly or unwillingly living on each other's territory and en-
meshed in each other's destiny. This fact has led me to cross
national boundaries and to bridge two conceivably distinct areas
of literary investigation.

I have attempted as far as possible to preserve an accurate
historical context in this book. World War II continues to hold
the world's imagination. For scholars and professionals in many
fields as well as for the general public it remains one of the
pivotal events of life in the twentieth century. In writing this
study I have sought to address myself to a relatively broad audience whose literary and historical knowledge may vary consid-
erably. This was a major consideration in fixing the historical
circumstances that helped generate the literary texts.

I have chosen to present the material of this book in topical
fashion. The chapters delineate areas of historical and human
experience. The literary texts, of course, do not always allow
themselves to be so neatly apportioned. The texts of Günter
Grass and Heinrich Böll's *Gruppenbild mit Dame*, for example,
are really frescoes that paint pictures of German society going
back long before the start of World War II and ending well
after its conclusion. The topical method of presentation has inevitably led to a dividing-up of many of the literary works
among the various chapters with the result that something of
the impact generated by the totality of these works may have
been sacrificed. That sacrifice, which I have sought to minimize
as much as possible, seemed less heavy a price to pay than the
redundancy of subject matter, the inevitable aridity, and the
loss of an overall perspective that would have followed from a
presentation organized around individual authors or texts.

The books I have chosen to include are not of equal literary value. Some, in fact, have greater value as historical documents than as literature, and I have included them for the historical relevance of the scenes they describe. A good historical setting, however, does not necessarily make for a good piece of literature. On the other hand, literature itself stands in ambivalent relationship to history. It can be a faithful mirror of historical reality or a distorting one. Literary and historical truth are not necessarily the same, and the truth of a literary work does not altogether depend on its historical veracity. Furthermore, literature may chose to deal with certain historical situations and to neglect others; or it may emphasize certain situations and de-emphasize others. In the end, of course, literature triumphs over history, whether the image it conveys be the real or the distorted one, making that image more lasting and more real, as Flaubert perceived over a century ago, than historical reality. Literary truth takes form in the contact established between reader and text. Out of that contact an artistic reality is apprehended. On an intellectual as well as on an emotional plane the reader experiences the events or situations described. He lives through them, interiorizes them, and personalizes them. In fact, he re-creates them, though the degree to which he can and must re-create will depend to some extent on the demands of the particular text confronting him. Literary criticism today has taken on perspectives quite different from those after World War I when the primary and often only criterion applied to a literary text on the war was its faithfulness to the historical reality of the battlefield.

Authors of novels or plays will on occasion take the liberty of adjusting historical facts or situations to suit their own purposes. If they are writing some time after the events, they may reshape historical material and use it to comment on some aspect of the world in which they live. Some of the texts considered in this book, moreover, reflect an author's personal vision and make no pretense at objectivity. But these texts also were generated out of the "matter" of World War II, and must be taken into account in the overall attempt to be objective. On the nature of literary and historical truth, Céline's "German" trilogy discussed in the last chapter of this book is a case in point. Though the three novels of the trilogy are ostensibly chronicle novels, they all show a hearty disregard for the constraints of time and space. These two factors may be critical to the historian but they need not be critical to the novelist. Céline's whole artistic structure in the first of the novels, *D'un château l'autre,* revolves precisely around the violation of these constraints. The chronological and historical structure would have been an impediment to expressing the intellectual, and even more important in Céline's case, the emotional truth at which he is aiming, and so he discards it. By the very nature of this present study, literary truth has necessarily been my primary concern.

In the interests of economy I have, with some regret, not included the original French and German texts of the citations quoted in this book. I am consoled, however, by the fact that the vast number of books from which these citations are taken are readily accessible in their original form to those who wish to consult them. Where published translations of works mentioned in this book already exist, I have generally used them in citing relevant passages. Unless otherwise indicated, however, the translations are my own.

I wish to offer special thanks to Professor Henri Peyre for his kind willingness to read the manuscript and the proofs and for his wise and constructive suggestions; and to Professor Germaine Brée for her attentive reading of the proofs and her carefully considered critical perspective. Very sincere thanks, too, to Tony Outhwaite, Sallie Reynolds, and Kathy Antrim for their always excellent editorial advice, patience, and encouragement.

Contents

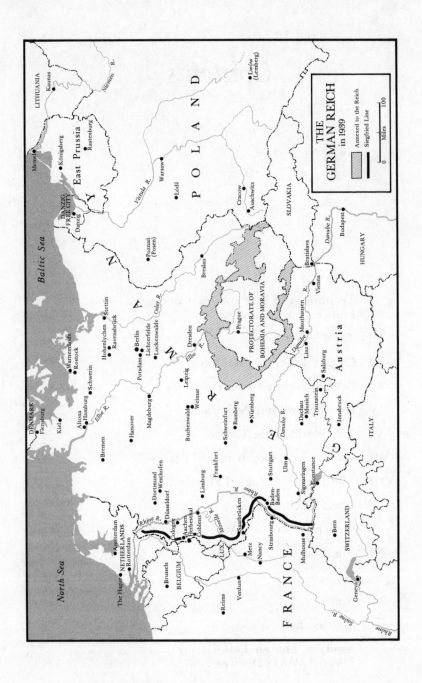

THE
GERMAN REICH
in 1939

Annexed to the Reich
Siegfried Line

Miles
0   100

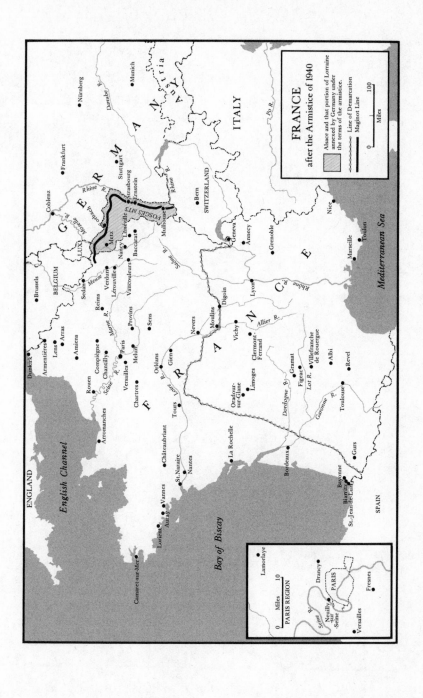

FRANCE
after the Armistice of 1940

Alsace and that portion of Lorraine
annexed by Germany under
the terms of the armistice.
Line of Demarcation
Maginot Line

0   100
Miles

ENCOUNTERS
WITH DARKNESS

CHAPTER I

Technological War and the Fall of France

By the end of May 1940, the fate of France had been sealed. Ever since the German invasion of Poland the preceding September, and even before that, the government and the military had been reduced to a state of continual debate, indecision, and intrigue. Certainly it would be inaccurate to say that France had been sleeping through the 1930s. By 1935 the Maginot Line, which journalist-historian William Shirer calls "the most formidable line of defensive works the world had ever seen," was virtually complete. It stretched across the northeastern corner of France from Alsace-Lorraine along the west bank of the Rhine and then westward to Luxembourg; and this Maginot Line, it was widely thought, would deter any German invasion of France. History, to be sure, had shown that since Roman times, and even as recently as World War I, the classic invasion route from Germany into France lay not across the Rhine, which provided a natural frontier that would make invasion difficult, but rather through Belgium. But this question, too, had been considered. Should Germany again invade Belgium, as she had done in 1914, French troops would simply have to move into Belgium to help out. Of course, many felt that France might first have to wait to be asked before taking such a step. In any case, to extend the Maginot Line along the Belgian frontier seemed out of the question. First of all, it would prove costly, and furthermore, it would leave the impression that France was abandoning Belgium to whatever destiny Germany might be preparing for her.[1]

Knowing that the Maginot Line was there bred a misguided and ill-timed sense of security in France. Unfortunately for France, the Line itself was conceived in light of the static trench warfare of World War I, and was intended to be nothing more than an impenetrable defensive entrenchment. When the German Luftwaffe attacked in Holland, Belgium, Luxembourg, and northeastern France early on the morning of Friday, May 10, 1940, the French were not prepared to meet the assault. The lessons of the blitzkrieg in Poland the previous September were lost on those who might have been in a position to help avert the impending disaster.

France declared war on Germany over the invasion of Poland late in the afternoon on September 3, 1939. But aside from the general mobilization that had already been ordered on September 1 and some movement of troops to the German border, very little happened for the next eight months. In Paris people settled in, not knowing what to expect at first and then adapting to the idea that they were simply going to have to wait to find out. The trains were full of soldiers; the Métro no longer made all the stops; people stood in lines to await the distribution of gas masks; movies, bars, and dancing halls were temporarily closed, and café patrons were expected to settle their bills immediately on being served so they could make a hasty exit in case of an alert. Jean-Paul Sartre had already left for Nancy from the Gare de l'Est on September 2, bound for military duty, and his friend and companion, author Simone de Beauvoir, who had been hoping against hope that war would not come, noted in her diary, quoted in *La Force de l'âge* (1960), that she had begun reading André Gide's diary of 1914.[2] Perhaps she expected it to give her some bearings.

In the east the "French army was poorly organized and inert," recalls Jean Dutourd in a series of memoir-essays published as *Les Taxis de la Marne* in 1956. Dutourd spent a very brief period in the army before being taken prisoner by the Germans in June 1940.

> The gunners settled down in the Maginot Line like apartment-house janitors, trailing about the corridors in slippers, playing innumerable games of cards under the silent guns, yawning from morning to night. The French army became so bored in its quar-

ters that actors and singers were sent to entertain it. . . . As the months went by, the war more and more began to look like a huge picnic that was smothering our frontiers with greasy paper and sausage skins.

On the night of September 7, some French forces crossed into Germany southeast of Saarbrücken and were subsequently reinforced. Germany was heavily engaged in Poland and mounted no real opposition against the French. Those German forces that were in the area withdrew to the shelter of their own defensive entrenchment, the Westwall, which the British called the Siegfried Line and the French "la ligne Siegfried," some eight miles north of the border. The French advanced about five miles on a fifteen-mile front, and then on September 12 were ordered to halt the advance and withdraw to the safety of the Maginot Line. What the French called a *drôle de guerre* and the Germans a *Sitzkrieg* had begun. Facing across the border, French and German soldiers watched each other almost playfully: ". . . the German soldiers sent the French friendly messages over their loudspeakers. To salve their consciences the French, through their own loudspeakers, shouted back, 'merde'."[3]

The German invasion of May 10, 1940, ended this "phoney war," as the British, in their turn, referred to it. Between May 10 and June 4, the day of the final evacuation of British and French troops from Dunkirk, German planes, tanks, and infantry overran the Netherlands, Belgium, and all of northern France from Luxembourg to the Strait of Dover.

Historians and politicians have been baffled by the limited use France made of her air power during the German invasion. According to testimony given to a Parliamentary Investigating Committee after the war by Guy La Chambre, the French Air Minister from 1938 to 1940, the French air force had a total of 3289 modern planes at the start of the German offensive, among which were 2122 fighters, 461 bombers, 429 reconnaissance and 277 observation planes. But only 790 fighters, 140 bombers, 170 reconnaissance and 210 observation planes—a total of 1310—were ever at the front.[4] Small wonder that so many in the French fighting force felt themselves betrayed. In *Pilote de guerre* (1942) Antoine de Saint-Exupéry, himself a French air force pilot, recalls that

> . . . the French army never saw French aeroplanes. We had roughly one thousand planes scattered between Dunkerque and Alsace. Diluted in infinity, so far as the men on the ground were concerned. The result was that when a plane roared across our lines, it was virtually certain to be German.[5]

What rapidly became clear in those spring days of 1940, despite the limited engagement of the French air force, was that this was going to be a new kind of war. Technology, particularly in the air, had made gigantic strides since the days of World War I, and the Germans were taking full advantage. But technology also placed new demands on the ability of the human spirit to survive.

The technological nature of World War II is reflected in the literature it inspired. Among those flying reconnaissance missions for the French air force that May was Saint-Exupéry. *Pilote de guerre,* which pulls together various details of his experience as a reconnaissance pilot, is a fictionalized rendition of one such mission to the city of Arras in northern France. André Malraux, too, who was already known as a novelist and thinker, tried to join up, preferably with the air force, but was rejected. He was admitted instead into the tank corps and stationed from November 1939 until May 1940 with a tank unit at Provins, southeast of Paris. He enlarged on the experience in *Les Noyers de l'Altenburg* (1943) in the story of his hero, Vincent Berger, advancing on the German lines in a tank in late May or early June 1940. A third book in which the writer or his hero functions locked up in a machine is Lothar-Günther Buchheim's *Das Boot* (1973). The story takes place long after the French defeat and is based on the author's experience as a naval war correspondent assigned to a German U-boat detachment docked at the naval station of La Baule-Saint-Nazaire in the outer harbor of Nantes in Brittany. It tells of a U-boat expedition late in 1941 from Saint-Nazaire out into the North Atlantic, then south to the Mediterranean and back to home port.

Technology had rendered the hand-to-hand combat and even the trench stalemates of World War I obsolete. Men were now fighting each other with machines, and only rarely did they see the enemy with the unaided eye.

Fighting the War in the Air

Pilote de guerre is a tale of the artist as pilot and technician. Physically confined to his aircraft for the duration of the flight, he is free only in his imagination to transcend the machine as he looks upon the ruin of his country below. His body is assimilated, as it were, by the machine. In the realization that, among other things, he is dependent for oxygen, and therefore, for life itself on the proper functioning of the plane's mechanisms, Saint-Exupéry concludes: "The plane is my wet-nurse. Before we took off, this thought seemed to me inhuman; but now, suckled by the plane itself, I feel a sort of filial affection for it. The affection of a nursling."[6] To some extent war has always deprived the soldier of his physical freedom: "the soldier's body becomes a stack of accessories that are no longer his property."[7] The novelty of this war lay in the fact that for the first time and on a large scale, men relinquished their freedom to a technology on which they were almost totally dependent.

The city of Arras was abandoned to the Germans by the British on the night of May 23, and the French commander-in-chief, General Maxime Weygand, used the British withdrawal as a pretext for calling off a counter-attack. When Saint-Exupéry begins his story of the last days of May 1940, it was for the French "a time of full retreat, of full disaster." According to Saint-Exupéry there were only fifty reconnaissance crews available for the whole French army, twenty-three of which were assigned to his unit. Each of these crews consisted of three men, the pilot, an observer and a gunner, and of the twenty-three crews, seventeen had vanished in the course of three weeks. In the light of these statistics, it was clearly absurd to attempt to fly over German-held Arras. His mission could change nothing of the destiny that was ravishing France.

> It was as if you dashed glassfuls of water into a forest fire in the hope of putting it out. . . . Throughout the closing days of the French campaign one impression dominated all others—an impression of absurdity. Everything was cracking up all around

us. Everything was caving in. The collapse was so entire that death
itself seemed to us absurd. Death, in such a tumult, had ceased to
count.[8]

Not everyone was capable of philosophizing. As May turned
into June, the roads leading from northern France to the south
were jammed with refugees fleeing the oncoming Germans.
Pushing down from the Somme, German troops entered Paris
on June 14. It has been estimated that by the third week in
June more than eight million refugees were strung out on the
roads of France. In Paris itself it is estimated that of its usual
five million only 700,000 persons were in the city on the day it
fell.[9]

In World War I and in every war that preceded it there had
always been a zone of fighting called the "front," where battles
were fought by men who had volunteered or been drafted for
the task. One of the standard structural techniques of the World
War I novel, whether it was Barbusse's *Le Feu* (1917), Remarque's *Im Westen nichts Neues* (1929), or to a degree, even
Hemingway's *A Farewell to Arms* (1929), was to shift focus from
the battlefield to the homefront and back again, in order to
dramatize the differences between the two, to make more
graphic by contrast the horrors of the battle and the naïveté,
pettiness, and the seemingly total inability of the homefront to
comprehend what was happening in the trenches. In that war
French and German soldiers could still go home on furlough
to a world relatively untouched by the experiences they had
been a part of. The first half of Proust's "Le Temps retrouvé,"
the last book of *A la recherche du temps perdu,* is based upon the
often frivolous concerns of wartime Paris. When he could obtain leave, the French soldier especially, fighting on his own
soil, had sometimes to withdraw only as much as several miles
behind the front lines to find life as he had always known it. In
World War II there was no such escape. Western civilization
has taught us that fighting war is an affair for men. But Western man must unlearn the lessons of his civilization. "For the
aeroplane, dropping its bombs on towns behind the lines, has
made this such a war as was never dreamt of."[10]

"Où est la guerre?" the soldiers seem to be asking in *Pilote de guerre*, in a way reminiscent of Stendhal's Fabrice avidly searching for his hero Napoleon and for the battle at Waterloo. The answer was that war was at once everywhere and nowhere. It was everywhere because it could no longer be confined to a front. It was nowhere because it could not be identified by those indicators that had traditionally revealed it. Saint-Exupéry relates the story of a French artillery officer entangled in a swarm of refugees trying to set up his "seventy-five" beside the road. Opposite him, a German who, missing his target, mowed down instead the refugees who happened to be in his line of fire. French women rushed upon the French lieutenant who was stubbornly attempting to hold his untenable position with all of twelve men and shouted at them: "Go away! Go away! You cowards!" Whereupon, the lieutenant and his men went away.[11]

War does not always live up to the expectations it generates. Tolstoy's *War and Peace* made that abundantly clear, and so did a whole body of World War I literature exemplified by Henri Barbusse's *Le Feu* and Erich Maria Remarque's *Im Westen nichts Neues*. But World War II, even more than other wars, failed to conform to people's imaginings. Because there was no front in the classical sense of the term, because women and children were immersed in the fighting as deeply and often deeper than the soldiers themselves, because the situation in France by late May 1940 seemed so entirely hopeless that it was simply not worth sending more reconnaissance crews to their death, the war that was being fought did not resemble a real war: ". . . no part of it makes sense. . . . not a single blueprint fits the circumstances. . . . the puppets have been cut free of the strings which continue to be pulled." The only thing left was to play at war, and play according to the rules, for "everyone knows what war looks like."

> Handsome horsemen transmit the orders—or rather, to be modern about it, motorcyclists. The orders ordain events, change the face of the world. The handsome horsemen are like the stars— they bring tidings of the future. In the midst of turmoil and despair, orders arrive, flung to the troops from the backs of steaming horses. And then all is well—at least, so says the blueprint of

war. So says the pretty picture-book of war. Everybody struggles
as hard as he can to make war look like war. Piously respects the
rules of the game. So that war may perhaps be good enough to
agree to look like war.[12]

In this context Saint-Exupéry recalls an incident that occurred
on base the night before he flew to Arras. He was driving in a
motorcar, and as he approached the aerodrome, he found himself face to face with the ridiculous pantomine of a sentry presenting his bayonet. "We are playing Cops and Robbers. . . .
We are abiding scrupulously by the rules of conduct prescribed
by the history books and the rules of tactics prescribed by the
war manuals. . . . We are playing at presenting bayonets to
German tanks. But the tanks are playing their own game."[13]

The mass evacuations in northern France were also part of
this game of making war look like war. Even in cases where
local officials were advised to halt the evacuations which could
serve no purpose in the end, they responded according to the
rules of wartime behavior that Western civilization had laid
down. Women and children were to be sheltered. Looking back
to a less civilized era, Saint-Exupéry's colleague Dutertre reflects: "The tragedy is that men have been taught that war is
an abnormal condition. In the past they would have stayed
home. War and life were the same thing."[14] But it would take
the local officials a month to adjust their consciences to the demands of a new age, and all the while they were adjusting their
consciences, the enemy was advancing.[15]

Finally, there was the shadow of death hovering over the
game. In the chaos that was France that May, death, too, had
its role to play. But it was a watered-down and shabby death
that appeared. Along with the towns and villages, hospitals were
being evacuated, and in the general evacuation "there is no real
death any longer. There are bodies that break down the way
cars do."[16] But death was by no means confined to the ill who
were removed from their hospitals. Daily it confronted those
who, in the prime of their health, were still playing at defend-
ing France.

The war scenario calls for dead people, and "we . . . were
agreeing to play the part of dead men merely because the show
called for dead supernumeraries."[17]

Though perhaps every war wittingly or unwittingly generates a romance of its own, World War I had gone a long way toward removing from the literature of war many specifically romantic elements inherited from the nineteenth century. *Pilote de guerre* consciously and consistently refuses the inspiration that romance and romanticism offer. Not content with robbing death of whatever heroism the war may have lent it, Saint-Exupéry removes himself and his plane out of the reach of romantic sensitivity. Nearing Arras he perceives some distant bursts of anti-aircraft fire and assumes that the Germans are trying to gauge his position and guide their fighter group toward him. From below, no doubt, he has already been observed for some time. "The German on the ground knows us by the pearly white scarf which every plane flying at high altitude trails behind like a bridal veil."[18] A pretty image! But just a few short chapters later he rejects and repudiates it, confusing the bride's veil with the train of her dress.

> It is hard to believe that I invented that disgusting literary image of a dress with a train. I couldn't have! For one thing, I have never seen the wake of my ship. Here in the cockpit, in which I fit like a pipe in its case, I can see nothing behind me. I see behind me through the eyes of my gunner. And then only if the intercom is working. My gunner never called down to me, "Adoring suitors aft in the wake of our train!"

The romance of the game has broken down. "Of course I should like to believe, I should like to fight, I should like to win. But try as a man will to pretend to believe, pretend to fight, pretend to win by setting fire to his own villages, it is hard to feel elation over pretense."[19] Historians and memoirists have commented again and again on the particular beauty of that spring of 1940 when France fell to the Germans, and the day assigned for the mission to Arras was one among many spectacular days. "It would be easy to write a couple of fraudulent pages out of the contrast between this shining spring day, the ripening fruit, the chicks filling plumply out in the barnyard, the rising wheat—and death at our elbow." Why not? Such ironic contrasts are well established in the domain of literature. But Saint-Exupéry deliberately rejects this one. "I shall not write that couple of pages because I see no reason why the peace of a spring day should constitute a contradiction of the idea of death. Why should the sweetness of life be a matter for irony?"[20]

When a man's world literally begins collapsing on all sides, and when he no longer believes in the validity of the work he is doing, where is he to find the bearings that will help him reconstruct his identity? Where will he find the words to help him understand and articulate his new experience? *Pilote de guerre* begins with a vision of the past, a vision of Saint-Exupéry's own childhood. "Surely I must be dreaming. It is as if I were fifteen again. My mind is on my geometry problem. Leaning over the worn black desk, I work dutifully with compass and ruler and protractor. I am quiet and industrious." The odors of the classroom, the sunshine outside, a tree branch swaying in the breeze—he can revel again, if only momentarily, in the "sense of security born of this dream of a sheltered childhood." But the dream soon ends. "The ruler, the T square, the compass have become weapons with which we shall build a world, triumph over an enemy. Playtime is over."[21] But as the book progresses, it becomes increasingly clear that, in another sense of the term, playtime continues, and that the geometric tools of the schoolboy have merely changed position and become the instrument panel of the plane. Now as then, the schoolboy defines himself in terms of his function. He does not think of the "war of the Nazi against the Occident,"[22] but rather of the possibility of wounds and the absurdity of flying over German-held Arras at 2000 feet. What is important is that he perform that function, that, like Camus's Sisyphus whose "rock was his thing,"[23] he do his job and fly over Arras.

Unfortunately for Saint-Exupéry, who by this time had quite a career in flying behind him—pioneering mail lines, being forced down among rebellious Arabs in the Sahara, and flying over the Andes—this flight to Arras did not even seem particularly adventurous: ". . . war is not a true adventure. It is a mere ersatz. . . . there is no adventure in head-or-tails, in betting the toss will come out life or death."[24]

With all sense of adventure gone, the job of flying to Arras degenerates into a mere rite. In executing the mission, the pilot does honor to that rite, but the rite itself is devoid of significance. Religious metaphor helps him to articulate this new experience. He feels like a Christian abandoned by grace.[25] When he dresses for his mission, it is as though he were a priest dressing for a religious service. But in this instance organs are added to his body that make a monster of him and rob him even further of his identity. Of course, France and her civilization, too, are being robbed of their identity. The pilot who can no longer see the "cathedral in which I live," dresses "for the service of a dead god."[26]

As the service progresses and the mission to Arras comes ever closer to completion, the pilot-priest of the cathedral France slowly but surely generates his own inspiration. For it is by his act that he unites himself with the sufferings and ambitions of the worshippers who make up the cathedral. He begins to understand things that were incomprehensible to him before. Certainly the villages of northern France that were burning from Alsace to the sea at Dunkirk could not for all that stop the German advance by even one day. But it was necessary to talk about sacrificing French villages, Saint-Exupéry admits, reminiscent of Proust who calmly resigned himself to the destruction done to Rheims cathedral during World War I. "When a war is on, a village ceases to be a cluster of traditions. The enemy who hold it have turned it into a nest of rats. Things no longer mean the same."[27]

Finally, burning Arras comes into sight, and the flames over the city are like a lamp in the nave of a cathedral. But still Saint-Exupéry is skeptical. "The lamp that was Arras was burning in the service of a cult, but at a price. By tomorrow it would have consumed Arras and itself have been consumed."[28]

As the plane heads back from Arras to the safety of the base, however, the pilot's attitude changes. Reverting to the image of the schoolboy at the start, he knows he will be able to report nothing of consequence to his commander and that he will flunk his examination. But as the feeling of oneness with the people of France takes increasing hold of him, he slowly comes to the realization that he has gone to war that day to preserve a certain light,[29] the light in the lamp of the cathedral perhaps, that lamp which in its religious symbolism is a sign of the presence of the real God. He has gone to war so that his own civilization, that "heritage of beliefs, customs, and knowledge slowly accumulated in the course of centuries,"[30] that heritage which was France, might continue to shine, however feebly, in the darkness. It is this civilization that opens up for us what Saint-Exupéry calls man's scope (*étendue*), the inner "distance granted him by the childhood home, by the chamber at Orconte,[31] by the field of vision of Pasteur's microscope; distance opened up by a poem." These are the "fragile and magical gifts that only a civilization can distribute. For distance is the property of the spirit, not of the eye; and there is no distance without language."[32]

The flight to Arras itself and later the book which it produced, and which, in turn, articulated the experience of Arras, opened up for Saint-Exupéry that inner distance to his own spirit of which he speaks. During the flight he had renounced his body and its fears, and in this renunciation had salvaged his spirit. He had renounced the individual in himself for the good of Man because of whom we are men.[33] How ironic that the technological machine of the airplane, notwithstanding its ability to soar above the earth, which might for its very technology be the perfect symbol of matter, should prove the instrument of so spiritual a discovery. Before his flight Saint-Exupéry had already ceased to be the "architect" of the cathedral; but realizing after Arras that the cathedral was more than the "sum of its stones," he would manage somehow to preserve the edifice intact. "Tomorrow we of France will enter into the night of defeat. May my country still exist when the day dawns again."[34]

In December 1940 Saint-Exupéry left Europe from Lisbon on a ship bound for New York, where he wrote virtually all of *Pilote de guerre,* publishing it first there in February 1942 and later that year with Gallimard in France. The book was banned by the German occupation authorities in Paris and withdrawn by Gallimard in February 1943. Saint-Exupéry remained in the United States until the spring of that year when he left to fight with the Allied forces in North Africa. On July 31, 1944, he flew his final mission, this one to the Grenoble-Annecy region of southeastern France. At forty-four he had already flown longer than his age would have permitted, and his superiors informed him that this mission was to be the last. It was, but in a way they could not have anticipated. Saint-Exupéry disappeared in flight.[35]

The War on Land

Vincent Berger, the central character in Malraux's *Les Noyers de l'Altenburg*, was able to see day dawn on France as he emerged from his tank, which had become stuck in a trap trying to make a foray against the German lines. In a very elementary way the sight it revealed gave him the consolation for which Saint-Exupéry was reaching. Berger functions as an alter ego for Malraux; and his experience, advancing on the German lines as part of a tank crew in late May or in early June 1940, is the one Malraux would have wanted for himself. He would have liked to be a hero, and Berger's adventure would have enabled him to play that role to the hilt. But at this juncture in his life art had to substitute for reality. In an interview with one of his biographers in 1973 Malraux concisely summed up his activities during the spring of 1940. The tanks at Provins where his unit was stationed southeast of Paris were unfit to be taken out of the training grounds. After a few maneuvers on foot and a bit of shooting he was slightly wounded on June 15, and the next day was taken prisoner at a point about halfway between Provins and Sens. During his first night in captivity he was housed together with other prisoners in Sens cathedral and later moved into a warehouse.[36] These were the facts. But Malraux, in the third and final part of *Les Noyers de l'Altenburg*, chose to write a substantially different version of his experience in the *drôle de guerre*. The fictionalized rendition was written in 1941, first published in Switzerland in 1943, and then brought out in limited edition by Gallimard after the war in 1948. Perhaps because of the aesthetic reservations he had about the book, he never allowed another printing. He did, however, use substantial portions of it, among them Berger's experience with the tank crew, which, except for several omissions, he transcribed almost verbatim, although in a different context, in the *Anti-mémoires* of 1967.

Like Saint-Exupéry, Malraux's protagonist allows the ma-

chine, however paradoxical this may seem, to solidify his relationship with the other men locked inside it and ultimately with
the concept of Man. As narrator Berger takes great care to introduce his three companions in the tank crew, Bonneau,
Léonard, and Pradé. But as much as he tries to individualize
them in his description, to a large degree they remain types
and even stereotypes, included only because they are necessary
to see Berger through his narration: Bonneau, the tough, whose
reputation is worse than the man; Léonard, the simple citizen
who knows how to think for himself, and who, suspicious of all
official pronouncements made by his superiors, considers the
Germans to be no different from people everywhere, an admixture of good and bad; and finally Pradé, a symbol of republican dignity,[37] who is less concerned with the progress of the
war than with the education and upbringing of his son now
being deprived of his father's presence and encouragement.
Pradé's son is his only vengeance against life,[38] a boy of eleven,
just the age Pradé himself had been at the time of World War
I. That war had prevented him from getting an education and
he does not want to see history repeat itself for his son. Ultimately, however, the narrator's concern is for himself, for himself as a part of humanity, to be sure, but a humanity that is
philosophically conceived rather than concretely individualized.
And if the narration plods ahead toward philosophical awakening at the conclusion, the narrator, not unlike the knights of
old, must suffer, struggle, and endure before the prize can be
attained. The war provides him with the test of his endurance
and the medium for his discovery.

War is an uprooting experience and, particularly when faced
with the possibility of the ultimate uprooting of death, people
will often reach back into the past in an attempt to define themselves, retrace their identity, and establish a continuity. Before
his flight to Arras, Saint-Exupéry drew upon the image of a
schoolboy working out a problem in geometry.[39] But neither
Malraux nor Berger ever seems to have felt uprooted in the
way Saint-Exupéry did, and even though the threat of death is
a real one as the tanks begin to advance, Berger states flatly,
"It is not true that one sees the whole of one's past life on the
point of death."[40] To describe the actual onslaught of battle

Berger, like Saint-Exupéry, reaches into the realm of metaphor, but the register is different. As he neared Arras, Saint-Exupéry found himself tempted to use the romantic image of the bridal veil to describe the wake of his plane and the pursuit of the German planes behind him.[41] Malraux was more of a realist and this kind of romantic imagery held little fascination for him. In his text, image and metaphor often have rather an informative function; that is, they impart what to most readers would otherwise be an experience completely outside their ken. Something the reader may have experienced or to which he can relate more easily helps the narrator at one and the same time to convey the experience and to humanize it. There is "no word to describe the sensation of advancing on the enemy, and yet it is as specific and as powerful as sexual desire or pain."[42]

As his tank advances, Berger becomes acutely conscious of man's relationship to the earth on which he is fighting. This consciousness is not a new one in the literary tradition of war. Remarque and Barbusse among others made it excruciatingly poignant in the exasperation of the trench stalemates of World War I. The earth can be a friend or an enemy. In World War I the rains made it an enemy for almost everybody. More disturbing, however, is the fact that in both world wars human beings had perverted the natural functions of the earth and made of it something it was not intended to be. "Nothing remained of the old harmony between man and earth: these cornfields through which we were lurching in the night were no longer cornfields but camouflage; the earth no longer bred crops, but traps and mines. . . ." In the *guerre mécanique* that was World War II, Berger in his tank recognized even before any encounter could take place that "the enemy was not the Germans, it was a broken track, a mine, or a tank trap."[43]

The mines mean instant death, and no one talks about them. Either you explode or you don't, says Berger, and so it is not a subject for conversation. The trench is another matter. As it turns out, Berger ends up caught in a kind of trench, a tank trap, and for much of the narrative he describes the attempt to escape. Much like Saint-Exupéry returning from Arras, he has begun to feel a sense of "communion in action performed at the price of blood."[44] He resorts to metaphor, and the metaphors he uses are gleaned from a simpler setting than the *guerre mécanique* of the tanks. Almost invariably they are taken directly from nature or from some pristine primeval setting that by way of the metaphor takes its revenge on the war and the tanks. When Léonard shouts out for Pradé his screams are "high-pitched yells like the cries of a bird in the cataclysmic silence. . . ." Meanwhile Pradé tries feverishly to manipulate the tank but succeeds only in tilting it excessively to the fore so that it sits in the hole "its tail in the air like a Japanese fish. . . ." He backs it out of that position and rams its rear into one of the walls of the trap so that the whole machine begins to vibrate "like an ax quivering in a tree trunk."[45]

Philosophically speaking, the situation in which Berger and his three companions find themselves, the tank trapped in a hole and the men trapped in the tank because they realize that to come out might be even more dangerous, is not unlike the one Camus chose to portray in *La Peste* (1947). Like the protagonists of *La Peste* the men in the tank know they must act, and eventually they overcome the inertia that took hold of them when disaster struck,[46] emerge from the tank, and survey their position. Part of one of the walls of the trap has collapsed and is now rising on a gentle incline, but the pit is covered with tree trunks, and the men, "petrified into Peruvian mummies" by each and every shell burst, are unable by their own brute force to move the trunks. So they retreat into their tank and try maneuvering it forward and up into the trunks. As the tank lunges to its task, the tracks finally gripping, it throws an unwary Berger, like a rock against the turret, "with the furious strength of a dying bull. . . ."[47] Again nature has explained the machine.

Berger and the three men, who in the course of the night have become his "oldest friends,"[48] soon enter a farming village the Germans have just evacuated and find sleep and shelter in a barn. Berger has come through the trial and is ripe for his reward. The morning awakening is to him what the flight back to his base was to Saint-Exupéry. The deadly night from which he and his companions have just emerged alive now seems to have been a "living night" (*nuit vivante*), that was like "a prodigious gift, like an immense germination."[49] It has given birth to new life, or rather, and more importantly, verified the con-

tinuation of the old life. The peasants have fled or been evacuated, but chickens still strut about in the farmyards.[50]
Life is quietly but confidently defying the ravages of war:
wood piled high for the next winter, orderly garden plots of
vegetables, wooden clothespins bobbing up and down in the
wind on empty clotheslines, wash that has been hung out and
is not yet dry, threadbare stockings, facecloths, farmers' or
workers' blue overalls, towels that bear their owner's initials.
Into this rural setting, still palpitating with life, the two enemy
armies had descended.

> We ourselves, and the Germans facing us, were no longer good
> for anything but manipulating our murderous pieces of machin-
> ery; but the old race of men which we had driven off and which
> had left behind its tools, its washing and its initialed towels, seemed
> to me to have risen, across the millennia, from the shadows of the
> night just past . . . .[51]

In his diary of the French campaign, *Gärten und Strassen*
(1942), German officer Ernst Jünger also noted, though without the philosophical speculations of Malraux, the vestiges of a
life that seemed to have stopped in its tracks. Jünger was forty-
five years of age in the spring of 1940, and his name was well
established as the author of the World War I novel *In Stahlge-
wittern,* published in 1920, and *Auf den Marmorklippen,* which
appeared in 1939. He had been a German nationalist but had
begun to have reservations about the National Socialist movement. Nonetheless, called back into service as an infantry captain, he was delighted at the rapid advance the German troops
were making. He had served with the German army in France
in World War I and remembered with regret how the Germans
in 1918 had hoped for just such an advance without being able
to bring it off. But now victory was clearly theirs, and Jünger's
only regret was that since he was not on the front lines, he
could not see much of the actual battle. What he did see were
houses demolished or partly demolished, with one façade removed at random and exposing interiors which still bespoke an
elegance and a life style no longer possible in Germany, especially the excellent stores of burgundy wine to which the German soldiers royally helped themselves. Tables were still set in

these houses, but the meals had been interrupted and the inhabitants had fled before the invader.[52]

Jünger's diary of the French campaign is not reflective in the way of *Pilote de guerre* or *Les Noyers de l'Altenburg*. In fact, Jünger shows remarkably little sensitivity to the sufferings and privations of French civilians. It simply does not seem to have occurred to him to dwell on it. Perhaps it is the role of the vanquished to be introspective and to reflect. Perhaps it is a question of temperament. No doubt, too, that in the Nazi state in which he lived, Jünger had to exercise caution in what he wrote. He spent the war with the German army of occupation in Paris in two stages interrupted by a tour of duty in Russia, and finally, in September 1944, he was back in Germany for good.

If Jünger could boost his spirits with burgundy, Cointreau, and champagne, the only boost many Frenchmen could give themselves during that spring of 1940 was a psychological and philosophical one. The morning after Malraux's Berger crawled out of his tank, he felt that life had been revealed to him for the first time, and it was "as powerful as the darkness and as powerful as death." Life had, in fact, triumphed over death, and death, as Malraux's work confirms again and again, need not be our ultimate destiny. By uniting with the life of the "race," the individual can triumph over that destiny. In that "biblical dawn," Berger had discovered man as the Hindus believe him to be.[53] He had understood that death was a part of life and that it could impart meaning to life. Years later for this very reason Malraux included Berger's story in a section of the *Antimémoires* in which he was discussing the faith and philosophy of India's Hindu multitudes. Malraux could only think "with bitterness of the men of our own land for whom death has no meaning . . . ."[54]

Berger's ultimate realizations about the structure and meaning of life provide tangible evidence of a spiritual rebirth after nine months of training that mirror the nine-month cycle from conception to birth, "the time it takes to make a man."[55] They also explain why Malraux placed the story of the tank crew at the end of *Les Noyers de l'Altenburg* even though chronologically it does not belong there. Of the book's three basic parts the first portrays the prisoner-of-war camp in which Berger finds himself after the debacle of 1940; the second, or text proper, considered here only for its relevance to the other two parts, is a flashback to some scenes from Berger's father's career as a university professor in Alsace and then as an officer in the German army of World War I; and the third part is Berger's experience with the tank crew which, from the chronological point of view, preceded the POW camp. In a prefatory note Malraux described *Les Noyers de l'Altenburg* as an incomplete piece of work and claimed that the remainder of the manuscript had been confiscated and destroyed by the Gestapo. Regardless of what may have happened to the manuscript and what other arrangement Malraux might have used to work out his text, the book can certainly stand as a novel complete in itself, albeit perhaps, as Wilbur Frohock cautions, not a novel in the traditional sense but a meditation in fictional terms on the subject of man's fate.[56] In this light it can even be considered as possibly one of Malraux's more interesting attempts at the genre. Far from being the fragmented piece Malraux would have us believe, the three parts fit together as a circular but organic discourse. Berger's discovery of the continuity of life and its victory over death fulfills the other two portions of the book and confirms his own father's insights in the second part: Berger's father has been participating in a conference at the old Altenburg priory in Alsace where the proposition has been advanced that there is no intercommunication between cultures and hence no valid foundation upon which to base our notion of man. Man has not always been the same; he has not always been identical with himself. Greek man has nothing in common with Gothic man who, in turn, has nothing in common with modern man. The idea is repulsive, yet neither Berger's father nor any of the other participants have succeeded in refuting it. To take some fresh air and distance he leaves the conference room. Once outside he gazes upon some old walnut trees framing the Strasbourg cathedral in the distance and recognizes in those trees that have been standing there since the Middle Ages, the possibility for endless change along with endless continuity. Perhaps like the trees man can be shown to change under the accidents of time and place. But his fundamental nature, the stuff of which he is made, always remains the same.

Frohock correctly points out that the proof is intuitive rather than logical.[57] In any case, it is analogous to the son's discovery as he sees life's remnants stubbornly persisting and triumphing over the destruction of war. The very similarity, furthermore, of the discoveries of father and son, made at different times and in different places, points toward a continuity.

The remaining first part of *Les Noyers de l'Altenburg*, set in a prisoner-of-war camp put together hastily first in Chartres cathedral and then at an old construction site nearby, begins to formulate the questions that will be raised and, after a fashion, resolved in the two succeeding parts of the book. After the defeat of France in June 1940, Malraux like his hero Berger and approximately one and a half million other French soldiers, was taken prisoner by the German army. The scenes Berger describes at Chartres are not very different from those that other writers describe in still other prisoner-of-war camps: the almost total disbelief, because of the sheer numbers involved, that the Germans actually intend to do what they seem to be doing—namely, taking captive the whole French army; and the wild rumors that begin to circulate among the men, who, in frustration at their own ignorance, paradoxically reach out for these rumors as a means of fixing their destiny and that of their country. President Paul Reynaud had gone to America. Old Marshal Pétain, the hero of Verdun and the last war, had taken over the conduct of this one, or had he perhaps been arrested? Hitler had said he would enter Paris by the fifteenth of June and peace would be signed before the end of the month.[58] Of course, that might mean they could all go home!

Food is scarce in the beginning and the soldiers treasure whatever canned food they have been able to save in their packs and even the crumbs of food they have already eaten and which remain in their pockets.[59] They spend their time eating little, speculating a lot, and writing letters to their friends and families. But in writing letters there are formulas to be adhered to, and the Germans assure them that letters not adhering to the formulas will not be sent. These formulas were typical of those soon used on the "interzone" cards that were supposed to facilitate communication between occupied France in the north and "free" France in the south. Only the barest essentials could be articulated. In Malraux's book a sign spells out what the men are permitted to write: "I am a prisoner —I am wounded. I am feeling fine. —I am well treated. —Affectionate greetings. — Cross out inaccurate statements. —Do not give an address. — Do not seal." Rumor has it that perhaps the letters will first go to Berlin to be censored.[60] In the end, regardless of how they are written, none of the letters arrive.

From behind the barbed wires of the camp, the French prisoners can see the first flow of would-be refugees returning home to Paris. Those traveling by car or cart force themselves not to look at the prisoners or merely wave "hello" with their hands, furtive and almost ashamed. The prisoners answer with slackened gestures. If occasionally a passing cyclist throws them a cigarette, a fight breaks out immediately over who will get it. The prisoners are reduced to pretty nearly animal status, performing animal functions with animal reactions. The metaphors used in the text speak for themselves. While they are in Chartres cathedral Berger and a tank companion manage to walk only by leaning on each other like "two entangled crabs." After they are herded into the camp the prisoners see a woman approaching the barbed wire fencing on foot from outside. She is carrying a bag, and sensing that she might be bringing them provisions, they dash toward the fence "with the hasty gliding of cats" toward a soft prey. When they go to sleep for the night, they retreat to their "dens."[61]

Under these trying and degrading circumstances Malraux began his search for man in *Les Noyers de l'Altenburg*. Substituting Vincent Berger for himself enabled him to use a third-person narrator, and this opened possibilities that a first-person narration would have excluded. Besides being more heroic than Malraux's, Berger's role carried affiliations with the role that Malraux's real father had played in World War I and thereby provided the kind of continuity he was seeking. The choice of an Alsatian as his major protagonist when his own family came from the Dunkirk area provided further advantages. Berger is a name that is equally at home in French and German, and because the hero is Alsatian he could, with little if any stigma attached to him in France, have had a father who served in the German Army of World War I. Alsace had then belonged to

Germany and the father, moreover, had expressly requested service on the Russian front. To him France and Germany were essential components in any understanding of the world of art and ideas, while Russia was indifferent.[62] With the deck of cards stacked in this way Malraux could be sure that Berger's father would not *a priori* be unpalatable to a French audience. Nor would the parallel discoveries of the son, serving in the French army some twenty years later. Like Saint-Exupéry Berger feels no particular animosity toward the Germans; in fact, he scarcely thinks about them. He thinks rather about doing a job that has to be done and about his own commitment to his fellow man. One of his father's comrades-in-arms had observed in World War I: "The Russian, the Frenchman, or the German isn't bad, . . . it's man in general!"[63] Friend or foe, all are men and that fact alone is more significant than all the differences generated by time and place.

To enhance the artistic vision of *Les Noyers de l'Altenburg* Malraux shifted the site of his own initial detainment as a prisoner of war from the actual Sens cathedral to Berger's Chartres. Perhaps more than any other of the great cathedrals, Chartres incarnates France. It is older than Rheims or Paris or Amiens and embodies to a greater degree the history and traditions of France as she emerged from the Middle Ages. One of the German soldiers guarding the prisoners inside Chartres cathedral is reminded of Bamberg in northern Bavaria, causing Berger to reflect that Bamberg is the German Chartres, that Bamberg cathedral is to German civilization what Chartres is to the French. "What misery to recognize our fraternal connection in between the calls of our wounded men to the sick-attendant and the noise of those boots moving away!..."[64] Under the vaults of Chartres and Bamberg two civilizations might have met. In *Les Noyers de l'Altenburg* they did meet, if only for a moment.

The War at Sea

Much more prosaic and less philosophical in its concerns than either *Les Noyers de l'Altenburg* or *Pilote de guerre* is Lothar-Günther Buchheim's *Das Boot,* made into a film of the same name in 1981 by Wolfgang Petersen. To a greater degree than

Berger in his tank or Saint-Exupéry in his plane, Buchheim's narrator and the U-boat crew are the prisoners of technology. For one thing, a U-boat can house a much larger number of men than a tank or a reconnaissance plane; and once submersion begins, the Commander and the hydrophone operator, through the instruments at their disposal, are the only ones on board able to maintain contact with the world outside. "The Commander can see the enemy, the operator hears him. The rest of us are blind and deaf." [65] Where the airplane was able to give new power and dimension to Saint-Exupéry's vision, the submarine reduces practically the entire U-boat crew to a subhuman level of perception.

The very size of the U-boat serves to depersonalize its crew. In a veritable tour de force, the narrator actually succeeds in mentioning and commenting individually on some thirty-eight members of a fifty-one member crew. But try as he will, he fails to infuse the breath of life into his characters. The book is spattered with bits and pieces of conversation that are mere fragments with neither substance nor development. To some extent, of course, these fragments are indicative of the way the characters function. The captain of the boat does assume something of a personality, but even he is none too loquacious. He has few illusions about his young crew. "You won't get much out of the children themselves. . . . After all, they're nothing but blank pages—three years' schooling, then drafted immediately, and the usual training. They haven't seen anything yet— nor experienced anything—and, besides, they have no imagination." [66] For a time during the war Buchheim did submarine duty as a naval correspondent. His narrator, who occupies precisely the same position and is, therefore, something of an alter ego, reverts in a not particularly imaginative way to the animal imagery typical of war novels. "I remind myself of a zoologist: the animals I'm studying have become accustomed to me." [67] But not even the Commander really knows his men, and after being at sea for over two weeks, confides to the narrator that the emotional life of most people is a mystery to him.[68] In any case, the U-boat is a microcosm of Hitler's Germany. It is not especially calculated to encourage free and open conversation.

The Commander is likeable enough, and despite the fact that

he is only about thirty years of age, the crew affectionately refer to him as the Old Man (*der Alte*). He obviously has little use for the Nazi ideology and has forbidden all discussion of politics at the officers' mess. He prefers to do his job rather than enter into discussions that could only bring on depression. He is like an artist at his work and his work is his one source of satisfaction.

From every angle the world of *Das Boot* is a depersonalized one, and if the captain and crew seem generally reduced to a two-dimensional level, this is even more true of the enemy. Already in Remarque's World War I novel, *Im Westen nichts Neues,* the narrator, Paul Bäumer, does not begin to realize that the enemy is a man little different from himself until he is physically confronted with the presence in his shell hole of a French soldier he has wounded. It had been easy enough to kill the abstract "enemy." It would not have been as easy to kill this young Frenchman whose papers identify him as a printer, husband, and father with the name Gérard Duval.[69] But the technology of World War I was primitive by comparison with that of World War II in which the extended use of machines provided ever greater possibilities for abstraction. The U-boat is a case in point. On one occasion early in the book, even before the start of the mission, several German seamen in the Bar Royal at Saint-Nazaire reflect on the ups and downs of their trade. Without qualm you shoot down the man who has a deck under his feet, it is only the poor victim struggling in the water who can make claim to your sympathy. "If it's only one man, you imagine it could be you. . . . But no one can identify with a whole steamer. That doesn't strike home."[70] Both Saint-Exupéry and Malraux's Berger learned to see beyond the abstractions of modern warfare, to rehabilitate man from the "ant-hill" and reintegrate him into the human community. No such rehabilitation occurs for the "animals" of Buchheim's boat.

Saint-Exupéry tried to reject romantic inspiration in telling his story; Buchheim goes one step further and debunks it. He takes the most classic of romantic images, the evening moon, and in a literary gesture reminiscent of the nineteenth-century poet Alfred de Musset's put-down of romantic exaggeration in the *Ballade à la lune,* twice disfigures the aging symbol beyond repair. Shuffling out of the Breton bar-cabaret on the night before embarcation, the narrator is jolted momentarily. "The white moonlight beyond the swinging door hits me like a blow. I wasn't prepared for light . . . My God! There's never been a moon like this. Round and white like a Camembert. Gleaming Camembert."[71] Even at its best there is nothing romantic about a Camembert, and the moon, far from being the *nourriture spirituelle* that it has always been in literature, is degraded to the level of a *nourriture terrestre* and a blow in the chest. The second instance occurs much later. The U-boat is well out at sea and preparing for an encounter with the enemy. Since it must ride on the surface before maneuvering into an attack position, darkness can be an asset in achieving surprise. But that particular night there is a bright moon, and the Old Man says, "Let's hope we get rid of that bastard before long!" Following the Captain's gaze and trend of thought the narrator notes in turn, perhaps a bit naïve and childlike, that the "moon shows a man's face: fat, round, baldheaded." "Just like a contented old customer in a whorehouse," adds the Second Watch Officer.[72]

With the exception of the First Watch Officer who had been a Hitler Youth leader, there is no indication that any of the men on board gives any thought or care to the cause for which they and the German nation are fighting. And since 30,000 out of 40,000 German U-boat men never returned from their missions, one might well ask what prompted so many young men to enlist. The Old Man provides what is probably the best explanation when he tells the narrator in his own characteristically ironic way, "We're what you might call the *crème de la crème*, the Dönitz Volunteer Corps." Admiral Dönitz, the once respected head of the German navy may have gone over to the Nazi "bigmouths" and the Führer. That Dönitz is toeing the Party line disturbs and irritates the Old Man, but even he admits there is one thing that remains in the U-boat service, and that is comradeship.

> It really attracts people. And more than anything else so does the feeling of belonging to an élite. You only have to look at the fellows on leave. They swell up like pouter pigeons with their U-boat insignia on their uniforms. Seems to have some effect on the ladies too...[73]

But even the noble ideal of comradeship, so important in the
literature of World War I, is denigrated in the mouth of the
drunken seaman Trumann, swaying through the Bar Royal and
pulling from his pocket a crumpled piece of newspaper showing the will of Lieutenant-Commander Mönkeberg. Mönkeberg
was reported to have been killed in action, but in reality he had
struck his head against the ballast tank of his ship one fine day
when he decided to take a swim. The Corps will now close ranks
over the dead Commander's remains. "All alike—one for all—
all for one . . . "[74]
Among the younger crowd of seamen gathered at the Bar
Royal on the night before embarcation there are some idealists,
to be sure, some "philosophically oriented youngsters with faith
in the Führer in their eyes . . . who practice intimidating looks
in front of the mirror," but they are summarily dismissed by
the Old Man as "chin-thrusters."[75] It was not idealism that gave
the great majority of these men the courage to volunteer for
U-boat service and it was not idealism that inspired those who
took their lives into their hands by shipping out on gasoline
tankers. As far as the Old Man is concerned, the latter are either
superhuman or subnormal. "Of course, they get lots of cash—
love of country plus a fat paycheck—maybe that's the best mix
of soil for breeding heroes." He adds dryly, "Sometimes the
booze is enough."[76]
World War II consistently refused to be heroic. Right from
the opening scene at the Bar Royal where the narrator surveys
the "assemblage of young heroes," he brings them under the
fire of his irony. They are "swollen with their own superiority
and crazy for medals." Vain to the point of exhibitionism, they
have no thought in their heads but one: "The Führer's eyes are
upon you—our flag is dearer than life." An incident from the
Hotel Majestic which serves as the officers' billet sustains the
ironic temper. "Two weeks ago in the Majestic one of them
shot himself because he'd caught syphilis. 'He gave his life for
Volk and Vaterland,' was what they told his fiancée."[77]
These are not the mythological heroes of old, and as long as
they are on shore the U-boat men find plenty of diversion in
the bordellos that flourish along the coast as well as in Paris.
Instead of going home to Germany two seamen, in fact, spend

their entire leave in a Paris whorehouse.[78] The Old Man is philosophic about such matters, "When you're scared, go get laid." And the narrator concludes: "That's the way it always is. The Führer's noble knights, the people's radiant future—a few rounds of Cognac washed down with some Beck's beer and there goes our dream of spotless, shining armor."[79] If they want a more meaningful relationship with a French woman the U-boat men run the risk of harassment. Such relationships were frowned on by the German authorities and the women risked punishment from the French as collaborators. Ensign Ullman's predicament is a case in point. He is secretly engaged to a salesgirl named Françoise from the flower shop in town. Françoise is pregnant but she does not want to have the child, fearful of the treatment she will get from the French.[80] The narrator himself has to discourage his girlfriend Simone from coming to port with him on the day of embarcation. "It would only cause trouble. The Gestapo idiots watch us like lynxes."[81]

Perhaps the two seamen who spent their leave in Paris knew what they were doing. Visiting family and friends on the home-front was risky business emotionally, and there was no assurance that a leave would provide any real diversion. A war-weary Paul Bäumer in Remarque's *Im Westen nichts Neues* goes home on leave to World War I Germany only to find his father wanting nothing more than to parade through town with Paul in uniform.[82] In *Le Feu* in World War I France, one of Barbusse's comrades, after managing with the help of an Alsatian serving in the German army to get behind the German lines, is about to enter his house in occupied Lens just north of Arras, when he sees his wife and a woman friend of hers talking and laughing with two German noncoms, his own child on a German's knee.[83] Buchheim's Commander, wise in the ways of the world in which he lives, prefers to be in France or on his U-boat rather than go back to Germany where he is engaged to "one of those Nazi bitches," a flyer's widow, eager to parade with him wearing his uniform and decorations.[84]

With his unit the Old Man is master. Though he cannot totally isolate himself from politics, he has ruled out questions about the meaning of the war and speculation on the chances of a German victory. What matters to him is the game he is playing and he plays it with expertise. The ships he sails are "living things with pulsing hearts of machinery" to be maneuvered and manipulated in a struggle to destroy or be destroyed.[85] The narrator wonders about his inner convictions, but the Commander does not give his cards away easily. At times the narrator views him as a "benevolent pastor" explaining the functioning of the ship's machinery, and at other times as a silent and uninvolved witness to the "liturgical antiphony" of orders being passed from the First Watch Officer to the tower. Like Saint-Exupéry this narrator is fond of religious imagery. When he watches two men in the officers' mess removing the cover from one of the batteries, he stares at them "as if they were altar boys performing at High Mass."[86] But the religious imagery is not sustained as it is in *Pilote de guerre*. At most it indicates a kind of ritual that the Commander and crew carry out, but here the ritual has no meaning. It is the ritual of a warfare in whose validity the participants no longer believe, warfare reduced to the bare elements of the game. The only stake is survival.

The game begins the moment the U-boat puts out from Saint-Nazaire.

> Our crew on the upper deck act out the standard farce—how wonderful to be on our way at last! And the ones left on the pier pretend they're dying of envy. You're off on this splendid cruise! You get to see enemy action and grab all the medals, while we poor bastards are struck here in shitty France frigging around with shitty whores![87]

But the Commander is an artist at his trade, and the game he plays is a good one. The ritual can be exciting, dangerous, and at times adventurous. With the help of modern technology, it can also be atrocious. The Commander torpedoes three and possibly four enemy ships, and the narrator is stunned by the succession of fiery explosions he sees on the horizon.

> I'm overwhelmed with horror at what we have done with our torpedoes. . . . How does the Old Man feel when he visualizes the mass of ships that he himself has destroyed? And when he thinks of the crowds of men who were traveling on those ships and went down with them, or were blown up by the torpedoes—

scalded, maimed, dismembered, burned to death, smothered, drowned, smashed. Or half-scalded and half-smothered and then drowned.[88]

In the end the U-boat returns, half-crippled itself, to the safety of Saint-Nazaire, and the ritual has had no meaning. It is a dead and empty form whose significance has evaporated, and those who have performed the ritual are in some ways like robots. The narrator seems to have foreseen this conclusion from the beginning in his haunting description of the U-boat's departure from France.

> The boat has freed itself from the pier, a dismal ferry on an oily black Styx, and with a cargo of leather-armed men on the anti-aircraft platform . . . . No exhaust visible, no engine noise. As though by a magnet, the boat is drawn from the pier.[89]

The Evacuation at Dunkirk and the Fall of France

The French fleet never had a chance to play its role in World War II, and the German conquest was established on land and in the air. After the initial German thrust of May 10, the outlook for France degenerated rapidly and at the end of the month the French were desperate. By Sunday, May 26, the British had made their decision to begin evacuating their own troops from France and were willing, theoretically at least, to take along those French troops who had made it to Dunkirk on the Channel coast. Dunkirk was the last Channel port still in Allied hands, and from their shore batteries the Germans were already close enough to shell the initial operations with long-range artillery fire. The French, in any case, were largely unprepared for a grand-scale evacuation, and in the next few days matters were further complicated by constant bickering with the British as to whether the evacuation would take place at all, and if so, under what conditions. On May 27 an agreement, in principle, was reached by French and British officers at Dover. On the twenty-eighth came Belgium's official capitulation. King Leopold had trusted his position of neutrality and did not request Allied help until the Germans had already overrun his borders and it was too late to stop them. The next day the

French First Army was authorized to retreat to Dunkirk for evacuation. But again problems arose. The British generally gave priority to their own and did not always show consideration for the French. In a few instances they actually forced French soldiers off the boats. On Friday, May 31, Winston Churchill flew to Paris to try to remedy the situation, and that weekend, despite the difficulties that continued to dog the operation, the evacuation gathered momentum.

Robert Merle's ironically entitled *Week-end à Zuydcoote* (1949),[90] adapted into a film of the same name by Henri Verneuil in 1964 and presented in English as *Weekend at Dunkirk,* is based on the events of that fateful Saturday and Sunday, June 1 and 2, 1940. It was not to be the kind of leisurely vacation weekend at the coast which the title suggests and which one might expect in early June, when spring in its fullness basks in the certainty of a summer yet to come. "In peacetime life is harmonious and composed. One meets the same people, one sees them again, one loses sight of them and then meets them once more. . . . But in wartime everything is unraveled, without connection, without continuation, without coherence."[91]

Not far from the chaos of France, of course, order and calm did still exist. It is only twenty miles across the Channel to England. The problem was getting there. As he approaches a road crossing near the coast, Merle's central character, Julien Maillat, a sergeant in the French army, notices an English officer directing traffic. "English to the right! French to the left!" "Anglais à droite! Français à gauche!" French and British soldiers did not always take kindly to each other, and Maillat's companion, a man from Béziers, objects instinctively. "We're still in France . . . . No Englishman is going to tell me what to do."[92] Maillat, in any case, is suspicious and fears that if he gets on the French line he will never see the cliffs of Dover. Because he can speak English he is able to persuade the British officer in charge to do something for him. Though the Englishman complains of having been insulted for the past hour by every French officer who has passed him, he takes a liking to Maillat and writes out a request for embarcation rights. But despite the note it is only by dint of sheer perseverance that Maillat manages to board a ship bound for England.

The ship no sooner lifts anchor than German Stuka planes push in for the attack. Maillat quickly realizes that in a few minutes the ship will become a blazing inferno, but while it is still within the harbor area, he has one alternative open to him: to jump the twelve meters from the deck to the water and swim back to shore. And he has to act quickly. Up to now he, like many others, has looked upon the war with an almost artistic detachment. People are passing value judgments on it as they would on a movie or a cup of tea. Or they insist on playing the role of spectator and comparing it with the last war. Earlier Maillat had observed an old man walking along the coast, who had perhaps wanted to see how they were making war this time around. It so little resembled the one in which he had campaigned, "la grande, la seule, la vraie." The specter of that war is haunting this one. Two weeks before, Maillat had run into a British MP in Armentières looking for the address of a bordello while the town was being bombed.[93] No doubt he remembered the World War I ballad about the Mademoiselle from Armentières and wanted to do no less than his ancestors had done. But for Maillat on his boat this is no time for reflections and comparisons. He jumps, and by the time he wades to shore it is already late Saturday. The beach is littered with a wreckage of human bodies that Merle describes with a vision almost as graphic as that of Barbusse or Ramarque on World War I. The weapons being used may have become more technological, but the human body is limited in the forms of disfiguration it can assume.

On Sunday morning Maillat spends considerable time stumbling around the beaches and then withdraws into town. His attention is arrested by a single house standing on a street that has been completely leveled. Entering the house he finds two French soldiers raping the young proprietress. The war seems to give license to the strong to do whatever they want. Maillat kills the pair, not failing to note the irony: "All that I have managed to kill in this war is two Frenchmen." Soon a truck passes by on its drive through the battered town picking up the bodies of the dead, and Maillat sustains the ironic tone of his narrative, observing that in this war the dead travel by motor vehicle while the living trudge amid the ruins on foot. "The

world is turned upside down," remarks a passing cyclist,[94] and
the two dead rapists are hoisted into the truck to lie with the
anonymous dead who had given their lives for *la Patrie*.

Week-end à Zuydcoote is not a fairytale like *La Belle et la bête* or
Cinderella. The young proprietress Jeanne refuses to leave her
house with Maillat. Though her sister has gone to live with relatives two kilometers away, she is tenacious, believing that as
long as she remains in the house it will not be bombed. But it
is bombed, and Maillat, who has abandoned all thought of getting to England and hopes to outfox the Germans by exchang-
ing his uniform for civilian clothes, dies in the shambles with
this woman who before her death eagerly gives him that for
which he has killed his two compatriots.

The weekend was over, but the evacuation proceeded for another two days; almost 53,000 French men were taken out on
Monday night and early Tuesday morning.[95] By Tuesday
morning the evacuation and slaughter at Dunkirk ceased, and
what was left of the French First Army surrendered to the Germans. On June 5 the Germans began their offensive on the
Somme and on June 10 the French government fled Paris for
Tours. Just the day before, General Weygand decided that in
order to "preserve its character as an Open City," the capital
would not be defended. Parisians were not apprised of the decision until June 13 when posters appeared on building walls.
On the fourteenth, German troops entered the city. According
to the terms of surrender, the local police would remain to
maintain law and order, and the population would stay indoors
for the first forty-eight hours of the Occupation.[96]

The government of Paul Reynaud which had fled to Tours
now fled to Bordeaux, and upon Reynaud's resignation two days
later, old Marshal Henri Philippe Pétain, who had led the
French army to victory at Verdun in World War I, was named
premier by President Lebrun. Reynaud had shared with Charles
de Gaulle the broad conceptions of a France whose empire extended beyond her continental borders, a France that might
continue the war from outside Europe in North Africa. But in
the end it was the defeatists who carried the day, General Weygand, the politician Pierre Laval who had been working for some
time for the formation of a government under Pétain, and

Marshal Pétain himself. On June 17, even before any talks had taken place, Pétain asked the Germans for an armistice. Jean Guéhenno notes sadly in his diary of the occupation years, the *Journal des années noires* (1947): "Now it is over. An old man who no longer even has the voice of a man, but speaks like an old woman, gave us notice at 12:30 this afternoon that during the night he had asked for peace."[97] On the afternoon of June 23 at Rethondes, north northeast of Paris, by the edge of the forest of Compiègne where the German empire had capitulated in 1918, France signed the armistice. The French delegation was represented by General Charles Huntziger, commander of the Second Army at Sedan. Adolf Hitler came in person to represent Germany. He seated himself in the same chair and in the same old railway car in which the victorious General Foch had received the German surrender almost twenty-two years before.

When the French soldiers heard Pétain's request for an armistice, many laid down their arms. One after the other the great French cities were officially proclaimed "open" cities and capitulated, offering little resistance and hoping to save themselves from destruction. A few like Sartre's Mathieu, the existential hero of *La Mort dans l'âme* (1949), the third volume of the trilogy *Les Chemins de la liberté,* would go on fighting for a few more days, to the bitter end. Fighting becomes for Mathieu a means of achieving spiritual freedom, a means of self-purification in the defeat. Killing the enemy is an act of self-assertion, something definitive for which he alone can assume total responsibility. In a way that perhaps no plane or tank or U-boat could duplicate, his rifle gives him an individual sense of power over life and death, the right and obligation to take personal credit for the revenge which in his anger he wishes to inflict not only on the Germans but on the world at large.[98]

By the terms of the armistice, metropolitan France was divided by a line of demarcation into two zones. The *Zone Nord* or *Zone occupée* comprised about sixty percent of the country including all of northern France from the Belgian border to a point somewhat south of the Loire and the entire Atlantic coastline and was to be occupied by the German army. The *Zone Sud* or *Zone libre,* as it was called, comprised the remainder of the country and was to be administered by the French government. Requisitions to Germany were stipulated in the form of food and coal.[99] French prisoners of war captured during the German advance and who numbered nearly one and a half million, were to remain captive until the conclusion of a peace in the west, which almost everybody in France seemed to think would materialize in a matter of weeks.

At 12:35 AM on June 25, according to the agreements signed at Rethondes, the war officially ended in France. On June 29, the Pétain government abandoned Bordeaux to the Germans who, according to the armistice, were given jurisdiction over the Atlantic coastal areas. Pétain established temporary headquarters at Clermont-Ferrand; but by July 1, due to lack of facilities at Clermont-Ferrand, he moved on to the health spa of Vichy whose great hotels provided more adequate accommodations. There, in the ironic and unlikely atmosphere of unreality generated by the renowned watering-place of the French upper crust, the government remained until the liberation.

The longed-for peace which the armistice of Rethondes was expected to bring was not immediately realized. Britain was not as eager as France to trust the Germans and feared they would arm the French fleet and use it in the fight against England. On the morning of July 3 Britain seized all French naval vessels at anchor in her ports. She rendered useless, at least temporarily, the French warships that were stationed in Alexandria, by discharging their fuel and removing parts of their gun mechanisms. And at the French naval base of Mers-el-Kébir near Oran in Algeria where the Atlantic fleet had recently been relocated from Brittany, she delivered her most deadly blow. The British wanted either to enlist the French fleet in the cause against Germany or else to remove it from the European theater entirely by sailing it off to the French West Indies. The French would only guarantee that measures had been taken to insure that none of their warships would fall into Axis hands. Late that afternoon the British fleet, with the support of aerial bombardment, opened fire on the helpless French warships. The entire fleet, with the exception of a few ships that managed to escape into the open sea, was destroyed. Some 1297 French sailors were dead.[100]

France was stunned. Pierre Laval, who had served three times as Premier in conservative governments in the early 1930s and had worked his way into the Pétain government, demanded an immediate declaration of war against Great Britain. In the end, Pétain contented himself with breaking off diplomatic relations. Freed from the responsibilities of war, Vichy could turn its attention to the question of administering unoccupied France.

On July 10, thanks in great part to the machinations of Laval, the National Assembly voted the Third Republic out of existence. The regime of Marshal Pétain, with Laval as second, could now assume full command in the *Zone libre*. The old hero of Verdun, whom many now simply and affectionately called *le Vieux*, had brought France the peace she desired above all else. "A country dumbfounded," recalls Pierre Seghers in *La Résistance et ses poètes* (1974),[101] "a population benumbed by the 'drôle de guerre', an overwhelming majority wishing only for peace. Peace at any price, a narcotic peace, peace as a suicidal surrender."[102]

Remembering the Fall of France

Inevitably the fall of France brought with it a sense of loss, for if it signaled the beginning of a new era, by the same token, it signaled the end of an old one. Claude Simon's *La Route des Flandres* (1960) is an attempt to salvage something from the dissolution that ensued. In a series of interrelated but temporally and spacially unconnected texts and with a free and ample use, reminiscent of Flaubert, of the temporally ambivalent present participle whose real time value is determined only by the tense of the verb that governs it, Simon has very appropriately all but annihilated the customary boundaries of space and time and thus sidestepped the convenient, if at times superficial, definition they give to things. The reader has the task of piecing together a plot from certain events that actually do occur and the recollections the characters have of these events. Like the characters the reader must become free to imagine and conjecture. Though there is no single narrator and, therefore, no constant narrative point of view, the largest part of the story is related by Georges, an ex-soldier in the French army, who participated in the collapse of 1940 and whose purpose it is to reconstruct the death on the battlefield of his unit commander, Captain de Reixach. De Reixach's death appears to have been a suicide and Georges, who had always been somewhat in awe of this nobleman with whom he had a distant kinship, attempts to piece together, out of the past, persons and events that might help him reconstruct de Reixach's life and death and throw some light on the suicide theory. Conforming very closely to the "guidelines" for the so-called new novel that Robbe-Grillet describes in his essay *Pour un nouveau roman* (1963), Simon never attempts to delve into the psychological make-up of his characters. They are seen from the outside and all the information assembled about them is gleaned through observation and listening. Even when they allow themselves to speculate on what they have observed, their conclusions are subject to verification in the observable world of what philosophers call phenomenology.

Even before the war it was clear that de Reixach had picked in his wife, Corinne, a bride whose nature and status in society were quite different from his own. What drew them together was their love of horses. There is strong indication that Corinne may have had an affair with their jockey Iglésia, and though de Reixach suspected a liaison he never fired Iglésia. For five years after the collapse of France, much of that time spent in a prisoner-of-war camp in Saxony, Georges has been conjecturing and dreaming about Corinne de Reixach, and the conclusions of his revery appear to lend support to his original suspicion that her husband's death had been a suicide. The war provided de Reixach with a convenient escape from his marital problems, and the confusion of the battlefield had made his suicide possible, disguising it under the mantle of heroism. To test his hypothesis Georges returns after the war to Toulouse where Corinne has remarried and carries on an affair with her. Together they reconstruct, as it were, the person of the dead officer, but even that reconstruction is inconclusive, and the affair with Corinne becomes yet another failure parallel to the defeat of the French army, the "objective correlative," Leon Roudiez has called it, around which the book is structured. For Georges and for the reader as well, the failure with Corinne assumes an even greater significance than what is historically the obviously more important defeat of France. For out of his affair, Georges had hoped to discover the truth about de Reixach's life and the manner of his death, and this attempt to discover the truth is the central issue of the book. De Reixach had centered much of his life before the war around his love of horses, and he rode a horse into battle in the spring of 1940. Technology has little role in this novel. Many horses died during the retreat, and throughout the narration the reader is brought back again and again in circular fashion to the image of a dead horse killed on the battlefield. But circling back to the horse yields nothing. As the dead animal's body decomposes it returns to the earth and becomes progressively less distinguishable from the ground on which it has fallen. Whatever intuitions it may have had about death have dissolved with it. If we can learn no certainties about the meaning of death from the death of the horse, we can learn nothing certain in regard to de Reixach's death either, and the result of Georges's investigation is a hauntingly empty and oft-repeated *comment savoir?*—"how can one know?"

What we do know is that the setting of the battle provided de Reixach with an excellent opportunity for the escape he may have been seeking. The war had been a "murder" and an "assassination" and not a war as men had thought of war heretofore.[103] The soldiers had stumbled about screaming and wondering where the front was. Georges's only proof of having actually been on a battlefield is not a wound from an enemy rifle, but rather the inadvertent kick he received from a nailed shoe. Perhaps the aggressor was not even a man but an animal. Indeed Georges feels himself being transformed more and more into the animal state and is reassured about his own mental condition only when he recalls having read somewhere in Latin verse that men could be changed into animals. Literature has presented such cases and so it is possible.[104] Through linguistic euphemism the military establishment has disguised the reality of war. The term "affair" replaces the expressions for fighting a battle or a duel, and instead of saying "the squad was massacred in an ambush," popular jargon has it that "we had a hot affair at the entrance to the village . . . ."[105] In a water image that is more reminiscent of the literature of World War I, since the French campaign of 1940 was fought under particularly sunny skies, the whole world seems to be dissolving in the rain, being absorbed by the water into a state of liquefaction.[106] Earlier in the century Proust had shown the destructive work of time on the world and on human beings. Water and the war now seemed to accelerate the dissolving process. In a gesture of nobility defying the ignominy of the situation, de Reixach drew forth his sword and may, himself, have stabbed it into his chest. But we cannot know for sure. Georges has failed to achieve certainty and we have failed with him. But though he has failed with Corinne and though the French army failed to repulse the German invader, the experience of the war and of the dead Captain de Reixach need not have been an utter futility. They can be saved from oblivion and thus endure. The text has preserved and perpetuated them. Thanks to the "incantatory magic of language, of words invented in the hope of rendering comestible . . . unnameable reality",[107] the text has saved them from the "incoherent, listless, impersonal, and destructive work of time."[108]

CHAPTER II

The French Army

A Lack of Enthusiasm for the War

By the time the armistice was signed at Rethondes, much of the French army had already come into German hands, either through capture in battle or through voluntary surrender. Article 20 of the armistice sealed the fate of that army. All French prisoners of war, some one and a half million men from Brittany to Alsace, were to remain in German custody until peace was concluded.[1] For some of the prisoners the humiliation was a painful one, but for none, no doubt, was it as painful as for the defenders of the Maginot Line stationed between the Vosges and the Rhine, who had simply been outflanked, and were never needed for the great battle that was to have defended France from German invasion.

For the majority of the French, 1939 and 1940 were nothing like 1914, and French soldiers did not go to war with anything like the same kind of enthusiasm. In the name of the older generation, Georges Bernanos wrote from Brazil where he had taken up residence in 1938: "Once again I feel that my country is going to war with the illusion of thereby being absolved of its faults, purified, renewed, reborn."[2] But for the soldiers themselves, even that illusion was lacking. "This time no Péguys or Barrès have infected the ranks of youth with their patriotic pox," Abel Tiffauges, the ambiguous hero of Michel Tournier's *Le Roi des aulnes* (1970) writes in his diary of "Ecrits sinistres." "The men who've been called up don't even seem to have any very

41

clear idea of why they're going to fight."[3] Jean Dutourd, for
one, "aged twenty years and six months," and taken prisoner
on June 25, 1940, "after having been a soldier for fourteen
days," found the return to peace a welcome change. The French
army was dead before the war began, he writes in *Les Taxis de
la Marne.* It had died of anemia in its own bed between 1930
and 1940, and so when Pétain "in his wisdom" had put an end
to "the absurdities of the war,"[4] it meant merely a return to the
normal order of things, to things as they should be. Crossing
Brittany in June 1940, Dutourd saw only disorder, the political
disorder of the *départements,* the human disorder created by the
flight of the refugees, and the material disorder of things removed from their habitual places: "we saw mattresses abandoned in open fields, which is not where mattresses belong.
. . ." France was being stretched taut, like a rope, and either
the tension would have to be relaxed or the rope would break.
"The rope slackened, to the great relief of everybody, when
Pétain announced on the wireless that he had asked for an armistice."[5]

A striking exception to this sense of indifference and even
defeatism is Pierre-Henri Simon's Jean de Larsan in *Portrait d'un
officier* (1958). De Larsan is a career officer, a graduate of the
military academy at Saint-Cyr, and unlike the majority of soldiers who were obliged by the state to play a role for which
they had little training, he already sensed war's approach while
still at Saint-Cyr and prepared for it as for a trade. Even more
than a *métier,* it was to be an "entrée en religion." But the narrator is quick to undercut de Larsan's élan. He is a fellow officer and prisoner of war in one of a number of camps in northern France where the Germans initially detained the captive
French army, and he serves as a foil to de Larsan. "If I understand you, my good fellow, I have the fortune and the honor
of having as a prison mate the last of the Christian knights."[6]
The words "prison mate" (*camarade de taule*) and the prison
camps of 1940, juxtaposed with the lofty idealism of the "dernier des chevaliers chrétiens," are enough to make de Larsan
himself admit that he is something of a Don Quixote. The narrator then drives his point home.

In idealizing war, you are contributing to its justification . . . it has never been, in any case, it can no longer be that great and loyal tourney that you imagine; it has become sordid and cruel, a kind of scientific butchering in which there are no longer soldiers facing soldiers, but engineers crushing villages, burning up with fire whole throngs of people. . . .[7]

But Jean de Larsan does not really learn. He escapes from the camp, goes on to other and later wars in Indo-China and Algeria, still trying to "live Corneille in the century of Kafka," and finally returns home to France, "broken in his soul, tired of having carried out honestly and lucidly his soldier's trade with the project of thereby saving man."[8]

The attitude of the average soldier did not change very much, at least not immediately, once the fight was over and the French army taken captive. Jacques Perret recalls in *Le Caporal épinglé* (1947) that after he and his fellow soldiers had been herded into a prisoner-of-war camp at the château de Vaucouleurs south of Verdun in the *département de la Meuse* in northeastern France, the thing that was uppermost in his mind was to get dry and to get something into his stomach. The defeat was everybody's problem and surely there would be time enough to think about it later.[9] For the individual soldier France was going to have to take second place.

Life in the camps was relatively easy. Jean Dutourd speaks again and again of the "sweetness" of life in the camps to which he was attached, first at Auray and then at Vannes, both in the southern part of Brittany. At least once, a wine party dragged on late into the night with the result that much of the next day was spent sleeping. At Auray regulations were lax enough to permit him to obtain occasional passes signed by both the French and German commandants and to go about the town on his own.[10] For the most part camp routines allowed for leisure without responsibility. Even in the eastern camps in Lorraine that Jacques Perret depicts at Vaucouleurs on the Meuse and then at Lérouville slightly to the north, and Sartre in *La Mort dans l'âme* in the famed glass-making town of Baccarat in the Meurthe-et-Moselle just southeast of Lunéville, conditions are certainly bearable. Perret alludes to the incessant rain which appears to have been one of the most annoying aspects of camp life. The weather was being capricious. The sunny spring days that favored the German advance in May and early June turned soggy as the French army settled into the various camps to brood over its defeat.

Though literature shows the average French soldier of World War II to have been apathetic at the outset, hostility to the ever-increasing and ever-visible German presence was, of course, something that could be learned. And once the defeat had become a reality, the French spirit of contradiction served to feed that hostility. "As long as the government was making war," Dutourd writes, "I was a pacifist. When it made peace and preached friendship with our enemies of yesterday, patriotism began to stir in my soul."[11]

One can safely say that insofar as literature portrays it, the defeat went down relatively well with the French soldier, at least in the beginning. Defeat, after all, meant freedom from responsibility. If anything, it was a stroke of luck! For the French soldier the war was over. He would be going home soon to take up his "real life" where he had left off. What a stroke of bad luck victory would have been, ruminates Dutourd. It would have meant months and maybe even years of fighting and then, after that, even more loss of time having to occupy enemy territory.[12] That task had now fallen to the poor Germans. The French soldier could look forward instead to a return to "normalcy," to the relative material prosperity and comfort of the late 1930s. Dutourd and his comrades felt themselves superior to the German soldiers because, as provisional prisoners, they would soon again be civilians. They had been the lucky ones!

> Our defeat also inspired us with a truly strange pride: the mere fact of being there, locked up and reduced to impotence and meditation, made us regard ourselves as men of wisdom. When we looked at the Germans, so busy, so self-important, organizers of nothingness, and still subjected to the antics of military life, we took ourselves for adults looking with pity upon the follies of children.

The Germans still believed in the war, but in the end the French had refused to lend themselves to the game. "Being in some way the more intelligent, we had given way, as grownups give way to the whims of children, with a resigned smile and a shrug of the shoulders."[13]

All in all, being a prisoner of war was not the worst thing that could happen. Dutourd also develops this theme in his novel *Au bon buerre* (1952) which takes a family of Paris dairy-shopkeepers through the vicissitudes of the war. When word arrives that Léon Lécuyer, the son of an old neighbor lady and customer, has been taken prisoner, the shopkeeper, Monsieur Poissonard, decides that this is indeed the best arrangement that could befall a soldier in war. After all, Léon will have cost his mother nothing all the while he remains a prisoner and soon will have his trip back to Paris paid for him.[14]

The Army in Defeat

As the French soldiers idled away the weeks following their internment in the prisoner-of-war camps, the reality of the defeat began to sink in. It had become part of their condition, and they were going to have to live with it. Dutourd goes so far as to say that in the national consciousness the very vocation of the French army of 1940 seemed to have been captivity rather than battle.[15] However this may have been, adjustment to the condition of captivity was something that in the end each individual had to settle for himself. But they discussed their condition, since they had little else to do in those weeks of waiting. One of the prisoners in Jacques Perret's camp at Vaucouleurs, a man named Ballochet, understates the case, claiming that it's a "pain in the neck to be conquered: it changes a whole lot of habits." Ballochet's neighbor, whom Perret designates only as "le voisin," thereby conferring on him an anonymity that enables him to speak for the group, responds more critically: "First of all, we haven't been conquered, mustn't say that! We've been sold." As narrator, Perret steps out of the discussion to add some insight of his own. It always gives pleasure to hear a "historical word," even if it has been "dropped through all the defeats in history. The legionnaire who fled the camp at Trasimene . . . also cried out: *Venditi sumus*, boys!"[16] But Ballochet has already cried out "Bravo!" For he has found a way out of the dilemma.

The tendency to shift responsibility is characteristic, too, of most of the soldiers in Sartre's long novel of the defeat *La Mort dans l'âme.* Some shift responsibility to ex-Premier Daladier, others to General Maurice Gamelin, the Commander-in-Chief replaced on May 19 by General Maxime Weygand, and others still to those among their comrades who had been less than eager to fight. Only Mathieu remains clear-sighted enough to admonish his colleagues a week before the armistice is signed: "[War is] each and every one of us, . . . made in the image of all of us. Men get the war they deserve."[17] In the end Mathieu accomplishes the task he set for himself as a point of honor and holds out for exactly fifteen minutes firing against the on-coming Germans.[18] He serves to counterbalance the scene in Bertolt Brecht's play of the French defeat *Die Geschichte der Simone Machard,* written in exile in California in 1942 and early 1943, in which French troops passing through the village of Saint-Martin, south of Paris, have to be fed posthaste because they can't wait to get out of the war zone.[19]

With few exceptions there were not many who decried the armistice. Jacques Perret experiences a vague feeling of shame but finds little support for his feelings in his internment camp.[20] For some, according to Pierre-Henri Simon's *Portrait d'un officier,* the battle rather than the defeat seemed shameful,[21] and this also seems to be the assessment of Sartre's Philippe, a young soldier who fled his army unit to return home and play civilian in a now occupied Paris. As a soldier Philippe had not shown particular courage. Unfortunately for him, he is a pacifist born into a family in which military courage is highly valued. He attempts to commit suicide by drowning himself in the Seine and is deterred only by the efforts of a homosexual named Daniel who happens to be passing along the quay at the right time and takes an interest in him.[22]

Philippe was not alone in fearing to face his family. The soldiers of 1940 were often the sons of the men who had fought in 1914, and, on the whole, the French army of World War I had put up a heroic fight. Even the Germans respected them for it. What would the grand old warriors of the Somme, the

Marne, and Verdun have to say to their sons who had brought home defeat and disgrace? The soldier of World War I may hardly have thought himself heroic as he struggled from his trench against the muddy terrain and the fire of an enemy he most of the time did not even see. But time had distorted some of the perspectives on World War I and romanticized them as time is wont to do. The French *poilu* had passed into legend. And even if the old soldiers had never personally thought of themselves as heroes, they knew that they had fought for France, that they had fought kilometer for kilometer to hold on to the very soil. In the camp at Baccarat in Lorraine where Sartre sets the entire second half of *La Mort dans l'âme,* an old army sergeant who had served in the trenches says to the young men whose captivity he now must share, we won our war and you lost yours. "I meant that you farted away in face of the enemy and you handed them France on a silver platter."[23] Jean Dutourd appraises the generation gap in this way: "The poilus of 1914 were fathers whose sons found them too heavy to bear. They had too much glory, and too much official glory. There was nothing left for anyone else."[24] Whatever the old soldiers thought of their sons, would not the general verdict soon be the same? Would not all of France soon talk of "les vaincus de 40, les soldats de la défaite?"[25]

If there is anyone in French literature who does not give a hoot what France will think, it is Michel Tournier's Abel Tiffauges. Tiffauges is a garage mechanic in Paris, and his attraction to young children is what starts him on the path of adventure. Every afternoon he picks up a little girl named Martine whom he has befriended and drives her home from school. One afternoon Martine is raped after she leaves Tiffauges's car and enters the courtyard of her apartment building. We never learn who really did it, but the little girl points an accusing finger at Tiffauges and his doom seems inevitable. When the case comes up for trial, however, the judge hands down a verdict of insufficient evidence for prosecution. Tiffauges has never admitted the crime, it is the third of September 1939, France is mobilizing, and Tiffauges's name happens to be among the first on the list of potential draftees. Pay back your faults on the field of honor, orders the judge.[26] Tiffauges is soon sped off to Erstein in Alsace where he will be attached to a group specializing in transmitting messages for the army by carrier-pigeon. His affection for his pigeons, at least in terms of sentimentality, approaches his affection for little children. As the victorious Germans draw near, Tiffauges's commander, Colonel Puyjalon, convinced that his men, uselessly massed against the Maginot Line, will be needed farther to the north, begins to move out with a few of them. But it is not long before he realizes that the Germans have overtaken them. When the Colonel discovers that Tiffauges has held on to one of the pigeons, he is ecstatic, wants to propose Tiffauges for a citation and send the following message to his men at Erstein: "My children, your colonel has fallen into the hands of the enemy after a fierce resistance."[27] Tiffauges, more concerned for the safety of the pigeons than the progress of the war, sends his own instructions for the good care of the pigeons still at Erstein. And while other French soldiers in other camps rejoice that for them the war is over, or try to reconcile themselves to the fact that they have been defeated and are now prisoners of the Germans, Abel Tiffauges calmly and silently rejoices that he may now be put to work for the enemies of the country that had mistreated him.

Hopes of Going Home

Once confined to the prisoner-of-war camps, the French soldiers entered upon a period of uncertainty. No one really seemed to know what the Germans intended to do with them, and all the camps were abuzz with rumor. In fact, the rumors concocted by the prisoners and preserved in literature are so numerous and at times farfetched they are virtually incredible. But then these soldiers had little else to do but wait and speculate. Of all the prisoners, Sartre's men in the camp at Baccarat seem to have fared the worst. There are frequent complaints about the quantity and quality of the food. But even for the men at Baccarat life has been simplified, reduced to little else but waiting. Indeed this waiting appears to sum up their whole army career. "They had waited for letters, for leave, for the German attack, and this was their way of waiting for the end of the war. The war is over and still they are waiting."[28] Brunet, a communist who hopes to turn the captivity of the French army to advantage and use the men's discontent to draw them to his cause, is helpless to do anything with them for the simple reason that they are not sufficiently unhappy. As long as they are not suffering and as long as they can still expect to go home they are useless to him.

Indeed they did expect to go home. Some were convinced that their liberation would be accomplished as early as the fourteenth of July.[29] It would be a nice gesture on Hitler's part, after all, to release the French prisoners for Bastille Day. Certainly it would be in Hitler's interest to gain, if not the love, at least the respect of the French people. He would not want to alienate them. In all the camps the talk continued, and so did the theorizing. There were rumors that America might declare war[30] and would indeed do so if the prisoners were not set free by the fourteenth of July; that de Gaulle was expected on the Côte d'Azur and would continue the fight from the south;[31] and a rumor spread by civilians fleeing to the south that Paris was in flames. Another rumor had it that since the Germans would soon be in Marseille, the prisoners would certainly be released by mid-August. Continental France ends in Marseille; after that there would be nothing left for the Germans to conquer. Perhaps they would seek to bring France into the Axis and rely on her prestige to help keep the United States out of the war.[32] There were even rumors that the Germans intended to free Brittany from France;[33] or, a rumor already in vogue before the internment of the French army, that they intended to create a United States of Europe with the result that the *petits gars* of 1940 would have accomplished what their papas had failed to do: abolish the nation states and with them war itself. In Paris, too, there were rumors. In Sartre's novel, after saving Philippe from suicide in the Seine, Daniel tries to coax the young man into spending the night in his apartment, telling him that if he does try to get home, he will probably fall on a German patrol, and since all Germans are purported to be pederasts, he will not stand much of a chance.[34]

It must be said that the Germans themselves encouraged the French prisoners to think that their return home was imma-

nent: " . . . morgen England caput, alles rétour Pariss! Kôg-
nac! Madam!" It is useless to write letters home, the sentries
inform the men in Perret's camp, they will be home before the
letters arrive.[35] All this seemed logical enough, for the Germans were taking everything that stood in their way, and many
soldiers and civilians alike were convinced that if France had
not held out, surely England would not be able to do so either.
Since England was just on the other side of the Channel, the
war would soon be over.[36] When new Austrian sentries from
the class of 1924 are assigned to duty in Perret's camp, this
seems an assurance that the Germans are becoming disinter-
ested in their French prisoners. Furthermore, it is rumored that
lists had been drawn up in preparation for the release of bak-
ers and electricians who would be more useful outside of the
camps than in them.[37] And both among soldiers and civilians
alike, the rumors of the terror the Germans were supposed to
be spreading enjoyed less and less credence. The idea that the
Germans would castrate the French soldiers, rape the women,
and cut off the hands of children was generally received for
what it was, propaganda left over from the last war.[38] People
as a whole had become more sophisticated and would have
blushed at the thought of swallowing wholesale all the "news"
that the media of both sides had disseminated between 1914
and 1918.

In short, it made no logical sense to think that the Germans
would do anything else but liberate their French prisoners at
the first opportunity. Pétain would not have it otherwise! To
feed them, first of all, even if the food was not excellent, cost
money.[39] Why, then, would anyone even try to escape? In some
camps, of course, one prisoner's escape meant that repercus-
sions followed for those who remained, and the loyalty and solidarity that began to develop among the prisoners acted as a
deterrent. But more often than not, moral deterrents were un-
necessary. In Dutourd's camp in Brittany the rumor was spread
that in two weeks all the soldiers were going to be demobilized
and given their trip home free of charge.

> This was the first time I heard talk about a paid journey home.
> It was not the last. I was to hear this remark dozens of times a
> day all the time I was a prisoner. Weeks passed by, England was

never invaded, peace never came, and discipline became more and more tyrannical, but nothing lessened the appeal of the free trip home.

It was because of this, and in the teeth of all the evidence, that five hundred thousand men refused to escape. What did that famous journey home cost in 1940? Possibly a hundred francs for some, fifty francs for others. This was the price, laughable even for poor men, which a third of the French army placed on its freedom and it found even that expensive.[40]

Driven by a need to find personal freedom, Dutourd resolved to escape at the end of July 1940.[41]

In a different camp Jacques Perret, less convinced than most that their liberation was immanent, makes a similar resolve. In order to help himself assess the future realistically, he seeks to place himself in the extraordinary position of Adolf Hitler, who has almost "two million" disarmed French soldiers in his hands.

. . . mon petit Adolphe, you are going to treat yourself to five minutes of a good time, you are going to take flight in high fantasy, play magnanimously or underhandedly, amaze the world and scandalize history; but he, such as I know him, is going to say to himself: "O Adolf, o Adolf . . . in short, what is he going to say to himself? . . . he has to make up his mind, a good German doesn't do things on the spur of the moment.

Perret draws his own conclusion: " . . . Hitler has the unheard of fortune to be holding two million French soldiers at his mercy, he will not let them go."[42]

One alternative to liberation was deportation to Germany. But to most, such a preposterous idea never occurred, and if it did, it was sufficiently absurd to dismiss out of hand. It does occur to Brunet, Sartre's communist, who knows that only when the French soldiers have been deported to Germany will their discontent enable him to arouse them to revolt. He hopes, therefore, that such a deportation will come to pass.[43] When Brunet tells a group of fellow prisoners that Hitler might send them to work in Germany, a fellow named Gassou calmly but confidently opposes him. "Work? Alongside the German workers? What'd the Heinies' morale be like after they'd talked with us a little? . . . The French workman is born cunning; he's a nat-

ural grumbler and stubborn as you make 'em; in less than no
time he'd have knocked the stuffing out of the Heinies; you
can be sure that old Hitler knows all about that. You can bet
your life he's pretty shrewd!"[44]

The idea of deportation to Germany also occurs to Abel Tiffauges, Michel Tournier's lover of children and carrier pigeons, who knows instinctively and rejoices in his knowledge,
that he is in the hands of destiny and that his star lies even
farther to the east.

Attitudes Toward the Enemy

One of the greatest surprises to descend on France in those late
spring and early summer days of 1940 was the fact that the
Germans were polite and correct. Those who were concerned
at first that civilization itself might be destroyed by the German
hordes were pacified. Dupieu, one of Perret's comrades in the
POW camp expresses the general feeling when he says, "I
thought I was going to see brutes and I see good people . . . ."[45]

For the French soldiers it was difficult to know just what attitude to take toward their German captors. One could always
say, of course, that the Germans were "idiots" and "wood heads";
but when you admitted that only a small number of them were
"arrogant fellows who bullied us" and that the majority were
"good-natured men who did not give a fig for the war and the
destiny of nations and who saw us only as unhappy fellow creatures," then it became more problematic to adopt a stance. According to Jean Dutourd, things might have been more cut and
dry had the situation been reversed and the French victorious,
for "we would have been ferocious. We would have been true
conquerors, violent, cruel, arrogantly trampling underfoot the
soil we conquered, taking the women and humiliating the men.
We should never have been accused of behaving correctly!"[46]

No doubt it was inevitable that the French soldiers should
make comparisons between themselves and their captors and
in so doing, attempt to salvage their own self-esteem and to
right the precarious psychological balance that had been upset
by the defeat. To the French the Germans of 1940 seemed in-

vincible. When Sartre's Mathieu finds himself in a position to shoot a German soldier isolated from his unit, he discovers a new truth: "the German army is *vulnerable.*" Like Orestes in *Les Mouches* after killing Clytemnestra and Aegisthus, Mathieu has accomplished his work. Paradoxically the dead German becomes proof of Mathieu's passage on the earth. Transfixed by an almost "religious fear" of the German supermen at the start of the attack, he now wants to kill others, since it is so easy, and to plunge Germany into mourning.[47] Even if the war is going to be lost anyway, as his comrade Pinette observes earlier, killing the enemy is a means of saving honor.[48]

If the Germans were strong in war so much the better for the French once the fighting was over. They could afford to feel less guilty over the defeat.[49]

Not only were the Germans strong, but they often cut an imposing figure in uniform. Of all the parts of that uniform certainly among the most imposing were the boots. "A man with jack boots is twice a man," Jean Dutourd states convincingly. The sight of German boots evoked either the admiration or the bile of the French. They saw in them the symbol of their misfortune. The German boots "represented exactly what they lacked and what had made the others the victors. One cannot lose a war in jack boots!"

Dutourd, for one, was unhappy about the French uniform as a whole. While the French soldier of World War I wore blue, his counterpart in 1940 wore khaki. World War I had proved to be a war stalemated in trenches, and this stationary war combined with the replay it was expected to enjoy, what with the fortifications along the Maginot Line, had determined the change in color: "the soldier clad in blue was thought of as coming from a distant horizon and mingling with the sky; but khaki, that base color, is intended for the man who withdraws into the earth, who sinks into it, who incorporates himself in the clay, who digs himself in." As for boots, a sedentary soldier guarding fortresses did not even need them.

To compensate for the lack of éclat in their uniform, the individual soldiers, all except "the most untidy, the most dirty" among them, attempted to achieve some kind of distinction. They found some way to achieve a *genre artiste.* Some tightened

their belts to an "inhuman" limit in order to swell their chests
and uniform jackets. Others practiced for hours the best way
to tie the *chèche* they wore on their necks. When Dutourd puts
forth the idea that a well-dressed soldier has more self-esteem
and in turn commands more esteem from his enemy, he is no
doubt correct. Precisely because the French felt deficient in
comparing their attire with that of the Germans, one more
wound among many, they sought some measure of satisfaction
for their egos in finding fault with the German uniform.[50]

The German uniform was green, and confronted daily with
the particular shade of that German green, some were quick to
take offense.

> The funny thing about the whole story is that they suppose their
> green uniform harmonizes pleasantly with the gamut of natural
> greens; maybe they think they have invented synthetic chlorophyll
> to die their clothing. No luck, kein glück (sic), it is precisely a
> green that goes against nature, and it is incredible that they have
> been able to win the war in our country with such a color. Maybe
> in their country nature has become accustomed to it, but here,
> everywhere this sham green makes a stain, in the foliage, in the
> grass, at every season. . . . The whole countryside is spotted by
> this shade of green, this mouldy green, this sick green. A hatching
> of larva in the process of eating up a beautiful tapestry.

As for German boots, when one didn't particularly feel like admiring them, one could always object with Perret that the German soldiers "sing with their boots and their heart isn't in it
because everything transpires in their feet . . . their song ad-
heres to the soil, no way to take flight . . . ."

One of the greatest sources of personal vindication Perret
discovers in his critique of the German uniform proves to be
the green knit gloves worn by the officers. Decked out in all
their military elegance, "arched torso and all, these good-looking
officers are wearing gloves of green knitting. They are so stupid, those gloves, so foolish, so foreign that I am all cheered
up because of them." Then savoring the irony to the very end,
he adds: "Of course, that doesn't stop them from being the
strongest if not the bravest, but what beautiful and good things

are they going to bring us, these champions of the new order in those hands of green knitting? I am now very comfortable about refusing everything without scrupule."[51]

Whenever the French wanted to redeem themselves in their own eyes and wipe out some of the sting of the defeat, the ultimate recourse for soldier and civilian alike characteristically focused on "l'intelligence française": the physical might of the Germans may have been greater than ours, but we are more intelligent. This confidence provided the French soldier with a sense of security. In one way or another, his intelligence would later come in handy when dealing with the Germans. Once Sartre's prisoners of war are settled in the camp at Baccarat, they take note that "the Germans didn't appear to be a bad lot"; and then, once they have reassured themselves on this point, their faces again begin to pour forth intelligence, "that specifically French *article de luxe*," and they expect they "could later use it to advantage with the Heinies to buy a few trivial concessions."[52]

On the whole, literature has shown the rapport between French soldiers and their German conquerors to have been as cordial as might possibly have been expected under the circumstances. On either side, few if any are enthusiastic about the situation, and both sides seem willing to make the best of it. Here and there a German noncom will mingle with the French assuring them that soon they will all be going "rétour nach Paris"; or commiserating with them, will repeat understandingly, "Krieg grosses malheur." As frequently as they are called *les Allemands,* the Germans are referred to as *les Fritz, les Chleuhs, les Frisous, les Fridolins, les Frisés,* and occasionally by the time-tested term *les Boches,* but it is rarely with any real hostility or animosity, at most with indifference or a slight condescension. In fact, the Germans are ungrudgingly given a certain respect where it is due: they are good workers, and precisely because they are good workers, they will put France back together again in good working order.[53] Very few of the French soldiers depicted in literature have strongly motivated political convictions, and even Hitler is on occasion brought in for his share of the limelight. At Baccarat a soldier named Livard, admitting that he is neither for nor against Nazism, says that it is simply not suited to the French temperament. Still and all, he concludes somewhat unrelatedly, "I will say this for Hitler, he sticks to his word." Another soldier, Gassou, seconds Livard and then tries to explain a bit more logically to the somewhat exasperated Brunet: "I agree with Livard: I don't like him, but I respect him, and that's more'n I'd say about a lot of people." The other men approve. "He loves his country, it's only fair to grant him that." "He's a man with an ideal. It's not the same as ours, but it's worthy of respect, just the same." [54]

At times one almost has a tendency to forget that the Germans were France's enemy. Jacques Perret's fellow prisoner Dupieu feels a kind of secret admiration for the Germans' clicking their heels, [55] and he is one of many who prefer to direct their hatred against their own officers. Whose fault is it, asks Sartre's Pinette, if we didn't fight? "It's the officers who lost the war." [56]

The English, too, come in for their share of derision. Jacques Perret at one point mulls over the idea of turning rifles against England if only the Germans would give the French their rifles back! Anything is better than captivity; and, after all, for a Frenchman, "shooting at the English is a natural tendency." [57] In another scene from Sartre's novel at Baccarat, the English fare a little better. A soldier named Lambert is provoked by a German Feldwebel trying to sympathize with the prisoners. "Poor Frenchies, where are the English?" Lambert waits for the sergeant to move on and then answers through his teeth: "Up my ass, that's where the English are, and you can't run as fast as they shit on you." Another POW, Moûlu, then steps in: " . . . maybe they will shit on the Fritzes, but it won't be long before they get shit on in turn, and dirty." [58] As it was, when things were really rough, the English had gone home! The French had seen them in operation. After the fiasco that ended in Dunkirk, the English were certainly not going to be the ones to hold out against the Germans. "It's easy for them to talk big when they're tucked away in their island, but just you wait until the Heinies cross the Channel! If we French couldn't hold out, it's a damn sure thing the Limeys won't win the war." [59]

The War and the Defeat as "Game"

Like so many other things in life, war is in many ways a game, and as in every game there are certain rules that have to be respected if the game is to be played properly. In a good game of war the victor must be strong so that he can play his role powerfully. He can also be magnanimous, kind, and understanding, but only on the condition that these qualities are not motivated by weakness of any kind. Only then does the victor permit the vanquished to play their role: they must recognize themselves as the conquered and their enemy as the conqueror. If they refuse to play their role the enemy will not be a conqueror at all. Napoleon learned this to his dismay when he marched triumphantly into Moscow expecting the city to be handed over to him officially by its magistrates, and found instead a virtual ghost town at his feet.

On the whole, the booted Germans of World War II did indeed look strong. While he looked upon the German uniform and the strength it seemed to convey, the average French soldier, as literature depicts him, appears to have been able more or less to play his part in recognizing the victor and in remaining submissive to him. But what if that uniform were removed? The German would then be no more than the Frenchman, and thanks to that special gift of French "intelligence," he would probably amount to less. As Sartre's POWs move on foot toward their internment camp and enter the town of Baccarat, they cross a bridge and suddenly stop.

> . . . millions of eyes were turned toward the river: five naked Heinies were splashing around in the water, uttering little shouts; twenty thousand gray-faced sweating Frenchmen, stifling in their uniforms, stared at bellies and buttocks that for ten months had been secure behind a rampart of guns and tanks but were now exposed to view with a quiet insolence in their fragility. So that was it: their conquerors were just so much vulnerable white flesh.

A low sigh runs through the crowd of prisoners. For even the vanquished need to retain a minimum degree of self-respect to play their role effectively. "Without the slightest feeling of anger, they had watched the progress of a victorious army perched on its triumphal chariots, but the sight of these naked Boche swine playing leapfrog in the water was an insult."[60] The scene could hardly bear too frequent a rerun!

By and large the French soldiers of 1940 were able to maintain that minimal standard of self-respect that enabled them to play out their role. Certainly there were incidents in which the French did not show themselves to be particularly *fiers*. Sartre draws one such example in a scene in which a blond, tanned, muscular German, bare to the waist and looking like "one of those young swells who ski, half-naked, at St. Moritz," sharpens his pocket-knife against his boot and begins cutting slices of bread from a loaf he has taken out of his truck, and throwing them over a barbed wired fence toward the hungry French. They, in turn, growl, grovel, and fight like animals in a zoo over the bread that the "master" is throwing them.[61] On the whole, however, the French soldiers seem to have maintained their own sense of dignity to such a degree that, almost paradoxically, many of them couldn't bring themselves to take the defeat seriously. For many of them, both war and defeat remained relegated to the level of the game, and it was only much later that they could even imagine them as having any deeper significance.

The importance of the historical moment became increasingly vague as the consciousness of war as a game gained precedence. Some of the soldiers began to find elements of the theater in their daily lives; and theater, of course, is also a kind of game in which actors and spectators can enter into a world of make-believe. That make-believe could be gruesome at times, but it was make-believe still and all, and that was in itself a consolation. A sense of theater enables Jacques Perret to look upon the fields of Lorraine as a stage which happens just then to be swarming with accessory characters in German uniforms. It can not be serious, after all; surely they will not be around for long![62] When his first attempt to escape from the camp is foiled, Perret manages to maintain sufficient detachment from his predicament to view it as if it were part of a scenario. The German noncom tieing him up "must have been a boy scout in his youth or a wrapper in a big department store." By letting the German play his role, "decidedly I am giving this man a

good evening; the movie goes on."[63] Sartre provides a similar
screen against which to view the last shots fired by Brunet's unit
and their final capture by the Germans. "It's just like a movie,
nothing looks real . . . ";[64] and Perret even identifies one of
the German sentries in his camp, a good-looking, blue-eyed boy,
as a movie-version Siegfried (a *Siegfried de cinéma*).[65]

In their defeat, the French soldiers played one role after another with marvelous dexterity. The child, who for the sake of
the war had become an instant adult, could revert again to
childhood, ready to be admonished by one of his own generals,
who tells him, as a father would, "not to *misbehave*." By another
stretch of the imagination, he could again become the adult
who in his wisdom had finally taken pity on the Germans and
given in, as adults will, to the foolishness of children.[66]

But what were so many of these soldiers if not boys suddenly
being asked to shoulder the responsibilities of men? They had
not been given time to learn their new role, and as a result did
not always know how to act. Shortly after the establishment of
the camp at Baccarat, the German authorities begin to allow
the prisoners to receive regular twenty-minute Sunday visits
from their families. The French soldiers, uncertain as many of
them are, of how their fathers will accept the defeat that their
sons have "imposed" on France, watch anxiously as the older
men enter the camp with a slow and heavy pace:

> . . . they had won their own war when they were young, and
> their consciences were clear. This defeat was not *their* defeat, yet
> they accepted it as their responsibility, carrying the burden of it
> on their broad shoulders because, when a man has produced a
> child, he has to pay for any damage it may do. They were neither
> angry nor ashamed, they had come to see what mischief the young
> hopefuls had been up to now.

The young soldiers stand there, not knowing what to expect,
waiting perhaps for a slap in the face.[67]

Introspection: The POWs Look at Themselves

A few skeptics aside, the French soldier of 1940, as he is remembered in literature, seems grateful enough for whatever

amenities the Germans may have granted him. After their internment in the POW camps, the initial and immediate reaction of many is to accept nothing from the Germans, but this reaction soon breaks down. Perret at one point refuses a cigarette offered to him by a German sentry, and yet, ten pages later, when his comrade Chaberlot tries to negotiate for a ration loaf with another sentry, and when the German nonchalantly gives him the loaf as a gift, good-naturedly adding some white bread to go along with it, Perret admits: "I already feel with sorrow that my heroism is starting to melt in my watering mouth." He decides that there are two basic solutions to such a dilemma. The Roman solution would be to trample the offering of the conqueror underfoot, the sportsmanlike solution to receive it as a handshake from the victor at the end of the last round. "The sportsmanlike solution has very numerous adherents." When Chaberlot offers to share the German's bread with Perret, Perret is forced to concede that "on the spot I forgot to notice a bitter taste."[68]

Either because they had exhausted their own capacity to resist or because they had developed, if not a liking for at least a certain understanding of the Germans and of their own need to get on with the enemy, some of the French soldiers ended up by learning a few words of German, just as the Germans had learned a few words of French. Passing among his comrades one day, Brunet finds one of them reading a book and from time to time consulting a huge volume nearby which turns out to be a dictionary. The soldier has decided to learn German.[69]

The reasons for which a Frenchman might learn a bit of German, however, were not always the same reasons that determined the Germans to learn some French. The constant repetitions, "Ein monat England capout, krieg fertig, allés rètour Pariss, Madam, kôgnak, compris?" or "Kapitalist, jude, nicht gut, compris? Franzose camarad, compris? Aber England, cheise!" lead Perret, for one, to conclude that "these formulas must figure in the German-French conversation manual in use in the German army . . . ." Perret takes an immediate and unequivocal stand against those German soldiers who used the French language to spread the Nazi propaganda. "I am willing to collaborate with the downright brute, but Hitler's missionary makes me vomit." Comparing the German army of 1940 to Napoleon's army, a comparison he will reject almost as soon as he has made it, Perret wonders momentarily: "If the warriors of the Year II also had this mania of sermonizing the conquered every evening of battle, I understand that Europe soon had its fill of that band of bores."[70]

The one group of French soldiers who encountered no language problems with the Germans were the Alsatians, and the Germans deliberately separated them from the French. Sartre shows them increasingly eager to speak their own language with each other rather than speak French. Even during the fall, before the war had escalated, Simone de Beauvoir noted in her diary (quoted in *La Force de l'âge*) on October 31, 1939, that already upon her arrival in Nancy everyone, including the soldiers, was speaking German. She had managed to get a pass to travel to Brumath near Strasbourg in Alsace where Sartre was stationed with his unit.[71] Sartre himself eventually ended up in the POW camp at Baccarat, though he does not play a role per se in *La Mort dans l'âme*. When the Alsatian soldiers in the novel are told "Thanks to the *Führer*, Alsace will return to the bosom of the motherland," some cry out "Heil!" enthusiastically, while others open their mouths to form the word but can't bring themselves to vocalize it.[72] Regardless of how the individual Alsatian felt, what was important was that the Germans had succeeded in driving a wedge between them and their French comrades-in-arms.

As time wore on, whatever divisions may have existed among French soldiers at large generally tended to fade away. Initially most of them saw their only obligation as to themselves. Perret's comrade Vincent is a farmer who, like the farmers of Hemingway or Remarque in the best literary traditions of World War I, can think only of going home to his farm to plant and harvest his crops. Another comrade, Dupieu, never encumbered by Perret's own scruples regarding the enemy, readily concludes a deal with a German sentry with whom he exchanges the Maginot Line insignia he is wearing on his uniform for half a ration loaf. After all, perhaps "the first duty of a prisoner is not to die of hunger."[73] The initial problems of

hunger and shelter in the camps were sufficient to occupy the
minds of the prisoners during the period immediately following their internment. But as conditions improved their nerves
relaxed. Once when Brunet is walking around among his comrades at Baccarat, he sees two of them lying completely naked
on a blanket sunbathing. He says nothing, but clearly the narrator speaks for him in assessing the new feeling in the camp:
"a mouthful of bread! A mouthful of bread and this sinister
yard, where a beaten army had been lying at its last gasp, had
been transformed into a seaside resort, a solarium, a fair-
ground." [74]

Discontent and Accommodation

Despite the slackened pace of life that on occasion seemed to
transform the POWs into a group of boys on holiday, minor
incidents recorded here and there attest to a strong if somewhat muted undercurrent of dissatisfaction and hostility. There
were, of course, a few overt attempts to escape, but, in general,
the kind of protest that evolved once the reality of the defeat
began to sink in was of a more subdued nature. When official
German time begins to be imposed at Baccarat, the "sacred"
time of Danzig and Berlin, as Sartre's narrator calls it ironically,
and the watches of the French prisoners have to be rolled back
an hour, even those who are wearing watches they have allowed to run down as a sign of mourning, fall into line. Yet
one day when a group of French prisoners, ravenous with a
midday appetite, ask one of their own sergeants for the time,
he tells them that it is noon even though official German time
reads eleven. He sends Gassou off to do kitchen duty, but Gassou returns almost immediately to report that the kitchens have
not yet opened. Some of the men begin to consult their own
watches, and when they see that it is only ten after eleven, they
realize that it is still too early for the kitchens to be open. That
may well be, the sergeant admits readily, but I am not going to
let go of French time just when France is "dans la merde." [75]

The times were unsuited to grand gestures. Jacques Perret
and his comrade Chaberlot decide that even if they do not particularly like the humiliation of performing such menial duties

as sweeping out the German lodgings, it is better to be alive broom in hand than dead carrying a rifle. Besides, there is more than one way of handling a broom, and a person does not have to choose the most energetic. And so they shuffle along, playing at sweeping rather than actually working.[76]

Even these mild forms of protest were perhaps healthy indicators, for they showed that the capitulation of the French army had not been a total one and that in their hearts the French soldiers had abandoned neither France nor themselves. A kind of *entente* had been established with the Germans. Neither side seemed eager to cause undue difficulty for the other, but both continued to keep a watchful and wary eye. The war being a time of heightened sensitivities, such an attitude could upon occasion produce almost comical results. At Vaucouleurs the soldiers go to wash in the river at the edge of the camp. Perret makes it quite clear that this is no romantic Arcadian stream but a veritable Ganges of men packed close together, scrubbing each other's backs, enjoying themselves and the water despite the crowding. Suddenly a German sentry's voice rings through the air. "Nix ligne Siegfried!" Perret looks around to see that his comrade Ballochet has hung a wash cloth on a nearby strip of barbed wire. The sentry calms down quickly, pleased at what seems to him his cleverness in preventing the French from appropriating the lyrics of a British war ballad about the soldiers hanging out their wash on the Siegfried Line and allowing these lyrics to assume a semblance of reality in a prisoner-of-war camp in Lorraine.[77]

Incidents such as these make it clear that French and German soldiers never lost sight of the fact that they were still enemies even though the hostilities had ceased. If Brunet at times despairs of ever raising the consciousness of his pleasure-loving French comrades above the concern for their immediate well-being, his despair is unduly pessimistic and premature, grounded only in his overly zealous wish to make communists of them all. They may not all have been ready to become communists, but certainly most of them had every intention of remaining thoroughly French. Their consciousness of their own solidarity as Frenchmen and more particularly as French prisoners of war seems in fact to have increased as the weeks wore on. More and more the majority began to believe, like the citizens of Oran in Camus's *La Peste,* that material salvation is not merely an individual affair but the affair of a united community. During one of the Sunday family visits to the prisoners regularly scheduled at Baccarat, for example, a French noncom effects a bold but simple escape. One of the prisoners, Cantrelle, who has learned of the escape before the others, tells them the story: "His old woman came to see him with a suit of civvies in her bag. He changed in a closet and then just walked out with his arm in hers!" Gassou does not quite know what to make of the escapade. At the very least it seems to him an ungrateful gesture toward the Germans who, after all, did not have to authorize the Sunday visits. A few others seem cautiously to share Gassou's reaction. Since they were all going to be liberated anyway, the noncom could have sat and waited like everyone else. A soldier nicknamed Le Blondinet best expresses the general feeling: "We're talking about a bastard who don't care whether he screws up twenty thousand provided he can do as he likes." Brunet is angered by all this talk. The only reason for the men's negative reaction is their own shame at not having done exactly what the noncom did. Testily he adds that he, too, is planning an escape. "We'll see whether anyone gives me away." Gassou counters soberly: "No one will give you away . . . you know that perfectly well, but when I get out of here, I'll damned well give you something to remember me by; because if you escape, you can be sure that we're the ones that'll have to pay for it." [78]

The story of the soldier rescued from camp by his wife is typical of an unending list of bittersweet ironies that at one and the same time plagued and charmed the life of the POWs. Another example is that of a soldier retrieved by his father who arrived at Vaucouleurs one day in his car and without subterfuge of any kind informed the commandant that he needed his boy to help with his business at home. Within the space of a quarter of an hour the son was promptly released into his father's hands. [79]

During their stay in camp Perret and his comrades are visited by an old American lady from the Red Cross, who looks "authoritative and maternal" in her beige raincoat and lovely gray hair. She has come to have the men write postcards to their families with assurances of their good health and agrees to take it on herself to mail the cards from Paris. She has already visited other camps and is winding up her tour. She has accumulated 50,000 postcards and is taking them to Paris in her van that very evening. The Germans had told the prisoners that it was useless to write since they were soon going to be released, but they eagerly avail themselves of the opportunity. Grateful to her as they may be, however, it is stupefying, all the same, to think that this old American woman can circulate freely on the roads of France and will be in Paris that evening, while they as Frenchmen are being detained as prisoners in their own country. "Greetings and good health": this is the message of the *armée vaincue,* the conquered army. They had gone to war to deliver Poland and now find they can be shot and killed, as indeed one of their number is, for urinating too close to the barbed wire fencing that encloses their camp.[80]

The Breakup of the POW Camps and the Trip to Germany

Despite all the hopes and all the rumors of an immanent liberation, for most of the prisoners freedom was still far off. By the end of the summer of 1940 trains rolling toward the east carried with them almost one and a half million French POWs about to be recruited for labor in Germany.[81] For most of them this was a fact not to be believed, and the pages of Sartre and Perret recounting that trip through eastern France and into Germany figure among the most pathetic and heartrending in the literature of World War II. As they head toward the cattle cars that are to take them away from France, all but a few of them still believe in their immanent liberation. This is to be the beginning of the trip home. The fact that all railway workers and Bretons from Perret's camp are excluded[82] should have been a clue, had the men been less intent on taking their hopes for realities.

En route to the trains they can see posters on the walls of local buildings showing a German corporal holding a French child in his arms. The soldier is fresh and healthy-looking, "as if he were doing a toilet soap commercial, and the child was radiant with happiness and confidence, a little thinnish no doubt, but one felt so much that the corporal guardian would soon give him the ample cheeks that his idiot mother hadn't managed to give him." At least the Germans were not cutting off children's limbs, and if the French soldiers were indeed going to be away for a long time, "it was good to be able to tell oneself that we were leaving our children in such good hands."[83]

Once the POWs were herded into the cattle transports the doors were shut, and until deposition in Germany the men could only stretch and strain at the garret-like windows in the roof of the cars to get a glimpse of the outside world and an indication of where they were actually going. With a kind of ironic good-humor Perret compares the crowding in the cars to the crowding in the Paris Métro, reaching into the realm of the familiar to help explain and alleviate the discomforts of the new and the fear of the unknown. He claims that the French soldier feels rather at home in an animal transport; and indeed the soldiers do seem to have accepted the situation with as much calmness and good grace as was possible under the circumstances.

After they were locked into the cars their first thoughts were for food, but however great their hunger, their need for empty ration cans was equally great. For men piled virtually on top of one another to be able to relieve themselves with a certain attention to cleanliness was no small feat but certainly worth the effort. With a little dexterity the ration cans could be unloaded through the roof window. Inevitably, though, there were accidents, compounded by the fact that many of the soldiers came down with diarrhea. Some renounced the effort and the ration cans entirely and on the spot simply did what they had to do. What Perret fears most is not the dirt or the stench or the enforced promiscuity of life in the transport cars; rather it is the loss of individual identity, and the fact that some of the men so early and so easily forget the most basic habits of cleanliness does not bode well.

A few, however, stubbornly retain traits of their individuality. Amidst the congestion, Perret notes that the NCOs managed always to remain together in a corner separated from the rest of the men. "Maybe they all have the same density," he reflects a bit sarcastically. Or again, there is the young reservist placidly reading *Les Orientales* in the huddle, who, not unlike Victor Hugo, is off "promenading" in the Orient while history is in the making much closer at hand.[84]

Trying to determine where they were going was, of course, an uppermost consideration. Both Sartre and Perret describe the agonizing situation of waiting to see whether the trains would take a left or a right turn at an upcoming fork, the soldiers inevitably relying for information on a comrade who knew the local rails. Slowly but surely the talk of their being taken to Germany was beginning to gain credence; and when they finally saw their destiny taking shape, some became angry, angry first with themselves for having allowed such a monstrous thing to come to pass. Others tried to joke bitterly. They tried to laugh and make their comrades laugh with them, like the soldier from the camp in Baccarat who talks about his "old lady" wanting "a kid." He isn't going to be around to give her one now. Now he'd have to write her to "get herself mounted" by the neighbor.[85]

Some are less philosophical. A young printer on the train from Baccarat, having reached a point of nervous exhaustion, wants to jump from the moving car and risk death rather than face internment in Germany. He is a communist, but "like a woman" has abandoned himself on Brunet's shoulder. Though uncertain after this display of weakness whether the printer can ever be a valuable asset to the Party, and debating with himself whether he has any right to prevent the man from jumping, Brunet, nonetheless, holds him fast. The printer asks for an empty can to urinate into, and while Brunet's attention is momentarily diverted, he undoes the hold and makes his leap. Almost instantaneously the Germans fire. Taking fright the printer tries to jump back into the car. Unlike Perret's group, the prisoners from Baccarat can see outside; they actually watch the printer running alongside the railroad car and they scream encouragement to him. He calls on Brunet again and again, and Brunet reaches out in a futile attempt to pull him back in, but at this moment the printer is cut down. Immediately but understandably the French prisoners forget any past kindnesses the Germans may have shown them. Among the Germans who come into the car to take charge of the situation the French recognize the *gros frisé* who had given them cigarettes when his colleagues were not looking and whom they had sort of befriended: he now has the eyes of a murderer. "The Frenchmen and the Germans glared at one another. *This was war.* For the first time since September '39, this was war."[86]

CHAPTER III

Civilian France in the Defeat

The War and the Exodus

The civilian population of France had been no more eager than were its soldiers to see France become involved in another war. The martial fervor that had excited the people twenty-five years before was gone, and gone, too, were the enthusiastic throngs and the atmosphere of parade that had sent the troops off to the front in 1914. To a great extent World War I itself was responsible for the change of heart. The deadly reality of that war had not measured up to the romantic ideals with which people had welcomed it, and they were not eager for a repeat performance. France had borne the brunt of the operations on the western front from 1914 to 1918, and the memory of it was still too vividly appalling. On September 12, 1940, after returning to Paris from the south eight days earlier, Jean Guéhenno wrote in his *Journal des années noires:* "Perhaps Hitler's genius consists in having understood that by playing on men's cowardice he could do anything he wanted during that period from 1930–1940 in which the memory of the Great War and its horrors left only fear alive in the European consciousness."[1]

Although many French feared another war, not everyone in the 1930s believed that Germany would start one. When Madame de Staël published her *De l'Allemagne* more than a century before, France fed on the visions of the peacefully idealistic and idyllically romantic nature of the Germany she portrayed, and continued to do so until that conception was blasted by the guns of the Franco–Prussian War in 1870. Again in the thirties, albeit certainly on a lesser scale, something similar seemed to be happening. "They made a success of German (anti-) war books," wrote Robert Brasillach, himself condemned to death in 1945 for collaboration with the Germans. From post-World War I Germany had come books like Remarque's *Im Westen nichts Neues* and then the films that were made from these books, notable among them being Pabst's *Westfront 1918* and *Kameradschaft* in which the Germans and the French had succeeded in establishing a dialogue. Projected on the screen were "gray images despairing of the fatality of war. In short, we were falling asleep."[2] In 1937 Brasillach and several of his friends managed to convince some French newspapers to help them defray part of the cost of a trip to Nürnberg to see the Nazi Party congress that was being held there. Brasillach returned enthusiastic about what he had witnessed, but his overall enthusiasm did not prevent him from retaining a certain lucidity. Taking note of the flowers adorning the balconies of German houses, he observed: "This people loves flowers. . . . It's always been what attracted the believers of the past, those who loved the 'good' Germany, the heavy-set Madame de Staël. Flowers do not preclude other realities."[3]

From the other end of Europe Franz Werfel, who was born in Prague and later lived in Austria until he was obliged to leave it in 1938, made a similar statement in his play *Jacobowsky und der Oberst* (1944), which he wrote in exile in California. The situation against which the play unfolds is the flight of a group of people from Paris to the southwest corner of France where they congregate after having "run" just about as far as they could from the oncoming Germans. In a café in Saint-Jean-de-Luz one of Werfel's characters, a stock type identified only as the Tragic Gentleman, reflects on the situation that has brought them to this extremity of Europe. "Damn Beethoven and Wagner! Damn German music! It is the exalted artillery barrage by which our souls were softened up for the Panzer divisions!"[4]

When the troops and the Panzers came in the spring of 1940, the inhabitants of the invaded territories reacted in different ways. Some remained calm and philosophical like the old man in Sartre's *La Mort dans l'âme* watching Roberville burn. "We had the Boches here in the other war and they didn't do much harm; they're decent fellows." And the countryfolk with him watched the blaze with an almost relieved sense of satisfaction, repeating over and over again, "It's peace, it's peace! . . . The war's over; it's peace."[5] But these, the calm, the stoical, the philosophical, were not the ones who left their mark on literature. Those who left their mark were the ones who simply picked themselves up and fled; millions of people from northern France pulled together their families and their belongings and headed blindly south. "It was no longer France, it was not yet Germany," writes Simone de Beauvoir in *La Force de l'âge*,[6] and since in their fear and anxiety these people did not know what to expect from the Germans, they ran from them as best they could.

Flying to Arras at the end of May, Saint-Exupéry was able to witness this mass exodus first hand.

> Looking down on those swarming highways I understood more clearly than ever what peace meant. In time of peace the world is self-contained. The villagers come home at dusk from their fields. The grain is stored up in the barns. The folded linen is piled up in the cupboards. In time of peace each thing is in its place, easily found. Each friend is where he belongs, easily reached. All men know where they will sleep when night comes. Ah, but peace dies when the framework is ripped apart. When there is no longer a place that is yours in the world. When you know no longer where your friend is to be found.

Those who had taken to the roads knew only one thing, they were going south. They knew not where and often they knew not why. Most often the mayor or some other local official had ordered their village evacuated, and so they went. "Somewhere in the north of France a boot had scattered an ant hill, and the ants were on the march."[7] In the south there would be no one to receive them, and even those who were initially well-disposed to helping the refugees find food and shelter became hardened with the passage of time. One could accommodate only so many.

The use of insect metaphors, ants (*les fourmis*) in particular, to describe the refugees and their clutter lining the roadsides

is a favorite both with Saint-Exupéry and with Sartre. Even
Werfel uses the term ant columns (*Ameisenzüge*) in his play, and
at one point Sartre develops the metaphor to provide a full
orchestration of sound imagery. "The insects crawled past,
enormous, slow, mysterious. . . . The cars creaked like so many
lobsters, scraped like so many crickets. Human beings had become insects."[8] That June not many thought to dignify the mass
rout to the south with the term exodus (*exode*).[9] This was reserved for a later time that was more leisurely and could afford
to be more reflective.

If one could prescind from looking at the general ugliness of
the hordes of people in flight, human birdlime (*glu humaine*) as
Michel Tournier calls it using still another metaphor,[10] and look
at the individual situations comprised in that general mass, one
can uncover the stuff of the entire range of human emotions.
They were sometimes tragic, comic, ironic, farcical, mercenary.

Sarah and her little boy Pablo in *La Mort dans l'âme* have hired
a chauffeur at Melun outside of Paris to take them in his car to
Gien on the Loire. The car runs out of gas and comes to a
standstill on the road twenty-four kilometers from Gien. The
cars they had been following all morning "stretched forward
into the distance in a cloud of dust. Behind them, horns, whis-
tles, sirens, a warbling of metallic birds, a hymn of hate." Sarah
and her chauffeur manage to push the car off the road, the
horns stop, and the flow of traffic continues. The chauffeur
declares flatly that now he will go no farther, even if she were
able to find him some gasoline. It is a foregone conclusion, of
course, that she will find none, since no one will stop for them
and lose his place in the line of traffic. In her frustration, Sarah
tries to prod the chauffeur by telling him that if he stays put
until the Germans arrive, they will deport him along with all
other able-bodied men; but her threat is without effect. "Well,
well, you don't say! And I suppose they'll cut off the kid's hands
and rape you, if they can bear to. All that is a lot of hooey; I
bet they're not half as bad as people say." He then tries to exact
the 200 francs she promised him as payment for the trip. Since
the trip has not been completed she is inclined to give him
nothing, but for the sake of peace ends up by giving him first
100 francs, then a second hundred, and then sets out for Gien

on foot. The sights she encounters are no more pleasant than the one she has just left. After a while she finds herself next to an old woman carrying a bundle who has probably fled some Paris slum and can hardly walk anymore. Kindness welling up in her heart, Sarah offers to assist. "I'm not giving my bundle to nobody," answers the old lady with a look of hatred in her eyes. "They don't want to be loved, they're not used to it," Sarah decides and she continues her trek toward Gien.[11]

Somtimes the Germans moved faster than the refugees, and tanks rolled past the winding caravans. But at other times whole German divisions floundered in the stew, and Saint-Exupéry observes that, Germans, who a short while ago were killing Frenchmen, were now giving drink to these refugees to slacken their thirst.

The refugees did not travel lightly. Everything that could possibly be crammed into their cars, trucks, or farm wagons accompanied them: all the relics of a peaceful French family life. But already the character of these precious possessions had changed. "Fling sacred relics into a heap and they can turn your stomach." Saint-Exupéry's attention is drawn especially to the old cars that line the highways:

> Of all these objects the most pitiful were the old motorcars. A horse standing upright in the shafts of a farm-cart gives off a sensation of solidity. A horse does not call for spare parts. A farm-cart can be put into shape with three nails. But all these vestiges of the mechanical age! This assemblage of pistons, valves, magnetos, and gear-wheels! How long would it run before it broke down?

Saint-Exupéry tells the story of a woman who approaches him one morning as he comes out of his billet. She wants help getting her car out of the garage. He asks her if she is sure she can drive it and she responds, "Oh, it will be all right. The road is so jammed, it won't be hard." But the road is not easy to drive and Saint-Exupéry estimates that the woman, accompanied by her sister-in-law and seven children, might be able to advance only from two to ten miles a day. Not to speak of gas and oil. He draws her attention to the fact that her radiator is leaking to which she responds that it is, after all, not a new car!

Her fate can be predicted. A few miles and she will run into half a dozen cars, stripping her gears and blowing out her tires. She and her family, beset by problems beyond their ability to cope, will start to cry and then give up. "They will abandon the car, sit down by the side of the road, and wait for the coming of a shepherd."[12] The allusion to the shepherd in a literary work so richly endowed with imagery and metaphor makes one think back on those happier times that pastoral poetry had painted in such mellow tones. The technological civilization that should have made life easier seems to have had the opposite effect. The cars that should have assisted the exodus impeded it, and now perhaps the shepherd would have to be called upon to help. The irony of the situation did not escape the artists. In his long film documentary on occupied France, *Le Chagrin et la Pitié* (1969), Marcel Ophuls captures memorable scenes of old cars stretching out on the highways as far as the eye can see. A civilization was breaking down, a civilization that had elevated the automobile to the level of a symbol.

Charity was not always offered during the exodus, and when it was, it was not always appreciated. Following the example of the Paris government which itself had taken to the roads, the Poissonard family in Jean Dutourd's *Au bon beurre,* slippery as the fish their name evokes, leave their dairy shop in Paris in June 1940 to set out in their van on the road to Bordeaux. Seeing a man in uniform on the way, they decide to offer him a lift. The soldier, however, turns out to be less grateful and cordial a guest than the Poissonards might have anticipated, for he drinks red wine without offering any to his benefactors, and Julie Poissonard quickly concludes: "The world is bad." In the future they will know not to pick up the first person who comes along simply because he is dressed in khaki and traveling on foot.[13]

Depending on background and status in life, some people found the exodus harder than others. For Werfel's Old Lady from Arras in *Jacobowsky und der Oberst* it is a veritable trauma to think that she has had to flee the city where her family has been living for centuries. Jacobowsky, however, a Jew who for years has been living as a refugee, views the events in a less tragic light. One remarkable feature of warfare is that it throws together the most unlikely group of characters, and Werfel has used this situation, with all its potential for comedy as well as tragedy—which he often rather skillfully intermingles—around which to construct his play, designating it as the "comedy of a tragedy." Jacobowsky grew up in Germany believing himself to be a German. With the advent of Hitler his belief proves futile, and he flees to Vienna, then to Prague, and finally to Paris. For him unlike the Old Lady from Arras the flight from Paris represents only one more stage, bitter and disappointing though it may be, in the larger adventure of his life.[14] For the Tragic Gentleman things seem less complicated. He is resolved to be a Parisian to the end and, therefore, simply to do what all of Paris appears to be doing—that is, leaving it.

> The Parisians walk, walk, walk. They are going to the stations, but the stations are dead, for no trains are leaving. And so the Parisians turn their steps and walk and walk through the long lanes of the suburbs, thousands, ten thousands, hundred thousands, all with bag and baggage, young women, old men, little tots and grandmothers, the businessmen and the doctors, the clerks and the lawyers and the keepers of the bistros, and the waiters and the barbers and the deserters, and the leaseholders of the houses and the janitors, and the streetsweepers and the dogs, and only the cats stay at home.

In twenty-four to forty-eight hours, the Tragic Gentleman continues solemnly, the Germans will be in Paris, and only God, Saint Denis and Sainte Geneviève, the patron saints of the city, know where all the refugees will be and what will have become of them. What is left behind will no longer be the Place de la Concorde or Vendôme or the Boulevard des Italiens, but only the empty façades.

> When the Boches march in, Paris will be a grimy casket, without even a corpse in it.... And I... I... was born in Paris and I belong to Paris and I go away from Paris... with Paris. And I don't want to ride... I want to walk with all the others and with the wandering boulevards, walk and walk, for hours, for days. For when the legs ache, the heart aches less....[15]

And so they left, from the north and the east and from Paris itself, all heading south, many without fixed destination. In Paris

apartments one can hear to this day the stories of those who
for some reason or another were not able to leave the city and
who were asked by their departing neighbors to take the keys
to all the doors in the building for safekeeping. Some had relations in the south; others like the characters in Werfel's play
and all those who on political, racial, or religious grounds had
to fear the Nazis, knew only that they had to put as much distance as possible between themselves and the Germans. They
fled to the southwestern extremity of the country, to Bayonne
and the surrounding area, "to stop up the cities and towns of
this accursed corner of French soil where all the scum of Europe has come together to gurgle away."[16]

The Civilians, the Bureaucracy, and the Defeated Army

Amid the confusion brought on by the German invasion, the
bureaucractic life of France, both in the prisoner-of-war camps
and on the homefront went on as usual. Jacques Perret even
finds it a source of consolation that during a time of so many
changes, this one facet of life should remain constant. In the
camps those who had always done the office work of the French
Army now simply continued to do it for the Germans.[17] In the
Werfel play, even before Jacobowsky and his traveling companions are finally overtaken by the Germans in Bayonne and Saint-
Jean-de-Luz, they are detained en route by a conscientious
French gendarme demanding their identity cards. Once it is
established that they have come from Paris he asks to see their
travel permits. Since their permanent domicile is in Paris, he
instructs them with the official dedication of a true *fonctionnaire*
to go to the police commissariat of their arrondissement in Paris
to request permission to change *département;* the commissioner
will, in turn, send their request to the Préfecture which will
send it on to the "Bureau Central Militaire de Circulation."
These are the ones who will finally decide whether or not the
refugees have the right to come as far as they have. The fact
that Paris is by this time in German hands, as Jacobowsky reminds him, cuts no ice with the gendarme. According to regulations, "You will . . . promptly betake yourself to Paris . . .
in order to comply with the officially prescribed procedure.

Otherwise you are circulating on this highway illegally, illicitly, and without permission of the authorities."[18] Fortunately Jacobowsky and his companions are able to keep the gendarme talking until his tour of duty expires for the day, after which he becomes humane enough to detain them no further. But their woes with French officialdom are not yet over. As the Germans extended their conquest, they simply enlisted the French civil service to work for them. One day Jacobowsky, his friends from Paris, and some new acquaintances made along the way are rounded up in a café in Saint-Jean-de-Luz and taken for questioning by the police. The arrest is made by a French police commissar, two French policemen, and two SS men. When the refugees protest that they are French and living in their own country, the commissar says meekly that he can do nothing. He has his orders.[19]

While the relationship between the civilian population and the bureaucracy, never the most cordial to begin with, was rapidly becoming more antagonistic than ever under the pressures of the defeat, the relationship between civilians and the army had been marred from the start of the fighting by frustration and misunderstanding. The flight of the refugees had made chaos of the conduct of the war. In their fright and confusion, people had often directed their hostility against their own army. Some reproached the soldiers for not fighting hard enough, others reproached them for fighting at all. And if the civilians began to resent the army, French soldiers, in turn, began to resent the civilians. For whether the civilians had taken to the roads or chosen to await the enemy at home, they quickly became a colossal nuisance. Since the homefront had become the battlefront, and since the battles, or more accurately, the skirmishes were taking place in front of people's windows or along the very roads on which they had hoped to flee, there was no longer any mystique surrounding the fighting. Familiarity breeds contempt, as the proverb tells us, and contempt was growing both for the war itself and for the soldiers fighting it. In World War I perhaps some civilians had seen too much, they had been too close to the fighting; but now just about everybody was seeing too much and many wanted to put an end to it as rapidly as possible. Since they could not end it, they fled from it. In Bertolt Brecht's play, *Die Geschichte der Simone Machard,* Père Gustave, an employee in a hostelry in Saint-Martin, "a small town on one of the main roads from Paris to the south of France," observes: "The crowds of refugees are ruinous for warfare. . . . When a war breaks out they ought to be moved to another planet, they're only in the way. One or the other has got to be abolished: the people or the war, you can't have both."[20] But this was not France's choice to make in 1940. Since neither the people nor the war was about to be "abolished," the people decided to fight the war in their own way, becoming in a vague sense, as Brecht suggests, an army unto themselves[21] and frequently an enemy, for all practical purposes, to the official army of France.

Sartre's *La Mort dans l'ame* is filled with small incidents depicting the hostility of the local population to the French army. Just before the end of the fighting, with enemy guns flashing in every direction, Brunet enters a sleeping village hoping to find a place to bed down for a few hours. He picks a house at random and descends into the cellar where he discovers a man, woman, and child hiding in fear. They know the Germans are near and the last thing they want is to be found harboring a French soldier. "I've got a wife and kid: I don't want to pay for any of your nonsense!" the man warns Brunet. In a very basic and elementary way the woman is even more hostile. There are some Frenchmen who are still fighting. Why is Brunet not with them? "Get out of here! You've lost the war, and now you're going to get us killed into the bargain!" When he informs the family that in light of the military fiasco he intends to surrender when the Germans arrive, the woman curses him as a "dirty bastard" for not continuing to fight with the others still out there, and as a "filthy coward" for endangering her life and the lives of her husband and child.[22] With unabashed defiance Brunet finishes a shave before taking leave of the panic-stricken trio and thanks them for their hospitality.

Abel Tiffauges in Michel Tournier's *Le Roi des aulnes* has a similar encounter. Tiffauges, his colonel, and another soldier come upon a local inn somewhere in eastern France where they hope to gain a brief respite from the fighting. But as the Germans come closer, they are told to leave the inn and head out into the open country. On account of his pigeons, Tiffauges is somewhat tardy as usual and soon finds himself without his companions. The innkeeper is dismayed. He certainly does not want the Germans to find a French soldier in his establishment. "He is going to chill his wine to welcome the Germans . . . ," reflects Tiffauges knowingly. The man is a businessman and for him the defeat will have more meaning than did the war itself.[23]

Since the army had not defended France's civilian population as it was "supposed" to, the civilians were in no hurry to set aside their anger and hostility toward the army once the fighting and the exodus were over. Sartre comments on the silence of one community in Lorraine watching the French soldiers, now prisoners of war, pass by.

> They were there now, on the doorsteps, their arms folded, silent: women with black hair, black eyes and black dresses, and old men, all staring. Confronted by these spectators, the prisoners straightened up, their faces became peaked and cynical, they waved their hands, they laughed and shouted: "Hello, ma! Hello, pa! We're the guys they drafted, the war's over, so long!" They passed with their greetings, ogling the girls, smiling provocatively, but the spectators said nothing, they just looked. Only the grocer's wife, a fat, good-natured creature, murmured: "Poor boys!"

One soldier from the north of France observes that it is a good thing they are not now in his part of the country, recalling again the hardness of the mercenary-minded northerners that Barbusse had already scathed in *Le Feu* in 1917. "They would be throwing furniture at us."[24]

When finally these same French prisoners are herded into the trains taking them to Germany, they wave from the cars at their countrymen whom they pass en route, many with handkerchiefs in hand to be sure their greetings will not be missed. But they receive no response. One soldier named André feels that the civilians could at least say *bonjour;* they had been happy enough the previous September when the troops had gone out to get their faces "bashed in." His somewhat more realistic colleague Lambert reminds him that they hadn't gotten their faces bashed in, but André will not be silenced; it is not the fault of the soldiers. They are French prisoners, and they deserve a greeting. The greetings are not forthcoming, however. An old man, seated on a folding camp stool, fishing, doesn't even take the trouble to look up at them.[25]

Ironically one of the few soldiers in literature who is offered some assistance by the local people turns out to be just the one who does not want it. As Abel Tiffauges in the company of other French POWs passes on foot outside of Strasbourg ready to cross the Rhine into Germany, young Alsatian girls living on the west bank of the river come from their houses to offer the French soldiers something to drink. The German guards surveying the movement would often close their eyes to these goings-on, but when one old Alsatian sets up a bucket and glasses on the sidewalk in front of his house, they feel he has gone too far. In the resulting confusion, a woman comes up and pulls Tiffauges into her house, offering him civilian clothing and a chance to escape. Since no role count had been taken at the outset of the march into Germany, he has a fairly good chance of success. Instead he thanks the woman for the glass of milk she offers him and resumes his place in the ranks.[26]

However gnawing and painful the general silence of the civilian population, which so many French soldiers encountered, perhaps it was better than the harangue fired off at them by one of their own sergeants in *La Mort dans l'âme,* a military man who had fought the war in 1914 and who still believes that soldiers are supposed to get killed in war.

> I saw it all coming a long time ago, I only had to look at you, the boys of 1940, the skulkers, the pretty boys without an ounce of fight in them. No one could so much as say a word to you; . . . Just you wait, I thought, one of these days there'll be a bust-up and what'll the little tough guys do then? The fat'll be in the fire then all right, I said. All the little ninnyhammers asking for a leave; when all the fuss about leave started, I knew the game was up. You little bastards were too spunky; the army had to send you home to get your babes to suck some of it off you! Did *we* have leave in '14?

When Lambert tells the sergeant that they are not interested in hearing his life story, he retorts: "I'm not telling you the story of my life, I'm just explaining how we won our war and you lost yours."[27]

Even before the defeat was completed French soldiers began to sense how little the nation would appreciate them. When Mathieu and his group of men find themselves being abandoned by their officers on the sixteenth of June, any illusions they might still have entertained start to crumble away. One unidentified soldier cries out bitterly, "They never liked us anyhow!" expressing something they had all been thinking for some time. Others join in. No, they never liked us, never. For them we were the real enemy, not the Fritzes. Even Mathieu, usually calm, cool, and collected, can't help but join the chorus. With the voice of the third-person narrator Sartre cuts short what was clearly an ongoing dialogue among the men. The narrator proceeds to speak on their behalf, articulating all their grievances in a kind of depersonalized interior monologue.

> Tongues were loosened, talk had become a necessity. No one likes us, no one: the civilians blame us for not defending them, our wives have no pride in us, our officers have left us in the lurch, the villagers hate us, the Heinies are coming up through the darkness. More accurately they should have said: we are the scapegoats, the conquered, the cowards, the vermin, the offscourings of the earth; we have lost the war, we are ugly, we are guilty, and no one, not one solitary being in the whole world has any use for us.[28]

Thus did this generation of French soldiers become, unlike the *poilus* of 1914, "the conquered ones" (*les vaincus de '40*).

Adapting to Defeat

The civilians adapted as best they could to the reality of a defeated and occupied France. If anything, the testimony of literature indicates that too many adapted far too readily and too well, and that many did so even before the new reality had become an established fact. The best way to adapt was to capitalize on the situation and turn defeat into material profit in the same way that some had turned the war into profit. In Bertolt Brecht's play of the debacle, *Die Geschichte der Simone Machard*, a deserter named Georges runs home to Saint-Martin before the Germans can capture him and defends his desertion without scruple. Aside from Germany's military superiority which would have made resistance futile anyway, he feels no sense of debt toward France. On the contrary, thanks to him France "has won something else": "A gentleman in Tours has made good money on my shoes and a gentleman in Bordeaux on my helmet. My jacket brought in a castle on the Riviera, and my leggings seven race horses. France was making a good thing out of me before the war even started." [29]

Brecht wrote his play in collaboration with another left-wing German writer, Lion Feuchtwanger, who was Jewish and who, with two grounds to flee the Nazis, found himself interned in France as an enemy alien after the war broke out and before he managed to emigrate to America. The Marxist-oriented Brecht clearly wished to indict the capitalist system as a cause for war, and given this purpose, he forged his characters well. Monsieur Soupeau, the proprietor of the local inn at Saint-Martin has reserves of gasoline hoarded away and refuses to make them available when the town mayor requisitions them. To the mayor's complaint that Soupeau has only been half-filling the pots of the soldiers and refugees streaming through Saint-Martin, he replies that he is running a restaurant and not a charitable institution. The play is structured around an alternation of realistic sequences and dream sequences. The mayor's sad reflection that only a miracle can now save France, since it is rotten to the core, ends the first realistic sequence. It is followed by Simone Machard's first dream which takes place on the night of June 14. Simone is a teenager whose brother is the only man from Saint-Martin to have volunteered for the French army. In her dream she leaves the ugly reality of the spring of 1940 and is transplanted back into what history has generally recorded as a nobler time in France and in which she becomes Joan of Arc, the Maid of Orléans. An angel who appears to her in the dream exhorts her to rally the people. "Now drum, and wake this people from its trance / Tell rich and poor take pity on their mother France." Unfortunately for Simone-Joan the real times are not disposed to heroic formulas that had seen their day long ago, and the first citizen she tries to rally to the cause turns out to be a disappointment. She tells him that his mother, France, is in danger, but he cannot think in these abstract terms. His mother was Madame Poirot, a washerwoman who had come down with pneumonia and for whom he had not had the money to buy medicine.[30]

From the start of the play it is quite clear that in the real world of 1940 people are ready to use patriotism for whatever purpose suits their fantasy and that the name France will cover a multitude of sins. Monsieur Soupeau refuses to place his trucks and his gasoline at the mayor's disposal because he intends to flee Saint-Martin and the oncoming Germans himself, and in order to flee in style he needs his trucks. Be reasonable, Philippe, he tells the mayor. "You talk about the property of France. What about my supplies, my precious china, my silverware? Aren't they the property of France? Do you want them to fall into the hands of the Germans?" But one of Soupeau's truck drivers, Maurice, sees through his employer's calculations. "It's not the Germans he wants to save his supplies from. It's the French."[31] And indeed, lest one immediately damn the Soupeaus of 1940, it must be remembered that the refugees were often hardly any more principled than they, as Brecht makes abundantly clear, stealing and lying whenever it was convenient and possible to do so. When Madame Soupeau, the mother of the proprietor and a deceitful and despicable character in her own right, asserts that thanks to the refugees' being sheltered in the town schoolhouse, it is "beginning to stink of sewage around here," that "the gutters of the northern cities are pouring their rats into our peaceful villages," and that Saint-Martin was "getting the riffraff from their cheap wine rooms," one realizes that though her lack of sensitivity is offensive, her assessment is not altogether untrue.[32]

Most of the refugees, whether they were the poor people or the business people like Soupeau, who eventually did manage to leave Saint-Martin, or the Poissonards, the shopkeepers from Paris, most in the end returned home, some within a few days, others a few weeks, some yet a bit longer. The Poissonards, who possess absolutely no charm of their own, find none in the departmental capital of the Gironde, as Jean Dutourd calls Bordeaux, to which they have fled. Unable to find accommodations in an area that is filled to the seams with refugees like themselves, they live for a week in their dairy truck. Jeannine,

the elder of the Poissonards' two children and an avid reader
though still a child, has had the foresight to bring along a collection of irrelevant reading for young girls with which to occupy herself. But then, persons older than she were doing similar things in their attempt to find escape and distraction—
Jacques Perret's soldier reads Victor Hugo's *Orientales* in a POW
convoy on the way to Germany; and the Immortal from the
Académie Française in Franz Werfel's play, who finds himself
no more than a refugee among mortals in southwestern France
in June 1940, plans his thirty-first book, to be entitled, "The
Provençal Art of Cooking under the Avignon Popes."[33]

Soon reports coming from Paris encourage the Poissonards'
return:

> The most important piece of news learned during four years of
> Occupation was that the Germans were correct. This news alighted
> in Bordeaux like a dove and smoothed many furrowed brows,
> including those of the two Poissonards, who had been tortured
> without respite by the thought of their beautiful dairy in the Rue
> Pandolphe (17th *Arrondissement*) being put to the sack like Byzan-
> tium.

The Poissonards pull themselves and their belongings together
and in two days return singing to Paris. At noon they arrive at
the Etoile where a group from the Wehrmacht is playing a kind
of funeral march. The Poissonards' young son Henri, called
Riri, is delighted as a little boy can be at the sight of soldiers.
Even his father, Charles-Hubert, is impressed. "What discipline! . . . It's not surprising they won the war." His wife, Julie, described a few sentences later as "ruminating like an ox,"
a woman who is every bit as dull as her husband in everything
that does not concern her dairy business, decides that, after all,
the Germans are men like all others. The joy of the Poissonards
is indescribable when they see the somewhat discolored yellow
letters of their shop Au Bon Beurre. "For two pins they could
have thanked the Germans." One of the first things they do
after putting on clean clothing is to wash their truck, dirty from
the trip. "We mustn't set the Germans a bad example. They
must see that the French also know how to behave." To their
first customer, a local woman named Madame Lécuyer who has

just recently received the news that her son Léon, a second-lieutenant in the French army, is now a prisoner of the Germans, the Poissonards hypocritically attempt to show themselves as good Parisians. "Well, they can't keep us from our dear old Paris, you see? Off we go for ten days and then here we are back again. Germans or no Germans, Paris is always Paris."[34]

Paris may always be Paris, but still and all something had changed if only in the visible German presence. During those few days in which Paris had found herself deserted by her own inhabitants she seemed to lose something in her lifeblood which she would not so easily regain even with their return. Those who had remained witnessed the changes first. "Nobody on the boulevard Saint-Germain; in the rue Danton nobody," wrote Sartre in *La Mort dans l'âme*, allowing the voice of the omniscient narrator to merge with that of the homosexual Daniel, one of those who had not left.

> The iron shutters had not even been lowered, the windows glittered: the proprietors had just removed the handles from the doors and gone. It was Sunday. For the last three days it had been Sunday; the whole week now, in Paris, consisted of one day. A ready-made, colorless Sunday, rather stiffer than usual, rather more synthetic, over-marked by silence . . . .[35]

Walking through the empty city, in which every window could become so many pairs of German eyes, Daniel feels himself to be the "warden of the Necropolis," a dead city in which the only colorful note is the Nazi flag flying from the Hôtel Crillon. But in other ways Paris is not dead at all, for the simple reason that it is now all his. For a brief moment in an interior monologue, Sartre allows him to appropriate the narrative voice entirely to himself. The Nazi flag, a blood-red rag with a circle in the center, "white as that of the magic lantern shining on the sheets of childhood," and "in the middle of the circle a knot of black serpents, Monogram of Evil," this flag would become "my emblem."[36] Just a little while before he saw a red and white poster that proclaimed, "We shall win because we are the stronger." Yet now they are all gone, the strong ones, not only Mathieu and Brunet whom he had known and whom he imag-

ines now to be either dead or taken prisoner, but also all the
others who for twenty years had been putting him on trial.

> . . . there had been spies even beneath his bed; every casual
> passer-by had been a witness for the prosecution or a judge or
> both; every word he spoke could have been used in evidence
> against him. And now, in a flash, stampede. They were running,
> the witnesses, the judges, all the respectable folk . . . . The walls
> of Paris were still clamorously extolling their merits and their pride:
> we are the stronger, the more virtuous, the sacred champions of
> democracy, the defenders of Poland, of human dignity, or heter-
> osexual love; the wall of steel will be unbreached, we shall hang
> out our washing on the Siegfried Line. The posters on the walls
> of Paris were still trumpeting a hymn of triumph that had gone
> cold. But *they* were running, mad with terror, flinging themselves
> flat in the ditches, begging for mercy . . . . They are running,
> they are crawling. I, the Criminal, reign over their city.

Suddenly in the midst of this long reflection he sees another
"them," the Germans, moving along in camouflaged trucks toward the Seine. What do they look like, these avengers against
a society that had oppressed him? "They were standing upright, images grave and chaste . . . standing stiffly, the inex-
pressive glances of their eyes resting momentarily on him. And
after them came others, other angels, exactly alike, looking at
him in precisely the same way." Though he is the only civilian
and the only Frenchman in the street, Daniel knows no fear;
rather he is prepared to surrender with confidence to these
foreign men who are "our conquerors."

> . . . Boldly he returned their stare, taking his fill of their blond
> hair, of their sun-tanned faces in which eyes showed like glacier
> lakes, their narrow waists, the unbelievable length of their mus-
> cular thighs. He murmured: "How beautiful they are!" He felt no
> longer earthbound: they had lifted him in their arms, they were
> clasping him to their chests and their flat bellies.

In his naïve ecstasy he imagines this to be the beginning of a
new world. Gone is the old society and the old law, and with it
the sentence that has hung over his head. Gone, too, and running for their lives, are the men who had defended that old
world, "those horrible little khaki soldiers, those champions of

man and the citizen . . . ." In a mental image that could be a scene from a last judgment tabloid, Daniel sees himself as the sole survivor of a disaster that has befallen the world, "the sole *man* confronted by the angels of hate and fury, the angels of extermination whose gaze invested him with the gifts of child-hood." As Daniel continues to watch the passing parade of the soldiers who are to be the new lawmakers, he especially notices one young German standing at the back of a tank and smiles at him. The German first looks at Daniel impassively, but as the tank draws away, he smiles back and reaching into the pocket of his breeches, throws out a pack of English cigarettes, which Daniel clutches so tightly that they snap. With all the Baude-lairean fascination for evil that Sartre shares, Daniel joyfully welcomes the German harbingers of the "Reign of Evil" about to begin. Indeed he "longed to be a woman so that he could load them with flowers."[37]

Shortly after this quasi-mystical experience Daniel runs into the young French deserter, Philippe, whom he saves from what might have been suicide in the Seine. Normally Daniel would not bring his pick-ups from Montmartre or Montparnasse back home to his apartment. But today is different. France is "screwed" (*foutue*), and now everything is permitted. Today the concierge along with most of the tenants of the building are in flight on the roads. Today Paris is empty. The French have left and he can do as he pleases![38]

But Daniel's rather simpleminded delight at the arrival of the Germans in Paris was far from universal, even among the Pa-risians who remained, and perhaps to no one did the German coming represent a greater tragedy than to the Jewish child who grew up to become the narrator of Serge Doubrovsky's *La Dispersion*. So traumatic, in fact, was that experience that its memory returns to haunt him years later when as an adult he has to deal with the loss to another man of a woman he has loved. This new suffering merges at first here and there with recollections of the other which it rather casually and superfi-cially evokes through various associations in the mind of the narrator. The recollection itself grows, however, until gradually but persistently it submerges, dominates, and in a sense assim-ilates the newer tragedy of the broken love affair. Doubrovsky,

writing in 1969, twenty years later than Sartre, uses situations
similar to Sartre's, the scene of the Nazi flag flying above the
Hôtel Crillon and the impression it made on an individual who
had been shunted away from the mainstream of society: Daniel, because of his sexual orientation, alienated from the old
society and, though he does not yet know it, certainly also from
the new; Doubrovsky's narrator, because of his Jewishness, from
the Aryan society that the German conquerors would seek to
create. The use of the metaphor of the serpents to designate
the swastika at the center of the Nazi flag is common to Sartre
and Doubrovsky, and so is the use of the object pronoun "them"
to designate the first real encounter of Daniel and the Jewish
child with the alien forces of occupation. But where Sartre uses
the personal pronoun *les,* Doubrovsky uses the more emphatic
disjunctive pronoun *eux* to represent the culmination of one of
the many verbal deliria (*délire des mots*) that characterize his
writing. The very momentum draws the reader into a vortex,
at one and the same time facilitating and coercing his participation in the spectacle. The passage describing that first encounter of the Jewish boy and the Germans in Paris in 1940
becomes in the hands of the narrator not simply the retelling
but the literal re-creation of the event.

Knowing that the Germans are on their way and hoping that,
since Paris has been declared an open city, they will not raze it
as they had razed Warsaw and Rotterdam, the narrator, now a
grown person, allows his vivid imagination of what the Germans would be like to fuse, in retrospect, in a series of non-
grammatical run-on phrases, with his memory of what they
actually were like during his first confrontation with their presence:

> . . . sweeping away everything, scattering everything, creating
> a void ringing with echoes under our skulls, lashing us with shat-
> tering noise, imperial, beaming, teeth shining, the pearly sap of
> their triumph dribbling from their lips, oozing from the pores of
> their smile, seated on trucks whose hoods had been rolled back,
> without making a gesture, their rifles between their knees, the
> whole boulevard full of them, our eyes full, our ears full: THEM.

Suddenly the scene shifts and the narrator again remembers
his lover on the Place de la Concorde. The sight of the im-

mense, empty square where he walked with her long after the war was over and the Germans gone, has triggered the association. That day she pointed across the square and asked him to identify a building in the distance. It was the Hôtel Crillon and again the narrator's memory is thrown back to 1940. He and his brothers, Charles and Marc, have come down from their apartment building, by now emptied of all its tenants who have fled the city. They walk into the rue Royale. Maxim's, of course, is closed, and the few pedestrians in the street seem to avoid each other's contact. On the Concorde a large black car has taken up position and is playing military marches from a loudspeaker mounted on its roof. Soon the loudspeaker stops, and all around the car, there they are, the Germans, coming on foot for the first time, *grandeur nature,* in true-to-life size.

> At the head, the trumpet fanfare, the brass, the drums in front, three across, and a few steps farther forward still, all alone, the general's standardbearer, and then, emerging from the Madeleine, stretching from one end of the square to another, over the bridge, beyond the Seine, the hammering of boots, dry, hard, implacable, many with field glasses around their necks, cartridge-pouch and holster, long grenade handles passing below the belt, the beating of boots, black, polished, impeccable, rifles carried stock in hand, heads at half-right, coming almost up to the knees, the regular breaking surf of the boots, the sun projecting a jungle of shadows onto the deserted pavement, multiplying the men and weapons in moving spots on the ground . . . the booted feet are rising and falling in cadence, the legion of centipedes without respite is crushing our pavements and our chests, the train of larva is stamping on Paris . . . .

The narrator seizes his brother Marc's hand which has shriveled in his own, and together they behold a

> . . . giant veil hiding pilasters and pediment over the whole width, over the whole façade, at the top of the Crillon, swirling without end on itself, coiled in an ecstasy of hatred, jet black serpent, cobra of the night, in the hideousness of the sunlight, tearing itself away from the pale gray shroud to leap over us, in us, in an exulting firewheel . . . gotten like a direct whiplash, triumphant, in the eyes, in the snout: THE SWASTIKA.[39]

Pétain and the Church

When the Parisians returned, those like the Poissonards simply adapted to the German presence, even hoping that the war between Germany and England, and therefore the occupation of France, would continue and that Germany would mount an attack on England as she had on France. The Germans would then be required to buy foodstuffs from France to supply their invasion force. Furthermore, if France had not been able to repel a German invasion, why should England be spared? A German conquest of England would soothe French pride. Still, not all could be so immediately mercenary-minded as the Poissonards, and as late as September 16, 1940, Guéhenno laments in his diary: "Poor Paris. Those lines at the store doors. And the tremendous silence of the streets. This is Thebes or Memphis, but no longer Paris. I decide to lock myself into my house and to go out as little as possible." [40]

The many French who made their peace with the Germans did so with the full encouragement of the venerable old Marshal who now officially, and more than anyone else, incarnated France. Many found it not only convenient but reasonable to rally to his cause in June 1940 and virtually throughout the four years of occupation. Looking back on those years in his preface to the *Journal des années noires* which he published after the war in 1946, Guéhenno sums up his own appraisal: "The crime of ex-Marshal Pétain was to make of dishonor a temptation for a whole people. There is no worse crime against man than to tempt him in his baseness and his cowardice." [41] In June 1940, France was interested in saving whatever could be saved, echoes Jean Dutourd in *Les Taxis de la Marne*, [42] and Pétain responded to that need. Few were in a mood to think about France's soul. One who did was Charles de Gaulle, but his voice was ignored. Thanks to Pétain everything was going to be all right. Pétain was going to give back to the prisoners of war their civilian life. Moreover, he represented the old French tradition of glory, whereas de Gaulle was relatively new and less known. All of France, or almost all, soldiers and civilians alike, were reassured that Pétain had done the right thing once they saw how "correct" the Germans were. "We found that we did not have to deal with a horde of savages after all, that civilization had not been destroyed, that France went on." One could accept material defeat and still maintain the nation's soul and spirit intact. "Pétain, the Père Goriot of France, the Christ of patriotism, had made us a gift of himself. France was the daughter of this blameless old patriarch—a prodigal, a shameful daughter." In selecting a literary antecedent for Pétain in Père Goriot, the long suffering father-figure whom Balzac describes as "the Christ of Paternity," Dutourd is only heightening his satire. One characteristic of Goriot that Dutourd does not evoke is the old man's selfishness amid all the apparent selfless generosity that he lavishes upon his ungrateful daughters. The selfishness and the selflessness abide together, neither able to cancel out the other. Perhaps the literary image is even more apt than Dutourd suspected. After the debacle, Pétain's Vichy regime organized a press campaign to blame Marcel Proust and André Gide for the defeat. France had read too many of their books, and they had "insidiously infused into the national soul the poison of renunciation and skepticism, so that our armies had been crushed." With the Vichy campaign against Proust and Gide in mind, Dutourd further develops the image of France as a wayward but repentant young girl, throwing herself into father Pétain's arms and tearfully begging pardon "for having read too many novels. They were the explanation of why a big brute had beaten her black and blue, poor thing."[43]

For the soldiers turned prisoners of war and bound for Germany the realization that Pétain was leading France to a great disappointment came early. They had never thought it possible that the old Marshal would so let them down.[44] For a large part of the civilian population that realization was slower in coming. A few, however, were critical from the start. As the Parisian refugees of Werfel's play sit in a café in Saint-Jean-de-Luz waiting for the Germans to overtake them, Pétain's "hollow" voice comes across the radio waves, interrupted by repeated fits of coughing, announcing that he has asked the Germans for peace. The nation has not been equal to its tasks, he reminds the French, encouraging them to tear themselves loose from their wanton past and take part in the building of a new Europe. The Tragic Gentleman, whose habitual pessimism at this point

sharpens his perceptions, explains to a little boy next to him:
"*That* is dear old grandpa with the ice-cold heart! *That* is Trea-
son speaking of Honor! *That* is day-before-yesterday's mouldy
victory! *That,* unfortunately, is a Maréchal of France! *That* is
Monsieur Pétain!"[45]

The politics of the Pétain government seemed all too frequently to go hand in hand with the politics of the Church, or
vice-versa. The Church had not played a very edifying role in
World War I if we are to believe the testimony of books from
France and elsewhere such as Barbusse's *Le Feu,* Romain Rolland's *Au-dessus de la mêlée,* Jaroslav Hasek's *The Good Soldier
Schweik,* and many others, and she appeared to be doing little
better the second time. In Perret's camp at Vaucouleurs, priests
are "content to pull out the malicious argument of a chastised
France, divine punishment, redemption in misfortune . . . ."[46]
At Sartre's Baccarat one Sunday morning a priest delivers a
sermon lambasting French workers and employers alike for their
materialism and greed, and telling the French prisoners of "la
France pécheresse," sinful France, who for the last quarter of
a century has forgotten both her duties and her God. It is because of this materialism that they have been beaten. Evoking
France's old and glorious title of "eldest daughter of the
Church," he reminds them that this is the France that has inscribed in the roles of history her magnificent succession of vic-
tories, but that it is a France without God that has come to
know defeat in 1940. France has been chastised, and now by
her suffering she must pay for her sins and "buy back" her way
to God. Interestingly enough, in choosing a verb like *racheter*
and its noun derivative *rachat,* the priest with oblivion anchors
his own lesson in a highly materialistic vocabulary. Brunet is
quick to draw a sarcastic parallel between "France, the eldest
daughter of the Church, and Pétain, the leader of the French,"
and reproaches Baccarat's curé for associating primarily with
the officers, and often with German officers at that.[47]

Both Cardinal Gerlier of Lyon and the recently appointed
archbishop of Paris, Cardinal Suhard, among other Church
leaders, publicly lent their support to the Pétain government.[48]
Of course, public support for Pétain was fairly widespread for
some time after the signing of the armistice. But in the prisoner-

of-war camps and outside them there were priests who took a line that many people were beginning to find offensive, or if not downright offensive, irrelevant to their present condition. At Perret's second camp at Lérouville one of the men responds to a sermon on the mystery of the Immaculate Conception by saying that the question of the Instantaneous Liberation would now also not be without its mystery.[49]

The French and the Germans Take Each Other's Measure

If they did not meet with a joyous reception in France, the Germans at least met with a generally "correct" one, if one can use the word which the French themselves so often applied to the Germans. Both sides seemed to be making a conscious effort to be civil to each other, and more often than not they succeeded. The meanly avaricious Madame Soupeau in Brecht's *Die Geschichte der Simone Machard,* who takes charge of the family inn at Saint-Martin for a brief period while her son is busy fleeing from the Germans, does more, in fact, than prudence and decorum dictate. She had refused to take in the refugees, but dressed in black though she is, gracefully opens her doors to the Germans. Obviously she has little choice in opening her inn, but as always with Brecht, there is a class issue here, and Madame Soupeau, a business woman of comfortable means, would rather receive polite and "well brought-up" Germans who preface their requests with "please" than hordes of desperate homeless refugees. The German officers are introduced to the town notables by Captain Fétain, a wealthy vineyard owner and a duke of Burgundy who is known to be a "secret fascist" and whose name is too close to that of Pétain to be a coincidence. Saint-Martin's mayor tries to decline Fétain's invitation to breakfast at the hostelry with the German officer in command, but Fétain knows that with the Germans in town he has the upper hand. The mayor capitulates, and Père Gustave comments knowingly: "They're selling France the same way as they sell their wine and hors d'oeuvres!" By the end of the breakfast, Madame Soupeau has offered the German officer the gasoline stocks stored on her property, and so the gasoline that had been refused for the evacuation of the refugees would have passed into German hands had not the girl Simone Machard, with visions of Joan of Arc in her head, set fire to it. But Simone is neither clever enough nor devious enough to lie, and soon all of Saint-Martin knows that she has committed the "crime." Fétain and Madame Soupeau determine to have her sent to a home for the feeble-minded, for the "least our guests can expect," warns Fétain, "is that we clean up the dangerous elements in Saint-Martin." One of the Soupeau truck drivers reminds them that they are doing the Germans' dirty work for them, but Madame Soupeau will hear nothing of Simone's patriotism. The girl must be punished for damage inflicted on her property. It is all well and good that another one of the truck drivers can offer a cigarette to a German soldier of the rank and file and that before long they can both declare the whole war to be "merde" along with Madame Soupeau, Fétain, and the German officer in charge. What is important is that the Soupeau family has owned the hostelry for 200 years. To Madame Soupeau that is patriotism, and from now on people like herself and Fétain will be calling the moves. "*We* are France."[50]

On the whole the Germans had no quarrel with the French who loved their country, provided this love did not translate into the kind of violence or destruction of which Simone's fire was to become a forerunner. Their general attitude toward the French population seems in no way to have been a hostile one. Werfel makes a few references to the German prejudice that every French woman is a flirt[51] or involved in what a Gestapo official dressed like a tourist calls a "French triangle," meaning she is sleeping with two men at the same time. But in the larger order of things, these accusations are perhaps not so serious after all, and certainly they were not shared by all Germans. A German first-lieutenant, in fact, immediately counters the "tourist" by saying that in the Bund Deutscher Mïdchen, the feminine equivalent of the Hitler Youth, they are supposed to "do it" in groups of four all the way up to twelve![52]

If anything, the Germans were still too dazed by their recent race across France to have "taken on the habits of victory," recalls Jean Dutourd of those first days and weeks following the defeat. And the French as yet knew nothing about slavery.[53]

Both sides needed time for their attitudes to jell and to learn the rules of the new game.

There was one issue, however, on which the Germans did not need any time for their attitudes to take shape, and this was the question of what to do with German refugees in France, many of them Jews, who had fled to France to escape Nazi persecution. According to the terms of the armistice, the French government pledged to hand these refugees over to the German authorities.[54] In the third and last act of Werfel's *Jacobowsky und der Oberst,* the Polish colonel Stjerbinsky and his French fiancée Marianne sit in the café at Saint-Jean-de-Luz awaiting their fate with their Jewish travel companion Jacobowsky and other exiles. Stjerbinsky is in possession of some secret papers that must be delivered to a liaison in London. In the café they make the acquaintance of an Englishman, an official in disguise named Mr. Wright, who, for all dramatic purposes, functions perhaps a bit too much like a *deus ex machina* ready to untie the knot. He is in Saint-Jean-de-Luz waiting with a ship off the coast, protected by the fog and the French harbor police, to rescue people like Stjerbinsky from the debacle. Because of Marianne's relationship to the Pole, Wright is willing to admit her on board for passage to England, but as for Jacobowsky, it is out of the question. Only English subjects and allied officers are being rescued from the collapse. No one else. Jacobowsky, however, has fled once too often in life and is now resigned to whatever destiny might have in store for him. Still hoping to be able to get him on board the ship to England, and having less to fear from the Germans herself, Marianne renounces her place for Jacobowsky; but Mr. Wright will have none of it. Jacobowsky is literally at the end of his rope after the German announcement of an immediate round-up of all non-Aryan aliens. He produces two little bottles of pills one of which contains some type of medication and the other a poison. When, despite the hopelessness of his situation, he casts the poison into the sea, Mr. Wright decides on the spot that England can use such a man and invites him aboard.[55] Marianne decides to remain in France where she can be of more use to her country than as an exiled wife living in an English hotel room. She will marry Stjerbinsky on the day of his triumphant return, when the marriage can take place in France.[56]

Like many of the French who have hitherto led a rather individualistic, carefree, and easy life, Marianne is beginning to feel a bond intensify between herself and her people. A desire to fight is beginning to well up in her as in many of her countrymen, a desire that would eventually culminate in the activities of the French Résistance.

CHAPTER IV

Germany—Life under the Nazis

New Realities

Though daily life in France underwent a series of changes after 1940, in Germany the changes had come much earlier. Adolf Hitler, leader of the National Socialist or Nazi Party, was named chancellor by President Hindenburg on January 30, 1933, and when Hindenburg died on August 2, 1934, Hitler, according to a law enacted by the cabinet, assumed the role of president. That title itself was quickly abolished and Hitler was officially called Reich Chancellor and Führer, his old Party name. On the night of May 10, 1933, thousands of students marched in a torchlight parade to a square opposite the University of Berlin and there burned some 20,000 books. Any book that could be construed as alien to "German thought" or to the Nazi conception of Germany's future was vulnerable, as was any book that might have an undermining influence on the German home or the "driving forces" of the German people. Thomas Mann, Erich Maria Remarque, Arthur Schnitzler, Stefan Zweig, Albert Einstein, Sigmund Freud, André Gide, Marcel Proust, Emile Zola, and many others went up in flames. General reading as well as the school and university system were thenceforth more closely scrutinized. Beginning at the age of six children of both sexes were brought into various levels of the Nazi youth organizations. At fourteen a boy entered the Hitler Youth (*Hitlerjugend*), where he remained until he was eighteen and fit for the Labor Service or the Army. Girls of fourteen were placed in the BDM, the League of German Maidens (*Bund Deutscher Mädchen*), where they remained to the age of twenty-one.[1]

The press and radio were censored and exploited by the government for propaganda purposes. On October 4, 1933, the Reich Press Law stipulated that every editor had to be a German citizen of Aryan descent not married to a Jew. Journalism was declared a "public vocation" and any deviation from government policy was prohibited.[2] As is true even today in most European countries, the radio was already a state monopoly, and so the task of enlisting it in the service of the Nazi state was easily accomplished.

Hitler began his public war against the Jews soon after assuming office by issuing laws that excluded them from public service, the universities, and the professions. On April 1, 1933, he ordered a national boycott of Jewish shops. The Nürnberg Laws of September 15, 1934, deprived Jews of their citizenship and relegated them to the status of "subjects," thus incorporating into the legal system the idea that Jews could not be Germans. Marriage between Aryans and Jews was officially forbidden and so were extramarital relations. As the years went on new laws were added to outlaw the Jew even further from German society.[3]

The Christian churches fared better, certainly, for with them there was no racial issue involved. But the pulpit was another form of media, and those who "misused" it to speak against the Nazi state had to be silenced. Thousands of arrests were made.[4]

But all was not grim in Germany in the 1930s. From works such as Robert Merle's fictionalized account of the life of an Auschwitz camp commandant in *La Mort est mon métier* (1952), Klaus Mann's fictionalized rendition of the rise of actor/director Gustaf Gründgens in *Mephisto* (1936), Leni Riefenstahl's film of the 1934 Nazi Party rally in Nürnberg, *Triumph des Willens* (1935), and even Inge Scholl's *Die Weisse Rose* (1953), a documentary written in memory of her brother and sister who were put to death in 1943 for their part in an anti-Nazi student movement of the same name in Munich—from these works and others it is quite clear that for many Germans Hitler's state brought relief, hope, and joy after the economic chaos that followed World War I with its poverty, inflation, and unemployment. Germans were working once again. Once again they could look forward to relative economic security, and after the political humiliation imposed on them by the Versailles Treaty, many felt they could again take pride in their country. People of all ages, children and adults alike, were inspired with the idea of working toward a common goal, which was the betterment of life in Germany.

Not everyone, of course, had the same idea of what a better life meant, and for those who refused to obey the government or who challenged its conceptions, there were the Gestapo and the concentration camps. Gestapo is an abbreviation of Geheime Staatspolizei, the Secret State Police, which was originally established on April 26, 1933, to operate in Prussia only, but expanded one year later when Field Marshal Hermann Göring placed it under the direction of Heinrich Himmler, whom Hitler had made head of the SS or Schutzstaffel in 1929. The SS together with the SA, the Sturmabteilung of storm troopers or Brown Shirts as they were called, formed the armed military wing of the Nazi Party. A series of rulings in 1935 and 1936 placed the Gestapo above the law and beyond the reach of judicial review. This meant that if the courts, which were already reduced to a state of subservience, should, nonetheless, on occasion hand down a verdict whose decision ran counter to the wishes of the Nazi Party, the Gestapo might intervene, as it actually did in the case of Pastor Martin Niemöller. When Niemöller was acquitted by the courts after eight months of prison on charges of "underhand attacks against the State,"[5] the Gestapo hauled him off to a concentration camp.

The concentration camps mushroomed during Hitler's first year in power, and by the end of 1933 there were already some fifty of them, not yet the mass extermination camps of the war years, to be sure, but places where a prisoner could be beaten or tortured. Some prisoners were simply put to hard labor, occasionally to the point of exhaustion and death; others were murdered outright as a result of the sadistic brutality of the torturers.[6]

Adapting to the New Realities. The Nazi Party.

Scholars may continue to speculate for years to come as to why the German people allowed a man like Adolf Hitler legally to

come to power in Germany or to stay in a position of power
once he had acquired it. Stefan Zweig, an Austrian writer who
considered himself, along with Romain Rolland in France and
others of their day, more of a European than a national of any
particular country, offered several explanations for Hitler's extraordinary success. In a memoir-essay called *Die Welt von Gestern*, written in exile, largely in Ossining, New York, and published posthumously, first in English translation in 1943, then
in German in Stockholm in 1944, he wrote: "Inflation, unemployment, the political crises and, not least, the folly of lands
abroad, had made the German people restless . . . ." At every
level and in every group there was a longing for order, and for
the German people "order had always been more important
than freedom and justice. And anyone who promised order—
even Goethe said that disorder was more distasteful to him than
even an injustice—could count on hundreds of thousands of
supporters from the start." So much for those hundreds of
thousands. But there were others who should perhaps have had
the foresight to squash the Nazi movement while it was still
possible to do so. Those people, Zweig objects, simply never
took Hitler seriously until it was too late. "Germany has not
only always been a class-conscious country, but within these class
ideals she has, besides, always borne the burden of a blind over-
estimation and deification of 'education.' " A few generals may
have gotten by without university training, but what Lloyd
George had accomplished in England, Garibaldi and Mussolini
in Italy, and Briand in France, that is, to rise from the ranks of
the people to the highest positions in the state, was not thought
possible in Germany. It was "unthinkable to Germans that a
man who had not even finished high school, to say nothing of
college, who had lodged in flop-houses and whose mode of life
for years is a mystery to this day, should even make a pass
toward a position once held by a Bismarck . . . ." [7]

Zweig left his home in Salzburg in 1934. After his house was
searched under police warrant with the pretext of looking for
subversive materials, he realized just how great the pressures
from across the German border were becoming. From then until 1940, when he emigrated to New York, while he resided
primarily in London, he traveled frequently and in the fall of

1937 flew back to Vienna to see his mother one last time before it was too late. Though by then Hitler had long since secured his base of power in Germany, and though Austria would fall under Nazi domination the following March, Zweig could not convince the Viennese that anything serious was in the offing, and he reflected sadly that those who were still wearing tuxedos to the opera and the gala social events of the city would in a few months be wearing convict attire in the concentration camps. But perhaps they were right to enjoy themselves while they could. Perhaps the "eternal light-heartedness of old Vienna" was indeed the best remedy. Those whose make-up allowed them this kind of carefree existence suffered only once, when disaster finally struck, whereas those who were too realistic and too farsighted suffered first in their imagination and a second time through the reality which in the end spared neither.[8]

Sooner or later everyone had to make some accommodation to life in the new Germany. For some this was more painful than for others, but there were those, especially in industry, for whom the adaptations were downright profitable. For Leni Pfeiffer, the central character of Heinrich Böll's *Gruppenbild mit Dame* (1971), as unpolitical a nature as there could be, adaptation primarily meant adjusting to the fortune or misfortune of friends and relatives more politically committed than she, and later, during the war, making do with whatever food supplies were available. To espouse the "forces of order" some joined the Party early, like Alfred Matzerath, the father of the midget Oskar, narrator of Günter Grass's *Die Blechtrommel* (1959), which was made into a film of the same name in 1979 by Volker Schlöndorff. Matzerath's entrance into the Nazi Party brings little change either to his own life or that of his household. Beethoven's picture is removed from its nail over the piano and replaced by that of Hitler, and Matzerath himself has to piece together a uniform consisting of a brown shirt, "shit-brown riding breeches and high boots," to go parading and drilling with his fellow Nazis on the Maiwiese in Danzig where the family live. Oskar's mother, however, is adamant that Beethoven's picture should remain somewhere in the living room, and the result is that "Hitler and the genius" have to look each other in the eye, with neither too happy about the situation. During the time between the end of World War I and the beginning of World War II, the free city of Danzig was a place where a German and a Polish population coexisted more or less harmoniously despite an increasing Nazi presence in the last years. Jan Bronski, Oskar's mother's Polish lover, for example, adapts readily to Matzerath's entry into the Party. He comes calling regularly on Sundays while Matzerath is out parading.

Some were idealistic in their adherence to the Party, others joined for purely personal advantage. In Albrecht Goes's *Das Brandopfer* (1954), the husband of the central character Margarete Walker joins the Party in the hopes that it may procure him certain advantages and spare him some inconveniences. He finds, however, that it does him even less good than it does Matzerath. Herr Walker has to report for military duty on the second day of the war with Poland.[9] For some like the habitually intoxicated trumpeter Meyn in *Die Blechtrommel,* joining the Party seemed to provide at least a temporary sense of direction, straightening out a crumbling moral and emotional life. In May 1938 Meyn renounces his gin and tells everyone he meets that he is starting a new existence.[10] But when the Nazis, who have their own code of morality, discover that Meyn has half-killed his four cats, stuffed them into a sack, and then put them into a garbage can to die, he is stricken from membership in the SA for conduct unbecoming to a stormtrooper and for "inhuman cruelty to animals." This despite his "conspicuous bravery" on the night of November 9, 1938.[11] On that night, the infamous Kristallnacht, Jewish synagogues, homes, and shops throughout Germany went up in flames in what was called a "spontaneous demonstration." On November 7 the third secretary of the German embassy in Paris, Ernst vom Rath, had been murdered by a young German Jewish refugee, Herschel Grynszpan, whose father had been deported with thousands of other Jews in boxcars to Poland.[12] Meyn helps set fire to the Langfuhr synagogue in Danzig but, as Oskar notes with characteristic irony, "even his meritorious activity the following morning when a number of stores, carefully designated in advance, were closed down for the good of the nation, could not halt his expulsion from the Mounted SA."[13]

That many people, before the war had started and after, joined the Nazi Party or used their position within the Party to justify acts that can only be termed psychologically sick is incontestable, and literature abounds with examples. Erich Maria Remarque's *Zeit zu leben und Zeit zu sterben* (1954) is the tale of a German soldier, Ernst Graeber, who returns home on furlough from the Russian front in the spring of 1943 at the time of the German retreat after Stalingrad and after the first heavy bombings of German cities in the west had begun. By chance Graeber meets a former schoolmate, Alfons Binding, who has become a Nazi *Kreisleiter,* a kind of district supervisor. Clearly Alfons has done well for himself and can afford to treat a friend to a spree, especially an old classmate like Graeber whose family home has been obliterated in the bombings and who cannot even find out whether his parents are still alive. The political and social climate in Germany has deteriorated by this time to such a degree that people hardly dare say anything beyond the absolutely necessary even to their friends, and Graeber regrets the irony that has made the first person willing to help him a Party bigwig. One of the first stories Binding tells him is about an old mathematics teacher they had had, who years ago had reported Binding for some vague "business" relating to a girl. Binding had pleaded with the teacher but to no avail: it was his moral duty to file a report. Binding's father had subsequently beaten him half to death over the incident. Now Binding has had a chance to even the score, and he had the teacher banished to a concentration camp for six months. "You should have seen him when he got out. He stood at attention and almost wet his pants when he saw me. He educated me; so I reeducated him thoroughly."[14]

A friend of Binding's, an SS officer named Heini, boasts openly of sadistically working off his anger on the inmates of a concentration camp he is helping to run.[15] And Frau Lieser, a committed Nazi who has been placed as a watchdog in the house of another of Graeber's school friends, Elisabeth Kruse, has been given part of her apartment for having denounced the girl's father and gotten him sent off to a concentration camp. To obtain control of the whole apartment she would denounce the daughter, too, if she could find an excuse for doing so. Frau Lieser is one of those fortunate ones whose personal ideals and aspirations march hand in hand with the times.

If people felt shortchanged in life for one reason or another, the Party provided a way for them to correct the balance. In Carl Zuckmayer's play *Des Teufels General* (1946), a flying ace named Harras has enjoyed both personal and professional success in life, all of which he has accomplished without the help of the Nazi Party. The Party people envy him his success, his girlfriend observes, especially his success with women. For in that area "they are way below zero."[16] For them joining the Party was a way of setting things right.

Living in Fear

Whatever may have been the motives of the Nazi leaders and however ill-equipped psychologically they may have been for the positions of prominence they assumed, they did in fact impose themselves on the German nation, and to such a degree that they affected virtually every area of German life. Fear so infiltrated daily existence that shortly before the end of the war most people could think about only one thing: how to survive. With the Americans at Germany's western flank in the fall of 1944, they knew the war could not last much longer. But worse than the war for many was the climate of fear that reigned inside Germany, especially during the last few months when, according to one of Heinrich Böll's characters in *Gruppenbild mit Dame,* "every minute someone was being hanged or shot, you weren't safe either as an old Nazi or as an anti-Nazi."[17] Some two years before the end, when the tide first began to turn against Germany, Remarque's Ernst Graeber, home on leave from Russia, found the domestic climate well nigh intolerable. It may be paradoxical though not really surprising that life on the front lines was freer than on the homefront. Under enemy fire life seems to take on a larger meaning, if the experiences created or re-created in literature, and particularly in the novels of World War I, are any guide. Then, as in World War II, the fighting man had neither the time nor the energy to concern himself with the often petty preoccupations of the society back home. Even before his westbound train has entered German territory Graeber gets a taste of what to expect. After the soldiers are put through controls by the German MPs, they begin grumbling among themselves, as "real" soldiers will, about the army of bureaucrats who have stayed behind. They are quickly admonished by one of the older noncoms: "At the front you can talk any way you like. But from now on you'd better shut your trap if you know what's good for you." When the train arrives at the German border, all the men are ordered out into a delousing station[18] and then informed of their responsibility, under penalty of severe punishment, to utter no criticism and to reveal nothing to friends and family at home of the time they have spent at the front. This is routinely accepted. But the next announcement is of a different order. Those heading for the Rhineland, Alsace, or Hamburg are ordered to step forward, and since there is no one from Alsace or Hamburg among them, the Rhinelanders alone step up and are informed curtly and without explanation that the entire Rhineland has been closed to soldiers on furlough. One man who has a wife and child in Cologne demands some excuse, but none is forthcoming. It is not his business to ask questions. He must choose another city to visit instead. What's wrong in Cologne? he asks the others, tears in his eyes. Why can they all go home and not I? Little by little as the train proceeds into Germany, the soldiers become aware that Germany has changed in their absence, that this is no longer the land they left behind and whose memory they have carried in their imaginations, that the scenes of destruction they witnessed in Russia were not unlike what they are beginning to see at home. Already on the night of May 30, 1942, the British "had carried out their first one-thousand plane bombing of Cologne,"[19] but of such large-scale bombings the soldiers at the front had known nothing. Just as they were told to reveal nothing about the front to the folks at home, so the homefront feared to reveal anything to the soldiers that could have political implications. After all, one could be sent to a concentration camp for so much as intimating that Germany might lose the war. The soldiers, however, happy in their ignorance, were simply glad to be back home. They try to explain away what they are beginning to see. Per-

haps there had been a few isolated bombs here and there. Like
the French prisoners of war headed for Germany in 1940, they
wave from their train to farmers in the fields, and like the
French they receive no response. Insulted, a noncom on Graeber's train jerks his window shut. "Oxen . . . . Village idiots
and milkmaids."

The train finally arrives in Graeber's hometown, Werden, a
city somewhere "in the middle of Germany" whose name ironically suggests growth or becoming. It is only thanks to a railroad official who announces the stop that he knows where he
is, for there is no more sign, no more station. Uncertain, Graeber at first hesitates to alight at what appear to be the outskirts
of the town since he knows the station is in the middle of the
city. Confused, he steps down from the train, nonetheless, and
finds that there is a bus waiting that goes on into the city. When
he asks the driver why the train no longer goes through to the
station, he receives a curt, matter-of-fact answer: "Because it
only goes this far."

Getting through Werden to reach his house is a totally dis-
orienting experience. Old landmarks by which he knew the lay-
out of the city have simply vanished. His own house in the
Hakenstrasse, whose remnants he finally locates after considerable ado, is a pile of ruins in a street of ruins. And the townsfolk are of little help. No one dares open his mouth. At last
Graeber finds a couple who were friends of his family and whose
children have all been killed in the bombings. "You don't know
what it has been like here during the last year with everything
getting worse and worse," says the father. "No one could trust
anyone else any longer. They were all afraid of one another."[20]

With increased surveillance and brutality, fear indeed escalated as the Nazi regime began to show signs of panic after
1942; but, in effect, Germany had been living in a climate of
fear for a decade. Many of her greatest writers, like Thomas
Mann and Bertolt Brecht and the Austrians Stefan Zweig and
Franz Werfel, had emigrated to America; Carl Zuckmayer had
fled Nazi Germany for Austria, but after the Anschluss of Austria to the German Reich, he fled again, first to Switzerland,
then France, and finally he, too, made his way to America. Max
Reinhardt and other theater producers and directors, many of

whom were Jewish, also left. Freud fled to London in 1938 after the Anschluss had made Vienna an impossible place for him to live. German cinema, which in the twenties and early thirties had occupied so prominent a position in the development of the art form, was so utterly destroyed by government manipulation that it has only in the last decade really begun to recover. The noted playwright Gerhart Hauptmann remained, however; and Leni Riefenstahl's films, whether she intended them to do so or not, embodied Nazi ideas on the function of the arts.

In 1933 Leni Riefenstahl made the film *Sieg des Glaubens* covering the fifth Nazi Party rally in Nürnberg. Though Hitler himself asked her to make the film, she later claimed she could not secure Goebbels's cooperation at the Propaganda Ministry and was dissatisfied with the footage obtained. In any event, Hitler asked her to do a film on the sixth Party congress in Nürnberg in 1934, and the famous *Triumph des Willens* was the result. Riefenstahl insisted on and apparently obtained complete artistic freedom in making this film. The following year she made *Tag der Freiheit–Unsere Wehrmacht* to placate the army which felt it had been neglected in *Triumph des Willens*.[21]

Music, the least political of the arts because it is the most abstract, was also the most firmly entrenched in German soil and suffered the least uprooting. Composer Richard Strauss and conductor Wilhelm Furtwängler among others had little difficulty continuing their careers under Nazi vigilance.

In 1936 after he and his family had emigrated, Thomas Mann's son Klaus published in Amsterdam the novel *Mephisto* adapted into a film of the same name in 1981 by Hungarian director István Szabó. Despite Klaus Mann's denials, the novel is clearly a satire on his former brother-in-law, the noted actor and director Gustaf Gründgens. Gründgens had married Mann's sister Erika, though the marriage had ended in divorce in 1929. Clearly Mann's hero, whom he calls Hendrik Höfgen, shifting the double *G* of his prototype's initials to the double *H* of his protagonist's, transcends Gründgens. A novel can never restrict itself to biography, for it carries with it its own momentum and its own dynamism. As a novelist, it is true enough, Klaus Mann maintains almost absolute control over his charac-

ters, allowing them very little freedom to develop themselves.
His interventions in the guise of a third-person narrator are
frequent and blatant; and when feasible, rather than allow his
characters to present themselves, he controls their presentation
to the reader through flashbacks and free indirect discourse
(*discours indirect libre*). But despite his rigid control Klaus Mann
was still enough of a novelist to have known that if it was only
a portrait of Gründgens he intended, the novel would not have
been the most appropriate genre. And so when he claimed that
his characters represented "types" rather than "portraits,"[22] he
was no doubt being sincere. The novel was published for the
first time in Germany in East Berlin in 1956, but West German
courts, still fearful in 1971 of injuring Gründgens's reputation,
even though the director had died in 1963, upheld the ban on
Mephisto's publication. When Rowohlt Verlag published the book
in 1980, it chose simply to ignore the injunction.

Hendrik Höfgen is one of those artists who elect to remain
in Hitler's Germany. He can not see himself as an emigrant,
starting from scratch in a country in which he would have to
learn even the language. As the years pass he becomes more
and more successful and powerful, and thanks to his co-star
Lotte Lindenthal, manages to ingratiate himself with the head
of the Air Ministry, a man named Männe, who is a hardly at
all disguised Hermann Göring. Männe makes Höfgen head of
the Prussian State Theater, but his success carries a price. He
must forevermore do the bidding of the Nazis. His own youth-
ful flirtation with communism must be eradicated as well as the
sexual liaison he had enjoyed in a sadomasochistic relationship
with a black African girl. She is deported, whip and boots and
all, to Paris, and Höfgen has made the age-old compromise with
the devil that Goethe enshrined in German culture. Not only is
Höfgen identified with Mephistopheles as the book title suggests, but he has become a Faust for the Mephistopheles he so
brilliantly incarnated again and again on the German stage.

Anyone who was to any degree a public figure had to exercise extreme caution. In *Der Totenwald* (1946) Ernst Wiechert
created the portrait of a writer of some renown whom he calls
Johannes, a name general enough, but a man whose experiences closely resemble Wiechert's own. In 1938 Wiechert's op-

position to the Nazi régime cost him several months of imprisonment in Buchenwald. Early one morning at the outset of the book, Johannes is subjected to a house search by the Gestapo. For four years he has held no public conferences; but more recently, on the occasion of the Austrian Anschluss, when Hitler himself had spoken of rights and justice, Johannes felt compelled to write to the local Nazi Party leader on behalf of the wife and children of a certain unnamed clergyman. The clergyman is never identified, but, given the description of his wide-ranging career from ship commander to preacher, his long imprisonment before a court acquittal, and his subsequent kidnapping and internment in a concentration camp by the Gestapo, he can only be Pastor Martin Niemöller. It is to his letter on behalf of the Pastor's family that Johannes owes the early morning visit of the Gestapo, "whose Asiatic methods have brought more blood and tears to the German people than was possible in a hundred years of western storytelling." In this commentary on Gestapo techniques made by an omniscient third-person narrator, there is a play on the same time-hallowed expression so often evoked against Germany by the western Allies during World War I, of the barbaric East versus the civilized West. Though the narrator remains distinct from Johannes, he is clearly Johannes's spokesman, and in the context of the whole narration they are both too cultivated and intelligent to accept such a ready-made cliché about the German nation; but at the same time, who could deny that the methods of the Gestapo had gone beyond what civilized people could imagine? What the search party hopes in vain to find is a written correspondence with the clergyman or with ecclesiastical authorities, and since Johannes has collected a mound of foreign stamps, they hope to find evidence of connections with German emigrés. Finding no such evidence they have to settle for Johannes's diary and letters from unknown people who made no secret of their feelings about the times. It is of no avail to Johannes to point out to his investigators that the laws of the Reich forbade the use of diaries that had the character of private monologues as matter for indictment. Like Pastor Niemöller Johannes is sent to concentration camp.

This was not a time for justice on any level in Germany. Free

elections in such a state were a myth, and Wiechert's narrator
reflects that only half an hour after the elections that authorized Austria's annexation to the Reich, all those who had voted
against the annexation were beaten half to death.[23]

Among the most blatant and scandalous of the injustices of
the Third Reich were those against the Jews. Lutheran pastor
Albrecht Goes's novella *Das Brandopfer* is the story of Margarete
Walker, proprietress of the only meat market in an unnamed
German city authorized to sell to Jews. In a structural tech-
nique harking back to the eighteenth century novel, she reveals
much of her tale in a long letter written to the narrator after
the war. It is easier for her to write this story than to tell it
aloud. The time she will spend in writing her letter and the
narrator in reading it give her a vague kind of assurance, furthermore, that the people of the story who are now dead can
for those moments return and dwell among us.

Her Jewish clientèle are restricted to making their purchases
on Friday evenings between five and seven, a time specifically
chosen by the Nazis because it interferes with the Jewish Sabbath which begins Friday at six. Since all forms of public transportation are forbidden the Jews and park benches are clearly
marked "Not for Jews," many from distant sections of the city
have to spend an hour or two on foot to reach Frau Walker's
store to buy what little they can with the ration cards they receive. The cards have different colors every month and are always stamped with a large "J".[24] Since the Jews are forced to
begin their Sabbath in a butcher shop rather than in a synagogue, a Rabbi begins on one of those Fridays to lead the congregation in prayer. Out of fear, the Jews have virtually stopped
talking to each other, on occasion they have even taunted one
another, but henceforth in Frau Walker's store they unite briefly
every week for a few moments of prayer. Frau Walker is only
too happy to accommodate them. But SS patrols often select
these Friday evenings to make their visits to the shop, and during one such visit a Nazi officer publicly humiliates the Rabbi,
who is taken off and is never seen again. For a few days Frau
Walker considers filing a legal complaint for trespassing against
the Nazi, but then she abandons the idea, knowing full well
that there is no chance of obtaining justice.

Thereafter there is no more public praying at the Walker meat market, but Frau Walker herself, remembering a word she learned from the Rabbi, sometimes greets her Friday evening customers with "Shalom" and thus tries to help them retain something of their Sabbath. One Friday two Nazi officers in uniform stride into the shop: in the higher ranking of the two Frau Walker recognizes the same giant of a man who had taken away the Rabbi. Even then he had seemed to her to evoke all the mindless, barbaric, and heathen terror of the giant Goliath of the Bible pitted against a frailer David. Unfortunately the biblical ending had not followed through, and now Goliath has returned, drunk and meaner than before. When he lights a cigarette and extinguishes it against the face of one of her clients, Frau Walker can hold her silence no more. Diplomatically confining herself to the facts of the situation, she draws the giant's attention to a visibly posted sign stating that smoking is legally prohibited on the premises. There are laws that even a Nazi must obey, and so he cannot find fault with her. In his drunken stupor, however, he looks at an old man in the line, a long retired judge, and, knocking his package out of his hands, tells him point blank not to eat so much lest he become too heavy to ascend "through the air" into heaven. His subordinate reminds him that he is on duty, and Goliath retorts that he is actually being rather nice to tell them that "they are soon going to go through the chimney." One younger woman, Frau Zalewsky, a musician's wife in her last months of pregnancy, has already put her bag on the floor and begun to tremble. The Nazi officer notices her and turns to his subordinate: " . . . Sara with the fat belly, she is—aren't you, Sara? —even grateful to me when I tell her that she shouldn't trouble herself about children's diapers, the sweet little shitty diapers." For Frau Zalewsky this is the last straw. Certain now that she is without recourse, she comes back later the same evening to offer Frau Walker the baby carriage that she has prepared for the child. Frau Walker has been good to her; perhaps one day she will be able to use the carriage. Frau Walker is left to reflect that if such things can happen, that "a woman who is expecting her baby must give away her baby carriage because a sentence of death has been placed without grounds on her and the unborn child," then there is no more hope of redemption, for such a wrong cannot be righted. The only remedy would be for everything to be cleansed thoroughly and purified by fire.[25]

Fire, the age-old purifier, even mightier and more dramatic than water, is not long in coming. In the British bombings that strike the city, amid the shrieking of air-raid sirens, Margarete Walker remains in her apartment, immobilized. With ironic coincidence it is a Jew wandering through the burning city that night who sees her through the shattered windows sitting at her table, engulfed in fire. When he manages to get her into the street, her face is already badly burned. He covers her with his overcoat and then leaves, as he had left his own family some time before, hoping that since he alone was Jewish the others would not be harmed. The attack is over for the time being and Frau Walker will be cared for. In a last minute reflection he returns to remove from his coat the yellow Star of David, which after 1941 all Jews in Germany were obliged to wear. Because of the star he had been denied the shelter of the city bunker. Frau Walker comes to, and recognizing him as her rescuer, begins to speak: "He did not accept it. . . . The burnt offering. . . . God did not accept it."[26]

Denunciations

While Frau Walker's heroism and compassion were not unique, she is somewhat exceptional in the pages of literature. Far more common seems to have been the realization that the individual in Nazi Germany could do nothing and for his own sake had best attempt nothing. Anyone—friend or family, passer-by, neighbor, colleague—might make a denunciation. The narrator's mother in Heinrich Böll's *Ansichten eines Clowns* (1963) claims in all sincerity to an *ad hoc* investigating committee, hastily gotten together after her ten-year old son has had a squabble with a fourteen-year old boy in the Hitler Youth, that she would turn her back on him if she really believed he called the other boy a "Nazi swine."[27] For many the only path was that of passive resistance. Witchcraft has it, wrote socialist Luise Rinser in the third brief narrative of her *Weihnachts–Triptychon* (1963), that one can kill a person on the night of a new moon by sticking a pin through that person's photograph in the area of his heart. On the third Christmas of the war in 1941, though there is no full moon and though she has no pin and photograph at hand, she wishes death on the man responsible for the "desecration" of Christmas. Though she has been forbidden to write, the Nazis cannot forbid her to think, and in her thoughts, though she does not name him in her narrative, she would put Adolf Hitler to death.[28] But in the end Luise Rinser was too outspoken and after being denounced by an old school friend, she was arrested in October 1944 and taken for several months' internment to a prison camp in Traunstein in Bavaria near the Austrian border and Salzburg.

Some filed denunciations from idealistic motives, some because denunciations worked to their benefit. The Nazi Party fanatic, Frau Lieser, in Remarque's *Zeit zu leben und Zeit zu sterben* may have denounced Graeber's girlfriend's father out of ideological motives after he said he no longer believed Germany could win the war, but the fact remains that because of her zeal she also secured a share of his apartment for herself. Lest the same fate befall her and lest she lose to Frau Lieser the one room she has been allowed to retain and end up in a concentration camp, is it not better for Elisabeth Kruse to turn on the record player when Graeber is visiting to muffle their conversation and prevent Frau Lieser from detecting something that might serve as material for a denunciation? It is better, too, to keep lights off during the air-raid emergencies in accord with the government directives that Frau Lieser religiously enforces.[29]

Children, too, could bring denunciations, and in Günter Grass's *Hundejahre* (1963), a schoolteacher named Dr. Oswald Brunies is reported by some of the pupils in his class for chewing the lemon candy-like vitamins called Cebion tablets that, beginning in the fall of 1941, were supplied for distribution to schoolchildren. The denunciation comes as no surprise. Brunies had asked Walter Matern, one of the book's central characters, just returned to Danzig from the Russian front, wounded and unfit for combat, to read a poem to the class instead of delivering the lecture about the fighting on the eastern front that he was supposed to deliver. In court several members of the class testify that Brunies had on occasion eaten candy in class, but never Cebion tablets. Unfortunately the teacher begins pulling Cebion tablets from his pocket and sucking on them right in the middle of the hearing. The book provides little justification for Brunies's absurd action in court. The story is narrated by one of his former pupils, Harry Liebenau, who himself testified on his teacher's behalf at the time of the hearing. Even though the story is related in retrospect and Liebenau is much older at the time of the narration, it is not uncharacteristic of Günter Grass's storytelling that the *Erzählungszeit* or time of the narration should shed no light on the *erzählte Zeit* or time narrated. As a result the whole presentation is rather naïve, innocent, and childlike; the reader sees what the child saw. Whatever may have driven Dr. Brunies to eat the Cebion tablets in front of the court, the fact that he never hung out the flag on state occasions like the Führer's birthday was of no benefit to him. Both he and Herr Kruse in Remarque's book die in concentration camps of alleged heart failure. Brunies's daughter Jenny receives a telegram announcing the death and Elisabeth Kruse a mailed invitation to report to Gestapo headquarters. Graeber, who by that time has become Elisabeth's husband, takes the dreaded summons to the Gestapo for his wife. He is asked to sign for receipt of a cigar box filled with what are purported to be his father-in-law's ashes. Both he and Jenny Brunies are instructed that no mourning garb or ceremony will be tolerated: mourning tends to undermine national morale. But from the moment her father is taken away, Jenny Brunies wears black.[30]

Getting by on the Homefront

By 1943 the German homefront became almost more treacherous than the battlefields of Russia. Remarque's Ernst Graeber, on furlough in Werden, cannot at first even locate his family home. The whole street has been bombed and a local air-raid warden informs him curtly that since the whole area has been scheduled for a clean-up, Graeber will be arrested if he remains. Out on the front Graeber had felt fairly immune to the snares of petty bureaucracy, but the warden retaliates bitterly.

"Do you suppose this isn't a front right here? . . . We have had six air raids here in ten days, in ten days, you front-line soldier!"[31] He clearly resents Graeber's coming home hale and hearty while his own wife lies dead under the rubble. Perhaps it is because the soldiers have done such a poor job on the front that catastrophe has befallen the homeland. Not long after this unnerving encounter shrill sirens scream out warning of yet another air attack.

The diehards, of course, remained diehards. The informer Frau Lieser sets up an altar to the Führer in her room replete with his portrait, candles, and a luxuriously bound copy of *Mein Kampf* resting on a swastika flag.[32] Her husband is serving with an army unit in Russia, and Graeber tries to reassure her that for the moment all is quiet in her husband's sector. But he has misjudged her priorities. All is not quiet out there, she snaps back. Her husband's group is in the thick of the fight and he is in the first line of fire. Graeber is only too well aware that such concepts as the front line no longer have any meaning in Russia, but to try to explain that to Frau Lieser would be futile.[33] The less one had to do with people like her the better. According to one of his old schoolmates, also home on leave, the less one had to do with anybody the better. Cynicism is becoming contagious, and the army barracks where Graeber spends his first few nights in town echo the mood. When one soldier offers him some prophylactics as a protection against disease during his leave, another interjects that since Graeber is an "Aryan stud with twelve thoroughbred ancestors . . . rubbers are a crime against the fatherland."[34]

But by 1943 some were already beyond cynicism. A couple who lost all their children in the bombings of Werden recall that the more conditions deteriorated, the more people became fearful and reticent. "Today each can think only of himself. There is too much unhappiness in the world."[35] The singer and actress Hildegard Knef, having lived through the war in Berlin, writes in her autobiography *Der geschenkte Gaul* (1970) that sooner or later everyone was bombed out and it was simply an unwritten law not to expect help from others.[36]

Angst increased, not the metaphysical *Angst* of the philosophers, but fear pure and simple, fear of the Gestapo, fear of one's neighbors, and eventually fear of the war itself. One of the characters in Zuckmayer's *Des Teufels General,* Diddo Geiss, the daughter of an opera diva, reflects: "We know no real joy. None of us. We are always uneasy—encumbered. . . . There is too much fear in everything. —And if one has no fear oneself, then there are always others who are afraid. This can't always have been this way?"[37]

As always there were a few who managed to be merry despite everything. One of them is Waltraut von Mohrungen, affectionately called Pützchen by everyone else in the Zuckmayer play. A girl from the BDM, she is a blithe spirit, or at least does her best to be. She claims that neither she nor any of the other girls intends to marry because getting married has become too much of a hassle: "all the proofs, Aryan blood down to your great-grandmother's big toe, health certificate, ability to bear offspring . . . it's all necessary on account of the race—but if you want to wait for all of this in the normal course of life, you could get old and rancid."[38] Not at all reflective by nature, she does not question the ideology. But she cannot accept the inconveniences and has decided to take whatever amusement she can find.

Not everyone could be so lighthearted, however, and not everyone could reconcile the goings-on in Nazi Germany with his own conscience. Pützchen's brother-in-law, pilot Friedrich Eilers, says that one gets used to one's job killing people, and his wife tries to support him by telling him that what he is doing is for the sake of the fatherland, the future, and a better world. But Eilers is not totally convinced. Recalling a few verses from the eighteenth-century poet Matthias Claudius, he asks: "Strange people we are, strange. Guernica—Coventry—and Matthias Claudius. How does that fit together?" His wife has a ready answer: believe and don't question. "Whoever believes will survive."

But believing was not always easy. Before the play is over Eilers is killed in a suspicious plane crash, and the Führer orders a state funeral.[39] Another air force officer, a man named Hartmann, in an apparent crisis of nervous exhaustion one day suddenly sputters to his commander, Harras: "It is all true what one hears. They are not horror rumors. I have beheld it with my own eyes. And they are the same—the same boys—the same ones who lived, dreamed, and sang with me in the Hitler Youth, spoke of ideals, of sacrifice and effort, of duty, of clean-living." In Poland Hartmann had run into one of his old school friends in the town of Lodz where he was awaiting a transport. He did not know the friend was part of an extermination squad, and when the friend invited him to come along, promising him a good time, Hartmann consented. "They shot at defenseless people—just for fun. They laughed when these people whimpered. . . . This has nothing more to do with war." Like a child in dilemma turning to his father or teacher for advice and consolation, he turns to Harras. Can everybody become like that? Could I become like that? Harras's answer is diplomatic and somewhat evasive but none the less profound because of that: for thousands of years man has tried to erect some kind of safeguard against himself, but the safeguard must not have been very sturdy since one lifetime was enough to destroy it.[40] Harras answers more definitively at the end of the play. He takes his plane up from the base in an unauthorized suicidal flight and is cut down. For Harras, too, though he could never be persuaded to join the Party, there would be a state funeral.[41]

Right or wrong, Harras chooses to die rather than stay and fight Hitler as the Luftwaffe engineer Oderbruck decides to do. Oderbruck reaches his decision the day he feels ashamed for the first time to be a German. He has no other reason, no family in a concentration camp and no ties of any kind with the Jewish community. Only shame. Others join him, some also out of shame, but others out of hatred or anger, some because they like and respect the work they had been trained for and can no longer stand by to see their work perverted, and still others because they want freedom for themselves or their brothers. Oderbruck is convinced that if Hitler wins this war, both Germany and the world will be lost. Harras encourages Oderbruck, but having himself become the devil's general (*Teufels General*) for Adolf Hitler, he has already selected his own form of resistance and reparation; his spirit is too drained to share that of his colleagues. Dramatically, the play has to end in a climax with the death of Harras. The audience knows his plane has been hit when Oderbruck intones in a low voice and with classical restraint the first phrases of the "Our Father." One can only guess what fate may await Oderbruck and his followers, who know in advance the futility of their resistance.[42]

The Call to Arms

Not all German fighting men thought themselves as glamorous as Sartre's Daniel imagines them in *La Mort dans l'âme,* watching them ride through the streets of Paris in June 1940. Many German men and boys found no more joy in the thought of mobilizing for the army than did their French counterparts. In Heinrich Böll's "Die Postkarte" (1952), one of eighteen stories written in the fifties and sixties and collected under the title *Als der Krieg ausbrach,* a young man named Bruno Schneider, early in August 1939, receives a postcard bordered in red and ordering him to report the very next day for an eight-week stint of duty. He is sitting at home in his mother's house eating a late breakfast of bread and butter when the card arrives. The food sticks in his throat, and his mother begins to cry as she had only once before in her lifetime, at the death of his father. Knowing that they are lying to each other, mother and son seek reassurance in the idea that Bruno will only be gone for eight weeks. Bruno tells his story in retrospect after the war is over, but as happens so often in Böll's writings about the postwar period, his characters cannot escape its memory. The past continues to live in the present. It refuses to be put away. One day Bruno discovers, quite by accident, a small postal receipt for registered mail bordered in red and now yellowed with age. Instantly it brings to his mind the fateful postcard that had summoned him to duty in 1939. He remembers being unable to finish his breakfast. Instead he retreated to his room to perform a whole ritual of senseless actions like opening and closing the drawers of his desk. At the moment when he was being forced to abandon his room, he needed the assurance that he was still in complete possession and control of it. But the postcard seemed to nullify that relationship. The room simply no longer belonged to him and that was all that was to it. His train to the army camp was to leave at eight that night, and though the railroad station was only fifteen minutes away, he left home at three in the afternoon. "Mother blessed me, kissed me on the cheeks, and as the house door closed behind me, I knew that she was crying."[43]

Germany had been systematically preparing her citizens for war for quite some time, and as the war drew near, propaganda was, if anything, intensified. In the story "Als der Krieg ausbrach" (1961), which lent its name to the whole collection of Böll's war stories, the narrator, an army recruit, remembers sitting in a movie theater on the last Sunday in August 1939, watching the newsreels for the week show "very unnoble-looking Poles mistreating very noble-looking Germans. . . ."[44] But despite the propaganda and the paramilitary organizations like the *Hitlerjugend* or the BDM or the Nazi Party itself which since 1933, and in some cases even earlier, had been putting Germans into uniforms of one sort or another, the war meant changes to which some people were just not attuned. One is the thirty-three year old Greck, a character in Böll's *Wo warst du, Adam* (1951), who in 1939 goes out into the field as an ensign-sergeant. Greck is an educated person with a prosperous career to look forward to. But the war cuts everything short. He finds that it is no longer sufficient to be a doctor of law and to have a professional position. "Now they all looked at his chest when he came home. His chest was only scantily decorated."[45]

The vast majority of people who were called upon to do military service in World War II did so without seriously questioning their summons. Still, a few like the book antiquarian's apprentice in Böll's *Gruppenbild mit Dame*, identified only as B.H.T., managed to avoid it. B.H.T. feels no need to justify himself to anybody by entering military service and aspires to no ideals that are not more amply satisfied by remaining in the bookshop. To achieve his ends he decides to follow the advice of a nun named Sister Rahel from whom he learns what to eat and drink in the form of tinctures and pills in order to be classified permanently as unfit when his urine is examined at recruiting time.[46]

For some, military service was a way out of a social or judicial predicament. It provides an outlet for Michel Tournier's Abel Tiffauges in *Le Roi des aulnes,* and for Günter Grass's Walter Matern, the character around whom *Hundejahre* is loosely struc-

tured, it provides a freedom and even license he could otherwise never have obtained. During his school days Walter Matern had befriended a Jewish boy named Eddi Amsel who used
to make scarecrows. When uniforms, especially the black and
brown ones associated with the Nazi movement, become an ever
greater part of the German street scene, Eddi develops a mania
for them. Since the Party's uniforms are available only to its
members, and since as a Jew Eddi cannot join the Party or any
of its organizations, the only way for him to get uniforms is to
have his friend Walter Matern join up. Walter is admitted to
the SA but later rejected for stealing while intoxicated. Like
Eddi he loves the theater, but his drunkenness even gets him a
dismissal from a local theater in Schwerin.[47] Matern is subsequently arrested in Düsseldorf, though the grounds for the arrest are never clarified in the book. With characteristic irony
Grass presents the entire mid-section of his text covering the
critical period of the Nazi rise to power and the war through a
series of "love letters" from Harry Liebenau to his cousin Tulla
Pokriefke, both members of the Danzig circle of friends, relatives, and acquaintances who populate the narrative. Liebenau
is not an omniscient narrator, and perhaps what was a rather
dangerous and precarious time becomes less gruesome in his
words because of his limitations as a person and as a narrator.
His neither profound nor philosophical mind enables him to
maintain an ironically matter-of-fact and sometimes even casual
stance. Liebenau claims not to know why Matern was forced to
spend time from May through early June 1939 in the cellar of
the Düsseldorf police headquarters. In any case Matern is officially a resident of Danzig, still technically a "free city" in the
aftermath of the Versailles treaties, sandwiched between Poland and Germany and supervised by the League of Nations.
His Danzig passport, together with his willingness to do military service, a willingness rapidly put to the test by an induction
order into the German army, save him from the Düsseldorf
police.

    As soon as Matern gets back to Danzig he turns up in the
yard in front of the Liebenau house and begins cursing loudly
at the Liebenau's big black shepherd dog Harras, calling it a
"Catholic Nazi hog." "I'm twenty-two dog years old, and I still

haven't done anything to earn immortality..." Harras is no ordinary dog, for he had sired the shepherd Prinz who was selected to be presented "in the name of the Party and the German population of the German city of Danzig . . . to the Führer and Chancellor through a delegation on the occasion of his forty-sixth birthday." The Führer had accepted Danzig's gift and henceforth kept Prinz along with other dogs of the same breed in his kennels. A letter of recognition and an autographed picture of Hitler that the Liebenaus have framed and hung in their carpentry shop inspire a number of converts to the Party from among the neighbors. And so for Matern to come home to Danzig and publicly revile Harras is no trifling matter. In the Liebenau shop machines begin buzzing furiously, and neighbors vanish into their apartments, for no one wants to hear what Matern is saying. Some denunciations are formulated, but in the end no one turns him in.

When Harras is found poisoned in August 1939, however, it doesn't take Harry Liebenau long to associate Matern with the deed. Harry and his cousin Tulla had seen a man approach the dog one night with some meat and urge the dog to eat it. From a distance and without explanation Tulla had also urged Harras to take the meat, but to Harry's rather simplistic mind Tulla always remains something of an enigma. Her generally ambivalent and unpredictable nature may be a reflection of the times in which she was raised and is certainly suited to their ambiguity. At any rate, neither he nor Tulla testifies against Matern, although Harry's father files a complaint. Matern, however, has an alibi, and proceedings against him bog down when two days later the war begins and he marches into Poland, saved from the prospect of punishment.[48]

Unheroic Heroes and an Unheroic War

Ostensibly the war began over the city of Danzig which Hitler was determined to bring back "home to the Reich."[49] By the terms of the Versailles treaties the Poles had been allowed to maintain a post office in Danzig, and in *Die Blechtrommel* Günter Grass, himself a native of that city, uses the Polish post office as the scene for the opening of the hostilities that developed

into World War II. More important for the novel, the battle of
the Polish post office, described in terms of a seduction scene
between the oncoming German tanks and the Polish fortress,
brings about the physical undoing of whatever ties may have
bound Oskar to Poland through his Polish "father," Jan Bronski. Some time before, Oskar's mother seems to have decided
to end the triangle she has constructed in this city where two
civilizations met, with Oskar's two "fathers," the German Alfred
Matzerath and Bronski. She begins eating fish of every variety
and preparation, and she continues eating from morning to
night until she becomes so ill that she is taken to the hospital
and dies.[50] Her lover Jan is an employee at the Polish post office, and Oskar is with him when the firing begins. They both
manage just in time to get under the cover of the building.
When the battle is over, Bronski and thirty other men who defended the post office against the Germans are rounded up
and executed. Oskar, only about fifteen and a midget to boot,
sees quickly which way the wind is blowing, and instead of pro-
tecting Bronski, points him out to the pro-German Home
Guards who take him prisoner, convinced that the Pole has
brutally taken this helpless innocent child into the thick of the
fighting.[51] Oskar's actions and attitudes are often mysterious,
as here, for he has always seemed drawn more to Bronski than
to his supposedly real father Matzerath. On several occasions
Oskar speaks of himself as being informed by evil or even by
Satan, though this is little more than an excuse and rationali-
zation for not facing the issues. By relating virtually the whole
story of *Die Blechtrommel* through the voice of the midget drummer Oskar, Grass has achieved an effect similar to, though more
spectacular and colorful than, the one attained by using Harry
Liebenau and his "love letters" in *Hundejahre*. To take the comparison further, where Liebenau is at times a bit dim-witted,
Oskar can be downright grotesque. Because of his apparent lack
of guile he is never repulsive; yet on occasion he displays such
ironic callousness that one wonders if his retardation is not more
than physical. Of course, Oskar does eventually wind up in a
mental hospital, and the reader knows this from the first page
of the book.

The heroes Grass has chosen for these two books are not

heroes in the classical sense of the term. Nor are they really the anti-heroes of modern fiction who would certainly disclaim all heroism if they ever thought about it. At the very outset of *Die Blechtrommel,* however, and in no uncertain terms, Oskar claims to be a hero in his own way,[52] and on several occasions further into the narrative he describes himself in messianic terms. In *Hundejahre* the problem of identifying a hero is further complicated by the fact that no one person dominates the narrative as Oskar does in *Die Blechtrommel.* The dogs, Harras, Prinz, and Pluto, together with the character Walter Matern can at most be said to operate as a kind of framework around which the story unfolds. "The dog stands central," Grass asserts at the beginning of the third section of the book.[53] But even this assessment is precarious, since for the most part the characters function independently of the dog or dogs "populating" their lives.

On a metaphorical level, of course, the term "dog years" used to designate the prewar, war, and postwar period in Germany is not without effect. The tin drum and its drummer Oskar, however, constitute an even richer and more powerful image. First of all, the narration is Oskar's, and for much of the story the tin drum functions as his primary vehicle of expression. Oskar received his first drum on his third birthday at which time he decided to arrest the normal growth of his body. The adults of the family later attribute his stunted physique to his having fallen down a flight of cellar stairs on the occasion of that third birthday, but Oskar consistently refuses to recognize the causal relationship. His drum, painted red and white, the colors of Poland, serves several functions: it enables Oskar to unite what he calls the two souls living in his breast, Goethe and Rasputin; it enables him to create and to destroy, to conjure up the past, to put a distance between himself and the sometimes serious adult world around him, and to free himself of responsibility to that world and ultimately even to himself. Oskar does not grow again until, approaching the age of twenty-one in 1945, with the Russians in Danzig as well as the returning Poles, he watches his German father Matzerath's burial in sandy Saspe cemetery and throws away his drum. The Oedipal conflict has been resolved along with the war. He can now proceed to the point where his white-enameled bed at the mental hospital will become what he calls the standard or norm by which he will make all his judgments and the goal toward which he will strive. This is just as he had said it would be at the outset of the narration and—since the story is related in retrospect from Oskar's hospital bed—just as it has been all along.[54]

In some ways the heroine around whose life Heinrich Böll chose to frame his long quasi-detective novel of the war period and its aftermath, *Gruppenbild mit Dame,* is like Grass's heroes. Her name is Leni Pfeiffer and for all practical purposes she is a completely insignificant person who happens to have lived through some rather crucial years in her country's history. Occasionally the times may elicit from her a noble and even brave reaction just as they might from any other ordinary human being. On Northrop Frye's scale of literary modes Böll's characterization of Leni Pfeiffer falls within the fourth or low mimetic mode. The hero is "superior neither to other men nor to his environment" and so "is one of us." For the most part *Hundejahre* can also be classified as low mimesis, though Oskar in *Die Blechtrommel* clearly belongs with the fifth and final or ironic mode. "If inferior in power or intelligence to ourselves, so that we have the sense of looking down on a scene of bondage, frustration, and absurdity, the hero belongs to the ironic mode."[55] In describing a war in which, with a few exceptions, heroic behavior was not the order of the day in Germany or in France, either because this was not a particularly heroic war or because war itself had lost its capacity to be heroic, the ironic mode has proven to be a very useful structuring device in fictional literature. In *Die Blechtrommel* it is the sustained point of view of the narration; in many other novels it has been used more selectively but certainly not without effect.

On September 1, 1939, when German soldiers marched into Poland, there were, by and large, no celebrations on the part of the civilian population. Nor were there any later on. A few pompous vestiges of World War I remained to the end, however. In Remarque's *Zeit zu leben und Zeit zu sterben,* when Ernst Graeber is ready to return to the Russian front after his furlough in Werden, he is surprised to see the troops still being given a musical send-off as the train prepares to leave. But by that time the new recruits are very young, "vegetables" and "cannon-fodder" a lance-corporal calls them, and the four musicians sent to play the *Deutschland-Lied* and the *Horst-Wessel-Lied,* a Nazi Party song commemorating one of National Socialism's first martyrs, play both songs rapidly and perfunctorily, giving only one verse of each.[56]

Though there was little enthusiasm among the general population, there were the usual expressions of support for the men, and letters and packages from their families. Letters from home had to be increasingly cautious, however, and after the bombings in Germany began in earnest, the civilians were often in greater need of packages than were the soldiers at the "front."[57] A girl named Elisabeth in one of Böll's stories, "Die blasse Anna" (1953), writes to her boyfriend somewhere with the German army, that she is proud he is in the army and sure they are going to win; but the soldier is not proud, and when he comes home on leave does not even bother to write to her. Instead he dates another girl who lives in his building.[58] In Günter Grass's *Hundejahre* Jenny Brunies allows her girlfriend, Tulla Pokriefke, to put nine leeches on her skin in the hope of preventing the fulfillment of a childish superstition that Tulla's brother fighting in France will otherwise bleed to death. Jenny faints during her ordeal, but after Harry Liebenau pulls the leeches off her and she revives, her only concern is that Tulla's brother will now be safe.[59]

Some German civilians like some French civilians inevitably made good profits from the war effort. In Böll's *Gruppenbild mit Dame* Leni Pfeiffer's father, Herbert Gruyten, who heads a construction company, makes a fortune building the Siegfried Line, the row of German fortifications that paralleled the Maginot Line on the east side of the Rhine. Business first begins a noticeable upward trend for the Gruyten firm in 1933, and ten years later no ratio can be established to measure its growth. Unfortunately for Gruyten a tax collector nabs him for irregularities in his finances and he spends the latter part of his career first as a construction worker operating a cement mixer with a penal unit on the French Atlantic coast and later clearing rubble after the air raids on Berlin.[60]

As the new masters of Europe, the Germans, or perhaps better said, some Germans, like Ernst Graeber's old school friend, Kreisleiter Alfons Binding, were able to help themselves to the luxuries among European products: canned turtle soup from France, canned asparagus from Holland, ham from Prague, Danish cheese, and so on.[61] Even people simpler than Binding had access to such things, food as well as fine handicrafts, if they had a husband or son or brother on military duty in occupied Europe. Only in Russia, as a haunting Brecht *Lied* recalls, did the German harvest turn bitter: from Russia the Germans sent back death.[62]

In the light of the sizeable emigration of German writers and the pronouncements they made against the Hitler regime, Stefan Zweig's claim that "almost all German writers" felt it their duty to support the advancing German troops and spur their enthusiasm seems somewhat unjust. Zweig charges furthermore that "they denied overnight that an English or a French culture had ever existed," and that compared to the German character and German art, they deemed what others had to offer "scant and worthless."[63] A few writers like Gerhart Hauptmann, to be sure, did opt openly to support the Nazi Party, but within the writing community Hauptmann was, if anything, in a minority. And if we are to believe what fiction tells us, even highly placed Nazi officials such as those in the entourage of the camp commandant of Auschwitz, let alone the writing community, were quite capable of appreciating the good things that came from abroad. It was certainly not the Party line, and they may not always have had the cultural formation that would have enabled them to appreciate good literature, but as Robert Merle indicates in *La Mort est mon métier*, they could appreciate other things, speak of France as a "marvelous country," and enjoy and revere the excellent quality of French cognac.[64] From these highly placed SS men to Oskar the tindrummer at another end of the spectrum there is a fascination with Paris and an admiration for it. Oskar's first contact with Paris comes from the shiny postcards sent or brought home by Sergeant Fritz Truczinski, the brother of Maria Truczinski who becomes Alfred Matzerath's second wife after Oskar's mother dies. Thanks to the postcards and his drum Oskar can conjure up a mild Parisian springtime, climb the Eiffel Tower, and enjoy the magnificent view of Paris as every good tourist was supposed to do.[65]

To many Germans, however, France also meant "brothels and
lewdness," reports Hildegard Knef, "and a respectable German
didn't even entertain the thought. . . ." A German could learn
nothing decent and respectable there. Her Aunt Emma, in any
case, had once been a cook in France, and that was a fact her
relatives discussed only in undertones.[66] This negative moral
attitude that many Germans had toward France is also visible
in Robert Merle's *La Mort est mon métier,* a psychological study
in fictional terms of the life of Rudolf Lang, the name of Merle's
protagonist whose life roughly parallels that of Rudolf Höss,
the actual commandant of the Auschwitz-Birkenau concentration camp in Poland from May 1940 to October 1943. Merle
devotes the first part of the book to an examination of Rudolf's
home life as a boy. His father is the stereotype of the Germanic
tyrant tolerating no disorder or infraction of any kind in his
household. On one of the rare occasions on which father and
son have a talk of any length and substance, Rudolf's father
tells him that he has decided that his son should be a priest;
this, in part, to atone for the sins that he, the father, committed
during a business trip to Paris before Rudolf's birth. Even now
it is only with disgust that he can pronounce the names of Paris
and of France. His religious fanaticism appears to date from
his return from that business trip. What actually transpired
during his stay in Paris can only be assumed from the general
statements he makes that Paris is the capital of all vices and that
after his stay there God had visited his soul. " 'I became ill,' he
said in a tone of incredible disgust, 'I took care of myself and I
was cured but my soul was not cured.' "[67] Rudolf does not become a priest according to his father's wishes. Perhaps he does
not even love his father, but he does revere him as one might
revere a god, and that reverence and obedience he later transfers to the head of the SS, Reichsführer Heinrich Himmler.
The negative impression of France his father bequeaths him
only sears deeper into Rudolf's flesh when Germany loses the
First World War in France and finds herself plunged into economic chaos.

When the Germans marched into France in 1940 there were

some who felt that they were paying back a debt that had been allowed to stand for over twenty years. In Böll's *Gruppenbild mit Dame* Alois Pfeiffer, whom Leni Gruyten eventually marries, takes part in the battle. He apparently thinks he has some talent as a writer and writes a series of descriptions for publication about the French campaign. They are overly rhetorical and pompous in nature and the narrator reserves the right not to comment on them. According to Pfeiffer it was up to the German soldier of 1940 to complete the task of those who had passed before him in World War I along the river Aisne.[68] But outside of his immediate family, no one, including his wife, seems to take anything that Alois Pfeiffer does or says very seriously. Leni, in fact, appears to have been much more attracted to her cousin Erhart Schweigert, but Erhart is timid with girls and never has time during his brief interludes from the army to make anything of that attraction. Both Erhart and Leni's brother Heinrich whose father does not want him to have to soil his hands with money and the dirty business of the family construction firm, meet their end together, facing a firing squad for trying to sell an anti-aircraft cannon for a few marks to the Danes. Heinrich was given the best humanistic education available in Germany and abroad, and, filled with lofty ideals, suddenly finds himself thrust into the often squalid reality of Hitler's war machine. "Too much Bamberg Rider and too little Peasants' War," reflects Lotte Hoyser, wife of Otto Hoyser who rises from the position of the elder Gruyten's head bookkeeper to that of his successor.

Among all the characters in Böll's book, Heinrich Gruyten remains among the most ambiguous, although he is potentially far more interesting than his sister Leni, whom the book is ostensibly about and who is at the center of the narrator's investigations. But if Böll was going to put together a fictional inquiry into the war years and their effect on the German people, he had to choose someone as ordinary as Leni Pfeiffer around whom to structure his investigation. People like Leni, unpolitical for the most part and on the whole relatively discreet, were the ones who survived. One thinks of Jean Giraudoux's Electra and Aegisthus's attempts to marry her off to a gardener in the realization that the gods do not strike the average citizen but only those who stand out from the multitude and can be distinguished from the rest. Unlike Leni, Heinrich was not meant to blend into the landscape. The letters he writes from the service to his family, without salutations or conclusions, read like military instruction manuals. Is this the revenge of an adolescent whose dreams have been shattered by the cruel reality of the world, or perhaps more to the point, the revenge of an adult son on his father who had so wanted him to be educated, his revenge on the system for which and under which his father is working and profiting? Heinrich shouts "Shit on Germany!" as he dies with his cousin Erhart, "two Bamburg riders," in the words of Lotte Hoyser, "who wanted to die together, and God knows they did . . . ." In the process and perhaps unwittingly, Erhart in his mother's eyes makes up for her husband who had failed to die in battle at Langemarck in 1914.[69]

Since Erhart cannot be for Leni, she marries in the spring of 1941 the vindictive and hawkish Alois Pfeiffer who was made a sergeant the year before when France was invaded. She refuses to wear white for the wedding ceremony. Alois has orders to report to his unit in the east on the very night of the wedding, and since he forces her to have conjugal relations with him half an hour before his departure, she writes him off as dead to herself even before he is killed a few days later in Russia and then she refuses to wear mourning.[70]

Not all Germans went to France with Pfeiffer's vengeful turn of mind. Werner von Ebrenach, a German officer billeted in a French provincial house in Vercors's *Le Silence de la mer,* reveres French culture to the point of adoration. And then there were those who did not want to be in the war at all, like the soldier-narrator of Böll's story "Entfernung von der Truppe" (1963–1964), who in his own words feels toward war as a pedestrian might feel toward cars.[71] Or novelist and short-story writer Alfred Andersch who in 1933 at nineteen years of age spent six weeks in Dachau as a communist, was subsequently drafted into the German army, and in his autobiographical *Die Kirschen der Freiheit* (1952) claims to have regretted not being able in 1940 to desert that army as it stood poised on the Rhine and ready to march into France. The river currents were too strong, and even if he had made it across, he would only have "bumped up against an army whose defeat was determined."[72]

If the Germans, in turn, encountered any real animosity in France, literature does not speak very much of it, at least not in the early stages of the Occupation. The French Résistance took time to develop, and for some time after the invasion of 1940 had been completed, relations between the German soldiers and the French population did not always turn sour. France was, of course, for the German army one of the early battles of the war, and to those Germans who had been there and who later found themselves on rail transports headed for Russia, France in retrospect seemed like paradise. On one such transport in Böll's *Der Zug war pünktlich,* rolling through what is described here and elsewhere as cheerless, unhappy Poland, a German soldier named Andreas is trying to remember the eyes of a French girl he had been smitten with and who lived on the fringes of Amiens. Andreas wound up for a time in a military hospital in Amiens, and when he got out, he went back to what he thought was the girl's house, but everything seemed to have changed. To his dismay he found a petit bourgeois Frenchman standing in front of the house, a pipe in his mouth and derision in his eyes. Everyone had fled; the Germans had plundered everything even though acts of plundering were supposedly punishable by death. The man knew nothing of the girl. The Germans had smashed his windows, burned his rug with their cigarette butts, whored on his couch. He had ample reason to resent them, but he could still feel sympathy for this German soldier trying in vain to locate his girlfriend.[73]

The spirit not only of France but of Paris itself may have been blunted by the arrival of the Germans, as Stefan Zweig says,[74] but if Paris was to become Greater Germany's amusement park as Rolf Hochhuth's play *Der Stellvertreter* (1963) indicates,[75] its spirit could not be allowed to deteriorate altogether. At least the Germans destroyed nothing in Paris, Ernst Graeber explains to his girlfriend Elisabeth.[76] But she is generally apprehensive about what the Germans have done in the occupied countries and fearful that once the war is over no one in Europe will want to receive them as visitors or tourists. She asks Ernst, who had been in the French campaign, if there is much hatred in France. "I don't know," he answers. "Perhaps. I didn't see much of it. Of course we didn't want to see it either. . . . We wanted to get the war over in a hurry and sit in the sun on the streets in front of the cafés drinking the wines of a foreign country. We were very young." [77]

The first soldiers who went into France seem on the whole to have been innocent enough, innocent at least to the extent that they had not yet experienced or participated in mass liquidations and other atrocities that many of them later came to know in the east and even in France itself. Events like the tragedy at Oradour-sur-Glane near Limoges came later. Most of the soldiers who marched into France in 1940 did so with a clear conscience. From Russia Graeber recalls those days with nostalgia in a kind of interior monologue in which his own voice blends almost imperceptibly with that of the narrator.

> The summer of 1940 in France. The stroll to Paris. The howling of the Stukas over a disconcerted land. Roads jammed with refugees and with a disintegrating army. High June, fields, woods, a march through an unravaged landscape. And then the city, with its silvery light, its streets, its cafés, opening itself without a shot fired. Had he thought then? Had he been disturbed? No. Everything had seemed right. Germany, set upon by war-hungry enemies, had defended itself, that was all. [78]

Obviously a point of view is always relative and from the French point of view the situation was certainly less than idyllic!

Of all the Germans who made it to Paris in one capacity or another during the years of occupation one of the more colorful is Grass's Oskar Matzerath. Oskar goes to Paris not as a soldier, naturally, but as part of a troupe of midgets who have arranged to play in the Théâtre Sarah Bernhardt and the Salle Pleyel. As a child Oskar had learned to shatter glass with the high intensity and pitch of his voice, and in Danzig had tried his voice successfully on the windows of local churches and once even on Nazi Party headquarters. In Paris he proceeds to do the same with French glassware from the time of Louis XIV to the Third Republic. The audience on the whole does not grasp what Oskar calls the historical significance of his act, [79] but lest one be tempted to attach an anti-French significance to it, one should recall the scene much earlier in Oskar's career, when his father Matzerath attends the Nazi mass meetings on the Maiwiese in Danzig. Oskar, thanks to his height which enables him to hide easily and his drum which enables him to set the tone, turns Nazi martial airs into rather innocuous Viennese waltz and charleston melodies.[80] In June 1944, just before the Allied landings in Normandy, Oskar and the troupe go out to the Norman coast to tour the Atlantic Wall, a series of fortifications that the Germans built on the Channel coast to repulse precisely the kind of invasion that is in the offing. To Oskar the somber and ominous-looking German pillboxes, squatting heavily on the gentle elevations overlooking the Channel, are like big toys. He domesticates them as children do today, crawling playfully and heedlessly over the huge gray humps: "And then we had our concrete. We could admire it and even pat it to our heart's content; it didn't budge." The pillbox, "shaped like a flattened-out turtle, lay amid sand dunes, was called 'Dora Seven', and looked out upon the shifting tides through gun embrasures, observation slits and machine-gun barrels."[81] When the invasion comes Oskar and his troupe leave France and hurry back to what by now can only be called relative safety in Danzig.

CHAPTER V

Roundheads and Peakheads

There are two peoples living side by side
Of quite a different racial origin.
You tell them by the contour of their skull.

Brecht: *Die Rundköpfe und die Spitzköpfe* [1]

Within the German mentality there existed a contradiction of moral and social values. Time and again since the end of World War II it has been asked how a people as civilized as the Germans could commit the atrocities they did throughout Europe from 1939 to 1945. The extermination camps were not established until well into the war, but beginning with Hitler's assumption of power in 1933, Germany had begun to accustom herself to atrocity directed against her own people. This is, of course, begging the question to some degree. Nonetheless, Stefan Zweig wrote that even though Freud was disappointed as a man by what human beings were capable of doing to other human beings, he was not surprised as a thinker.[2] With the possible exception of Robert Merle's *La Mort est mon métier*, the literary texts do not propose specifically to answer the question. What they do instead is present material depicting the atrocities and show various reactions to them. In so doing, of course, perhaps they break ground after all for a way to understanding.

In Rolf Hochhuth's *Der Stellvertreter* a Jesuit priest, Father Riccardo Fontana, in the entourage of the papal nuncio's office in Berlin, puts the question directly to SS officer, Kurt Gerstein. Gerstein is one of the historical figures, along with Pope Pius XII, Adolf Eichmann, and a few others, whom Hochhuth took into his play. Gerstein joined the SS after he himself had been interned in a concentration camp, supposedly to be able better to fight the Nazis, spy on them, and investigate at first hand the rumors of their atrocities.[3] For Hochhuth's Gerstein, Hitler is the destroyer of Germany and, at obvious risk to himself, he is willing to defy Hitler by harboring a Jew named Jacobson in his Berlin apartment. To Father Fontana's question as to how a people that had produced Goethe and Mozart could become so brutal and savage, Gerstein answers:

> We Germans are no worse than other Europeans. First of all the great majority have no specific knowledge about the killings, though, of course, a lot of soldiers in the East have watched the massacres, and the whole nation looks on while Jews are shipped out of the cities like cattle. But anyone willing to help—what can he do? Are we to castigate a man who does not want to die for others?[4]

Gerstein then proceeds to specifics. When the Berlin factories were informed by the police that all Jewish employees were to be sent to Auschwitz, 4000 Jews managed to disappear before the police made their descent, and those 4000 were hidden and fed by Berliners, every one of whom was risking his life in the process. As for scoundrels, they can be found everywhere.

> In Holland the Dutch police are working hard to round up every Jew; in France they don't cooperate with so much zeal, but still they do their part. In Hungary too, but worst of all in the Ukraine ... The Ukrainians shoot the Jews themselves. . . . Only on rare occasions can a Jew in Poland find a place outside the towns. His kindly neighbors turn him over to the German murderers for a small bounty.

Gerstein admits that the Germans must bear the greatest guilt, for their leaders conceived the program against the Jews. But as "for the *people*—the other peoples hardly are much better."[5] The historical Gerstein eventually met his end in France under cloudy circumstances that do not warrant a detailed investigation here. In brief, on last account he was in a Paris prison[6] and there were reports of his suicide, though Hochhuth himself is more inclined to believe, from reports that reached Gerstein's widow from Paris, that he "was one more of the still uncounted Germans and Frenchmen who were arbitrarily killed in France after the liberation of 1944. Not many of those resistance fighters who after the entry of the Americans took savage

action against defenseless fellow countrymen and German prisoners truly deserved the honorable name of resistance fighters.
. . . ." However, Hochhuth also allows for the possibility that Gerstein may have been hanged by hardcore SS men who realized how committed he was to giving the Allies a total accounting of what he had seen.[7] However Gerstein may have met his end, the Jewish community of Paris revered him sufficiently to have his name inscribed on a memorial to the victims of fascism.[8]

The character who plays the role of Gerstein in *Der Stellvertreter* says in defense of the German people that they had "no specific knowledge about the killings" that were going on both inside and outside the German Reich. The key word here appears to be "specific." In Günter Grass's *Hundejahre*, when Jenny Brunies's father is taken off to the Stutthof concentration camp near Danzig, she immediately begins to wear mourning. Theoretically she has no right to do this, since "in those days you were allowed to wear mourning only if you could produce a stamped and certified reason. You were allowed to mourn for fallen sons and deceased grandmothers . . . ," but the arrest of Dr. Brunies for "unseemly conduct and crimes against the national welfare" would not have been an acceptable reason to the rationing office where, in the clothing section, permits could be purchased for wearing mourning.[9] Jenny knows intuitively that once her father has been taken to Stutthof, he is gone forever; and when she receives official notice that he has died of "heart failure," she can neither believe the alleged cause nor show surprise at the final outcome. But in the Third Reich one did not talk much about one's belief—or disbelief—in such things.

Some, nontheless, may have been less resigned to their fate than Jenny Brunies. In Remarque's *Zeit zu leben und Zeit zu sterben* after Elisabeth Kruse's father has been taken away, she and Ernst are out walking one evening when they stumble across a contingent of concentration camp inmates laying pipes in a street in the half-darkness. The inmates are wearing striped suits with numbers on them. Throwing caution aside, Elisabeth suddenly moves toward the group, scanning their dead faces in the hopes of finding her father. Graeber has all he can do to pacify the two young SS guards whose duty it is to keep the prisoners isolated from contact with ordinary citizens. One had to learn to lie to perfection in Germany in those days. Using as a pretext the story that Elisabeth has earlier lost a brooch and has now returned to look for it, Graeber manages to gain enough time for her to survey the whole line of prisoners.[10] Her father is not among them.

Though the general public may not always have known exactly what transpired in the concentration camps, certainly it knew of their existence and had at least some suspicions of what was going on in them. In 1943 flyers distributed around Munich and other German cities by the student resistance movement Die Weisse Rose, indicated, quite clearly that there was a vague and general familiarity with what was happening. The ringleaders of Die Weisse Rose were executed in rather summary fashion and their associates sentenced to prison terms.[11] But they had spoken out. In Günter Grass's *Hundejahre* Harry Liebenau in some of his "love letters" to his cousin Tulla writes of the village and camp at Stutthof and of how that name has begun to be reflected in popular parlance. "If you don't keep that trap of yours shut, you'll end up in Stutthof," people say. But what did "ending up in Stutthof" really mean to the people of Danzig? Certainly it did not mean the same thing a New Yorker means when he says "You'll end up in Creedmore or up the river in Sing-Sing" to someone who has little likelihood of ending up in either a state mental or correctional facility. "A sinister word had moved into apartment houses, went upstairs and downstairs, sat at kitchen tables, was supposed to be a joke, and some actually laughed: 'They're making soap in Stutthof now, it makes you want to stop washing'."[12]

At the Kaiserhafen battery outside Danzig there was a factory and in front of the factory a large mound joined by railroad tracks to other railroad tracks that had been built right into the Stutthof concentration camp. The area began exuding a sweet smell that lodged itself in the taste buds and could not be eradicated. Once during Harry's tour of duty at the battery when he, Tulla, an air-force auxiliary named Störtebeker, a tech sergeant, and some other companions are out sporting in the area of the battery, Tulla, never one to mince words, suddenly declares as she looks at the mound in front of the factory, "That's a pile o' bones." The attempts of Harry and some of the others to contradict her only increase her certainty. "Bet you it's bones. And what's more, human bones. Everybody knows that." Somewhat braver and for once more clearsighted in retrospect as a narrator than he was as a participant, Harry writes: "No one talked about the pile of bones. But everybody saw smelled tasted it." And Tulla is going to prove it conclusively. When one of the fellows bets that they are not human bones, she dashes off toward the mound, gliding easily under the barbed wire. The others can see the crows rise up as Tulla bends down, and when she returns, what she brings back is a human skull. A portion of the lower jaw is missing, but there can be no doubt that it is human. The tech sergeant slaps her on the cheek and the skull falls without breaking, bouncing twice among the weeds. The tech sergeant wants to know no more and orders the boys back to their barracks at the battery. Tulla wastes no time thinking about the skull; she has proved her point. Besides, she is more interested in getting pregnant, either by Störtebeker or by the tech sergeant, both of whom, however, usually prefer to give other "proofs" of their existence by shooting dune rabbits.[13] They are adolescents, and life has to go on, side by side with death. But in writing his "love letters" Harry determines that neither he nor Tulla nor anyone else will so easily be allowed to forget.

Stutthof had 2698 inhabitants. They made money when soon after the outbreak of the war a concentration camp was built near the village and had to be enlarged again and again. Railroad tracks were even laid in the camp. The tracks connected with the Island narrow-gauge railway from Danzig-Niederstadt. Everybody knew that, and those who have forgotten may as well remember: Stutthof: Danzig-Lowlands County, Reich Province of Danzig-West Prussia, judicial District of Danzig, known for its fine timber-frame church, popular as a quiet seaside resort, an early German settlement. In the fourteenth century the Teutonic Knights drained the flats; in the sixteenth century hard-working Mennonites moved in from Holland; in the seventeenth century the Swedes several

times pillaged the Island; in 1813 Napoleon's retreat route ran
straight across the flats; and between 1939 and 1945, in Stutthof
Concentration Camp, Danzig–Lowlands County, people died, I
don't know how many.[14]

The deaths that occurred in the Stutthof concentration camp
are part of the European experience, a fact that neither Günter
Grass nor his narrator can forget or ignore, a fact that must be
remembered along with so many others in the long and tur-
bulent history of his native Danzig which Grass has resurrected,
as it were, in his books.

Many Germans believed that it was their country's sacred
mission to save herself and the world from Russia and communism. To accomplish this end they were prepared to undergo
whatever hardship and privation the government deemed necessary. As to their consciences, they could follow the example
of the Rhenish baron in Hochhuth's play who says that he can
still be a good Catholic, since the Pope in his wisdom, by not
meddling in internal German affairs, has spared him the necessity of being a bad German.[15] Some believed that it was essential for the German people to find enough *Lebensraum*. Hildegard Knef, a bit simplistically perhaps but not without effect,
recalls that as a child she was never really able to grasp what
this meant since she had never seen a real crowd in Berlin except at Christmas on the Potsdamerplatz and at the beach at
Wannsee in July. She learned early in her life that questions
only spelled trouble, but she could restrain herself no longer
when one day at school her chemistry teacher described the
homesickness of all those ethnic Germans living in eastern Europe and South America who wanted only to come back within
Germany's borders. Would it not be better, she asked aloud, if
they stayed where they were and where they had enough room
to live?[16]

The question of who was German and who should be included in the German state is a thorny one, long and heatedly
debated in nineteenth century politics and philosophy. It is not
the purpose of this book to sort out the issue. Suffice it to say
here that Hitler developed early in life, and particularly after
the years he spent in pre-World War I Vienna, an abiding con-

tempt for the Jews and the non-Germanic elements, notably the Slavs, who made up the Austro-Hungarian empire. And with that contempt came a conviction in Germanic superiority. As Chancellor he succeeded, as Bismarck never had, and as many late nineteenth century Pan-Germanists wished he had, in uniting the whole German *Volk* or people in one political state. As elaborated in the later part of the eighteenth century, the *Volk* was essentially a cultural concept, and its members shared not only a cultural but also a spiritual affinity. Jews could become a part of the *Volk* by taking on its values. This was precisely what assimilated Jews in Germany had done. Not until the 1870s and 1880s were racial overtones applied to the term. This is not to say there were no anti-Jewish feelings before that time. But the racial element now made it impossible for Jews to become Germans. Indeed for those who subscribed to the racial theory, as the Nazis later did, it became essential if Germans were to preserve their identity as a *Volk* to minimize if not actually prevent any admixture of Jewish or non-Germanic blood.[17]

In the Nazi state people generally avoided talk about who should live in Germany and who should not, certainly in public if not in private. They had jobs, and that was more than many of them had had in the days of the Weimar republic. On the whole they had enough to eat even though they shopped with ration coupons, and they were able to eat more or less what they wanted until later in the war when the bombings made it difficult to obtain certain items. Even toward the end of the war one did not speak of malnutrition, for that would have been considered defeatist.[18] Böll's Leni Pfeiffer, at any rate, refuses to forgo her fresh crisp breakfast rolls and even manages fairly late in the war to be able to drink a decent cup of coffee. Coffee was the luxury that people seemed to prize and envy most of all.

By that time Leni is a war widow, tainted by the scandal over her father's business dealings, and she finds herself working in an establishment that manufactures funeral wreaths. She is surrounded by a motley and potentially explosive entourage including her boss, Walter Pelzer, an inveterate though frequently benign Nazi who in his earlier days used to allow people

to bribe him for not denouncing them; Liane Hölthohne, a
Jewish woman in disguise and a Rhenish separatist to boot; Ilse
Kremer, a communist; three rabid fascists; two neutrals; and
the gardener. For all of them the nine o'clock morning coffee
break is one of the important moments of the day. Each brings
his own, reports Walter Pelzer; some have only ersatz coffee
and others a blend of real and ersatz in the ratio of one to ten
or one to eight. Leni always has a ratio of one to three, while
Pelzer himself sometimes drinks his coffee pure. In any case,
ten individual coffee pots have to be prepared, and the only
one whom everybody trusts enough to do this is the communist, Ilse Kremer. No one trusts the three fascists, Marga Wanft,
the Schelf woman (known in the book only as such), or Heri-
bert Kremp, who would have switched coffees to their own advantage. One particular morning late in December 1943 or early
in January 1944, a Russian named Boris, who has been in a
Nazi camp for Soviet prisoners of war and released into Pelzer's custody through the intervention of an influential friend
and some Party bigwigs, shows up for work just as the coffee
pots are being distributed. Leni, who has never thought in political terms of Jews, Russians, or anyone else, offers the Russian, since he has no coffee, a cup of her own. She had absolutely no inkling, Pelzer later maintains, of the highly political
nature of her act. She had done what for her was simply the
most natural thing in the world. Already the aroma of her one
to three blend has aroused the envy and jealousy of some of
her colleagues, and it would have taken little to induce them to
lodge a complaint against her for violation of the war economy,
though Pelzer insists that by this time the police are only too
glad to see people get their ounce or two of coffee. But still, to
some of her co-workers Leni's action is too much, and the Nazi
Kremp, in an eruption of hitherto suppressed rage, goes up to
the wall on which he always hangs his artificial leg, grabs it, and
dashes the Russian's cup to the floor. Marga Wanft and the
Shelf woman clearly approve, the two neutral women remain
neutral, and Ilse Kremer and Frau Hölthohne look on with
understanding. Only the old gardner Grundtsch, who is considered an oddball anyway, begins to laugh.

Leni makes the first move to resolve the situation. She picks up the cup, washes it slowly and carefully, refills it, and then hands it to Boris. Sweat standing on his forehead, Boris thanks her and begins to drink. Frau Hölthohne breaths a sigh of relief, Kremp mutters something about Bolsheviks and a war widow, the two Nazi women snort with indigation, and Ilse Kremer, realizing that now Leni has no more coffee, pours her a cup of her own good coffee which came from her Nazi brother stationed in Antwerp, saying that Leni needs a drink to wash down her bread.[19]

Boris eventually becomes Leni's lover and the father of her son Lev, a "Holy Family" trio, according to witness Lotte Hoyser.[20] The child is born in the last days of the war when everything seems upside down. Leni is too unpolitical to have been influenced in one way or the other by her Russian lover. There is simply nothing there for Boris to undermine, and he himself is unpolitical enough to wish for nothing more than a bit of domestic happiness with Leni and his little son.

Racial Theories and Their Results

Foreign influence, to the extent that it existed, cut little ice in Nazi Germany, and the Frenchman in the POW camp in Sartre's *La Mort dans l'âme* who said the Germans would never bring French soldiers as laborers into Germany because the French would undermine German morale, was wrong on both counts.[21] Contacts between foreign laborers and German citizens where they occurred remained for the most part politically harmless. In Günter Grass's *Hundejahre* French laborers eventually replace their German counterparts working in the icehouse at the Schickau shipyard near Danzig. Jenny Brunies had often gone up to the German ice haulers and asked them to let her touch one of the big blocks of ice. One day she, Harry Liebenau, and his cousin Tulla pass by the icehouse and observe that the French ice haulers shoulder the ice blocks the same way the Germans had done before them; they even look like them, cubical in stature and with the same purple faces. They are called "foreign workers" (*Fremdarbeiter*), and the children do not know if it is permitted to talk to them. But Jenny is learning French in school and approaches one of the Frenchmen with a polite "Bonjour, Monsieur," to which he very courteously replies, "Bonjour, Mademoiselle." Jenny curtsies, as German children often do, and in her best French asks the ice hauler if he will allow her to go into the icehouse for several minutes. "Avec plaisir, Mademoiselle," the Frenchman responds graciously. As though in a perfectly executed ballet fantasy, Jenny performs another curtsy and says, "Merci, Monsieur," giving her hand to the French ice hauler who leads her into the icehouse. The other haulers laugh and joke, but Harry and Tulla begin counting slowly and decide that if Jenny is not out by the count of 200, they will shout for help. Jenny and the ice hauler reappear at 192, still hand in hand. She curtsies to him once again, carrying off a chunk of ice in her left hand, licks it, and offers to share it with her friends. Liebenau tries licking it, but Tulla is not interested.[22]

Adding to the normal uncertainty and caution that often accompany dealings between people of different origins, the Nazi racial theories created enormous tensions in the way Germans viewed non-Germans—and for that matter, in the way they viewed their fellow Germans as well. Bertolt Brecht makes a mockery of such theories in an allegorical play entitled *Die Rundköpfe und die Spitzköpfe,* conceived shortly before Hitler came to power and published first in abridged form in English in 1935 and then in the complete version in German in 1938. In the play the inhabitants of a fictitious country are divided by the shape of their skulls. Just as so-called Aryan Germans were trying to suppress the non-Aryan elements in their society, so the Roundheads seek to suppress the Peakheads.[23] Racial theories operated at every level of German society, and both in Germany and in the occupied lands the Jews bore the brunt of them. As applied to non-Jews the Nazi theories were more subtle and provided material for endless debate. Remarque sets a scene early in *Zeit zu leben und Zeit zu sterben* in which Ernst Graeber and other troops on furlough from the Russian front arrive at the German border where they have to be deloused. As they sit naked, picking dead lice off their bodies, an inane discussion arises, provoked by a man whose wife has apparently been made pregnant by a Russian prisoner of war. The man is not sure how to handle the situation upon his return. Russians are Aryans, says one of the soldiers, so let your wife have her child, the Fatherland needs Aryan children. The Russians are not Aryans, counters another, but Bolshevik "sub-humans." But how can this be true? Germany was once allied with the Russians, retorts the first soldier. The debate winds on tortuously. Only Poles, Czechs, and Frenchmen are sub-humans. The Russians were once Aryans and not sub-humans, at the time when Germany was allied with them. Even the Japanese are now Aryans, yellow Aryans! But now that Germany is at war with Russia, all Russians are sub-humans. The poor man who wants to know what to do about his wife and her child is more confused than ever and leaves the others angrily. One of his colleagues, however, cannot resist adding yet one more tidbit to the general state of wisdom prevailing: according to the latest data in racial research, a Frenchman might perhaps have been a better choice for the job than the Russian, since the French are only half sub-humans.[24]

Among their own, too, the Germans made distinctions, and the child who was what was thought to be German-looking, blond and blue-eyed, enjoyed a definite favoritism. *Lebensborn* homes ("fountains of life") were established in different parts of Germany and in some of the occupied lands, notably in Norway, to encourage the birth and provide for the care of children conceived of Nordic-looking parents. Marriage was certainly not required of women admitted to give birth in these homes, and little concern was shown for the morality of the conceptions involved. What counted was the production of healthy Nordic children, as many as possible, and to that end the *Lebensborn* establishment directed its efforts. France got a *Lebensborn* home at Lamorlaye near Chantilly.[25]

Fortunately for herself, Böll's Leni Pfeiffer is both blond and blue-eyed, and for two years in succession, at the ages of eleven and twelve, wins the title of "most German girl" in her school, a title that is awarded by a roving commission of racial experts. Once she is almost named the most German girl in the city but has to cede first place to a Protestant minister's daughter whose eyes are of an even lighter blue than her own. Leni, alas, is not a good student, however, and twice has "volunteered" to repeat a year. For a while the school administrators consider sending

her to a special school for slow learners, but it would hardly do
to inflict such a remedy on the most German girl in the school.[26]
Leni does join the BDM, though she detests the brown uniforms, which remind her of the scatological preoccupations of
one of the nuns, Sister Rahel, with whom she has trained at
school and who thinks she can predict the girls' scholastic
achievements on the basis of their stools. But Leni's attendance
at BDM meetings grows sparse, especially after her unit is com-
mandeered by a forceful young Catholic woman who has decided to infiltrate "this business" and get to the bottom of it.
She structures whole evenings around the rosary and the reci-
tation of songs to the Virgin Mary. Leni has nothing against
religious observances per se, but for two and a half years, she
had endured convent-school piety and found the experience
sufficient. Nonetheless, when the Catholic woman is denounced
by one of the girls, Leni and twelve other pupils deny stead-
fastly that they had sung songs to the Virgin at the BDM, and
thus they spare the young woman "considerable suffering."[27]

Toward Jews the attitude of the civilian population was a
mixed one. Once the Nazis legally attained power with Hitler's
rise to the Chancellorship in January 1933, a whole series of
perverse though, at least initially, often unsystematic "con-
sciousness-raising" efforts, official and otherwise, were aimed
at making the German population aware of who their Jewish
neighbors were and at progressively alienating the Jew from
German society. Initial boycotts of Jewish businesses were carried out pretty much at random by local SA units, but an official nationwide boycott was organized for April 1, 1933. These
boycotts were followed by attempts to Aryanize Jewish businesses which were often either closed on some legal technicality
or simply forced to sell out. The April Laws of 1933 effectively
restricted the ability of non-Aryans to maintain their position
in the medical and legal professions as well as in the civil service. In addition, the laws restricted the entrance of non-Aryans
into these fields of endeavor and their access to the *Gymnasium*
(German secondary school), the technical institutes, and the
universities. In May 1935, Aryan ancestry became a prerequi-
site for entry into the armed services, and in mid-September of
that year legal measures brought to bear against the Jews cul-

minated in the so-called *Nürnberger Gesetze* or Nürnberg Laws promulgated at the end of the Nazi Party rally held in that city. While Jews theoretically retained their *Staatsangehörigkeit* (state citizenship), they could not hope to attain the new rank of *Reichsangehöriger* (Citizen of the Reich), to which only Aryans could aspire. The Nürnberg Laws attempted to regulate sexual relationships and intermarriage between Aryans and Jews. Marriages between Germans and Jews were made illegal, for all practical purposes, as were extramarital relations between them, which were punishable by prison terms. To avoid sexual enticement between the two groups, Jews were forbidden to employ a German housemaid under the age of forty-five, and violations of this law were punishable by a year in prison or by a fine or both.

At this point in the drafting of the legal arsenal, it obviously became critical to define exactly what constituted a Jew. From the time of the April Laws of 1933 when a child with one Aryan and one Jewish parent was still considered Aryan, to the complex decree passed in November 1935, supplementing the Reich Citizenship Law, those who had sought to temper the Nazi drive lost ground. A completely Jewish person, one who had four Jewish grandparents, or a three-quarters Jewish person, one with only three Jewish grandparents, was legally considered a Jew and, consequently, subject to the Nürnberg Laws. A half-Jew, one with two Aryan and two Jewish grandparents, was legally considered Jewish if he adhered to "the Jewish faith, he was married to a Jew, he was the child of a marriage with one Jewish partner, or if he was the offspring of an illegitimate union between a Jew and Aryan. Someone with two Jewish grandparents, if he was not legally Jewish on the basis of these four conditions, was legally a 'Jewish *Mischling*.'" The *Mischling* was neither Aryan nor Jewish, and an official commentary to the Nürnberg Laws published in 1936 made it clear that the aim of any legal solution was the disappearance of the "*Mischling* race." Finally, in January 1, 1939, Jews were barred from operating retail or wholesale enterprises as well as independent artisan shops.[28]

The Jews living in Germany became known as "guests" of the German people, as Goebbels referred to them in a speech in

1933,[29] or simply as the "non-Aryan population."[30] Animosity
was directed against them less because of anything specific that
they were doing than because of who and what they were. In
Ilse Aichinger's *Die grössere Hoffnung* (1948), a pathetic and often
heart-rending novel about the fate of a group of Jewish children in the Third Reich, the central character, a little girl named
Ellen, learns that her ancestors are to blame for whatever suffering and discrimination she must endure. These things have
nothing to do with her personally, and there is absolutely nothing she can do to redeem herself from them. Jews are different
and have to be kept apart from other Germans. In Albrecht
Goes's *Das Brandopfer,* Jewish children asking their little friends
to come and play with them are told: "My momma said I can't
play with you anymore. German boys don't play with a Jewish
kid. . . ."[31]

Hildegard Knef remembers the racial indoctrination she received at school, learning in detail the characteristics of the different races and learning to recite the reasons why she herself
was Nordic. One day when a girl in her class named Margot
Wiener, whose name clearly was not Nordic, disappeared, the
teacher simply explained to the class that Margot had moved
with her parents.[32]

To accent their difference from the rest of the population,
Jews were obliged after 1941 to wear a yellow Star of David
sewn onto the sleeve of their outer garments. Some may have
worn that star with pride, but for children especially, it is always painful to be different. In a series of episodes surrealisti-
cally presented, for the most part, in a dream-like sequence in
which she annihilates the barriers of time and place, Ilse Aichinger shows us how a little girl with two "wrong" grandparents
comes to grips with her world. Ellen's mother has left her in
the care of one of her grandmothers to go off somewhere across
the sea where Ellen now cannot follow because a war is raging
and the borders have been sealed. She makes friends with several other children, all of whom have at least three or four
"wrong" grandparents and who have been waiting for seven
weeks on a quay in the hopes of spotting a drowning child who
might come floating down the canal so that they can save it.
They will dry the child and then bring it to the mayor who will

be pleased to recognize their good deed, pardon them their grandparents, and permit them once again to sit on all the city benches which have been forbidden them and to play in the park. Ellen is more realistic than the others. What if the drowning child should never come down the canal?[33] The reader, older than Ellen and further removed from the events, will be more realistic still. Even if an occasion should materialize in which the Jewish children might prove themselves a benefit to the community, would the state relax the laws in their favor?

When the people in Ellen's world begin wearing the star on their garments, Ellen wishes to do so too, admiring the shape and the bright color. Ellen is only part Jewish, however, with only two "wrong" grandparents, and her grandmother reminds her that she should be glad she does not have to wear the star. But Ellen is not to be put off. One day when her grandmother is out, she clumsily sews a star onto the left side of her coat and runs down the steps of the building. One of her friends, Georg, is having a birthday and she wants to buy him a cake to help him celebrate. For weeks she has been eyeing a particular kind of cake in the windows of a local café. She knows its price and makes sure beforehand that she has enough money to buy it. Entering the glass door of the café she puts her money on the counter and asks the saleslady for the cake. At once all the clients in the shop stop eating. The eyes of the saleslady are fixed on the star, and hatred emanates from her face. Perhaps the price has gone up, Ellen ventures; she will return directly with more money if that is what is needed. "Get out," the saleswoman admonishes coldly; and when Ellen doesn't budge, the woman threatens to have her arrested, screaming at the child, "Be glad that I am letting you go." Ellen looks around her for help, but there is no one to help her. Everyone is looking at the star, some laughing scornfully. Others have a sympathetic smile on their lips, but even they will not help. Ellen, who had wanted to be like her friends and had envied them their star, realizes for the first time the meaning of that star and its price. Now perhaps she can better understand Georg who had been looking forward to the fifteenth birthday celebration that his family had been planning for weeks. His joy would have been complete were it not for the star.[34]

One of Ellen's friends, a girl named Julia who for some time has disassociated herself from the other children, manages to get a visa to go to America. Ellen hopes that through Julia she can send greetings to her mother. Ellen herself has spoken to the consul earlier about obtaining a visa, but there is no one to witness for her, and the consul tells her with the ambiguity of a Delphic oracle that each one must give himself his own visa. His meaning is clarified in the example of another friend, Anna. Anna had also come to bid farewell to the group. Thinking that she, too, is leaving for America, Ellen expresses the wish to join her someday, to go to America, to her mother, and to freedom. Freedom, Anna observes, "is there where your star stands." The consul would have approved. Julia then asks if she and Anna might be traveling together. Anna's answer comes haltingly, but she finally brings herself to say the words that no one in those days dared say. "The direction is different. . . . I—I have the summons for Poland." [35]

Ilse Aichinger's book is filled with images of suffering and forebodings of death that alternate with images of a hope and joy that will triumph over death. Dream and reality intertwine. On a trip to the Holy Land that the children dream about and enact, as children are wont to enact their dreams in the games they play, one of the boys notices that a plague has broken out, but no one else seems to be aware of it. When Albert Camus published *La Peste* in 1947, he certainly had in mind, among other things, the four years of German occupation that had just ended in France; and when Ilse Aichinger in 1948 had one of her characters use the same word in German, the metaphorical allusion to the malady which the German people had contracted from their Nazi masters is inescapable. In the Europe of World War II no one held a monopoly on the plague.

But even the plague had its consolations. On their trip to the Holy Land, which in the context of the novel appears to be a kind of extraterrestrial haven rather than the geographical Holy Land itself, the children are determined to seek out their ancestors and demand that they make good on their responsibility for having created them. The children meet Columbus playing with a globe of the world and tell him with the simplicity of children to whom all things are possible, that they are seeking "those who were." Columbus informs them that there are no such people but only those who are and those who are not. Those who are, are always, for being is not destroyed, and being is the "passport for eternity." A philosophical consolation, certainly, and perhaps no more than that. But it was the only thing Ellen and others like her had to hold on to as they sat in their homes waiting for the Gestapo to come and take them or their loved ones away. Like Ellen's friend Hanna who had always dreamt of owning a home on the Swedish coast, they knew that their dreams were being shattered and that for them such things as houses on the Swedish coast could never exist.[36]

Ellen's grandmother, too, is waiting in her apartment. She has traded her fur coat for some poison that may still save her in time from whatever ultimate suffering is standing between her and her death. Ellen manages to snatch a handful of the poison from the old lady, enough to prevent her from inflicting damage with the portion she still holds, and promises to give her the rest only after she tells one last story. Ellen knows that once her grandmother has told the story, Ellen will be released from any obligation to surrender the poison. Grandmother tries to tell the story but is unable to put it together and begins to doze. Ellen herself then assumes her grandmother's role and begins reciting the story of Little Red Riding Hood. By the conclusion of the tale she allows fantasy and reality to intermingle and asks her grandmother as though she were the bad wolf of the story, if she really wants to eat the poison. Just as Ellen decides that after all her grandmother is really her grandmother and cannot have been devoured by the wolf, a sound of footsteps echoes in the corridor; and her grandmother, thinking the footsteps are meant for her, again calls for the poison. Now there is no time for nonsense and dreams! She is clear-headed and firm. Ellen obeys, feeds "her grandmother with the poison like a sparrow its young," and breaks down next to her bed. The steps come nearer, stop momentarily, and then are gone.[37]

Another fictional personage who chooses suicide as a solution is the toy merchant, Sigismund Markus, in Günter Grass's *Die Blechtrommel,* whose store provides Oskar with his drums.

Sometime before his death Markus encounters difficulties when he turns up at the cemetery to pay his respects for Oskar's mother and is forcibly ejected by the dissolute trumpeter Meyn and a local baker. On the infamous Kristallnacht, when Jewish synagogues and businesses throughout Germany were ransacked, Alfred Matzerath takes Oskar by streetcar to the Langasser Gate in Danzig to see the burning of the Langfuhr synagogue. Firemen look on, taking care only that the flames do not spread to the neighboring buildings. Matzerath stays to warm his hands in the public fire set outside the destroyed hull of the synagogue for the burning of books and ritual objects taken from the building, but Oskar is more concerned for the source of his drums and slips away. By the time he gets to Markus's shop, he sees that the same firemen who are now at the synagogue had already paid their visit to Markus. On the window they had scrawled the words "Jewish sow" and then kicked it in with their boots. When Oskar arrives a contingent of firemen, dressed in SA uniforms, is still at work in the store. Some have taken down their pants and are relieving themselves on the toy sailing vessels, the monkeys, and the drums; one, who is cutting open dolls, seems disappointed to find nothing in them but sawdust. Markus himself is beyond their rage. When he heard them crashing through his shop window, he had gone to sit down at his desk in a back room where he kept his office and here Oskar finds him with an empty water glass in front of him.[38]

One escape that was at least theoretically open to the Jews of Germany in the years preceding the war was emigration. In *Le Dernier des justes* (1959) André Schwarz-Bart tells the story of a family of Polish Jews after World War I seeking a haven from the pogroms that beset them in their native land. Ironically when Benjamin Lévy thinks about choosing a home in exile he passes over England, America, and France and decides upon Germany. England is an island, and that geographical fact alone seems to indicate a position fraught with insecurity; America will separate him by a whole ocean from his family and gives rise, furthermore, to visions of the Biblical dance around the Golden Calf; France is tainted with memories of the not so distant Dreyfus affair. But in Germany, he has heard, the Jews

are well and agreeably established. They are so well assimilated
into the mainstream of German life and culture that many consider themselves more German than Jewish.[39]

Benjamin Lévy ends by settling in the Rhenish town of Stillenstadt, suggestive of any small to moderate-sized German city,
the name itself evoking in sound and significance an aura of
peace and tranquility. There he opens a tailor shop. Stillenstadt
is not free of anti-Semitism, but to Benjamin Lévy coming from
Poland, the Jews of Stillenstadt are, if anything, conspicuous
for the degree to which they have become assimilated Germans; and by being especially nice to the German customers
who frequent his shop, Benjamin hopes to remove any feelings
of anti-Semitism they might be harboring. Once he is sufficiently established, Benjamin has his parents come from Poland
to live with him, and even among the Jews of Stillenstadt, the
arrival of their co-religionists from Poland creates a sensation.
In their manners, dress, and general way of being, the newcomers might have stepped in from another world. But gradually they, too, adapt more or less. Benjamin prospers modestly
and marries a timid local girl of Jewish origin who is known
throughout the book as Mademoiselle Blumenthal, perhaps because she never manages to become a real woman in the image
of her mother-in-law, in whose shadow she is always condemned to stand. He has two sons and later a daughter named
Rachel. The elder son, Moritz, is too German for his grandparents' liking, but the younger one, Ernie, seems more amenable
to their influence.

After Hitler's ascent to power in 1933, the Jews of Stillenstadt bear the brunt of Nazi fury. There are neither communists nor social democrats in town, and so all efforts can be
directed unmitigated against the Jews. Little Ernie Lévy gets a
foretaste of what is to come when one day one of the children
in the group with whom he plays suggests that they play the
trial of Jesus. Ernie is the most obvious candidate for the role
of the Jews screaming for the release of Barabbas and the crucifixion of Christ. Fantasy and reality are never very far apart
in the minds of children, and it is not long before Ernie finds
himself cursed by his comrades, boys and girls alike, as the killer
of Christ and the murderer of God. He is beaten and struck

unconscious by a rock aimed at the back of his neck. Soon thereafter Ernie's grandmother says: "We should never have left Poland. . . ."[40]

It is not long before the Lévys begin to see roving SA bands marching in the street. They make detours to avoid them on their way to the synagogue. During one of the services some uniformed Nazis actually congregate in the synagogue court-yard and as the worshippers emerge, begin jeering and casting a few stones. Several German windows facing onto the court-yard are flung open and the Nazis pause momentarily. Monsieur Krémer, the schoolteacher, rebukes them publicly for their conduct, but they are not so easily put off. An older woman from the congregation, Madame Tuszynski, unable to contain her fury any longer, steps forward and vehemently begins to revile the Nazi leader in her heavily accented German. Their dialogue is brief, and in no time the woman is knocked to the pavement, her wig falls from her head and her collarbone is broken. With a bravery beyond his boyhood years or perhaps because of them, Ernie advances toward the triumphant Nazi, but he is struck in turn and held up to ridicule as the "defender of the Jews."[41]

As time passes life in Stillenstadt becomes increasingly diffi-cult for the Jews. Moritz is thrown out of his gang despite his German bearing; certain stores are declared off-limits; even a crippled beggar, aptly named Monsieur Moitié, whose thighs were ripped away by a French shell in World War I and who is begging in the street, manages to be "man enough" to summon his energy and shout an anti-Semitic insult at Ernie who has paused a bit too long to look at him.[42]

At school, too, the situation deteriorates. In Stillenstadt as elsewhere Jewish children have begun to be called "guests," and not infrequently they are beaten up during recess by the *Pimpfe,* the elite among the Hitler Youth in the class. The teacher, Monsieur Krémer, holds rigidly to his belief in the fundamen-tal innocence of children and refuses to see the reality unfold-ing around him. Regimes come and go, after all, and he can teach Schiller under any of them. Fascism means the "rule of the tavern in the streets and in the government." It cannot last. Stillenstadt's synagogue is burned one night, and the other teachers begin beating the Jewish pupils; but to the old humanist Krémer, the Nazi policies are too manifestly absurd to be around for long. Soon Germany will punish the "bad boys" and send them back to the bars and prisons from which they have come.

Krémer's naiveté is his undoing. When Ernie Lévy receives first prize in German and Ilse Bruckner the first prize for singing, Kémer arranges a "tea" for them in his home; but when it subsequently becomes known that Ilse is seeing Ernie Lévy, her mother forbids her any further contact with the Jewish boy. Her cousin Hans Schliemann scrawls hostile words and obscene drawings on the classroom blackboard. Already Kémer has alienated the teaching staff, none of whom including the headmaster are speaking to him any more; and so it does not come as a surprise to anyone when he is replaced by Monsieur Geek, who has come directly from Berlin. Monsieur Geek further isolates the Jewish "guests" from their Aryan hosts by putting them in the last row and separating the two groups by an empty row of chairs. One particularly Jewish-looking child is held up to public ridicule for his facial characteristics. Monsieur Geek's attempts to break the pride of the Jewish children continue unabated, and when Ernie meets Ilse after class, as they have continued to do despite the parental prohibition, Hans Schliemann and his gang of *Pimpfe,* apparently alerted by Ilse in advance, burst in upon them, spit on Ernie, remove his pants, and curse his Jewishness. For the first time in his life Ernie Lévy knows the meaning of hatred. A few years later, with the events of the Kristallnacht seared into their memories, the Lévys understand fully that it would be better to be German in France than Jewish in Germany; and so, while it is still possible to emigrate, they set out for Paris, crossing the Rhine over the bridge at Kehl on November 14, 1938.[43]

Initially it had been the hope of many Nazi visionaries and planners that what they perceived as the "Jewish problem" might be alleviated by emigration. Some Jews like the Lévys did indeed emigrate, and it is estimated that between 1933 and 1938 approximately 150,000 Jews left Germany. That left some 350,000 who remained, more than half of whom were over the age of forty-five.[44] To uproot oneself at that age is obviously more difficult than for the young. Furthermore, alien permits were required for residence abroad, and since the world had not yet fully recovered from the trauma of economic depression, foreign countries saw to it that these permits were not issued and thus kept their doors closed to Germany's Jews. Since German Jews were primarily urban, middle-class business and professional people, even those countries that were in need of farm workers or skilled laborers feared that their economies might not withstand an influx of these prospective new immigrants.[45] On May 13, 1939, German authorities permitted the SS *Saint-Louis,* chartered by the Hamburg-American Line to set sail from Hamburg with a passenger list of 937 German-Jewish refugees, men, women, and children. The refugees hoped to find a haven in Cuba, many of them in the hopes of eventually making it from there to the United States. The boat anchored in Havana harbor on May 27, but after negotiations with the Cuban government collapsed, it set out to sea again on June 2 and for four tension-filled days cruised up and down between Havana and a point north of Miami. When it became clear that neither Cuba nor the United States would grant landing rights, the *Saint-Louis,* with no other alternative, began to sail back across the Atlantic, arriving in Antwerp, Belgium, on June 17. Thanks in great part to the compassionate efforts of the German captain, who allowed them to debark before the ship returned to Germany, the refugees were scattered among Belgium, Holland, France, and England. In the end, of course, some of them found their way into the concentration camps anyway.[46] But the whole story of the emigrants on the *Saint-Louis* is an exceptional one. Despite the severity of the persecution against them, the majority of German Jews remained. They remained, wrote Stefan Zweig, "out of loyalty or laziness, out of cowardice or out of pride. They preferred to be degraded at home rather than to degrade themselves as beggars abroad."[47]

Poet, novelist, and short-story writer Elisabeth Langgässer was one of those who remained. She had been a teacher, but since she was declared a "half-Jewess" (*halb-Jüdin*), was notified in 1936 that she would not be allowed to practice her profession. She was closely watched by the Gestapo but managed to escape arrest because she was married "in Christian wedlock" to an Aryan. Her daughter Cordelia, however, born out of wedlock to a Jewish father, was taken away and sent ultimately to Auschwitz.[48]

The fear, hurt, resentment, and hatred of those times are incorporated in Langgässer's work. In a short-story called "An der Nähmaschine," published posthumously in 1956, she describes the plight of a *Mischling*, Frau Behagel, living like herself in Berlin toward the end of the war as the wife of an Aryan husband. She is an archaeologist by profession but has been directed by the labor board to work in a sewing factory a good hour's subway ride from home. She has never used a sewing machine in her life, performs poorly on the job, and is held up to ridicule. But as a *Mischling* she can do only one of two things: sew or help clean up rubble from the bombings. Frau Behagel's supervisor settles her case promptly, sending her off to the rubble and telling her "with kindness" to spend her time doing the things she understands.[49]

Just as little Ellen's fate in Ilse Aichinger's *Die grössere Hoffnung* is preferable to that of Anna bound for Poland, so Frau Behagel's fate is preferable to that of Elsie Goldmann in another of Langgässer's short stories, "Untergetaucht," published in 1948. Elsie appears one day at the house of an old school friend named Frieda, her handbag covering her star, and asks to be admitted, "but only for just one night." Since it is to be for only a night and since they had been school friends, Frieda agrees, despite the forebodings of her "thoroughly kind soul" of a husband Karl. But the nights multiply, and with a parrot in the house who spends his day calling out Elsie's name, Frieda and Karl become increasingly anxious. They know they must get rid of Elsie, but to whom can they send her? Tensions mount. Frau Geheinke, the wife of the local block warden, begins asking questions. Frieda reassures Elsie that with her straight nose and straight hair she does not look at all Jewish, and one day Elsie comes back at her point blank: if Frieda were obliged to wear the star, everyone would take her for a Jew, dark and heavy as she is. The arrival of the Gestapo, who come to take Elsie away, puts an end to the situation. To save her hosts from complications, Elsie first throws a blanket over the

parrot's cage and then presents herself to the Gestapo, standing by her explanation that she had just entered the house
through the garden and back door, believing it to be empty.
The story is told by Frieda to a lady friend after the war in a
beer room at a suburban train station, probably just on the edge
of Berlin. The narrator overhears their conversation, acting as
an intermediary between Frieda and the reader. Langgässer no
doubt chose this somewhat intricate structure to create an "al-
ienation effect" (*Verfremdungseffekt*), enabling the reader to take
distance from the characters. With it she also created a means
for the narrator to establish the setting and provide a commentary. Frieda herself is too shallow and too insensitive to reflect
in any meaningful way on her story as she sits drinking beer
with her friend.[50]

To stay and take the consequences is not an alternative as
Ernie Lévy sees it in Schwarz-Bart's *Le Dernier des justes*. For him
there are only two paths of escape, suicide or emigration, and
he tries both. In 1932 sometime after Monsieur Geek's arrival
as the new schoolmaster, Ernie slits his wrists and jumps from
the bathroom window of the family apartment to the ground
below. He has to be taken to the Jewish section of the hospital
in Mainz where he remains for two years under intensive medical care before returning home to Stillenstadt. Schwarz-Bart
appeals to statistics to show that though the percentage of German Jews who committed suicide in the last years before the
collapse of the Nazi Reich was virtually nil, there were hundreds
of schoolchildren in 1934 who succeeded in bring their young
lives to an end.[51]

Besides Jews others on occasion also chose suicide as a means
to end their persecution. In September 1942, the greengrocer,
Albrecht Greff, a friend of the Matzerath family in *Die Blechtrommel*, decides to hang himself after receiving a court summons to appear on a morals charge. Though he is married,
Greff apparently gets whatever erotic stimulation he needs from
his position as head of a boy scout troop, and it is in the uniform of a boy scout leader that he is found hanging.[52] As usual,
Oskar's drumming, which would often be callous were it not so
impish, removes all sense of moroseness from the event. Because he is the ever-likeable Oskar, a midget in body and a

trifle enfeebled in mind, his sensitivities appropriately trimmed to his particular narrative task, Oskar is consistently able to relate and comment on subject matter that in the mouth of another narrator would only too easily become either ponderous or pathetic.

For those people in the Third Reich who had no stigma, political or social, attached to them, life simply went on. The "precarious barrier between thief and gendarme" was wearing very thin at times, and certainly there were not few among those at the helm who had started their careers closer to being thieves than gendarmes. Things which had not been wrong before became wrong now. One might, for example, "earn" one's death by listening to a foreign radio broadcast[53] or, once the war broke out, by intimating too loudly in a public streetcar that the war would soon be over. And yet even after the heavy bombings began, life went on, though it had to do so in the ruins. Bureaucracy, too, continued to function in its characteristically heavy and blundering way just as it did in France, making what for many were already desperate situations even more inhuman.[54] In Berlin "bombed out" passes were issued to allow people to take shelter in the municipal bunker where they lined up as at a bus stop, and those who were more than just simply bombed out received "totally demolished" cards if they could prove to the right person at town hall that they were indeed "totally demolished."[55]

Many people were becoming enraged and bitter at the continued massive bombings after 1942 and especially after 1943 and at the "pigs" who were dropping their bombs indiscriminately on a civilian population.[56] Hildegard Knef's mother, who was staying in a small town outside Berlin, wrote her that both day and night there were bombers in the skies overhead en route to Berlin. When one of them crashed in a neighboring village the farmers went out and beat the pilot to death.[57] After one of the air raids on Werden, Graeber sees what first looks like a slaughterhouse behind a stone wall. But a slaughterhouse would have been more orderly, for there animals were killed according to prescribed regulations; whereas here there are victims mangled, mutilated, and crushed, particularly a whole group of children with their limbs torn and twisted in every direction.

A woman behind him stares at the children saying only that such a deed can never be forgiven, neither in this world nor in the next. A passing patrol forces the spectators to move on, and Graeber thinks about how he has seen many more dead children in France, Holland, Poland, Africa, and Russia. All those dead children, too, had had mothers who cried for them.[58]

Graeber returns to Russia after his furlough only to find the Russian offensive and the German retreat more intensified than when he had left. He wonders whether perhaps the fighting would end once the German army was forced to retreat behind its own borders. But no one in the Germany of World War II would be willing to make the mistake that had been made at the end of World War I. No one would accept responsibility for a defeat and then run the risk of being accused a week later of having betrayed the Fatherland. This time the defeat would have to be total.[59]

CHAPTER VI

The World of the Camps

The Realities of the System

Shortly after the Nazi *Machtübernahme,* or takeover of power in 1933, a network of concentration camps sprang up in Germany, and as German hegemony spread throughout most of continental Europe, they appeared in Austria and in eastern Europe as well. France was spared the erection on its soil of anything like the infamous Auschwitz camp in Poland, but French citizens did not all escape the horrors of the concentration and extermination camps. The road to the Nazi camps began at the prison and processing center at Drancy outside of Paris, and for those who came to know it, it was quite adequate a substitute for the camps themselves. From Drancy the prisoners were taken to the Gare de l'Est and placed aboard railroad cars for the trip across the Rhine.

It has been said many times over that the horrors of life in the camps cannot be described, and many people still object to their being used as matter for fiction. The judgment and the objection have a certain validity. It is always difficult if not impossible to make others see and experience what we ourselves have seen and experienced. In the case of the camps the problem is compounded since the general reading public has never been exposed to anything even remotely resembling them. There exists no personal agglomeration of memories, images, and sensations able to sift and respond to the descriptions of these experiences. Difficult as such descriptions may be, how-

ever, they have been attempted again and again, in fiction as
well as in documentaries, and they constitute the corpus of holocaust literature. In that the novel creates a world unto itself,
it may indeed be the ideal form in which to portray the experience of the concentration camp. The novel is not necessarily
bound by the conventions of any particular reality; instead it
creates its own reality, a world based on the "real" world, to be
sure, but apart from it nonetheless, and governed by its own
laws. If the "univers concentrationnaire," as survivor David
Rousset calls it in his book of the same name, is a world closed
to conventional reality, then perhaps only another closed world,
yet one still accessible to the public, can describe and evoke it.

As always it is the writer who must take the intitiative, and
whether or not the reader is expected to make some contribution of his own, the writer must create the situations and structure them in such a way as to sustain the reader's interest or
engage his sympathy. Holocaust literature has been written by
survivors as well as by those who never set foot inside the camps.
Their techniques vary as do those of any other group of writers. What has motivated them all, however, to one degree or
another, to describe the indescribable, is a desire to bear witness for the living as well as for the dead, to show "how deeply
and terribly outside forces can take hold of man, even to his
core," and to show, too, that "there was something at the core
that was untouchable and inviolable."[1] Ernst Wiechert wrote in
an afterword to *Der Totenwald* that he had dedicated his book
as a "memory to the dead, as a sign of infamy to the living, and
as a warning to those yet to come."[2]

Wiechert was arrested by the Gestapo in 1938 and spent several months at the Buchenwald concentration camp near Weimar. *Der Totenwald* presents his experience in the form of a
fictionalized autobiography. The title is itself a play on the name
Buchenwald, the "forest of birches" which had become a "forest of the dead," as people in Thuringia, the province in which
Weimar is located, used to call the camp in their midst. From
the beginning the fictional character Johannes, the author's alter ego who sees and endures what Wiechert himself had seen
and endured, can only regret the events that have conspired to
put Germany in the position in which she now finds herself. A

single people who speak the same language, who once prayed to the same God, who went through the Thirty Years War and the "Great War" together, whose mothers or grandmothers sang the same songs at evening time, is now divided not by wealth and poverty, by religion and paganism, by two languages, religions, or natures, but by nothing else than a "political dogma, by a paper calf, erected for adoration. . . ." Henceforth nothing else that one had done in life counted but the honor or dishonor one paid to that paper calf. Between the two worlds thus divided there is no mutual understanding. "They excluded each other. Enmity was set between them from their earliest conceptions."[3]

The concentration camps were the material result of the divisions that existed within German society. Those who eventually found their way into the camps could be categorized in six basic groups. All received a "uniform" consisting of a pair of pants and a jacket of low quality synthetic material, vertically striped in blue or gray, a shirt, a pair of undershorts, one pair of woolen socks, a pair of heavy lace shoes, and a visorless cap that had to serve for both summer and winter. The six groups were distinguished from one another by the color of a triangular piece of cloth sewn onto the jackets and pants. Ironically enough, even these groups were not equal in terms of the degree of "respect" they could muster. Those awarded the highest consideration were those who wore the red triangle of the political prisoners. This was a broad classification covering people of all religious or other persuasions that happened to be in political opposition to the ideals of the National Socialist Party, or members of parties that had once vied with the Nazis. These included old democrats or social democrats and communists. Common criminals wore green and came next in the camp hierarchy, to be followed by those unwilling to work who wore black; homosexuals wore pink; radically pacifist Jehovah's Witnesses, known as the "Bibelforscher," wore purple, and Jews yellow. Jews could also qualify for any of the other categories, and many ended up wearing the black triangle along with the yellow one, the two sewn together in such a way that they formed a Star of David. Prisoners who managed to be released from the camps and then confined for a second term after a

new arrest were given a small stripe to wear under their triangle, and those deemed in need of special punishment as a result of one infraction or another wore a black dot next to their
triangle.[4] The blind got two black dots, and some even had the
word *Blöde* stamped onto their sleeves signifying that they were
feeble of mind. Even the stripes of a prisoner's clothing might
be differently arranged according to the credit he had, and veteran prisoners often wore old army uniforms, torn and patched,
of blue, green, and gray.[5] The inmates knew no privacy of any
kind, since they were all housed together in various barracks
which they either constructed themselves or which were already available upon their arrival. It is one of the curious ironies of the time that after their liberation from the camps many
survivors found it difficult to adjust to the relative privacy of
normal life.

   The first group of convicts that Wiechert's Johannes sees at
Buchenwald, shorn and dressed in zebra stripes, reminds him
of a "tired, stumbling herd of animals, without hope, without
home, even without face, so much did they resemble one another in the gray monotony of the picture they presented." On
one hand the prisoner was totally stripped of his individuality
while on the other, distinctions that had maintained if not actually fostered some sense of individuality in the outside world,
were upheld and even embellished in the new one. Johannes
himself was given a red triangle and the number 7180;[6] and
while a number, especially to one as firmly rooted in humanistic thinking as Johannes, might appear to be a travesty of the
human being's right to an individual name, numbers could paradoxically still convey a sense of individuality to their bearers.
The "univers concentrationnaire" was a world apart from the
normal world, and in the new society that it created, it is perhaps not so strange that new designations should have appeared. Even the SS who administered the camps under the
direction of Reichsführer Heinrich Himmler held new ranks
that paralleled those of the army, but whose names were quite
different. It is not without irony that this new world, so many
of whose inhabitants were rapidly reduced to little more than
half-starved skeletons, should have given birth to a society organized on so paramilitary a basis. There was all the traditional military concern for hierarchy and order, there were even

work details and frequent marches to and from the *Appellplatz*, the flat parade ground on which roll call was taken. But the only battle that most of the poor inmates of these camps would ever fight was the daily battle to survive against fear, torture, and starvation.

Those who had an ideal to sustain them in their battle for survival enjoyed a decided psychological advantage. In 1935 André Malraux published a novel with such a character for its hero, *Le Temps du mépris*, the story of a German communist named Kassner. Ever since Hitler had assumed the Chancellorship in Germany, Malraux had been active in organizing French intellectual circles to combat Nazi excesses. On January 4, 1934, he even traveled to Berlin with André Gide in an aborted attempt to see Goebbels and secure the release of three Bulgarian communists implicated in the Reichstag fire of the preceding February. The Bulgarians had been theoretically acquitted but still not released. While Malraux claimed to his biographer Jean Lacouture that he had actually seen Goebbels in Berlin,[7] the Gide documentation of the Berlin expedition indicates quite positively that the meeting with Goebbels never occurred since ". . . Gide and Malraux went to Berlin at the moment when all the ministers were meeting in Munich and could not reach those whom they wanted to see." Furthermore, in *Littérature engagée*, a collection of Gide's political writings and addresses, there exists the published copy of a letter that Gide and Malraux jointly addressed to Goebbels on January 4 and deposited the same day at the ministry on the Wilhelmstrasse in lieu of the personal visit which never occurred.[8]

Like many French artists and intellectuals of the period, Malraux was fascinated by the promise of the communist experiment going on in Russia and saw it as an alternative to German Nazism. Gide had already dealt with the question, a bit naïvely perhaps, in March 1933 when he said in a speech prepared for the *Association des Ecrivains et Artistes Révolutionnaires*, the AEAR, which consistently attempted to protest the events taking place in Germany: "in German terrorism, I see a revival, a recapturing, of the most deplorable past. In the establishment of Soviet society, an unlimited promise of the future."[9] Essentially Malraux agreed with Gide on this point, and out of the opposition between communism and national socialism as he understood them, came *Le Temps du mépris*. By Malraux's own admission it lacks the complexity of a true novel,[10] and thirty years after it had first appeared, he did not seem to think highly of it as an artistic work.[11] The communist hero Kassner is an anti-Nazi intellectual originally from Munich but at the time of the narration residing in exile in Prague. The tone is established at the outset in Malraux's dedication "to the German comrades" with whom he had been in contact. They had wanted to convey to him what they had suffered and "what they had *preserved*" despite their suffering. This book was to be theirs. If one is going to be a comrade, one must be a comrade in something or because of something, and even though Malraux never actually joined the communist party, the idea that brought him together with the "German comrades" was their mutual allegiance to communism. Certainly if one were writing in 1935 simply to oppose Nazism, one could have found other victims of its terror with whom the general French reading public would have been able to sympathize far more easily than with the communists. But clearly Malraux's purpose in writing *Le Temps du mépris* was at least as much to win support for communism as to condemn the totalitarian measures adopted by the Nazis in Germany.

Malraux was shrewdly aware of the magnitude of the problem that some French writers, and especially Gide, were stumbling against in their attempt to support communism. Those who were nourished in the French tradition of individualism and feared for the integrity of the individual in a communist state needed reassurance, and in *Le Temps du mépris* Malraux tried to give it to them:

> The individual stands in opposition to society, but he is nourished by it. . . . communism restores to the individual all the creative potentialities of his nature. . . . It is difficult to be a man. But it is not more difficult to become one by enriching one's fellowship with other men than by cultivating one's individual peculiarities. The former nourishes with at least as much force as the latter that which makes man human, which enables him to surpass himself, to create, invent or realize himself.[12]

Malraux invented Kassner to illustrate this theory. After spending nine days under arrest in a Nazi prison awaiting death and searching desperately for a way to make his death useful, nine days of mental anguish that was far more painful than any physical torture inflicted by the Nazis, Kassner is suddenly and unexpectedly released. The Gestapo guards inform him that his arrest had been a case of mistaken identity, that the "real" Kassner has confessed, and that he is now free to leave. Kassner realizes that another comrade must have assumed his name and taken his place on the Gestapo list. That comrade was willing to be put to death either to spare others from torture or to free someone he considered more important than himself. On his flight back to Prague, Kassner senses that only in the loving and unifying embrace of his wife, herself a worker in the cause against Nazism, can they together try to make good the loss of the dead comrade who had sacrificed himself.

What Kassner has accomplished is to transcend the sub-human level to which his incarceration had reduced him, and which Malraux indicates on a metaphorical level by a series of insect images applied to prisoners and jailors alike and that diminish the prison, *une fourmilière,* and the "human condition" that it evokes. Water metaphors suggest another level on which to read the text. During his incarceration Kassner has a nightmare in which a vulture is shut up in his cage with him and tears at his flesh. Visions come to him of earlier revolutionary days in China and particularly visions of the Yang-Tse River flood. The revolution, the flood, and the vulture combine in his dream. Space and time are annihilated, and a flooding death chant submerges the vulture and the prison. One is tempted to draw an analogy with Prometheus, bound in punishment by Zeus, who sends an eagle to feed on his liver, especially since Malraux specifically describes Kassner's liberation from prison as a return from hell and thus gives it an otherworldly dimension. Free in mind but bound in body, Kassner is not unlike the Greek hero. By returning from hell he does what is not permitted to mortals and acquires a further resemblance to Prometheus who defied the gods to give mankind the fire it was not permitted to have. Unfortunately Kassner does not have the stature of a Prometheus. The twentieth century is not heroic as were the days of old.

Water can act as a purifier but it can also function as an agent of death. In his confinement Kassner's visual range is more or less limited to the area within the walls of his cell. He must rely on his hearing for any information from the outside. For a time he tries to decipher some sort of code in the systematic banging of a comrade in a neighboring cell, when suddenly the banging stops and is replaced by other more stifled sounds. "But something confused and distant, like sounds under water, was taking place in there, was making him tremble in the night."[13] The comrade is being beaten, and the muffled sounds Kassner hears are created by the flesh and blood of his battered body striking against the wall of the cell. The dullness of the sound can only be compared to that of sounds made underwater. Despite the contentions of at least one critic,[14] death associated with the water imagery in this book is not a retreat in the form of a return to the womb. It would be satisfying to think of Kassner's nine days of imprisonment as a parallel to the nine-month confinement of a human embryo to its mother's womb. And it would be satisfying to think of his liberation at the end as a parallel to the end of the nine-month birth cycle. But Kassner's prison is no womb. While the womb represents a stage of dependency in which a human embryo lives immersed in water, the womb also brings shelter and security. Here the water image brings with it only a slow and ugly death. According to philosopher and critic Gaston Bachelard, this use of water imagery is appropriate. "A being given over to water is a being in vertigo. He dies at each minute, without intermission something of his substance is destroyed. Death on a daily basis is not the exuberant death of fire which pierces the sky with its arrows; death on a daily basis is death by water."[15]

That Malraux was a bitter foe of Nazism needs no confirmation here. But his treatment of the Germans in *Le Temps du mépris* and elsewhere reflects a moderation that is noteworthy. He highlighted the figure of Kassner, centering the book almost exclusively on him, while the nameless Nazi prison guards remain steeped in shadow. The book is more a *récit* than a novel, and given its narrow scope Malraux had to curtail his focus. Had he given greater exposure to the jailors, he would only have generated an anger and hatred against them that would have distracted the reader's attention from Kassner. It was not

Malraux's style, furthermore, to portray people hatefully. Rather he wished to portray people working out their individual idealisms. In *Le Temps du mépris* Kassner's idealism runs counter to that of the Nazis and there is no room for both. Malraux says in his preface: "If I had to give Nazis the importance I give Kassner, I should obviously have done so in terms of their basic emotional drive—nationalism."[16]

To a greater degree than Kassner, Wiechert's Johannes is able to maintain contact with the world outside and with his own inner being, as he whiles away the time in a Gestapo prison awaiting internment at Buchenwald. Nearby, a church bell tolling the quarter hour reminds him of the bell of the town hall in some French city where twenty years earlier he lay wounded and awaiting sleep. A literary man himself, he remembers scenes from literature that help him see more clearly through a difficult present—Gorky, Büchner, the Count of Monte Cristo. His day begins at six in the morning with a sometimes friendly, sometimes not so friendly, "Aufstehen!" called out to the accompaniment of a key rapping on his cell door. For some, breakfast consists of coffee, rolls, butter, and an egg—as in a little hotel, Johannes remarks not unhappily. On Tuesdays and Fridays a man comes by with a shaving knife, and on those days Johannes is permitted visitors. Most of these meager amenities cease, however, once he arrives at Buchenwald, and the only literary comparisons that even enter his mind there are fleeting recollections of Dostoyevsky. In prison he was able to seek strength and comfort in the past, but at Buchenwald he can afford to think neither of past nor future, he is content merely to survive one day at a time. When he first hears the name Buchenwald, it sounds rather pleasant, and he remembers the countryside as the one where Goethe once walked with his friend Charlotte von Stein. But these thoughts are soon overwhelmed by starker realities.[17]

These realities are of the kind that greet the reader on the opening page of Remarque's *Der Funke Leben* (1952). "Skeleton 509 slowly raised its skull and opened its eyes. It did not know whether it had been unconscious or merely asleep." 509 remains still and listens for a while, playing dead in accord with an old concentration camp rule and hoping in this way to escape any lurking danger. It was a "simple law of nature known to any beetle." Only at the beginning of the third paragraph does the author change from the neuter pronoun *es* referring to *das Skelett* to the masculine pronoun *er*.[18]

The setting for the minor trauma 509 has just experienced is the concentration camp Remarque calls Mellern, "dozing" peacefully in the sun. "The large Appellplatz, that the SS humorously called the dance floor, was almost empty." All that can be seen are four people hanging from sturdy piles that have been driven into the ground near the entrance gate. Their hands are tied behind their backs, and they have been raised by means of ropes so that their feet no longer touch the ground. Their arms have pulled loose from their sockets, and two stokers from the crematorium are amusing themselves by throwing little pieces of coal at them, to little avail since by now the victims are unconscious. To the left of the gate sits an SS officer named Breuer who is having some cake and coffee at a little round table he has had set up for himself. It is spring 1945, and real coffee is hard to come by in Germany. People make statements about themselves in what, when, or how much they eat. Unlike Leni Pfeiffer in *Gruppenbild mit Dame* sharing her coffee with the Russian Boris or the girl Jenny Brunies in *Hundejahre* trying unsuccessfully to share with her friends the ice she had gotten from a French ice hauler in Danzig, Breuer is content to eat alone. Unlike Jenny's father and his Cebion tablets or Oskar Matzerath's mother and her fish in *Die Blechtrommel* both of whom ultimately die either directly or indirectly because of what and how much they eat, Breuer eats because he has made others die. He has just strangled two Jews who had been idling for six weeks in a bunker reserved for special punishments. Sleepily he listens to the distant strains of the Strauss waltz "Roses from the South" being played by the camp band. It is camp commandant Neubauer's favorite selection.

This opening scene from *Der Funke Leben,* packed almost to the point of contrivance from an artistic perspective, sets down in five paragraphs of unequal length, none of them excessively long, many of the dominant themes of concentration camp literature. As noteworthy as the themes themselves are the narrative style and structure, both of which rely more heavily on irony than on any other fictional device to present the situation and evoke the desired mood. The reader is thrown directly into the story, *in medias res*. He is curious to know something about Skeleton 509 and perhaps even feels sympathetic toward him as a victim. The idea that a human being should be reduced to the level of an insect is repulsive, and precisely because it is repulsive, it is one of the prime metaphors used by Remarque and other authors of concentration camp literature in their attempt to make the public come to grips with so gruesome a subject. The fact that the SS refers to the *Appellplatz* as a dance floor is also ironic, but this was in fact standard terminology. At times the SS seem to have had a propensity for irony, either as a means of enhancing the torture of the inmates or as a means of blunting their own consciences. Himmler is said to have told his men, upon inspection of one of the Polish camps, that though they knew what it meant to see hundreds or even 1000 corpses lying together, they had still known how to remain decent human beings and thereby written a glorious page in German history.[19] Unfortunately the irony of his statement was probably lost both on Himmler and on his audience.

To describe Breuer's strangling two Jews as a "deed done for the well-being of society" (*menschenfreundliche Tat*), is also bitterly ironic, particularly in the light of Breuer's sadistic character as it develops in the book. As the spring of 1945 wears on and the liberation of the camps becomes immanent, Breuer one night wakes up from his sleep and decides that he needs some adventure. Pulling on a pair of boots over his pyjamas, he goes into cell number 7 where he has been keeping one of the prisoners under special torture for some six months. The prisoner, named Lübbe, has been "nourished" for days with nothing but salt herrings and salt water, and lies unconscious in his cell, chained hand and foot to a radiator. A watering can is sufficient to revive him; and Breuer, after smoking a cigarette with his victim and telling him just how close he has come to regaining his freedom because of the Allied advance, proceeds to kill him with a hammer. Lübbe does not scream, he has never screamed, and Breuer knows that he cannot let the night end without making someone scream and wail and moan. He finds his candidate in cell number 4.[20]

The stylistic irony in Remarque's opening passage is complemented by a structural irony in which the cringing existence of
Skeleton 509 is juxtaposed with the peaceful drowsing of the
camp itself. This ironic justaposition is, in turn, complemented
by Breuer's strangling the two Jews, and this brutality is con-
trasted with his drinking a cup of real coffee, eating cake, savoring the raisins in it, all the while listening to the strains of
the Strauss waltz played in the distance, probably by a group
of inmates specially selected because of their training in civilian
life. They were the camp orchestra or what was called in the
terminology of the day *die Lagerkapelle*.

Since the "univers concentrationnaire" was a world apart, it
is not surprising that it gave birth to a vocabulary of its own.
The camps formed a separate realm that was of this world and
yet outside of it, and the language of the authors who wrote
about them with all its irony and metaphor is no less curious
than that of the camps themselves. Wiechert's term *Totenwald*
may have originally been a simple popular mimic for the name
Buchenwald, but its use in a literary context suggests some hidden and mysterious domain in a horror-inspired fairy-tale. The
parallels drawn from the insect and animal kingdom that dot
the pages of concentration camp literature find echo in Wiechert's "animal transport" and "human freight" (*Viehtransport* and
Menschenfracht), that describe Johannes's passage through Bavaria and into Buchenwald. The commandant of the *Totenwald*
was an SS named Hartmann, who happened to be a minister's
son, and Wiechert capitalizes on that bit of irony by repeatedly
referring to him as the *Pfarrerssohn*. From the mouth of this
"minister's son" come words like "dung birds" and "wild pigs"
(*Mistvögeln* and *Wildsäuen*), referring to the inmates. According
to Johannes's fellow prisoner Karl, the expression in Dachau is
"dung bees" (*Mistbienen*). The theme seems capable of infinite
variation. Once the prisoners had been robbed of their humanity, it was no doubt easier to torture or kill them. Anthropologist Germaine Tillion, who was associated with the Musée de
l'Homme *résistance* group in Paris, arrested in April 1942 for
her implication in *résistance* activity and sent to Ravensbrück
north of Berlin at the end of October 1943, recalls that the

term "piece of jewelry" (*Schmuckstück*) was used to designate the most forlorn and decrepit of the prisoners.[21]

One of the minor characters in *Der Funke Leben,* an SS officer named Steinbrenner,[22] describes the arrival of a group of invalids crawling into the camp gates at Mellern as a "turtle race" (*Schildkrötenrennen*). These are people who collapsed en route to the camp, and since prospective inmates are not permitted to help one another, the invalids are on their own. They struggle as best they can, like wounded birds, to make their way into the camp, for they know that if they do not make it through the gates they can expect a shot in the neck to put an end to their efforts. Steinbrenner is sadistically and thoroughly amused at the ironic eagerness of the prisoners to get into the camp. Two shots fired at random into the air above the crawling pack seems to demoralize at least one of the stragglers. "Another sixty seconds," screams Steinbrenner. "One minute! In one minute the door to paradise will be closed. Whoever is not inside by then will have to stay out." As though really intent on watching a race, Steinbrenner has been betting on one particular bald-headed man and is elated to see him make it through the gates on time, but some others including the demoralized man, who simply lies down on the ground, his face in his hands, are less fortunate and are shot. Another officer, a colleague of Steinbrenner's identified only as Robert, prides himself on having shot forty people from this transport alone. The fortieth victim manages twice to turn around and look at Robert, hoping perhaps to avoid his fate. But Robert is not to be dissuaded. "As you wish," he tells the man and shoots him point blank in the face. Steinbrenner's admiration for this colleague, who is only a few years older than he and appears to have achieved something of a record, knows no bounds.[23]

Not only the extermination camps like Auschwitz were equipped with ovens to burn the dead. Even in the more "humane" camps like Mellern, people died what was called a "natural death" and their remains had to be disposed of. The crematoria were not always referred to by name. Both officers and inmates frequently used the phrase "going through the chimney" (*durch den Schornstein gehen*) for whatever euphemistic value it may have had. At Auschwitz, the largest and most dreaded of the extermination camps, however, camp commandant Rudolf Lang, the fictionalized recreation of Rudolf Höss in Merle's *La Mort est mon métier,* directs special efforts toward maintaining a proper attitude and decorum. He never uses words as crude as those of the minister's son at Buchenwald; the inmates are *les patients,* and the actual extermination process including the gassing of the inmates and the disposal of their remains is *l'action spéciale.*[24] Once the bodies of the inmates of the different concentration camps were burned, the ashes were not always returned to their individual families as were those of Remarque's Herr Kruse and Grass's Dr. Brunies. When there were no survivors or the SS had no interest in seeking them out, the ashes were sometimes used for fertilizer.[25]

Staying Alive

Life in the camps was dominated by one overriding concern and that was to stay alive. Some like Wiechert or his alter ego Johannes managed to get by with only a few months in the camps; others like Remarque's 509 had been in the system for ten years, and a Czech boy named Karel in the same book had lived most of his life in the camps, having come through childhood and into adolescence in no other world but this one. Because of the conditions of life—heavy labor, poor nourishment, beatings and other punishments—all the inmates were able to observe changes taking place in their bodies: Johannes notices his heart weakening, his feet swelling; 509 for all his six feet of height, weighs only seventy pounds. For four months he has been living in a separate section of the Mellern camp reserved for those too weak to work and called the "Little Camp" (*das Kleine Lager*), though its official title was the *Schonungsabteilung,* a kind of intensive care station. With an irony typical of this world, there were few inmates who managed to survive more than two weeks of intensive care. Those who did called themselves "veterans," but even the veterans did not usually survive indefinitely. One, a university professor named Joel Buchsbaum, cannot even be delivered *in toto* to the crematorium. In the process of his "education" toward becoming a "useful hu-

man being" he has sacrificed three fingers, seventeen teeth, his
toe nails, and a part of his genitals lost through an injection of
hydrochloric acid.[26]

In the barbaric world of the camps Jews, in particular, were
denied their human status; "they were not even animals. They
were only vermin that are trampled under foot." One of the
medical doctors making his regular rounds in the *Totenwald*
never even bothered to look at the sick, but only paraded
through their midst, and before he arrived the Jews who were
present among the sick had to hide themselves, for the doctor
could not even bear the sight of them.[27] Of course, even in the
minor prison camps such as Traunstein in southern Bavaria
where socialist Luise Rinser spent several months toward the
end of the war and where people were detained for less serious
offenses against the Nazi state, medical care was a mockery.
Those who sought relief from their ailments, Rinser writes in
her *Gefängnistagebuch* (1946), were summarily diagnosed by the
camp physician and not infrequently dismissed with the words
"prison psychosis" (*Gefängnispsychose*).[28]

It appears in literature to have been common knowledge
among the prisoners that gassings occurred at some of the
camps. New arrivals in Mellern, told to undress and prepare
for the baths, knew that in a matter of seconds they had to
reach a decision that could spell life or death. They did not
know what kind of camp they were in, but if it was an extermination camp, then it was better to feign a collapse, since the
unconscious were generally not herded into the baths with the
others. The ultimate concern was to live, and every moment
counted, every delay in the death sentence was critical. There
was always the chance one might survive, since all inmates were
not killed, not even in the extermination camps. If the camp
were not an extermination camp, any signs of collapse could
still be fatal, since one might be considered useless and simply
cut down with a bullet.[29]

For the Czech boy Karel, in *Der Funke Leben*, Mellern is not
his first abode. He has grown up in the camps; he was at
Auschwitz and knew that at Birkenau, the smaller component
of the Auschwitz-Birkenau complex, when people were told to
take the baths and given face cloths, they were going to be

gassed.[30] One of Robert Merle's commandant Rudolf Lang's primary concerns is to mask the knowledge of the gassings from the prisoners. But his techniques do not always succeed.

On an informative visit to Treblinka Lang is told by camp commandant Hauptsturmführer Schmolde, his SS rank parallel to that of an army captain, that the prisoners know what is in store for them. Treblinka is close to Warsaw, and even in the Warsaw Ghetto there are some who know. On Himmler's orders Lang has supervised the construction of his own camp from scratch, transforming a muddy marshland situated between two old Polish army camps, one at Auschwitz, the other close by at Birkenau, into a concentration and extermination camp complex that by the end of the war was the pride of the Nazi system and the bane of Europe's oppressed. To Auschwitz are sent the Jews and to Birkenau prisoners of war.[31] One of Lang's major thrusts in returning from Treblinka to Auschwitz-Birkenau is to preserve intact the "secret" of the gassings, first of all because they are supposed to be secret, and by virtue of his upbringing Lang cannot deviate from an order, and secondly because the inmates themselves are more malleable when ignorant and can be dealt with more efficiently..

Among the inmates of the camps there were the haves and the have-nots just as in the outside world. There were ways of obtaining certain privileges, especially food, for a black market system existed. Wiechert's Johannes in *Der Totenwald* is allowed to receive money from relatives which enables him to buy food supplements.[32] Others like the veterans of the special care unit at Mellern in *Der Funke Leben* sometimes manage to barter to their advantage. One inmate named Lohmann offers his companions his gold tooth before he dies; for them that tooth can mean several more days of life. As a rule every gold tooth is officially registered upon entry into camp and extracted before its owner is sent to the crematorium. As Germaine Tillion reminds the reader in her account of the women's concentration camp at Ravensbrück, the camp system was essentially designed not only to be self-supporting but also to register profit. However, Lohmann has lived in Mellern for seven years and claims that at the time of his arrival gold teeth were not yet subject to registration. Furthermore, he had paid for his tooth long before coming to Mellern and did not want it to fall into the hands of the SS. A fellow-inmate, Leo Lebenthal, who manages some never fully explained contacts both inside and outside the camp, strikes a bargain with some whores from the nearby town who make regular visits to the SS. They always come at night and with a little discretion are able to throw food to Lebenthal through the barbed wire fencing. Still another method of survival is that chosen by a young boy named Ludwig who is fed to capacity by two homosexual lovers, both of whom belong to the camp "aristocracy" and are themselves better nourished than most.[33]

Though a few people like Lebenthal were able successfully to fend for themselves as well as their colleagues, it was not always feasible to come to the aid of one's fellow inmates. The basic unwritten law at Mellern was that a life could not be protected when to do so would endanger the lives of a dozen others. 509 is fortunate that his comrades are willing to risk their own necks for him when he incurs the wrath of one of the supervisors. They arrange to give his number to another inmate who has just died. The supervisor would, of course, still be able to recognize 509 if he saw him, and so the inmates take advantage of the confusion created by one of the Allied bombings and the foggy atmospheric conditions that accompany it to kill that supervisor.[34]

Curiously enough, 509 is the only prisoner at Mellern designated by a number. All the others have names. While this discrepancy does nothing to further the credibility of the narrative, it does represent one possible solution to the artistic problem facing Remarque; namely, that of retaining the number system actually used in the camps on one hand, and of peopling his book with numbers on the other.

One rule of camp life that most inmates strictly adhered to was not to volunteer for anything. To volunteer was naïve, and those who had experience with the camps knew that volunteers frequently never returned, regardless of what it was they had volunteered for. When SS officer Weber visits the special care unit at Mellern in the company of a doctor offering hospital attention to six men who would volunteer for it, no one except for a few newcomers steps forward. Weber then orders 509 and another comrade to fall out and stand with the volunteers; they refuse and are beaten half to death for their resistance and confined for several days to the camp bunker. An inmate could never admit to having been beaten, and when 509 is questioned sometime after his release from the bunker by officer Weber himself about the origin of his wounds, he answers meekly that he has taken a fall.[35] Truth in the concentration camps was like truth in Orwell's *1984*. One could affirm what was not just as easily as one could deny what was. The conventions were known, and both the SS and their prisoners adhered to them. Both knew that promises made by the SS or the Gestapo had the "same value as the promises made by dreams in the night."[36]

The SS was aided in its task of administering the concentration camps by inmates wearing every color of the camp insignia who worked for them in policing and beating up their own comrades.[37] They functioned as *Kapos* on camp police details and even as members of the *Sonderkommando,* the special detachments in charge of burying the dead. On his visit to Treblinka Rudolf Lang is astonished to learn that the *Sonderkommando* there is composed entirely of Jews, some of whom are so well cared for they even manage to look athletic. "Everything is possible here," camp commandant Schmolde reminds him.[38]

Indeed Schmolde had a point. Frequently prisoners who were artists, especially musicians and even sculptors, were sought out to enrich the lives of the officers. Wiechert's Johannes is given permission to have all his published works ordered for the camp library at Buchenwald, and their number causes a sensation among the Nazis on the other side of the barbed wire partition. They did not think it possible that a man wearing a number could be capable of such productivity, and more than once Johannes has to assure an astounded *Scharführer* or platoon leader that he has written these books all by himself. Johannes, in turn, marvels at his fellow prisoners who have managed to form a whole band replete with violins, mandolins, and guitars, and who spend evenings playing their music.

Not all were so fortunate as those who were permitted to practice their craft, regardless of the constraints under which they worked. One Sunday during a roll call in the *Totenwald,* a

Protestant minister begins preaching loudly from a window in the bunker to which he has been confined. Sunday services, however, are not permitted in the camp, and the minister is quickly stopped.[39]

Roll call itself was one of the most important functions of the camps. It was a time when the officer in charge could strike with hand, stick, or boot anyone not particularly to his liking. It was an ironic time when the prisoners' lives, which ordinarily were of so little consequence, suddenly assumed inordinate value if one of them should fail to appear on the *Appellplatz*. Since escape by night through the barbed wire fencing was virtually impossible, an absence meant that a prisoner had committed suicide either by running into the electrified barbed wire or by hanging himself from a tree or that he had been hidden by his comrades. In any case he had to be found, and until he was, punishments were sure to rain down on the others. Anna Seghers's *Das siebte Kreuz*, first published in English in New York in 1942 and then in German in Mexico in 1943, tells a similar story. Seven inmates, despite the odds against them, escape from the camp at Westhofen southeast of Dortmund, and for those who remain the flight of the seven means a cut in food and sleeping blankets, increased working time, and long interrogations animated by threats and beatings.[40]

Rations could be and were cut, however, under other pretexts as well, even though the pretexts at times had little to do with the camp or the inmates. In the "univers concentrationnaire" the logic of cause and effect was suspended as thoroughly as in any of Kafka's works.

When Allied bombs begin to fall in greater number on the nearby city, work loads at the camp in Mellern in *Der Funke Leben* are increased and free time suspended, since the prisoners are used to help in the clean-up. After one of the bombings, for no logical reason, the Jews of the camp are denied bread for two days. Even among themselves inmates could be cruelly illogical. A Catholic inmate at Mellern by the name of Ammers, knowing that his death is near, asks for a priest. Leo Lebenthal's perfectly innocent question seeking to ascertain what kind of priest the man wants serves Ammers as a pretext to launch into an anti-Semitic diatribe blaming the Jews for everything including the concentration camps which would not have come into being had there been no Jews. "I am dying because you damned Jews devoured everything that was coming to me. And now you do not even want to get me a priest. I want to confess. What do you know about that? Why do I have to be in a Jewish barracks? I have the right to Aryan barracks."[41]

One of Rudolf Lang's superiors in *La Mort est mon métier,* conscious of French history as he could be only in a French book, reminds Lang that Napoleon once said that "impossible" was not a French word. "Since '34 we are trying to prove to the world that it is not a German word." And indeed the Germans were succeeding. Anything and everything had become possible in Germany. Large transports were organized, the infamous *Nacht und Nebel Transporte,* designed to arrest people under the cover of "night and fog" and to deliver the human cargo by rail right into the extermination camps. Once he really has Auschwitz-Birkenau functioning, Lang calculates on submitting 2800 *unités* or units, the term he uses to describe the condemned, for the *action spéciale* every twenty-four hours.[42]

Incongruities of all kinds were realized daily. Communists were brought together in the concentration camps and united as they might never have been in the outside world. They were an organized and energetic group who worked together with the other inmates but never trusted them completely. In *Der Funke Leben* 509 is approached on separate occasions by two communists, Lewinsky and Werner, but always prefers to remain free from any attachments, particularly from attachments to a totalitarian party. The Nazis have been a sufficient lesson. Werner, moreover, is as convinced that the world will one day belong to the communists as the Nazis had been that it would belong to them, and admits openly to 509 that under a communist regime, new concentration camps would probably have to be erected for some of those who opposed the party. 509 refuses his overtures categorically.[43]

Romance, too, could blossom incongruously on the barren landscape of the camps. In *Der Funke Leben* Ruth Holland is imprisoned in the women's compound at Mellern. Because she had once been beautiful, she had been forced to render services to the German soldiers and some Ukrainians fighting with them and so was allowed to live. Two years before the book opens she had met Josef Bucher while he was working as a carpenter in the women's compound. Since that time they have met regularly, though secretly, standing for a few moments together on opposite sides of the barbed wire that separates the special care unit, where he is being held, from the women's camp.[44]

Playwright and novelist Jean Genet, who was a veteran of the French prison system and always something of a social nonconformist, said after a trip to Germany in the 1930s that he felt ill at ease there. Since the whole country was being run by gangsters, he found himself unable to assert his individuality as he did in France by running counter to the law.[45] Genet's point is well taken. Under a regime such as that of the German Nazis good can equal bad and bad can equal good with disturbing facility. Often it was a circus feat to be able to dance between the ropes and survive. Even the normal and honorable discharging of one's professional obligations could bring disaster.

The story of a medical doctor named Berger imprisoned at Mellern is an example. Berger was sent to Mellern for having once treated for syphilis a man who subsequently became a high Nazis officer. Berger is fortunate enough to get off with a concentration camp sentence, but only because he has succeeded in persuading the Nazi that he believes the man's problem to have been caused by an infection contracted during the previous war. One of Berger's colleagues involved in the same case does not fare as well. The Nazis simply have him shot.[46]

Administering the Camps: The SS

The fear that was a part of the daily life of concentration camp inmates, fear of the unknown, the unexpected, and the unpredictable which could materialize at a moment's notice, was also part of the lives of the SS officers who administered the camps. Although any attempt to compare the two worlds would be ludicrous, Remarque's use of an omniscient third-person narrator enables him to straddle both. Mellern's commandant, *Obersturmbannführer* Bruno Neubauer, his rank corresponding to a lieutenant-colonel's, is a case in point. His position allows him to create a comfortable existence for himself, his wife Selma,

and his daughter Freya. Selma has bought shoes, a dressing
gown, and some elegant armchairs from France, lace from Belgium, and a fur coat and blanket from Warsaw. Neubauer even
owns a commercial building that is worth at least 200,000 marks
in the early spring of 1945. In 1933 it had belonged to a Jew
named Josef Blank who had asked 100,000 marks for it and
complained that even at that price he was taking a loss, but
after two weeks in a concentration camp Blank had sold the
building for 5000 marks. Neubauer eases his conscience with
the conviction that he had in essence dealt fairly with Blank,
since he could certainly have gotten the building for nothing if
he had turned Blank over to the SS. The transaction had been
legal, furthermore, and if Neubauer had not bought the building himself, someone else from the Party would have done so
for less money or none at all. This little material step forward
in the world is nothing more than his personal revenge against
the Party "big shots" who had started from nowhere.

But Selma Neubauer is not as appreciative as her husband
would like her to be. The intensified bombings of the city put
her nerves on edge. She is not a stupid woman, and the reality
of the bombings stands in flat contradiction to government
promises of victory and revenge against the enemy whose planes
were not supposed to dare enter German air space. Not unlike
the inmates of her husband's camp, she soon realizes that
promises made in the German Reich are worthless. One day
when the screech of the air-raid alarm sirens seems particularly
loud and piercing, Selma Neubauer and her daughter leave
their house in town despite the air-raid shelter that has been
built into their cellar and go up to Neubauer's camp to be with
him. Convinced that the Allies will not bomb the camps, she
expects to find a measure of security there. Her arrival coincides with that of a fresh transport of prisoners diverted to
Mellern because the extermination camps for which they were
destined lie too far to the east, and conditions are too unsettled
to permit their unloading. What Selma Neubauer sees appalls
her. Bruno has been leading a double life, so to speak, and in
no way is Selma prepared for the sight that meets her eyes. She
cannot stop staring at the pitiful new arrivals. Reading revolution in the faces of his wife and daughter, a revolution he can

ill afford to provoke in the presence of another SS officer, Neubauer puts his family off with the explanation that the arrivals have been sent to Mellern for rehabilitation. Remarque ends the scene with dramatic abruptness, and the reader is not permitted to witness Selma's reaction to this lie. That she recognizes it as a lie is certain, but she also loves her husband, or at any rate, had loved him once.

When Selma Neubauer finally perceives that the end is approaching in Germany, she begins to lay plans to persuade her husband to flee to Switzerland with her and their daughter and some jewels she had purchased over the years without his knowledge. Jewels, unlike real estate, were transportable, and the house could be written over to their daughter without arousing too much suspicion. The Jews were a sufficient example to her that one must know in time when to leave a place, and she is determined not to be caught as they had been. But Neubauer does not appreciate either the idea of a flight, since he and his family are not outlaws, or the comparison with the Jews. Selma herself, he tells her, is behaving like a Jew who would cut someone's throat for gold. But she can no longer be deceived. "Jews cut no throats. Jews take care of their families. Better than many Germanic supermen." Aware now that she will have to act alone before it is too late, Selma one day takes her daughter and flees, leaving her husband a letter containing the address of a village in Bavaria and inviting him to follow.

When he discovers what his wife has done, Neubauer feels abandoned. He had thought of himself as one of the most humane of the camp commandants, and Mellern was certainly no Dachau or Buchenwald, not to speak of the extermination camps. Even before Selma's desertion, however, he has begun to have some misgivings about the future. Once when he goes into the city to inspect the bombed ruins of the commercial building he "purchased" from Josef Blank just after the Nazi takeover, he finds Blank wandering around in the same area and cannot help feeling a certain resentment at having paid Blank good money for the building and gotten a pile of ruins in return. He is almost about to ask Blank why he is not in a concentration camp when a sudden premonition checks his impulse. Is it possible that people like Blank will rise up again?

Judging by the physical aspect of the human wreck standing before him, it seems unlikely, but one had best be prudent. And so instead of arresting Blank, Neubauer offers him a cigarette. Blank may some day be useful to him as a witness.[47]

Other camp commanders, too, had their problems. When it becomes apparent in Anna Seghers's *Das siebte Kreuz* that all seven escapees from the camp at Westhofen will not immediately be overtaken and returned to camp or otherwise accounted for, Commandant Fahrenberg begins to fear for his career. Even at the end when Georg Heisler is the only one of the seven still free, Fahrenberg can neither eat nor sleep. He has had cross beams nailed at shoulder level to seven already topped plane trees so that the trees resemble crosses awaiting their victims. But Fahrenberg's dream of making the crosses into instruments of crucifixion is never fulfilled. The tale of the seven escaped inmates ends with the seventh chapter: Heisler never returns, and Fahrenberg is replaced by a less melodramatic successor who immediately has the crosses cut down.[48]

The problems an SS officer encountered in the administration of the camps were made to the measure of the position he occupied. For Rudolf Lang, the realistic and self-disciplined commandant of Auschwitz in *La Mort est mon métier,* they are at times staggering. As requirements come through from Himmler in Berlin for ever greater rapidity and efficiency in the extermination of the victims who arrive in increasingly unmanageable numbers, Lang knows that he must find ways to meet the demands placed on him or suffer the loss of his career if not his life. Through patient and painstaking research and experimentation he proves himself equal to the task. But for Lang life has always been a stern schoolmaster, and it is, in effect, Merle's unstated premise in *La Mort est mon métier* that the man's background made him what he was. After a harsh upbringing at the hands of a religious and patriotic fanatic of a father, distraught by the political and economic debility of Germany and by the continuing prospects of his own unemployment, Lang joins the Nazi Party early on, along with many other malcontents. He is grossly disappointed at not being assigned to the German resistance units sabotaging the efforts of French occupation troops that the Versailles treaties had stationed on the west bank of the Rhine. He is, nonetheless, given the task of executing a schoolteacher who has betrayed one of the leaders of the German resistance, Leo Albert Schlageter. In 1923 the French shot Schlageter who became one of the early martyrs to the Nazi cause. But the Nazis are not yet in power, and Lang and two comrades in the teacher's execution party are sentenced to ten-year prison terms. It is because of Lang's prison experience, in fact, that Himmler has chosen him for work in the concentration camps. Accepting the arguments of Hitler and Himmler that Germany must exterminate the Jews or be exterminated by them, he never once has any regrets about his job. At one point, though, he seeks a transfer to the Russian front; but since that transfer is not approved he remains at Auschwitz until December of 1943 when he is named to the post of inspector of the camps and moves with his family to Berlin.[49] Like Neubauer at Mellern, Lang becomes ever more distant from his family. Perhaps the very nature of his work is enough to alienate him from normal society. Evil, like greatness and power, brings solitude. Jean Genet expresses this idea in *Pompes funèbres* (1947) when he bestows lavish admiration on Adolf Hitler for having attained in his lifetime the pinnacle of solitude.[50] Solitude is one of the greatest complaints of Lang's wife Elsie during their stay at Auschwitz, though in her case it is imposed rather than self-generated. She knows nothing of the gassings, has noticed only the unpleasant smell that never seems to leave the air, and attributes it to the factories located in the Auschwitz area. Her mind is set straight by a slip of the tongue of *Standartenführer* Kellner, who is on an informational tour of the camps. His rank is equivalent to an army colonel's, and on orders from Berlin Lang is obliged to entertain him. At table Kellner unwittingly alludes to the ugliness that he feels is the chief drawback of the camps, particularly the ugliness of the people who are to be gassed.[51] When Elsie is finally able to confront her husband alone, she is aghast. But she is no Selma Neubauer to challenge her husband, and Lang, a stronger man than Neubauer and more rigid, would never have permitted it.

Local Citizens and Their Response to the Camps in Their Midst

The essential rule governing relations between inmates of the concentration camps and the world outside was that they should

see as little of each other as possible. The SS deemed it un-
healthy to let German civilians see too much of the prisoners
and unwise to let the prisoners see too much of the destruction
befalling German cities, especially after the tide began to turn
against Germany.[52] Even the limited contact afforded by work
details that took prisoners outside their camps was not available
to all of them. Those destined for rapid liquidation in the extermination camps were never permitted to work on the outside.

Insofar as they thought about each other at all, the feelings
of the inmates for the civilian population living near the camps
and those of the civilians for the camp inmates were not always
of a friendly nature. From behind the barbed wire at Mellern,
509 has looked down for ten years on the city below. He has
never been inside it, knows it only from the elevation of the
camp site, and begins to hate it. The contrast between the still
relatively free life-style its citizens enjoy and the inhumanity of
the camp is too much to bear with equanimity. After a while,
however, even this abstract hatred subsides. Real things like the
struggle to find a crust of bread become more important.[53]
Aside from a few details about the lives of the SS officers running the Mellern camp, Remarque gives little insight into the
attitude of civilians living in its vicinity. East German writer
Anna Seghers's book, on the other hand, is structured primarily around the escape of an inmate named Georg Heisler, from
the Westhofen camp, and it unfolds, therefore, essentially in
the surrounding area. Initially when the camp was first constructed, some of the local citizens showed annoyance at having
a concentration camp planted "right in front of their noses";
but there were compensations: the camp brought business and
money. When it becomes clear that for a start Heisler has chosen to hide in his own hometown near the camp, some of the
townspeople as well as those from the neighboring area, however, are angered. After a period of three years they have slowly
become accustomed to having the camp in their midst but they
do not like being reminded of it. Heisler's escape forces them
to think, and the more they think the more it seems to them
that the camp is being erected anew, for a second time.[54] New
walls are in fact constructed and new barbed wire fences com-

pleted; there are new interrogations. Why does Heisler have to involve them in his escapade?

Heisler was first arrested and taken to Westhofen early in 1934. Some years before he had abandoned his wife Elli and their child, and no one including his family knew his whereabouts. Ironically the notice of his imprisonment from Westhofen is the first sign Elli has had of him. She has more or less relinquished any thoughts of sharing a married life with Heisler, and so when she receives a permit to visit him some time after his incarceration, she does not welcome it. Nonetheless, she feels obliged to go to Westhofen. The SS grants the permit in the hope that the sight of his wife will induce Heisler to talk and thus achieve for them what beating, kicking, hunger, and imprisonment in total darkness have not achieved. But Georg and Elli have never really shared each other's thoughts and do not do so during this visit either. Their conversation is limited to questions about their child and Georg's family. Both seem moved, however, by the unaccustomed experience of their togetherness and are not prepared to separate when the announcement comes that their visiting time is over. Elli's father has accompanied her to the camp and waited for her return in a local inn just outside the compound. When she arrives, the innkeeper, his wife, and two other women are present. Elli can remember nothing of how she has gotten back to the inn. One of the women pats her shoulder, the other strokes her hair. The innkeeper's wife picks up Elli's hat which has fallen to the floor and blows the dust from it. Not a word is spoken, for the realities of Westhofen are too close. "As silent as was her lament, just as silent was the comfort she received."

People were afraid of one another, and Elli soon notices that people begin to avoid her. And for good cause. An old friend Heinrich Kübler, who had visited her in her apartment, is kidnapped, beaten until he loses consciousness, and taken to Westhofen because the Gestapo have mistaken him for Heisler whom they expect after his escape to go back to see his wife. Heisler's relatives are watched, and Elli's father is summoned to Gestapo headquarters for interrogation. A fellow-worker tries to console him for the ill that has overtaken his family. "This can happen everywhere, Mettenheimer. . . . This can happen

today in every German family." Elli's sister whose marriage to
Otto Rainers, a bank clerk by day who does double duty as an
SS man at night, has been more successful than Elli's, warns
her that one day Elli too might be arrested.

In times like these even family and friends had to be shared
with the State. Neither Georg Heisler's mother nor his brother
know quite what to say in the presence of the youngest son,
Heini, who has been completely taken in by Nazi doctrine.
Trying to console his mother over Georg and not even imag-
ining that she can feel love for someone who has defied the
Nazi state, Heini tells her to forget that Georg ever existed.
The older of the two boys is more sympathetic toward Georg
even though he himself joined the SA in disgust after five years
of unemployment. But he is unable to speak forthrightly to his
mother until Heini has gone.[55]

In the course of Georg Heisler's wanderings through town,
he is seen and recognized in a snack bar by two young boys
wearing Nazi caps. Each of the boys knows that the other has
recognized Heisler as an escapee. The boys had once been very
good friends, but a time has come when, for fear of betraying
themselves, they can no longer seriously discuss anything, each
not knowing for sure whether the other has changed. After
Heisler has eaten and left the establishment, one of the boys
remarks that his friend could have earned a reward for turning
Heisler in. Staring each other in the eyes they admit that neither could have betrayed him. Neither of them has changed,
and the boys leave the snack bar with their old friendship renewed.[56]

One of Heisler's old friends Paul Röder is good enough to
hide him for a few hours in his own apartment. Röder's wife
Liesel, unaware of Heisler's identity and thinking she is doing
no more than receiving her husband's guest, does so graciously.
Upon Georg's departure Paul roams the city in search of other
contacts who might be willing to do something for Heisler. But
Liesel has to be warned to keep a tight lip, and when she is,
fear makes her almost hysterical. She has never been a good
liar, and certainly there will be questions, if not from the Gestapo then from the caretaker of their building who keeps informed about the activities of the house, since he himself could

be subject to questioning.[57] Paul Röder soon pays for his generosity or folly, as one might have it, by his own internment at Westhofen.

The End of the Camps

The concentration camps were not soundproof from the outside world. During the early years of the war, prisoners at Mellern are quite well informed of the progress the Germans have made, but as victory becomes scarce, Neubauer refuses to allow newspapers to be brought in and withholds information of the German retreats from the camp radio.[58] As the bombings increase, however, and work details from the camp are requisitioned to help remove the rubble, the prisoners are able to witness first hand the havoc war is wreaking on Germany and they draw their own conclusions. On one venture outside Mellern while the SS is marching a detachment of laborers out into the city to assist in the clean-up, air-raid sirens begin to wail. Many of the prisoners still have reactions healthy enough to make them instinctively want to take shelter. But the SS guards order them to stand still where they are. If they try to flee, they will all be shot. Meanwhile the guards themselves take cover in an adjacent cellar. After the air raid passes they creep from their hiding places and order the prisoners to unearth four of their comrades caught in the rubble. Three are dead. Then the prisoners are put to work freeing others trapped in the ruins, this time, German civilians. One man with a Hitler mustache pleads for their help. "Bitte! Meine Herren!" The prisoners are unaccustomed to being addressed so politely. But though the mustached man has promised in his desperation to give them some reward for their assistance, he flees as soon as he is freed. "Too funny!" reflects one of the prisoners named Goldstein, breathing heavily after the work he has done. Camp inmates were freeing civilians![59]

Finally the end which had been so long in coming seemed at last to be arriving. Many prisoners had to summon up their last ounce of will power to survive. Luise Rinser, arrested late in the war, awaited the Nazi defeat with eagerness. On October 22, 1944, ten days after her arrest, she noted in her *Gefängnis-*

tagebuch, the diary that she had begun to write in secret and was constantly obliged to keep in watchful hiding, that the power of the word would serve to "insulate" her from the "naked experience of imprisonment."[60] For communist Willi Bredel the need to write was more a need to speak out. Since he could not write during his imprisonment at Fuhlsbüttel on the outskirts of Hamburg in 1933–34, he had to content himself with making mental preparations to write, eventually recording his experience in fictionalized form in *Die Prüfung,* which was first published in 1935 in the Soviet Union. For some, hatred had been a means of survival; others, particularly in the more severe camps, were too broken to hate. Still others, at least in the beginning, preferred to take refuge in ignorance, unable to cope psychologically with the reality of what was happening.[61] Some had decided that if they should come out of the camps alive, they would have to forget in order to go on living. Attempting in *Der Funke Leben* to console Ruth Holland's anxiety over the sexual services she has been obliged to perform during her imprisonment, Bucher reminds her that the experience of the camps was an abnormal one and that normal rules of conduct could not obtain. A new moral code had had to be invented.[62] Some preferred not to forget, knew they could not, and indeed used their crying inner need to give testimony of their suffering as a psychological impetus to their own survival. Just as Stendhal conceived of the novel as a mirror reflecting whatever lay in its path, so did Wiechert's Johannes in the testimony of *Der Totenwald* become a mirror, absorbing everything he saw in order one day to be able to bear witness.[63] Neither Wiechert nor Johannes had to wait until the end of the war for his liberation. Others were less fortunate, and many, 509 among them, realized that their inner resistance was all they possessed in a world which had deprived them of all else. Some would live for the revenge they hoped to wreak, as does the Jew Jacobson who eventually finds his way to Auschwitz along with most of the other principal characters in Hochhuth's *Der Stellvertreter.* An inmate of Mellern named Ahasver proposes that camp prisoners should resolve to meet and maintain contact so as not to lose each other in the future. But most seem to have decided that though they should indeed not forget, they did not want to make a cult out of their experience.[64]

For the officers of the camps, Germany's defeat had quite different implications. Among the SS at Mellern reactions vary. One officer worries whether he and his colleagues will receive pensions since they had never learned a trade that would make them marketable in the outside world; another hopes to escape to Spain or South America; one hopes that all the inmates he has beaten since 1933 are dead but cannot be sure; others hope that the inmates at Mellern will give them a favorable report. In the confusion wrought by the approach of American troops, fanatics like Weber and Steinbrenner free themselves from Neubauer's command. Together with their men they pour benzine over the barracks housing the special care unit and then set them ablaze shooting the inmates as they emerge.[65]

Neubauer himself has prepared an heroic surrender for these unheroic times. He has never considered his actions to be of a criminal nature and is convinced he will not have to spend much time in detention, perhaps only a brief period in some castle with men of his rank until the transfer of power has been accomplished. He will surrender militarily. In earlier times—he thinks of Napoleon III at Sedan—officers surrendered their daggers; perhaps he should surrender his revolver? That hardly seemed appropriate. Neubauer has no pattern to follow and the proper scenario for a surrender in 1945 seems to be eluding him. No one thought to prepare for this eventuality. In any case he will not give the Hitler salute. A simple military hand salute will be more fitting. In the end were they not all military men and colleagues, the Germans and their enemies alike? At Mellern Neubauer has always thought of himself as somehow being at the front. He is formally handed over to the Americans in his own headquarters by his chauffeur Alfred. He never anticipated such a betrayal.

The Americans have little patience for Neubauer's ceremoniousness. One of them is a corporal who speaks perfect German, and Neubauer, unable even at the very end to accept the reality of the Reich's collapse, immediately conjures up visions of the German Bund in America. The corporal, however,

though he is working with the Americans, is a German born in
Frankfurt. Neubauer requests permission to leave his headquarters dressed in soldierly attire, but as far as the corporal is
concerned he is no soldier. Neubauer explains that it is his Party
uniform jacket he wishes to wear, is granted permission to do
so, and marches off with a few other SS officers to carry away
the charred remains of those who had died in Weber's last escapade. He walks over to the compound where those requiring
"special care" have been housed. The surviving inmates recognize him but can do no more than stare. They separate to form
a path for him, and not one hand or voice is raised against him.
To the Americans Neubauer repeats over and over again what
became a litany at the end of the war: he has only done his
duty, has done always and only that which he had been ordered to do; he has tried to do his best; he has been humane.[66]

If others denied personal responsibility for what they had
done, Rudolf Lang in Merle's *La Mort est mon métier* is an exception. As the former commandant of the Auschwitz-Birkenau
camp, he is ready to take upon his shoulders, as he believes any
true leader must, full blame for all that has transpired under
his administration. Of course, he, too, has acted on orders, and
he feels betrayed by Himmler whose suicide failed to set an
example for his subordinates. Just before the final debacle Lang
is demobilized and given papers stating that he had been a
lower-ranking naval officer and was a farmer in civilian life. He
goes to live on a farm where he works for eight months before
the Americans catch up with him and arrest him in March 1946.
He puts on his old SS uniform which he has carefully kept and
goes off with his arrestors, repeating the same testimony first
to them, then at Nürnberg, then at his final trial after extradi-
tion to Poland. He tells what he knows, hides nothing, and de-
nies nothing. He can ill understand the mania of the Poles who
have witnesses brought from all over Europe to testify against
him, since he has no intention of denying anything. Only once
during his trial does a discrepancy of any kind arise. When the
prosecutor accuses him of having killed three and a half million
people, Lang rectifies the number to two and a half million.
What the prosecutor takes for cynicism is no more than Lang's
habitual desire for exactitude. Just as he had been concerned

for doing what was correct and proper when as commandant he had a Christmas tree erected at Auschwitz, even though one of his officers had ventured to remind him that the inmates might have preferred to have their rations doubled instead, he now shows perfunctory concern that his wife Elsie and their children not be mistreated. There is little sentimental attachment; they are his family and he owes them certain obligations. He receives letters from Elsie and is able to write in return, relieved to learn that she and the children have not, in their turn, been placed in a concentration camp. Lang is sentenced to die at Auschwitz and is hanged on one of the gallows he himself had had erected, as unmoved by his own fate as he had been by that of so many others.[67]

The story of the concentration camps of the Third Reich is one of the most dreadful in the long history of humanity. What Merle has attempted to do in *La Mort est mon métier* is to show the psychological grounds on which a world such as that of the camps could have been built. In the process the reader never really becomes sympathetic toward the hero, or anti-hero, as one might prefer to call him. Lang is too cold, unemotional, and unfeeling a character. He is also the narrator, and his narration, conforming to his temperament, is cold and logical, too. Perhaps it is his honesty and his conviction in what he is saying that serve to hold the reader's interest. To understand may not always be to pardon, as the French proverb would have it; but to try to understand is an important first step in preventing the world of the concentration camps as they existed in Germany from 1933 to 1945 from anywhere taking form again.

André Malraux claimed to have said one day to Georges Bernanos that with the creation of the camps Satan visibly appeared on the earth.[68] This kind of spiritual language was more suited to Bernanos than it was to Malraux, but even a nonbeliever like Malraux could see the Nazi camps as a blatant manifestation of that kind of absolute and eternal Evil that all religions in one way or another have confronted.

CHAPTER VII

The German Occupation of France

The New Pace of Life

While the German homefront was being pulverized into a battlefield with the bombing of the cities, the French homefront became a battlefront of a different order. Certainly Nantes and Rouen were bombed by British planes, and between 1942 and 1943 three-quarters of Lorient was razed. But by and large death was not an overt presence in the city streets and the countryside—yet it was there, nonetheless, physical as well as spiritual death, the kind Germany had known since 1933. "Everything is dying without being seen," wrote Jean Guéhenno in his *Journal des années noires* on May 9, 1941, "and without provoking the reaction of horror and resistance that a bloody death would provoke."[1] Elsa Triolet, Résistance writer and wife of poet and novelist Louis Aragon, describes in "La Vie privée" (1945) the life of a painter, Alexis Slavsky, during the Occupation. Alexis was dedicated to his art, or at any rate professed to be, and would simply have liked the war to pass him by so that he could continue his work. But this war passed no one by. "The illusion of security behind walls was a vestige of time passed. Today, when it is not a bomb that breaks open a house, it is a cop."[2] And when it was not the Germans who did the policing, it was the French themselves.

On the whole the French adapted to the Occupation. In a short essay first published in London in 1945 and entitled "Paris sous l'occupation," Sartre wondered whether the British would understand him when he said that the horror of the Occupation was intolerable but that the French, at the same time, came to terms with it extremely well.[3] Some did so better than others, and some even made the adjustment with incredible ease. The very young, as always, seem to have adapted the most readily. Guéhenno was a lycée professor in Paris during the Occupation and by March 1943, if not earlier, began to observe an ideological division between himself and his students. "My faith itself, my hope, all that resists in me and says 'no' annoys and irritates them." What he told them of another time and another France appeared to them as fruitless talk; perhaps it was their instinct of self-preservation or the will to happiness at any price that animated them and made them adapt, whether they wanted to or not, to their country's misfortune. "They have a kind of vital interest in despising everything they lack and believe they will continue to lack."[4]

Generalizations, of course, are always a bit risky, and like any other group the young were not always of one mind. At age seventeen Francis de Balansun in Jean-Louis Curtis's *Les Forêts de la nuit* (1947) is assisting Résistance fighters to cross the demarcation line just beyond a town the author calls Saint-Clar below Bordeaux in the Pyrenees, in the occupied zone of southwestern France where the novel unfolds. Francis knows the terrain and runs less risk than the *résistants* should they try to cross the line unassisted. Though his family is no longer wealthy, Francis is of noble lineage, and his father instilled in him a sense of history and patriotism. But the old Count de Balansun has made his peace with the Germans and knows nothing of his son's activities. One cannot tell the truth to the old, agrees one *résistant*. They understand nothing of the times, and simply have to be allowed to dwell in the past.[5] For most people there was little choice but to move with the rhythm of the times,[6] and this usually meant some form of accommodation to the German presence. As a parish priest tells another *résistant,* this one in Roger Vailland's *Drôle de jeu* (1945), the Allied landings were too long in coming. People could not afford to spend their lives waiting for that day.[7]

Accommodation often meant simply accepting the defeat and the Pétain government at Vichy. Count de Balansun and many others like him, often perfectly upright and respectable people, glorified old Marshal Pétain. Thanks to him, after all, France would be assured of an honorable position, even though she would be relegated to second place in the new Europe the Nazis were creating.[8] If the majority of workers and peasants were *résistants* in their general attitudes, as Sartre maintains in an essay on French collaboration, "the conservative bourgeoisie was Pétainist and careerist."[9] For many, like the Paris businessman Pierre Michaud in Marcel Aymé's *Le Chemin des écoliers* (1946), their own businesses and families were a sufficient preoccupation to take their minds off the world and its doings. At times Michaud almost envies the German soldiers strolling around Paris like tourists, relieved at least temporarily of their family responsibilities.[10] But larger business concerns could not always afford quite so easily to ignore the new realities. Werner Rings points out in his study on collaboration and resistance in German-occupied Europe, *Leben mit dem Feind* (1979), that a number of important French firms rapidly made their peace with the Germans in the weeks following the armistice. In July 1940 Chaudron-Renault applied to the French Ministry of Aviation for permission to build several hundred trainers for the *Luftwaffe;* in August, Gnome et Rhône, France's largest aero-engine manufacturer, offered to supply the Germans with engines and spare parts, while Schneider-Creusot made a deal to supply them with bomb components.[11]

Some sought not to change anything in their personal lives and found that they had changed in spite of themselves. Such is the case of an older man who serves as narrator and his niece in Vercors's *Le Silence de la mer* (1942). Vercors is the pseudonym that Jean Bruller used in the Résistance, one of the many fictitious names Résistance people assumed in order to protect themselves and the anonymity of their work. Vercors finished writing the story in October 1941, and published it in 1942 with Editions de Minuit, the clandestine press that he himself helped found. One day in November 1940, the narrator and his niece find themselves obliged to billet a German officer, Werner von Ebrennac. The name is obviously not German and perhaps the officer is a descendant of one of the French Protestant émigrés of the seventeenth century. At any rate, he seems decent enough. Like many French, the niece is determined to let

her life go on as usual, and if that means living under the eyes
of the enemy, she will do her best to ignore him. Silence was
France's best weapon. The young woman sets herself to sewing,
and throughout the book continues to sew, accomplishing her
task mechanically and at times almost feverishly.[12] "With a tacit
agreement we had decided, my niece and I, to change nothing
of our life, were it the smallest detail: as if the officer did not
exist; as if he had been a ghost."[13] The French could, of course,
choose silence for themselves, but they were powerless to impose it on the enemy, and this particular German is undaunted.
On numerous occasions he comes to speak to them in the par-
lor, telling them of his life, his admiration of French culture,
his hopes for what he naïvely calls a marriage between France
and Germany. They feign indifference to him, but it soon becomes quite clear that despite their rigid silence, neither the
narrator nor his niece will be able to maintain their indifference to the end. Whenever they do not hear him in his room
at the accustomed evening hour, they are concerned as any
family might be over one of its members not yet returned to
the fold.[14]

Silence was the most immediately accessible form of protest.
When there was no necessity for personal contact with the enemy, silence could come easily and many took advantage of it.
People spoke of the Germans in terms of "they" and "them" (*ils*
and *les*). "At first the sight of them pained us, and then, little
by little, we learned not to see them, they had taken on an
institutional character," Sartre recalls in "Paris sous l'occupation," himself back in Paris after March 1941, having been released from a German POW camp. The Germans had become
a part of the street scene that one observes every day without
according it any special attention.

> What put the finishing touch on making them inoffensive, was
> their ignorance of our language. A hundred times I heard Pari-
> sians express themselves freely on politics in a café, two steps from
> a lonely German sitting at a table, his eyes vacant, in front of a
> glass of lemonade. They seemed to us like household furnishings
> rather than men.

Parisians may have vowed not to break their self-imposed silence toward the Germans, but at times they found it inhibit-

ing, for as Sartre admits, "we *weren't being natural.*" Sometimes a German soldier would come up to a pedestrian and politely ask directions, and almost inevitably, though he might curse himself for it later, the pedestrian would give some kind of response. Depending on the circumstances he would either give the German his directions or simply tell him, "I don't know." Sartre reports one incident involving a German colonel whose car had overturned on the Boulevard Saint-Germain. Ten Frenchmen near the scene of the accident rushed to his aid and tried to free him. They may well have hated the occupier, but "was that man an occupier lying crushed under an automobile? . . . The concept of an enemy is only completely firm and clear if the enemy is separated from us by a barrier of fire."[15]

More than one author has commented on the sadness of the Parisian street scene. Lines began forming at shop doors, and by mid-September 1940, Jean Guéhenno had already decided to shut himself in and go outdoors as little as possible.[16] Sartre recalls that there were neither cars nor pedestrians in the streets and when Parisians did have to go out, they rarely strayed beyond their own neighborhoods. Paris, furthermore, was no longer the capital of France; it was cut off from many of its provinces as well as from England and from America. All that remained was a Europe that "filled us with horror." In Paris itself, "Everything was hollow and empty." The paintings had been removed from the Louvre, the representatives no longer sat in the Chambre des Députés, the senators no longer sat in the Senate. The theaters continued to function under the watchful eyes of the Germans as did the races and other public events, but for all this Paris was only an "artificial showcase."[17]

In February 1942 Guéhenno wrote of the "boredom" of life in Paris, the unheated houses and the food that those fortunate enough to have relatives in the provinces would periodically receive from them.[18] In *Les Epées* (1948), on the other hand, Roger Nimier has a cynical army captain named de Forjac look back on the war and the Occupation once it was all over and say:

> One thing will prevent the French from avoiding the next war, that is the fact that they were not bored in the course of this one. And now they are bored. Destruction, even if the others were

responsible for it, was much more exalting than reconstruction. They suffered. But the simple and continual boredom of the trenches, for example, was absent. Bombs killed civilians? Yes, but how interesting the civilians became! The prisoners alone knew the true stuff of which wars are made.[19]

There is no doubt that the Occupation was a time of strong emotions in France, and in a small town called Jumainville in Jean-Louis Bory's *Mon Village à l'heure allemande* (1945) these emotions surface readily as relations of one kind or another become inevitable between the German occupier and the local population. Some of the women of Jumainville love some of the Germans, others hate them, as do some of the men; some men collaborate and others resist; some have business dealings with the Germans, while others fear them or are disgusted by them or by one another. But whatever else one might say, Jumainville is alive during those four years of occupation, and when it is about to come to an end, the suspicion arises in some circles that the local citizenry may find the postwar period pale, drab, and boring by comparison.

Rations, Restrictions, Bombings, and Other Disruptions

Whether or not it was interesting, life in Paris and the provinces was certainly different from what it had been. First of all, there were the changes in the consumer economy caused by rationing and price inflation, which were as much the result of the war still going on in Europe as of the Occupation itself. Before the end of the first year of the Occupation, there was rationing of bread, meat, and fats; coffee, wine, and tobacco were not always easy to come by; and turnips and plain noodles cooked only in water became regular staples at the Parisian dinner table.[20]

These changes required a certain amount of flexibility and practicality. Elsa Triolet's Alexis Slavsky has such a fear of the rationing tickets that he never touches them and would starve were it not for Henriette, the woman with whom he is living in a village an hour from Lyon, who sees that there is always sufficient food in the house for him to eat. Once, however, in Henriette's absence, he does venture to use the tickets, albeit with misgivings.[21] He is as inept when it comes to the rationing system as he is in all practical matters of life. Jean Guéhenno speaks of having to stand in line at the mayoralty in April 1941, to change his ration card. From that time on only physical education teachers were entitled to card T permitting them 350 grams of bread per week, and since one pound is equivalent to approximately 453 grams, this represented substantially less than a pound. Teachers in the humanities like Guéhenno, who dealt only with words, merited card A and only 200 grams of bread.[22] But one person's loss is another's gain and to Julie Poissonard, standing behind the counter of her dairy shop in *Au Bon Beurre,* the rationing system brings something of a boon. It assures her of a regular clientèle. When certain customers remark somewhat menacingly that the dairy shop is doing all too well given the official shortage of supplies in Paris, that such prosperity cannot last, and that everything has to be paid for in the end, Madame Poissonard, so different from Frau Walker in the German meat store in Albrecht Goes's *Das Brandopfer,* lets it be known that those who are not happy doing business with her need only go elsewhere. No one had been asked to sign up at the Bon Beurre and any name could be removed from the list of customers.[23] In all fairness, of course, Madame Poissonard's clientèle is also in quite a different position from that of Frau Walker's Friday-night Jewish customers.

By January 1941, Guèhenno recalls, even the rationing tickets were of little use. Since the stores were empty, the tickets had lost their purchasing power.[24] As products became scarce, furthermore, their prices rose. By the spring of 1944 Parisian women were complaining of the rarity of silk stockings. "Other women," according to Roger Vailland's narrator in *Drôle de jeu,* "adapt and even become more beautiful with a bit of rusticity, but a Frenchwoman's beauty has nothing wild or savage about it . . . ." Rather than wear stockings of mediocre quality that did not show them off to their best advantage, many Parisian women preferred to go bare-legged, and some removed the hair from their legs and then tinted them.[25] By March 1944, Parisians were allotted only fifty grams of butter per person, and real coffee commanded the luxury price of fifty francs a cup, with the unofficial value of the French franc throughout

the war at an average of fifty to the dollar.[26] In early August
of that same year, just before the liberation of Paris, a kilogram
of potatoes, when they could be found at all, cost forty francs,
a kilogram of green peas forty-five, and a kilogram of butter
1000 francs.[27] Despite the hardships incurred by the people of
Paris, the Résistance agent Marat in *Drôle de jeu* is able to observe as late as the spring of 1944 that the majority of Parisian
women are still remarkably elegant,[28] a credit to their good taste
and *savoir-faire*. But it was getting ever harder to maintain the
quality of life. In April of that year, when Marat checks into
the Hôtel Bristol in the Faubourg Saint-Honoré, the only one
of the large Paris hotels not requisitioned by the Germans, he
is surprised to find enough hot water for a bath. Hot water is
an unaccustomed luxury. This is a time when a typical student
meal consists of two small portions of vegetables cooked in water
and a tiny piece of plain cake.[29]

One of the ways to beat the system was to deal on the black
market, which could benefit buyer and seller alike. When Marat
pays a visit to his former girlfriend Mathilde in the spring of
1944, she can offer him some Lucky Strikes, which had been
smuggled in from Spain and of which she has an abundance.
The current asking price in Paris was 750 francs for a box of
fifty,[30] and early in August of the same year, according to *Les
Forêts de la nuit*, Algerians with faces that "looked like those one
sees in police files" were offering Gauloises cigarettes to passers-
by at 100 francs a pack.[31]

Charles-Hubert Poissonard in *Au bon beurre* is quick to spot
the advantages of the black market and the rationing sytsem to
a businessman like himself, and early in the Occupation decides
that it might be well to stock up and offer for sale all products
subject to rationing. Though in principle he is running a dairy
store, he begins selling meat that he has been able to obtain by
dint of his initiative and realizes profits up to double his original outlay. When butter becomes rancid and eggs spoil, rather
than discard them he simply sells them at a lower price. Moreover, butter could be "stretched" with margarine and sold to
clients only too happy to procure what the Poissonards tell them
is a special butter from the Charente, northeast of Bordeaux,
and which spreads extremely well. The Poissonards even water

their milk as much as 20 percent, until police inspectors catch
them, fine them 20,000 francs, and close the Bon Beurre for a
month.

If some of the other stores in Paris were completely stripped
of provisions at various times during the Occupation, this is
never once the case at the Bon Beurre. On the contrary products multiply as time goes on, and even the storefront is eventually redone in marble veneer. What provisions Charles-Hubert
does not get through normal channels in Paris, he obtains in
Normandy where he makes regular excursions in his little van.
Even the Norman peasants, traditionally tight and mistrustful,
are unable to get the better of him.

Behind her counter Julie Poissonard is what Jean Dutourd
calls a modern Themis, insensitive as justice itself to the individual needs and problems of the forty odd people who come
to stand in line every day in front of her store. In principle she
distributes strictly what the ration cards call for and no more.
If a client complains of the difficulty of adhering to the limitations the cards impose, Julie gives a lecture on the need to
economize. After all, if France has been defeated, whose fault
is it? The question is a rhetorical one and needs no answer, but
Julie concludes aloud that it is necessary to learn to eat less.
Once, however, after having made her point, she promises
Madame Halluin, one of her clients, a supplement of half a
liter of milk for her little boy the next time she comes. Generosity well-timed and well-placed could pay off in the long run.
Some of the customers complain of the meager rations they are
receiving and the food substitutes they are being asked to buy,
which the Poissonards keep in regular stock: saccharine, forbidden before the war but now suddenly recommended by the
faculty of medicine, a sticky black substance called grape sugar,
white chocolate, powdered eggs, and crushed date nuts that produce a powder called Datima, as well as an alternative to standard honey and another to grated cheese that was called *Sprin-
galine* and reputed to be superior to the real thing. But not
once during the four years of the Occupation do the Poissonards change their own eating habits. What Julie Poissonard gives
as her assessment of life in Paris early in the Occupation, she
could easily have given again at the end: "As far as I can see,

people look quite happy and things might be a lot worse." Neither she nor her family have ever lacked for material goods, and since they are concerned with politics only insofar as it affects their material life, there is little to complain about. Indeed they even rejoice to some extent in the fact that there is a war going on with England: the Germans are spending money to carry on that war, and some of the money is being spent in France, both on the construction of the Atlantic Wall in Normandy and on food provisions for the German army. Pétain is no fool. In the end the French will be the ones to gain. And furthermore, their satisfaction over a war with England has historical justification. England is the hereditary enemy of France. One has only to think of Joan of Arc! [32]

The Poissonards, of course, are business people, and not everyone enjoyed their advantages. But in their own way the citizens of Saint-Clar in Jean-Louis Curtis's *Les Forêts de la nuit* are equally as shrewd. A bartering system springs up between the townspeople and the local peasantry. Game, eggs, and fruit are exchanged for a pair of sandals, spices, coffee, a new pair of shoe soles, a letter of recommendation, or private lessons of one sort or another. When the local butchers begin slaughtering animals on the sly, the whole town becomes party to their activities, and in Saint-Clar the only victims of the food crisis during the Occupation are two women who are drunkards and cannot manage to maintain their prewar supply of wine, now restricted to one liter per week. Rather than adapt they commit suicide. According to the narrator the rest of the community eats too much and too well.

> Haunted by the specter of famine, admittedly fairly remote, the Clarois rapidly developed an existential philosophy shorn of ontological or eschatological concepts, but containing a moral of remarkable solidity, despite its brevity. They consented . . . to put the free flame of intelligence under a bushel . . . and to reduce their entire being temporarily to the humiliating functions of a digestive tube. The Clarois gorged themselves.

Eating can be a way of forgetting a present misery or a way of compensating for it. Especially in times of adversity it can be a means of asserting one's unchanged material solidity or even one's superiority over others, certainly material, if not also spiritual. For the Clarois, no doubt, it served on different occasions all these functions. The official suppression of the meatless Friday by a papal bull only encourages and confirms them in their pursuit.[33]

Restrictions in occupied France were not confined to the realm of food, however, and not all of them could be so easily circumvented. Urban transportation in Paris was curtailed as was railroad transportation into the provinces. Since gasoline was scarce, there were no taxis, and the city bus routes were eliminated one after the other. Eventually half the Métro stations were closed,[34] and on August 13, 1944, with the Allied liberation of Paris immanent, the whole Métro system was shut down.[35] As a substitute for taxis, a new type of vehicle came into being. It was called the *vélotaxi* because it was composed of a bicycle or a tandem to which a kind of sedan chair on wheels was attached, and it was capable of carrying one or two passengers. Some thought the *vélotaxis* immoral and found it offensive to the dignity of the human person to be obliged to pull people who remained seated. But those who rode in the *vélotaxis* paid a good price for the service, and Jean Dutourd remarks that it was rather ironic that during a period when so many more serious outrages were being committed against the dignity of the human person, especially against the Jews, this particular one should have been singled out.[36]

People who wanted to leave Paris found the railroads operating on abbreviated schedules. In 1944 only one express per day made the trip between Paris and Lyon. The trains that continued to run were often excessively crowded and uncomfortable, especially when some of the compartments were sealed off and marked with signs that read "Nur für die Wehrmacht," indicating that they had been reserved for German military personnel. The trains were not always safe, furthermore, especially as the Occupation wore on and resistance to it mounted in intensity. And those trains that were not derailed by the Résistance might be crippled by the British RAF looking for convoys or locomotives to riddle with machine gun bullets. Both Sartre and Beauvoir recall returning to Paris from Chantilly when their train was machine-gunned by the RAF. He dates the event in July 1944, she August 11. But the circumstances are exactly the same and so they are almost certainly talking about the same train, especially since Beauvoir writes that she and Sartre were together on it. The train was only a suburban passenger train, and when three dead and twelve wounded were counted in the first car, the remaining passengers began to vent their anger at the British. In this war, however, the British were not the real enemies of France, and in general people tried to temper the blame against them.[37]

The midnight curfew was another novelty to which Parisians had to adapt, and in times of stress that hour was advanced. In September 1941, after several German soldiers had been cut down, curfew was set for 9 PM,[38] and that December, when still more attacks against German soldiers were occurring regularly in Paris, curfew was sometimes pushed up to five or five-thirty in the afternoon. Punishments were occasionally meted out specifically to those *arrondissements* in which the attacks had taken place. Guéhenno reports, for example, that on December 3 the eighteenth *arrondissement* in Montmartre was placed under curfew at 5:30 PM after some German officers had been killed by a time-bomb in a local bordello. When attacks came against German officers on succeeding days, all of Paris was placed under curfew on December 8. No one was allowed to go out between five in the afternoon and five the following morning. The Métro stopped running at five-thirty, and all restaurants and other establishments catering to the public closed at that time. At six-thirty people looked out at the empty streets from their windows and made signs to one another. No one could believe this was Paris. Two days later with the early curfew still in effect, Guéhenno lamented that again all of Paris would be going to bed at ten, like a child being punished. On December 16 the curfew was rolled back to midnight once again, but General Otto von Stülpnagel, the military governor of France, announced fresh reprisals in the form of fines against the Jews of Paris along with the execution or deportation to Germany of a large number of Jews, communists, and anarchists.[39]

In *Drôle de jeu* Roger Vailland shows a crowd of people from the eighteenth *arrondissement* in the early spring of 1944 waiting out the night until the twelve o'clock curfew, huddled around the entrances to the local Métro stations. Several nights before, English bombers had attacked the Gare de la Chapelle, and several bombs had fallen on the periphery of Montmartre and some working-class apartment buildings had been destroyed and about 500 people killed. The Métro stations would provide a good shelter in case of an alert, especially the deepest ones like that at the Place des Abbesses.[40]

One of the earliest and most important air attacks around Paris was the British bombing of the Renault factories on March 3, 1942, in the suburb of Boulogne-Billancourt on the southwestern edge of the city. From higher ground in the Place des Fêtes in northeastern Paris, Guéhenno witnessed the raid, and on the following day he wrote:

> Yesterday evening during moonlight the English bombed the Renault factories at Boulogne-Billancourt. A massive and sustained bombing, really the first that we have undergone. To see better I went . . . to the Place des Fêtes, but even from there little could be seen. Nothing but the shell flares, the gleam of fires from the other side of Paris, and twice, above the square, two planes like shadows on the clouds.

The people with whom Guéhenno spoke that evening were not at all indignant. On the contrary, it was hard for them to hide their joy. Responsibility for the damage could be shifted from the British to the Occupation authorities who had not even sounded an alert. Still and all, there were some 100 dead and more than 500 wounded.[41]

In *Féerie pour une autre fois II,* subtitled *Normance* (1954), Louis-Ferdinand Céline describes a more general air attack on the Paris area, including a raid on the Renault works. British and American bombings in northern France increased in 1943, and the bombing or series of bombings which Céline witnessed and out of which he created his narrative most probably took place in 1943, particularly since later, in *Rigodon,* Céline himself speaks of having seen the bombing of the Renault plant in 1943. With a heedlessness to geography not uncharacteristic of *Rigodon,* he locates the plant at Issy, just across the Seine from Boulogne-Billancourt. During World War I Renault had been engaged in the manufacture of tanks, and during the Occupation, the Germans pressured the company into producing armaments once again. This, of course, made it vulnerable as a target for Allied bombing. By April 1943, Renault had gradually recovered from the British bombing of the year before and had been able to resume production. It was bombed again, this time by the Americans.[42] The bombing at Renault constitutes only a very small part of the general fireworks over Paris that Céline describes in *Normance,* but he lays the blame for it and for the overall attack squarely on the RAF.

Unlike Guéhenno's description in the *Journal des années noires* which is intended as factual testimony, Céline's description is intended to be a re-creation of the event. It is a preparation for three much more powerful frescoes of destruction consisting of *D'un château l'autre* (1957), *Nord* (1960), and *Rigodon* (1969), which documented his flight into exile as an accused collaborator through a war-ravaged Germany in the second half of 1944 and the early part of 1945.

Céline began writing his account of the Renault bombing after fleeing from Germany to Denmark in 1945. He was condemned by the French judicial system in 1950, and only after official amnesty came in 1951 did he return to France where he finished *Normance* and published it in 1954. He had witnessed the raid from the windows of his apartment in Montmartre in the northern part of the city. But as each new blaze ignites in different parts of town, the reader has the impression of watching the "show" as though he were right next to the bombing site, whereas in point of fact he is closeted with the narrator in Céline's building. The physical destruction raining down from the sky is paralled by events of a physical and social nature in the building. Not only does the narrator's furniture begin to "waltz" around in his rooms, but many of the tenants leave their apartments and take refuge in promiscuity and intoxication in the cellar. The destruction of the social fabric is portrayed through the unveiled attraction of the narrator's wife, Lili, for a somewhat larger than life cripple named Jules, and this attraction heightens the eroticism that danger can and, in this case, does arouse. As long as possible, however, the narrator's focus remains trained on his window and the spectacle outside. And it is this spectacle in *Normance* that is overpowering. As always it is animated by Céline's narrator, a thinly disguised alter ego who spares nothing of his characteristic, unabating drive and energy to make the reader see what he has seen. Céline's work is always much more than a simple *témoignage* or eye-witness account, and from the literary point of view it is not particularly important to know where exaggeration ends and factual truth begins.

> Look at the bombs Lili! Look! They're above Renault!... There are planes discharging tons of explosives!... white... white butterflies of planes!... one of these blazes above Renault! the height of the clouds! blue flames!... orange!... green!... and giant candles in a zigzag...

One of the planes flying away from Renault seems to brush the roof of the narrator's building, and with a classical Biblical image he transforms the scene into an archetype of destruction: "conditions like those of the Flood have to be present for an eight-story house to be shaken this way!... from top to bottom the house is trembling!..." An old wardrobe bouncing from one wall to another threatens to crack under the strain. Outside the attack is still going on: "it's hellish!... I am trying to make you understand!... and I can't leave the window!... The houses . . . are rising up in the wake of the planes!... exactly! they are following them! taking off after them!" Big buildings and small ones were just "flying off," "yellow!... green!... blue!... and boom! into the air! everything is shaking!... the whole cluster is quivering between the stars!... you can see jonquil stars... the sky looks like a sea of jonquils..." Paris is a "sea of fire"; in fact the whole sky is a "lacework of fire," and the Butte de Montmartre, the hill on which Montmartre stands, "a crater in full eruption." The whole scene is something of a sort of mud pie, a "grande bouillasse" the narrator calls it, but it is also "a fairyland" (*une féerie*); and even though he claims to be a "simple eyewitness" and not a painter, the narrator confesses: " . . . I am astounded at the colors!... I am saying to myself: it's luxurious!... This doesn't happen every day!..." For those who had the artist's eye to see them, the bombings could be spectacular. In Germany, too, Albert Speer, an architect who had become Hitler's minister for armaments and war production, could not help being dazzled, as he looked down on the British bombings in Berlin late in 1943, by the spectacle of light created by the parachute flares that the Berliners called "Christmas trees," by the explosions that followed, and by the flames caught up in clouds of smoke.[43]

Bombings like the one Céline describes were among the reasons for the midnight curfew. The enforced lights-out made it more difficult for Allied bombers to spot their targets. Despite the general inconvenience, a few people made personal use of the curfew, like one of Marat's acquaintances from the Résistance in *Drôle de jeu*, a young man named Frédéric who is trying to keep tabs on his girlfriend Annie. Normally Annie reads late into the night and does not retire before two or three in the morning. Even though her curtains are always drawn to conform to official defense regulations, some light still always filters through the closed shutters. Passing by her house one evening just before midnight and seeing no light in her windows, Frédéric knows that she is not home and, therefore, will not return before morning. The bells of a nearby church remind him of the midnight curfew, and during the quarter hour of tolerance accorded people on the street he has just enough time to find a room near the Gare d'Orsay. His girlfriend spends the night with Marat.[44]

If one was caught on the street by the approach of the curfew and did not wish to spend the night alone, there were always the local bordellos or "dancing bars" as such night establishments were sometimes called. This is what Gérard Delahaye does one night in *Les Forêts de la nuit*. He has come to Paris from Saint-Clar to court Hélène de Balansun, Francis's sister, and feels particularly despondent over her seeming indifference.[45] For Philippe Arréguy, also from Saint-Clar and also in Paris, on the pretext of taking some courses, the curfew turns out to be an asset. Bolder and more aggressive than Gérard, he finds himself one night in Hélène's apartment, and wanting to spend the night with her, uses the curfew as an excuse and refuses to leave. He has no intention of being snapped up by what was known as the Agence Todt,[46] named for Reich minister of munitions Fritz Todt, which recruited men for the construction projects of the Organisation Todt, the construction unit of the German Army that had built the fortifications along the Siegfried Line and was building fortifications in France, or by the STO, the Service du Travail Obligatoire, which enlisted young French men for labor and deported them to Germany. France itself was changing physically under the Occupation. In December 1940, Guéhenno complained that street names were being altered without advance notice. Directional signs printed in German began appearing everywhere, and in Toulouse the Place Jean-Jaurès became the Place Philippe Pétain. A little over a year later in January 1942, he noted that one by one the statues of Paris were disappearing, taken away to be broken down for armaments. Empty pedestals remained in the middle of city squares. At the Paris opera house German officers attended in great number and during the intermissions would stroll around the lobby, as people still do today in Vienna and other cities of central Europe, in the halls off the main galleries, generally walking in twos, threes, or fours and all moving in the same direction. Unconsciously the French followed suit, says Guéhenno, and entered into the procession. "The boots impose their rhythm."[47]

Until the American landings in North Africa in November 1942, the two zones into which France had been divided at the signing of the armistice continued to exist side by side, and even after the landings in Africa when the Germans decided to occupy the free zone of France, the line of demarcation remained. It served as a focal point for adventure in fiction and non-fiction alike. Lyon eventually became the center of Résistance conspiracy, and since it was located in the free zone, the conspirators often needed to cross the line to get back to their work in the occupied zone in the north. Crossing the line for some, however, was simply a means to escape. Léon Lécuyer, a French POW escaped from Germany, whose adventures are related as a kind of sub-plot side by side with the life of the Poissonards in *Au bon beurre*, crosses the line at Chalon-sur-Saône upon fleeing his mother's Paris apartment where the Germans had come to find him after Julie Poissonard filed a denunciation against him. Plot and sub-plot intersect three times in the novel, and each time the Poissonards emerge victorious. The first intersection occurs at the time of Julie's denunciation; the second at Vichy where the Poissonards go to pay a citizen's visit

to Marshal Pétain and by chance catch a glimpse of Léon struggling to free himself from the grip of four policemen who have
just apprehended him on suspicion of plotting to assassinate
Laval; and the third time occurs after the war and the Occupation are over, when they have Léon dismissed as a teacher
from a Paris school because he has failed their son, Riri. Like
Monsieur Homais, the progress and career-oriented pharma-
cist in *Madame Bovary*, the Poissonards with their realism and
good business sense triumph over all adversity, and this is their
final victory. But Léon is no Emma Bovary. He is too much of
a simpleton to evoke any real sympathy on the part of the
reader. When he crosses the demarcation line, Léon seriously
entertains visions of being a conspirator. But the crossing is
anti-climactic, and Dutourd finishes it off in one brief sentence.[48]

From the free zone there was only one way, authorized for
the general public, of corresponding with the north. The government printed up and circulated what were called "interzone
cards," and Guéhenno gives a detailed description of them in
his *Journal des années noires* on February 21, 1941.

> The text is printed in advance and we have the permission only
> to retain or cross it out as the case might be. It provides for a
> man's being "in good health," or "tired" or "slightly or gravely ill"
> or "wounded" or "killed" or a "prisoner." So much for the animal
> state. As to its needs, the animal has permission to have "need of
> provisions or money." Finally, the average Frenchman being at
> times, as everybody knows, a competitive animal, it is indicated
> that he can "have entered school...," that he has "passed."
> That is all. After that, "Affectionate thoughts. Kisses." We can
> love neither more nor less.

Guéhenno notes further that one card out of two was rejected.
A card sent by his daughter Louisette to her grandfather was
returned with a blue crayon mark pointing out her mistake.
She had written that Guéhenno was "tired." That was permitted, but she had added "like last year" and that was not.[49]

Léon Lécuyer, for all his simplemindedness, fares somewhat
better in his attempt to write to his supposed girlfriend in Paris,
a young woman named Emilienne who already has a lover
named Jojo. The interzone cards are "completely printed up";
one needs only to fill in the blanks. But where Guéhenno saw

only the possibility of crossing out the inapplicable items on the cards, Léon uses almost all the options to his advantage: "his imagination inspired him with surprising madrigals that opened up" between the acceptable formulas.

> Lyon, November 27, 1940
>
> My body is IN GOOD HEALTH, I am never TIRED of thinking of you but my heart is ~~SLIGHTLY~~ SERIOUSLY ~~ILL~~ WOUNDED by delicious memories of you. Nevertheless I have KILLED the love in me. I shall not be a PRISONER of your charms much longer, cruel one. I sometimes wish that Jojo were DECEASED. I think of your alabaster body, of your pretty lips which leave me WITHOUT NEWS. THE FAMILY of my feelings is more tragic than that of the Atridae. Black IS WELL suited to my soul. I have a great NEED OF PROVISIONS of kisses. My spirit is as full of tears as a treasure chest is OF MONEY. Poor Léon is GOING TO SCHOOL of adversity. HE HAS PASSED the examination of woe. KIND REGARDS. Mad LOVE from one who has never ceased to adore you.
>
> Léon[50]

The card arrives in Paris intact!

As people became accustomed to it, the demarcation line gave rise to amusing stories in which the French often successfully matched their wits against the opponent. Guéhenno tells one such story that took place in the railway station at Digoin on the Loire in east central France. Some workers from the south had just finished unloading requisitioned material of one kind or another, and the German Feldwebel or sergeant on duty at the line had neglected to verify the delivery. One of the workers in a broad southern French accent calls out to the German: "Heh, conqueror! Come on, there's work for you here." The Feldwebel is offended and tells the Frenchman to lay off. "I have already told you not to call me conqueror. . . . it's ridiculous."[51]

Getting across the line or sending something across, however, was not always a joking matter. While publisher and Résistance poet Pierre Seghers was allowed to cross the line in 1943 without apparent difficulty under the pretext of business affairs, he reported in 1940 that the Germans were awarding the *Ausweiss* or permit necessary to cross the line "with a liquid dropper."[52] In February 1941, Jean Guéhenno waited two months for permission to send money from Paris into the free zone, and at the end of May of the same year when he was thinking about going south to spend the vacation with relatives, he had little actual hope of getting there. The most recent regulations on traffic across the line permitted children to go and see their parents and vice-versa, but there was no provision made for collateral relationships. By August 11 he had, nonetheless, still not abandoned the project. But his attempt to obtain the *Ausweiss* turned out to be futile. He was on the subway at five-thirty in the morning and by six had arrived at Occupation headquarters on the rue du Colisée in the eighth *arrondissement* off the Champs-Elysées. But that was much too late; 300 people who either lived in the area or had spent the night sleeping in the corridors of surrounding buildings were already there before him. Since Guéhenno was apparently unwilling to go to such extremes and since the curfew did not permit people to be on the street before five, he realized that he might as well abandon the idea of obtaining the *Ausweiss*. Furthermore, as the authorities only examined some fifty cases a day, he presumed that at least 200 of the early arrivals were there for the third or fourth time. People began to squabble, each one claiming to have a relative with a more serious illness than the next. Those Guéhenno calls the luckiest could claim a death in the family and brandished telegrams that enabled them to pass to the front of the line. Eventually Guéhenno was informed that only urgent cases were being considered and that consequently his own did not even merit examination. After two hours of waiting in line he left.

He finally did make it to the south in July 1942, after an absence of two years and in the capacity of chaperon for a school convoy of eighty little children. French and German authorities were supposed to have confirmed a seat for each child in the convoy, but mistakes had been made on both sides, and some forty children in all had to be left on the platform when the train left Paris. At the line of demarcation, papers were examined; and when they finally arrived in the free zone, Guéhenno was a bit astounded and saddened by the sight that met his eyes: "a strange country, a sort of principality where everybody

. . . seemed to me to be in uniform."[53] Six-year-old children were regimented in youth programs, and war veterans were wearing legion insignia or the *francisque,* the Frankish battle-axe adopted as the symbol of the Vichy government. The sight is reminiscent of Günter Grass's descriptions of the German citizens of Danzig in the thirties, walking to and parading on the Maiwiese in their uniforms. Guéhenno asks sadly, Where is France?

Protest and Distraction

With the defeat and the German occupation, France entered into one of the darkest periods in her history, and her writers use the image of night and darkness over and over again. In many respects this was the same night, and even nightmare, that had descended seven years earlier on Germany—brought on, for many of the French, not so much by the rationing of food or the inconveniences in transportation and communication, but by constant fear of the police, the German Gestapo and their French counterparts in the Milice, the interrogations, the roundups in the streets, the shootings, and the deportations.

When the Germans invaded France they brought with them the machinery of the Nazi police state. In addition to their own Gestapo they were often able to recruit the French to do much of their work for them. The policing became particularly ominous as the Résistance increased in size and activity, and known Résistance fighters were handled with particular brutality. If many in France were impressed at how "correct" the Germans were, Jean-Louis Curtis points out in *Les Forêts de la nuit* that "the Gestapo was the other side of Germanic correctness."[54] The prison at Fresnes in the suburbs of Paris was taken over by the Germans and organized as a detention center for political prisoners, and the name Fresnes together with that of Drancy, the prison outside of Paris that was transformed into a processing center for Jews, struck fear into the heart of France.

One did not have to be a *résistant* or a Jew to know the terror that had come to France. To a greater or lesser degree it affected everyone. On his return from Arras, Saint-Exupéry spoke of France as a cluster of traditions uniting the nation. The Occupation, by putting people against a wall and forcing them to make the kind of choices that people should perhaps never be asked to make, pushed them into ambiguities that worked to undo those bonds. This was a time of heightened sensitivities, a time when political and moral convictions became polarized as perhaps never before, and when individual acts began as never before to take on political and moral significance. Situations that had never seemed in need of questioning now began to be questioned, and new situations arose for which no response had been formulated. Under the strain the loyalty of family and friends sometimes collapsed. Jean-Louis Bory illustrates this graphically in *Mon Village à l'heure allemande*. The opening scene unfolds in the house of the Boudet family in Jumainville where daughter Elisa has just been slapped by her father for listening to an English radio broadcast. If the Germans got wind of the broadcast coming from the Boudet house, at the very least an interrogation would be sure to follow. But Elisa is young and impetuous and determined for once to oppose the fears of her father and other more prudent townsfolk. Monsieur Boudet reprimands her for using the word *Boche,* and that night Elisa flees into the street where before the houses of Jumainville, shut and dark after an eleven o'clock curfew, she repeats "dirty Boche" to her heart's content. Her father is by no means pro-German, but he maintains a business relationship with the Germans. Even he abhors the town collaborationist, however, a pastry-maker with the obsequious name Lécheur, who defiantly listens to loud German radio broadcasts at his open window. One day Boudet receives a small package in the mail wrapped in brown paper: a little wooden coffin painted black and inscribed with a cross painted in white on the lid. Earlier, after receiving just such a coffin, Lécheur hanged himself, and Boudet's coffin contains an appropriately suggestive little piece of rope. Eventually Boudet's farm is "pillaged" and his granary set on fire, but he never follows Lécheur's example. Instead he burns his little coffin. Elisa, however, almost disowns her family, revealing to her father a secret her mother had imparted to her before she died. She is not Boudet's real daughter, nor is she the sister of his son Auguste, an often dislikeable and arrogant boy who by the end of the book joins the Milice. Other townspeople are not any more rigidly principled than Boudet. Madame Germaine, Boudet's second wife, described as being a "brothel unto herself," takes pride in having slept with a number of nice Austrian boys who were among the first troops sent to occupy Jumainville and in having made them cry out in their heavily accented French, "Matame Chermaine, Matame Chermaine, Merte Hitler, Merte Hitler."[55] Mademoiselle Vrin, a spinster who plays the organ at church, secretly lusts after her beloved Austrian Ernst long after he has left Jumainville. The town pastor elicits a mixture of emotions, mostly negative, from his parishioners because of his unqualified support of the forces of law and order which, at that particular time, meant the Germans.

At different times, Bory allows each of his motley collection of characters to tell his or her own story, personalizing and giving narrative voice, somewhat in the style of a Greek chorus completely secularized, even to the village itself, and directing the whole cast through a kind of super-narrator, a third-person coordinator indistinguishable from the author. No doubt Bory saw this as the best way to handle the contradictions arising in Jumainville as a result of the Occupation. The characters are free to some extent to present themselves to the reader, and with a few exceptions, all, including the German commander Siegfried Baumann, emerge as basically likeable people surviving in a difficult time as best they know how.

In the plight of their daily lives people craved either hope or distraction, and it does not seem unreasonable to say that if everybody had been arrested who listened to the BBC, the whole country would have been in prison. Literature, theater, the movies, and the world of the intellect sometimes provided outlets for the frustrations of daily life. In *Drôle de jeu* Marat finds students eager to discuss recent productions by the Comédie Française of Corneille, Racine, Marivaux, and Claudel's drama of earthly renunciation and celestial reward, *Le Soulier de satin*.[56] Though Claudel had written the play much earlier, he gave it to the Comédie Française for production for the first time, significantly, in 1943. In *Les Forêts de la nuit* Count de Balansun busies himself with historical research on Gaston le

Roux, a figure out of the Middle Ages, and the townspeople flock to their movie house to see German actress and singer Marika Rökk amid the splendors of Vienna and the music of Johann Strauss.[57] Guéhenno speaks in his war diary of his work on Rousseau and his readings in Goethe and Nietzsche,[58] while Simone de Beauvoir settled in at the Bibliothèque Nationale in July 1940 to read Hegel or in cafés in Montparnasse and Saint-Germain-des-Prés to work on *L'Invitée* (1943), or as the weather grew colder, to keep warm.[59]

Before the Résistance became organized, simpler forms of protest against the Occupation sometimes gave dimension to people's lives. On June 14, 1941, many Parisians wore black ties to mark the first anniversary of the German entry into their city. On that day, Guéhenno wrote, the Germans had been in Paris for a year, like robots serving a machine, not really knowing why they were still there. They complained of the glass-eyed Parisians, the "Parisiens aux yeux de verre," who refused even to take notice of them in the street. A little girl wearing a black ribbon in her hair at school was brought before the headmistress and asked why she was in mourning. When she answered that she was in mourning for Paris, she was suspended for a week for lack of "social consciousness." "The 'sens social' today is a sense of dishonor."[60]

This may have been the kind of dishonor Sartre had in mind in *Les Mouches,* which Charles Dullin staged in 1943 at the old Théâtre Sarah Bernhardt, renamed the Théâtre de la Cité in 1940, since the Nazis refused to allow the name of the Jewish actress to flash across the Place du Châtelet even though she had been dead since 1923. Clearly not at liberty before the German censors openly to show the Parisians their dishonor, Sartre reached into Greek mythology to the story of Orestes and Electra avenging their father's death. Not altogether unlike the Parisians wearing black on that June day in 1941 to commemorate the first year of the Occupation, the Argives of ancient Greece have been in mourning for fifteen years when the play opens, and for fifteen years they have dressed themselves in black. They know that their queen Clytemnestra had taken Aegisthus as her lover while her husband Agamemnon was away fighting in Troy, and they know that she and Aegisthus planned and carried out the murder of Agamemnon on the day of his homecoming. When the first old Argive woman accosted in the play is asked by Jupiter for whom she is mourning, her answer is even simpler than that of the little schoolgirl in 1941: it is the custom of Argos.[61] Like the Argives, the people of Paris may not always have wanted to talk of their shame, but it lived there among them, waiting to be recognized, if only by the symbol of black ties and ribbons. Perhaps one day the Parisians would be delivered of their shame as were the Argives by an avenging Orestes, or perhaps like Orestes some would take it into their hands to deliver the others. Orestes's end is, of course, not a totally happy one; he is pursued by the Erinyes who, in turn, must avenge the crime of matricide. However, *Les Mouches* transcends the time in which it was written; and while Sartre certainly wished to expose what he saw as the communal guilt of the French for the state in which they found themselves under the Occupation and wished to make them acknowledge their responsibility for it, he was also addressing man in a broader context. To seek an exact correspondence in wartime Paris for everything that occurs in *Les Mouches* would be reductionist and an error in critical perspective.

In addition to black, people wore different combinations of red, white, and blue in their dress, drew crosses of Lorraine, the symbol of Free France adopted by Charles de Gaulle, in chalk on the *pissotières* of Paris, or cut *V* for victory, *H* for honor, or still more crosses of Lorraine into their Métro tickets and then threw them onto the sidewalk as a silent reminder to all passers-by. The Germans tried to adopt the *V* as a sign of their own victory, but that particular gesture did not always catch on in France. Guéhenno mentions seeing a young beggar playing the *Marseillaise* on his accordion at the poorly lit Châtelet Métro station on December 11, 1943, as proudly as possible given his condition. The Germans who passed by him were indifferent. Occasionally one of them probably even made a small offering to what Guéhenno, reacting somewhat bitterly and defensively and perhaps with hypersensitivity, calls this image of France. On the first November eleventh after the Occupation began, the day that marked the armistice ending World War I, pedestrians strewed flowers at the base of Clemenceau's statue on the

Champs-Elysées, and on German orders French policemen removed them.[62]

Individual Contacts between Occupied and Occupier

While some Frenchmen tried to ignore the Germans, others did not. In the world of the arts, many attended the cultural activities sponsored by the Deutsches Institut. Ernst Jünger, during his two tours of duty with the German occupation army in Paris, associated quite freely with people like Cocteau, Marcel Jouhandeau, and Céline, among many others. Of course Jünger, a recognized writer himself who also spoke French, was a rather special German. Nonetheless, even for those French who wished to have nothing to do with the Germans, silence was not always possible. Wherever one went, one saw them. On spring Sundays when many Parisians would take to the Bois for a stroll or, if they were of the younger set, rent a little rowboat and go out onto the lake, they found that the Germans had virtually monopolized the boats and were maneuvering across the lake in what looked like squadrons.[63] In the provinces, where German officers were frequently billeted with private families, and both sides had to deal with each other on an individual basis, impressions were formed that could not always remain indifferent. The old man and his niece in Vercors's *Le Silence de la mer* were especially determined to resist the advances of German officer Werner von Ebrennac billeted in their house. But when Werner takes leave of them, a disappointed and broken man who has volunteered for service in Russia, knowing from the reaction of his soldier colleagues that his hoped-for marriage between France and Germany can never take place, silence is vanquished. The old man hears his niece, perspiring under the impact of the scene, utter her first spoken word to the German, a barely audible "Adieu."[64] Werner has succeeded, perhaps too late and to no avail, in conquering the silence of France personified in the woman who has been forced to give him lodging. Though Vercors makes no further use of the water image contained in his title, it is significant that *la mer* is feminine. In his extensive treatment of water imagery in literature, *L'Eau et les rêves,* Gaston Bachelard observes that water can be life-giving,[65] an extension of the womb. Perhaps in Vercors's book the life that abounds in the silence of the deep could ultimately have borne fruit, but the text ends and we do not know.

A good cross-section of French public opinion can be seen in Marcel Aymé's *Le Chemin des écoliers* where reactions to the Germans vary from hatred simply because they are in France to gratitude for performing what some consider a service France should have performed for herself but did not—namely, to rid the country of her communists, Jews, and free-masons. One character even goes so far as to put on the German uniform and volunteer for service in Russia only to find that his concierge refuses to speak to him and that his former friends spit behind his back.[66]

The majority of citizens had more moderate reactions. Madame Lécuyer in *Au bon beurre* contents herself with giving a German the wrong directions in the street or refusing the seat offered her by a German on the Métro.[67] Even though he recognizes his own pettiness, Guéhenno took immense pleasure in making a confused German, asking for directions to Notre-Dame, look utterly foolish. With a wordless gesture, even though he understood German, he pointed at the cathedral towers staring both of them in the face.[68]

Beginning in 1943 one of the regular customers at the Bon Beurre is a German soldier by the name of Hans Pfeiffer. Hans is a peasant from Brandenburg, and like so many peasants in the history of the literature of war, is so totally unsuited to his present job that his figure in uniform appears a travesty. He left his home and family in Germany in despair, believing the war to be a monstrous thing. He made it through the Belgian and French campaigns of 1940 without firing a shot, and since he was thirty-seven years old, was allowed to remain in Paris rather than go off to the Russian front. The first conjugal infidelity the good Lutheran Hans has ever committed against his wife occurs with an employee of the Poissonards, Léonie Jacquet, who gives herself to him for two pairs of silk stockings. In two weeks, Jean Dutourd exclaims half-seriously, giving way to a prejudice that dates back at least as far as Madame de

Staël, Hans has learned more in matters of love than he could ever have learned in Brandenburg.

Hans continues to frequent the Poissonards even after they rid themselves of Léonie, having found her troublesome and argumentative. He tries to make friends with the regular clients by giving them items to which he has easy access, cigars, cigarettes, and candy. Charles-Hubert Poissonard accepts the cigars, Emilienne, the young "mistress" of Léon Lécuyer, the cigarettes, and Julie Poissonard and the new salesgirl who replaces Léonie, the candy. Madame Lécuyer and another customer Madame Halluin, trying as hard as possible to avoid eye-contact with Hans, refuse everything "with dignity" (*dignement*). Having played Santa Claus Hans next tries to make friends. In broken French he tells the assembled group that he likes France, to which Madame Lécuyer replies with quick French wit that the feeling is not reciprocal, and Charles-Hubert, knowing that with his limited French vocabulary Hans cannot understand half of what is said, tells him in a soft and smiling tone that belies the import of his words, "La France . . . elle t'emmerde"— "France shits on you." Conscious of maintaining a good profile in front of her customers, and being just sufficiently anti-German to be able still to remain polite, Julie reminds her husband that there are ladies present in the shop. Naturally none of this discourse has offended Hans, who most likely has understood none of it, and in any case, would not have wanted to understand. He takes up the theme of the sadness of war and shows photos of his wife and three children whom Madame Lécuyer, Madame Halluin, and Julie Poissonard mock rather unkindly. Only Emilienne, always touched at the sight of children, finds them cute. But Hans is no match for the group. His is a slow mind despite his goodness of character, or perhaps because of it; and in addition, he is clumsy in French. When he tells them he wants to learn French and asks them to teach him, both Mesdames Lécuyer and Halluin are incensed. "These Germans think they can get away with anything . . . Teach him French, indeed! Whatever next? He'll be wanting to marry my daughter, I suppose," exclaims Madame Halluin. "Give us back Alsace and Lorraine . . . After that, we'll see,"

retorts Madame Lécuyer. Charles-Hubert comes to Hans's rescue and professes to give him a French lesson by making him
repeat self-deprecating and insulting vulgarity that brings
laughter to the whole shop. Hans is elated and convinced as he
leaves, that friendship can triumph over national boundaries.
If people would only give each other their hands, war would
be eliminated. Once he is gone, Madame Lécuyer lets fly a stubborn "Mort aux Boches," death to all Germans, and in the ensuing discussion the group declares that after the victory the
Germans should all be castrated so that their race will perish,
that Germany should be occupied forever, and that Hitler
should be delivered over in a cage to the Jews. Madame Lécuyer recalls, furthermore, that Hans has the head of a brute,
the neck of a butcher, and the hands of a strangler. The Poissonards take a very French delight at having put on such a
good show. The real victors of the war are still the French! The
Germans are heavy, there is no doubt, and not subtle as the
French are.[69] This whole ironic, witty, sarcastic, and amusing
scene, amusing, that is, to everybody except Hans, had he been
able to grasp it, might be excusable, despite its insensitivity, a
relatively harmless way of letting off steam. What is inexcusable
is the Poissonards' subsequent conduct toward Hans. After receiving a continuous stream of provisions which they have gladly
accepted from the German, they never once in the ensuing year
and a half invite him to their table. As time goes on and the
Germans continue to suffer reverses in the war, the Poissonards become more and more reluctant to receive Hans in uniform. They know they must move with the times, and when
liberation is finally at the door in August 1944, Charles-Hubert
manages to lure Hans into the cellar of the Bon Beurre where
he locks him up and then hands him over, kicking at his legs,
to a local FFI unit, the Forces Françaises de l'Intérieur, the name
given in 1944 to all Résistance units fighting the German occupier. This was one German he could chalk up for the Résistance![70]

Men like Père Boudet in *Mon Village à l'heure allemande* and
even Charles-Hubert Poissonard cooperated to the extent that
their business interests dictated. Other men, especially those who
joined the Milice, often had psychological reasons in addition.

Boudet's son Auguste, for example, though not well developed as a character in the book, bears obvious scars of frustration, familial and social, and is always the one others do not seem to listen to. In the play *Morts sans sépulture,* first performed in 1946 and published in 1947, Sartre's *miliciens,* too, even though their characters are not developed to the same degree as are those of the *résistants,* are clearly no match for their adversaries, either intellectually or morally. The fact that one of them named Pellerin takes particular delight at the prospect of torturing Henri, a *résistant* who had been studying medicine when the war broke out, is indicative of the kind of revenge he is seeking against society. Pellerin left the lycée at thirteen and has been earning his living since then. There was no one to pay for his studies.[71]

The Milice was created by the Vichy government in January 1943, and placed under the direction of Joseph Darnand who was a member of the Waffen SS. The Milice was composed entirely of French and, according to Pierre Seghers in *La Résistance et ses poètes,* did as much harm to the French Résistance, if not more, than all the German organizations combined.[72]

It goes without saying that the French had little sympathy for the Milice, and so, very typically, Jean Genet has made an effort in *Pompes funèbres* to try to understand and even like them. The book is ostensibly a funeral rite on the death of Genet's lover, Jean Décarnin, a twenty-year old communist killed on the barricades by what Genet calls a "charming" young collaborator on August 19, 1944, less than a week before the liberation of Paris. In the agony of his loss, Genet wrote *Pompes funèbres* which he wanted to be the "prismatic decomposition of my love and grief,"[73] in the hope of achieving some kind of catharsis. Genet is fascinated by Décarnin but fascinated, too, by all the other colors reflected in the prism to be decomposed, and therefore fascinated by the one who may have killed his lover. In the exploration of these opposites, the killer and the victim, he hopes to construct some type of synthesis that will enable him to surmount his lover's death and go on with life. One day Genet leaves Jean Décarnin's mother's house where she is harboring a German soldier named Erik Seiler who is her lover, and where on the same visit he has also run into Jean's attractive but cruel-looking brother Paolo who is in the

Résistance. Genet goes to a movie hoping to achieve some peace of mind. Across the screen flickers a picture of a young *milicien* being overpowered on the rooftops of the city by a French soldier. The audience goes wild at the sight of a close-up of the traitor; a woman next to Genet begins thrashing about, cursing these bastards who should have their guts ripped out. Predictably, Genet's reaction differs from that of the audience: to him the woman is odious and the audience along with her.

> Neither the world's laughter nor the inelegance of caricaturists will keep me from recognizing the sorry grandeur of a French militiaman who, during the insurrection of Paris against the German army in August 1944, took to the rooftops with the Germans and for several days fired to the last bullet—or next-to-last—on the French populace that had mounted the barricades.

Genet finds his own hatred of the *milicien* so great and beautiful it becomes equivalent to the strongest love. He decides that this is the boy who killed Jean, baptizes him Riton, and desires him, hoping at the same time to play a trick on destiny and on Riton himself, by investing Riton with the love he had felt for Jean.[74] Already Genet sees Riton as a flower of the highest mountains, an *Edelweiss,* having perhaps ironically achieved, in the splendid isolation with which he has surrounded himself, the white and noble purity that the German name conveys. For Genet, killing is the symbolic representation of evil. By the act of murder one attains ultimate evil and hence ultimate solitude. In the person of Adolf Hitler, Genet admires the ultimate evil and ultimate solitude of which his mountain retreat at the Berghof in the Bavarian Alps becomes a symbol. Riton, too, is now alone. Virtually all of Paris hates him.

It is Riton's hatred of France, which, Genet asserts, he rightly confuses with hatred for society, that has made Riton join the Milice, and Genet admits that the Milice was mainly recruited from hoodlums. That Riton should at one point compare himself to Joan of Arc,[75] approaches blasphemy, but again, it is a step toward that dissection of opposites that Genet is seeking in the decomposition of his prism. Only after each of the opposites is known and tested and lived can the prism become whole again.

Perhaps it would be too simplistic to say that hunger alone drives Riton into the Milice; but he joins one day after eating a cat that he has killed out of hunger. As a *milicien* he will command the attention of a society that has refused to give him attention before. Out of his own sense of abandonment and deprivation in childhood and his subsequent experiences in the underworld to which they had driven him, Genet creates Riton and identifies with him.

Genet claims to be amused by recording the shame of a country to which he belongs and which, nonetheless, brings tears to his eyes when it suffers. In a similar way Riton is amused at the idea of shocking a Paris Métro car by allowing the German soldier Erik Seiler to engage him in an immodest position, with Erik's chest square against Riton's back, the thighs of both firmly joined, and Erik's cock hard against Riton's buttocks. Riton is experiencing what to him is the pleasure of submitting to a male, a soldier, and a German all at once, and both he and Erik derive pleasure from braving the disgust of the people who are powerless to do anything against them.[76] Perhaps there was a time when Riton would have asked only for acceptance from these people, but apparently he has not received it and so he compensates for it by isolating himself from them. At the same time, ironically, he is isolating himself from the Germans who have no respect for someone who can betray his own country. Meanwhile it has remained for Genet to experience for three years the "delicate pleasure of seeing France terrorized by kids between sixteen and twenty."[77]

But not everybody was of Genet's turn of mind. And above all, not everybody was willing to make the effort to try and understand what motivated others. When Madame Germaine in *Mon Village à l'heure allemande* sees her stepson Auguste in Milice uniform for the first time, she can barely bring herself to look upon him as a human being. Perhaps in the end even the Milice cannot bring him the kind of recognition he needs.

Besides the Milice there were other ways open to the French to do the Germans' dirty work for them. Louis Crevaux in Carl Zuckmayer's *Der Gesang im Feuerofen* (1950) is an example. Crevaux is an unemployed good-for-nothing who, as a child with father unknown, was raised at community expense. He is frus-

trated by his inability to find work and by the loss of social
prestige that unemployment carries with it. He is frustrated,
too, in his attraction to Sylvaine Castonnier, one of the local
girls in a village called Haut-Chaumond at the foot of the
Savoy Alps where the play unfolds, for Sylvaine's affections turn
instead toward Sylvester Imwald, a German radio operator assigned to the military detachment in town. The action of the
play takes place at Christmastime 1943, and focuses on a
Christmas dance sponsored by the Jeunesse Nationale in nearby
Villiers. Since the Résistance has been active in the region, any
gathering of young people might be regarded by the German
authorities with suspicion, but permission is accorded, nonetheless. Selfishly determined in his bitterness to kill in others the
joy he cannot share, Louis Crevaux approaches the Germans
with a list of all the townspeople involved in resistance activity
who would be in attendance at the dance, and the temptation
to liquidate them all in one fell swoop is too much to resist.
Crevaux had said that if he knew with whom Sylvaine was
keeping company he would slowly burn them alive, and now
his chance has come. A cold Nazi officer named Lutz Sprenger,
about to replace the more affable and congenial commandment
Major Mühlstein, moves into action and directs Imwald to
transmit a message ordering the beginning of a "military" un-
dertaking with the code name *Aktion Feuerofen.* Imwald's suspicions had been aroused earlier, and he had expressly asked Sylvaine not to go to the dance, but she was adamant.
Unfortunately distress does not make him imaginative. He sends
the signal announcing the start of *Aktion Feuerofen,* and the castle in which the dance is being held is burned down, with all
the people in it. Ignoring the possibilities for a dramatic confrontation with himself that could have existed for Sylvester
Imwald, Zuckmayer has him obey orders unflinchingly, albeit
somewhat dumbfoundedly. Since he does not confront himself
and cannot, one assumes, confront his superiors, he does the
next decent thing which is to go and die with Sylvaine in a
romantic and rather touching scene in which images of life and
death alternate poetically: the Christ child's birth and the flames
engulfing the lovers who can only look forward to death as a
rebirth into spiritual life. The spiritual dimension of this *Liebes-*

tod naturally escapes Crevaux, present to witness the disaster he has wrought. He had sworn that if he could not have Sylvaine then nobody would have her, and screams that now she is his offering and therefore belongs to him.

Somewhat like Goethe's *Faust,* Zuckmayer conceived of this play as taking place simultaneously on a heavenly and on an earthly plain and consequently transcending the particular circumstances of occupied France in which he set it. A chorus of angels, played by the same young men and women who die in flames at the end, opens the drama, and the local French and German policemen are played, not without effect, by the same actors and have the same names: Albert and Martin remain the same in both languages, but when appropriate, George(s) becomes Georg and Pierre Peter. The angels establish early on that it is Earth which must function as judge in matters of human conduct, and so it is a particularly biting comment when Sprenger tells Crevaux who appears after his bloody deed with the symbolic biblical brand mark of Cain on his forehead:

> Serves you completely right! You were always a mangy dog
> . . . . Jealous even of dead life. Nothing to be done about it.
> That which does not love you, you will not have, not in heaven,
> not in hell, and certainly not on earth. And if you are born bad,
> then no one will make you good, no priest, no woman, no child,
> not even your own mother.

Knowing that his own people have no use for him, Crevaux seeks to attach himself permanently to the Germans, reminding them that he has served them faithfully: " . . . I have been your ear, your eye—" But Sprenger responds curtly, "Now you are our refuse." Yet even for Crevaux perhaps there is hope. At the very end his old mother arrives to comfort him and persuades him to lay down his weapon before the townspeople who have come to handcuff him.[78]

For women to get on with the Germans was often a simpler matter than it was for men, and the examples provided in literature are manifold. To some degree in *Mon Village à l'heure allemande,* but more especially in *Les Forêts de la nuit,* intimate affairs with German soldiers seem to have offered some provincial women their more interesting distractions during the

Occupation. In addition to a local businesswoman in Saint-Clar who publicly attends the movies in the loge of the German commandant, there is Fernande Arréguy, the brash mother of Philippe last seen here trying to seduce Hélène de Balansun in Paris. Fernande defies the respect of the citizens of Saint-Clar by carrying on a progressively more open affair with a German non-commissioned officer until one summer day in 1943 she is caught sunbathing in immodest attire next to the German on the banks of the Gave de Pau. The spectators who form on a nearby bridge to look down at the offending couple expect a thunderbolt from heaven to punish "such scandalous audacity." If Madame Arréguy does not fall ill with an avenging disease, they hope at least one day—the day of accounting that is sure to come—to put her into the pillory themselves. Her fellow townswoman Madame Costellot becomes more and more pro-German as she reads more and more anti-British articles, and in as dignified a way as possible "suffers" the discreet courtship of German officer von Brackner. It is her personal revenge for having been snubbed by some English tourists at Biarritz before the war. Still another townswoman, the widow Madame Delahaye, raised in the tradition of Romain Rolland and Rabindranath Tagore, feels herself "too well brought up" (*trop bien élevée*), to ignore the German lieutenant Friedrich Rustiger whom she has been ordered to billet. Furthermore, Rustiger is a cultivated man with a highly developed appreciation of music whose adoration of Mozart and Bach corresponds to her own. She makes her entire record collection available to him for which he kisses her hand devotedly; and, taking her cue from literature as so many had done before her, Cécile Delahaye thinks she is living an unpublished chapter of *Jean-Christophe*, Romain Rolland's long, early twentieth-century novel about a German musician who came to Paris.

Perhaps one of the best summaries of life in Saint-Clar during the Occupation is given by Madame Costellot to Count de Balansun.

> Look around you, my poor friend, and name one of them who has not at some time spoken to a German! Why, the Germans are a blessing to Saint-Clar. The tradespeople exploit them for all they

are worth. The peasants welcome them with open arms, while they would shut the door in your face, Balansun, if you came to beg for six eggs. The shopgirls run after them. The schoolboys take free German lessons from them. The men joke with them in the cafés. In a word, the whole of Saint-Clar is out to make much of the occupants. And those who profess to hate them admire them secretly. . . . I'm not saying that the people of Saint-Clar like the Germans. I am saying that they accept them, out of calculation, self-interest, or simple inertia.

But Saint-Clar may be somewhat exceptional, and von Brackner wants to award the town a medal for civic merit in view of its good conduct toward the Germans.[79] Yet even in Saint-Clar there are rumblings which someone like Madame Delahaye is too sheltered and too naïve to notice.

One of the tenderest stories of the Occupation is Wolfgang Borchert's "Marguerite," first published posthumously in 1949. Borchert was born in 1921 and at the age of twenty was sent as a soldier to the Russian front. Some letters that he wrote too frankly voicing his negative opinions about Hitler and the war earned him a death sentence, from which he was later pardoned so that he could be sent back to Russia, and eight months in prison. Because of poor health he was released from military service but imprisoned again for having told jokes considered offensive to the Nazi state. The war, the prolonged imprisonment, and the lack of adequate nutrition immediately after the war contributed to Borchert's premature death in 1947 when he was twenty-six years of age.

"Marguerite" is the story of a somewhat naïve and unimaginative German soldier in occupied France, who also functions as the narrator, and his impetuous young French girlfriend. The tone is established in the first two paragraphs: the German knows little about Marguerite except that she comes from Lyon, that she is seventeen years old, and that he loves her. He makes virtually no attempt to penetrate her background. But Borchert's customary techniques: his economy of words, his brief sentences, and his refusal to bring to light any but the most factual details of the story, details that can be apprehended by eye and ear alone, are responsible for his achieving in the space of just

a few pages the story's very high level of emotion. A more reflective and intellectual narrator would have analyzed the facts,
but thereby run the risk of lessening their emotional impact.

It was theoretically forbidden for German soldiers to take
French mistresses, and so the relationship with Marguerite was
complicated from the start. When the lovers leave a café and
go out onto the street and kiss, they are interrupted by a German lieutenant, who tells them they cannot kiss this way in broad
daylight! Since the narrator is also a German, he immediately
accepts the justice of the reproach, but Marguerite does not. In
apparently very good German she tells the lieutenant that indeed they can kiss if they want to, and to a man such as he, she
would not give kisses even in the middle of the night. Fortunately the officer goes on his way without noticing that Marguerite is French.

Marguerite can be very French indeed, and perhaps it is this
quality that endears her to the narrator. Once in a movie house
they see some Paris firemen marching to celebrate a jubilee.
The German, trained in good military tradition, finds himself
laughing at the funny way the firemen are marching. Marguerite is irate over his laughter; she simply gets up and finds herself another seat.

In the third and last scene the lovers stand by a river, probably the Seine, since the story appears to take place in Paris
even though the location is never specified. Remembering the
scene, the narrator delivers a marvelously poetic fantasy
description of the river sailing with the night and whisking the
couple off to an unknown land. Unfortunately, at the time the
story takes place he is unable to respond on Marguerite's level.
To her the river smells of love, but to him only of grass, river
water, fog, and night. Suddenly a German patrol passes by,
shining a flashlight on them. The patrols are out looking for
underaged girls who, according to the narrator, blossomed at
night in the arms of soldiers like flowers in the parks. Marguerite's appearance seems to satisfy the patrol leader, for he
is about to depart when something about her arrests his attention and he asks her for identification. German women did not
make up the way French women did. "That's just what I
thought!" he snaps after looking over her papers. " . . .

Frenchwoman, such a paint box," and then takes down her lover's name.[80]

The narrator knows that this infraction will cost him at least four weeks confinement to barracks, not to mention other punishments. When he tells Marguerite that he will be unable to see her for the next month, she is appalled at his cowardice. She could not know just how impossible it would be for him to slip over the barracks fence. She goes off into the night informing him with brutal frankness that she will return to her room, wash her face, make herself pretty, and find a new lover. The narrator returns, dejected and sentimental, to his barracks. The heroic Cornelian conflicts between love and duty are no more. Instead narrator and reader alike are left with a lump in their throats with little choice but to swallow eventually, and then go on.

Occupied France, too, had to go on; those who could adapt easily and those who could not; those who collaborated, those who resisted, and those who for all practical purposes did neither; those who turned the Occupation into material profit and those who suffered its privations. It was a time of testing, when all these people with their different convictions and different degrees of conviction had to live side by side and when often quite ordinary men and women found themselves called upon to show their mettle.

CHAPTER VIII

The Jews in Occupied France

Life in occupied France was especially difficult for the Jews and became progressively more so as time went on. Even more immediately critical than the situation of French Jews was that of German Jews living in exile in France who, by the terms of the 1940 Armistice, could legally be repatriated along with all other Germans who had sought refuge there. Herschel Grynszpan who in 1938 assassinated the diplomat Ernst vom Rath attached to the German embassy in Paris was among the early victims of the Armistice provision.[1]

Before the invasion of 1940 France continued to play her noble historical role as a haven for refugees. But the German Jews she received found themselves straining against an increasingly tortuous bureaucracy. More and more they were made to feel the double stigma of a nationality and a religion different from those of the majority. When the Lévys in André Schwarz-Bart's *Le Dernier des justes* arrive in France after fleeing Stillenstadt, they are housed by the Comité Juif d'Accueil, the Jewish Committee of Welcome, in suburban Montmorency north of Paris. Benjamin and his two sons Ernie and Moritz soon find employment in a Jewish tailor's shop in town to which they travel every morning in a pitching and rolling double-decker train called a *tacot*. Sometimes people stare at them a bit, but there is no overt hostility, and occasionally a fellow commuter will even nod at them amiably. On the way home the three Lévys can walk into any bakery they like without harassment and pick out what they want. To Benjamin this is living.

But even in Paris the quality of life soon deteriorates. As it becomes clearer that war is going to be inevitable, gas masks are requisitioned for all the workmen riding to their jobs in the *tacot*, but the German Jews in exile are excluded from the general distribution. Ironically their passports, too, which are already marked with the swastika, carry the added notation "Jew." By August 1939, no one greets foreigners anymore on the *tacot*, and even if it is not said outright, the idea of a possible internment seems to be on everyone's mind. One day the newspapers announce that war has been declared. Upon arrival at the Gare du Nord, Ernie feels slightly unwell and uses this as a pretext to leave his father and brother and go to the Caserne de Reuilly on the rue de Reuilly in the twelfth *arrondissement* to enlist as a stretcher-bearer. On the way out of the barracks, he naïvely thanks a little old lady who pins a patriotic emblem on his chest. It isn't his thanks that she wants, however, but a contribution of one franc twenty-five for the Napoleon patch she has given him.

In the letter he writes to his family advising them of his enlistment and telling them that as a result he will not be coming home, Ernie is much too self-effacing to admit that it is on their behalf that he has made his decision. As a rationale he uses the Germans and what they did to him, reserving his real motives for a postscript: "In this envelope you will find eight certificates from the city clerk. For every one of you there is proof that your son, grandson or brother has enlisted in the French Army. Take good care of them, because with them you too are a little bit French, and they won't be able to put you into a concentration camp."

Two days later Ernie finds that in the ranks of the 429th Foreign Infantry Regiment sergeants born in Dresden or Berlin look at him with irritation, and a native Burgundian lieutenant tells them all he wants no one playing the role of the "alien-draped-in-the-folds-of-the-tricolor." Until further notice they are confined to quarters.

Ernie's regiment puts in regular appearances at the battle scenes in the spring of 1940, though he himself spends as much time or more beating the regimental drums rather than bearing stretchers. Stretcher-bearers are also required to be musicians, and since he is unable to play anything else, Ernie is given the drums. That May he receives a letter on the Ardennes front informing him that his whole family has been interned. A Paris neighbor has written the letter, making it clear how painful a thing it is, but that this kind of internment is not aimed at the Lévys alone. In time of war it was customary in France to inter enemy aliens to maintain law and order, and if German Jews were Jews, they were also Germans. A restrained letter from Ernie's father describes conditions at the internment camp at Gurs near the Spanish border. The camp at Gurs had originally been opened in 1939 to house refugee Spanish republican militiamen, but after the armistice in 1940 it took in some 12,000 foreign Jews, most of whom were German. Between 1940 and 1942 approximately 1000 deaths were recorded, and from his father's letter Ernie quickly deduces that "what was customary in France conformed at times to the best German tradition." In 1941, according to Schwarz-Bart's novel, came the announcement of the complete transfer of all internees at Gurs to Nazi concentration camps outside France.[2] Historically, however, this date seems a bit early. Although the press in the Occupied zone announced the deportation of Jews from France to the east on December 14, 1941, the first trainload of Jews did not actually leave France until March 27, 1942, and Robert Paxton, historian of the Vichy period, notes that even from camps in the Occupied zone the "first systematic deportation of stateless Jews . . . began in May and June, 1942."[3]

Gurs was not the only Jewish internment camp, and in his anger at what the French did to the Jews, Serge Doubrovsky in *La Dispersion* lists some forty centers in all where either alien or French Jews were imprisoned, both by French authorities. "Camps. Very much French. With guards and police with blue eyes and long mustaches, descended straight from the Gauls, certified pedigree, before a notary public."

As in Germany, the tragedy for individual Jews in France, even for those who were citizens through birth or naturalization, lay in the fact that there was nothing they could personally do to establish their worth in the eyes of the authorities. Little Ellen in Ilse Aichinger's *Die grössere Hoffnung* perceived the problem accurately when she understood that she had two "wrong" grandparents. As all victims of racial repression the Jews were considered to have been born "wrong" and there was nothing they could do to justify their existence and make their birth become "right." In *La Dispersion* the family of the principal narrator, of Russian Jewish extraction, tries in vain to justify its existence in France and its right to the protection of French law. The father, simply referred to as Père, had come from the Ukraine before World War I and was bound for America, but once in Paris he decided to stay just as he decides to stay in 1940 rather than cross the demarcation line into the south. Crossing the line would mean raising thousands of francs, and, furthermore, he is a naturalized French citizen. His naturalization papers were signed by Laval himself. In 1914 the family had provided the French army with three soldiers including the father; the other two died, one of an illness contracted at the front in 1914, the other of wounds sustained in battle in 1917. In 1940 the family gave four prisoners of war, all of them now in Germany. How much does that weigh? asks the narrator in a rhetorical question whose answer, one knows, can only be "nothing." What Ernie Lévy had learned a decade before in Germany, Doubrovsky's narrator, a schoolboy of eleven at the beginning of the Occupation, learns now: it does not matter that he is an excellent student in everything but mathematics and that he has carried off the first prize in French among other subjects. His grandparents were "wrong," and they were contaminating him from beyond the tomb. He has a Jewish cast of features; he is a Jewish "type" which he, still smarting from the scars of his childhood, is infuriated to find recognized by a boy in Venice years after the Occupation is over.

What would it mean to cross the line, moreover, to be in the free zone? "[F]ree IN WHAT WAY? Pétain. Laval. . . . A real difference. Elegant gangsters. No executioners German style, no. Distinguished torture, anti-Semitism the Guermantes way. Pardon, a nuance, not at all alike, the French way."[4]

Even before the Occupation, the old Third Republic had already started making life difficult for Jews by imposing stringent security restrictions. After May 1938, fearful of high unemployment, the government sought to limit the labor force by voting itself temporary power to intern all males between the

ages of eighteen and forty-five who were not citizens and then
put teeth into the measure by revoking the citizenship of 15,154
Frenchmen naturalized since 1927, among whom were 6307
Jews. In his study, *Vichy France,* Robert O. Paxton states that
the government of Marshal Pétain began setting up a "purge
and quota system" long before the Germans applied any pres-
sure on it. Effective as of October 3, 1940, the *Statut des juifs*
forbade Jews to assume positions in elected bodies and excluded them from positions of responsibility in the civil, judicial, and military services, as well as from teaching in the public
schools, reporting or editing for the newspapers, and directing
films or radio programs. On October 4, police prefects were
authorized to intern foreign Jews in special camps or assign
them a fixed residence. Jews were to be excluded entirely from
the *département de l'Allier* surrounding Vichy. Beginning in May
1940, the Germans did their part in the occupied zone to the
north by assigning *gérants* or provisional administrators to manage all enterprises whose owners had fled, and then forbade
Jews who had fled to return. On October 18, 1940, *gérants* were
assigned outright to all Jewish property, and the following April
26 these *gérants* were empowered to sell Jewish properties to
Aryans or to liquidate them and return the proceeds to the
State.[5]

Doubrovsky notes that in the publication industry in the occupied zone Jews were exempt from the restrictions when it
came to disseminating matter of a strictly scientific import,[6] but
beginning in August 1941, they were no longer permitted to
own radios. Instead they were to exchange them for a receipt
at the local *mairie.* After December of that year Jews were not
permitted to change residence or travel outside their own *département.* The narrator's family learns just how difficult it can
be to obtain a legal change of address when his father seeks to
move them officially from the eighth *arrondissement* in Paris
where he has a tailor shop to the *département de Seine-et-Oise* outside the city where his wife has inherited her father's property
and where the family is already living. He writes a polite and
respectfully humble letter to the *Préfet de police,* and the only
answer he receives comes in the form of a summons addressed
to the narrator, then a boy of twelve, from the Paris offices of

the "Direction des Etrangers et des Affaires Juives," a variant for the central office for Jewish affairs in the Pétain government, established by the efforts of Admiral Darlan, commander of the French fleet from 1936 to 1940 and Pétain's designated successor from 1940 to 1942.[7] The father is furious but also frightened. Playing the game, he writes the Préfet that his son has been declared a resident of the *département de la Seine* in Paris by oversight and that a certificate of residence has already been delivered for the Seine-et-Oise by a local police commissariat. The error is now in the process of being rectified.[8]

Only a month after the Germans arrived, Paris saw the Jeunes Gardes, wearing blue shirts, gloves, ties, and boots, appear in groups in the streets to put up fliers calling for the downfall and death of the Jews. Like the Nazis before the war in Günter Grass's *Die Blechtrommel* the Jeunes Gardes bashed in the windows of Jewish commercial enterprises, sacked the displays, and beat up the salespeople. Doubrovsky does not show us these scenes, he merely informs us, with unrelenting energy and animation. Doubrovsky's fascination for and facility with words, the "délire des mots," is matched most closely by Céline. For both of them, the "delirium" comes very close at times to degenerating into a harangue, although in some of his novels Céline is spared that fault by his incredible powers of description. Ironically Céline often used his "delirium" for purposes that were the very opposite of Doubrovsky's—as a vehicle for spewing out his anti-Semitism.

In Doubrovsky's book several stores located in the neighborhood of the narrator's father's shop begin sprouting signs declaring that they are French stores and henceforth entrance is forbidden to Jews. During the winter of 1940–41 a big yellow sign with the black letters *Jüdisches Geschäft* appears at the entrance to the building housing the father's tailor shop. This time it is official, and there is no question of erasing it. Soon another sign, this one red and black, is affixed under the yellow and black one, announcing to the public that though the store is Jewish it is being managed by an Aryan (*Direction assurée par un commissaire-gérant aryen*). The *gérant* turns out to be an Alsatian named Jung, with short blond hair and sapphire-blue eyes, the ideal Aryan for the job who, to his credit, first appears somewhat embarrassed by his new position. He alone has the right to approach clients who come to be outfitted, many of them for uniforms, ironically enough, since the father has always catered to the uniformed trade. The *gérant* alone can proceed "with the imposition of Aryan hands on Aryan buttocks." Père is now confined to the rear of the apartment, a virtual prisoner in his own house, working not the normal ten to twelve hours, but fourteen and fifteen hours per day. To the presence of the Alsatian *gérant,* is added that of a man named Richter, "a collector of Jewish enterprises, as others of postage stamps." He reviews the books and pockets 75 to 80 percent of the profits. After his arrival the father is only an employee. All this for a stupidity (*une connerie*), the narrator laments, that his father, bound for America, had committed in 1912 when he crossed the French border in Lorraine and instead of giving his first name as Ivan, Isidore, Dmitri, Joseph, or Fédor had said "Israël."[9]

As in Germany, Jews in France were increasingly isolated from the general population, and Guéhenno wrote on January 31, 1942, that his barber was a "little Jewish worker" who "no longer has the right to cut hair." He could not exercise any trade that would put him in contact with the public, and so, once night fell, he cut the hair of fellow Jews in the neighborhood to earn a living.[10] The list of amenities forbidden to the Jews also increased as time went on and began to rival the restrictions existing in Germany: pools, theaters, movie houses, concerts, restaurants, cafés, bars, museums, libraries, public expositions, sports matches, parks, etc. As of February 1942, writes Doubrovsky, Jews were forbidden to go out of doors between eight in the evening and six in the morning while for other people the curfew only began at eleven or at midnight.[11] After May 28, 1942, all Jews in the occupied zone were obliged to wear a yellow Star of David sewn onto their garments at chest level, and though Pétain expressly forbade the extension of that ruling into the unoccupied zone, he was overruled after the Germans crossed the demarcation line that November.[12] "To wake up a nigger," reflects the enraged and outraged narrator of *La Dispersion.* "For everybody's knowledge, an advertising sign on one's front, a trademark on one's skin, in one's skin." Only the last car in the second-class section of the Paris Métro remained available to those obliged to wear the star.[13]

Simone de Beauvoir claims in *La Force de l'âge* that in the cafés she frequented in Montparnasse and Saint-Germain-des-Prés she never saw anyone wearing the star and that her Jewish friends and acquaintances who were in the habit of coming to the Café de Flore continued to do so as before. It can be argued, of course, that in the cafés Simone de Beauvoir was living in a somewhat rarefied society. If one refused to wear the star one could be arrested like the stationery-dealer Whemer in Vercors's "L'Imprimerie de Verdun" (1951). Whemer has altered his identification card and is nabbed by French authorities. His case serves as a forerunner to that of Dacosta, another Jew working for the owner of a small printing press and whose name is Vendresse. Vendresse is a member of a Verdun veterans organization called the Amicale des Vieux de Verdun, and is convinced that with the greatest of all the Verdun veterans, Marshal Pétain, in the seat of government, all will be well. He even encourages Dacosta not to register as a Jew, only to find both himself and his employee hounded by another veteran, Paars, who wishes to rid the printing profession of Jews. Recognizing that matters are coming to a head, Dacosta goes into hiding, but young Frenchmen of the new order threaten to take away Dacosta's wife and children if he is not found. Not believing such a thing to be possible, Vendresse dares them to try. They dare, separating the children from their mother who tries to throw herself from a window; but they take her along with them. She is later gassed at Auschwitz.[14]

But even wearing the star and strict conformity to all anti-Jewish regulations was no guarantee of immunity from persecution. In 1943 Isaac Rappoport, a shirt merchant in *Au bon beurre* operating a store on the Champs-Elysées and living with his wife, mother, and daughter on the rue Saint-Senoch in the seventeenth *arrondissement* beyond the Etoile, naïvely feels himself forgotten by the authorities and safe from all danger. His family, on the other hand, feel less safe and think it better not to venture out of doors. Isaac's father had come to France from a Jewish suburb of Cracow after the downfall of the Austro-Hungarian monarchy when Cracow again became part of Po-

land, and its little Jewish community trembled for the future.
Following the wisdom of a central European proverb that speaks
of living the good life "like God in France" (*wie Gott in Frank-reich*),[15] Isaac's father headed for Paris. Even after his father
died in 1932, Isaac remained in Paris, though his brother estab-
lished himself in New York and various other relations located
in Buenos Aires and Panama. In truth, Isaac is too attached to
his business to leave Paris, so attached and involved, in fact,
that he has neglected to have himself naturalized. Thus he finds
himself in occupied France in the unenviable position of being
a Jew without a country (*Israélite apatride*). In the same slightly
ironic and mock-serious style in which author-narrator Jean
Dutourd presents the experiences of his other characters and
thereby makes the sometimes crass and dreadful story of the
Occupation somewhat more palatable to the reader, he recounts the downfall of Isaac's family almost as a biblical stroke
from on high. As Isaac returns one evening to the rue Saint-
Senoch, his concierge greets him with the announcement that
the Gestapo that afternoon had taken away his wife, his mother,
his daughter, his radio set, and two hams that he had been
storing in the house, not to mention money and jewelry. Rappoport faints at the news, and the concierge pulls him into her
rooms. Though the Gestapo have sealed the Rappoport apartment, they no doubt still intend to come and get Isaac. The
concierge has had some business dealings with the Poissonards
and is holding for safekeeping some of the products they had
acquired illegally, so she goes with Isaac to Charles-Hubert
Poissonard for advice. Poor Rappoport's lament explaining his
predicament to Poissonard is as good a commentary as any on
the abominable state to which the Jews had been reduced.

No! No! It's not possible! Some misunderstanding there must
be! They had no reason. Why should they arrest the poor things?
They have some mistake made. They've mixed them up with some
other people. We Rappos have never done anything wrong. Never,
I swear before God! We've always worn the star, haven't we, *Madame la concierge*? I always in the end coach went in the *métro* as
they order. And never, never, I swear, has any of us ever been
into a shop forbidden to Jews or any other *verboten* place.

He concludes in a pleading voice, "The Germans are just, aren't
they? . . . They won't keep Mesdames Rappoport if they can't

find anything against us." Knowing that his family has been taken to the prison at Drancy, the thought occurs to him in his desperation that maybe he should go there to explain.

> If I go, they'll probably release them, will they not? What can they possibly with a little girl of thirteen and an old woman of seventy-five want? Madame, Monsieur, what do you think? People don't get arrested without reason in the twentieth century, in France? All the more since we're very fond of Germany, we are. There are Rappoports in Germany, good citizens and all that, cousins...

Charles-Hubert Poissonard is never very sensitive to anything except money, and he expresses his initial irritation in an aside to the concierge. Rappoport's intuition warns him that if he is to get anywhere with Poissonard he had better start talking money, and immediately Poissonard becomes receptive. "That night, Charles-Hubert felt quite genuinely prepared to move heaven and earth for the Jews." Back at the dairy shop his wife joins in. Jewish or not, she says, they are all brothers. Nevertheless, Charles-Hubert has no intention of putting Isaac up for the night at his own place. Instead they will put him up in a building on the Boulevard Saint-Germain whose concierge is indebted to the Poissonards. Since it is only ten o'clock and the curfew close does not fall until midnight, the change of residence can be accomplished forthwith. Immediately Julie unstitches the star from Isaac's garments, and Charles-Hubert asks by what name he would like to be known on the new identity card he will procure for Isaac on the morrow. Isaac feels a distinct pleasure in taking on a name that will confer nobility and without hesitation chooses Raoul de Sérigny. After all, suffering has to offer some compensation! The entire transformation costs him 3000 francs. The next morning Charles-Hubert has no difficulty finding a Corsican in a bar on the Place Blanche who for 500 francs gives out identity cards issued at Cambrai where bombings have reduced the archives to ashes and made verification impossible. Rappoport gives the Poissonards another 5000 francs to send packages to his family at Drancy. He does not know that his family received nothing for this money, that they remained only twenty-four hours at Drancy before being sent to Auschwitz where they all died in a month and a

half. "Out of humanity" the Poissonards hide this news from
Rappoport who comes to the Bon Beurre every second day until January 1944, when despite her husband's objections, Julie
Poissonard decides they can no longer accept the money Rappoport has been giving them for their packages every week.
Sooner or later he would find out that his family is no longer
at Drancy and the Poissonards would appear less than honest.
Charles-Hubert has to concede to his wife's good sense. All in
all this Jew Rappoport, together with a ham that he had given
a *résistant* at the end of 1943, will look good on his record come
the day of liberation.[16]

If a Jew dared to be more audacious than Isaac Rappoport
he might on occasion not wear the star. If he could avoid being
caught, a whole world of amenities that other people took for
granted opened up to him. When France was defeated in 1940,
Ernie Lévy in *Le Dernier des justes,* who had enlisted in the French
army, manages to escape German captivity, and eventually
makes his way back to Paris and to the Jewish ghetto in the
Marais stretching out on the right bank behind Notre Dame
cathedral. He has spent considerable time roaming the Rhône
valley, and when he gets back to Paris, Stars of David are flour-
ishing all over the Marais.

> On every shopwindow a six-pointed star alerted the Christian
> stroller. These stars were also displayed on the breasts of furtive
> pedestrians, who glided along the walls like shadows, but here
> they were pieces of yellow cloth the size of a starfish, sewn above
> the heart and bearing a hallmark of human manufacture: "Jew."
> Ernie noticed that the children's badges were the same size as the
> adults' and seemed to devour the frail chests, their six points dug
> in like claws. Ernie couldn't believe the sight of these tiny branded
> livestock . . .[17]

Ernie befriends a lame Jewish girl after rescuing her from the
hands of two French "patriots" who were pawing her and
laughing. Golda Engelbaum, of Polish Jewish ancestry, has been
a refugee in almost every country of central Europe, and now
she has only one impossible wish left, and that is to walk with
Ernie through Paris without their stars. And so they do this one
Sunday afternoon in August 1943, when the weather is warm

enough to enable them to shed their outer garments with the stars sewn onto them. On the banks of the Seine in the shadows of one of the bridges, Golda stuffs their jackets into her shopping bag and covers them with a newspaper. "Holding hands, they strolled along the Seine as far as the Pont-Neuf, where in a delicious anguish they mounted the stone stairs to the surface of the Christian world."[18] Neither of them has ever been to a movie before, and since they are not wearing their stars they are free to enter. Ernie has seven francs, but Golda decides the movies are too expensive, and they settle for an ice-cream cone instead. Later they go home and make love for the first time, and as it is past the hour of the Jewish curfew, Ernie decides to accompany Golda home. They have to hide at one point, she in a doorway, he pressed against a shadowed wall, to avoid a passing street patrol. The next day Ernie goes over to the Engelbaums' apartment after Golda has missed the noon rendezvous they had planned, and when he arrives at their door he sees that the apartment has been sealed. The concierge is waiting for him on the ground floor, holding in her hand a broken harmonica that at the last minute Golda had thrown her for "the young man" and which one of the arresting officers had first examined and then stamped on. "I wanted to tell you before," says the concierge, explaining why she had not called to him when she saw him enter the building. "But this is the third time I've had Jews, and it's better to let people go upstairs first."

This is not the first time Ernie has seen an apartment sealed off either, and concluding, no doubt, that he has nothing better to live for, he goes to Drancy, hoping there to join his beloved. Schwarz-Bart describes Drancy as a very ordinary, quiet, and peaceful Ile-de-France town in suburban Paris, where nothing seemed to indicate the existence of a prison camp oozing with suffering, whose very name was enough to cast a spell of dread over Jewish children. On his arrival Ernie Lévy simply goes up to the gendarmes posted at the entrance gate of the prison and asks, since he is Jewish, to be let in. But people did not normally volunteer for Drancy, and the guards do not know what to make of this unusual request. Thinking he must mean that he wants to visit someone inside, they suggest that, though visits per se are not permitted, Ernie might leave packages. They might even be able to make a deal with him. In a bantering tone they tell him that one can get into Drancy but one cannot get out. When Ernie informs them that this is precisely what he wants, their humor subsides abruptly and gives way to an appalled silence. Quickly Ernie understands that these guards consider themselves responsible only for receipt of the "merchandise" delivered by the Gestapo and in no way wish to be implicated in the task of rounding it up. They are offended by Ernie's request and by his presumptuousness at presenting himself without waiting for an appointed day and hour which the Germans would decide. He gains his admittance to Drancy only after a low black sedan drives up to the camp entrance bearing a short man in a Tyrolean hat before whom Ernie grasps his star with his right hand, tears it from his jacket, and flings it onto the street. The man in the Tyrolean hat, wanting to ascertain Ernie's "real" reasons for wanting to enter Drancy, has him taken in and beaten unconscious. After that Ernie remains.[19]

Once inside he finds some of the bitter ironies common to life in the camps. A Catholic doctor, who has recently discovered he is one-eighth Jewish and is acting as a male nurse in the infirmary, finds it ironic that Ernie should have sought admission to the camp of his own volition; but it is no less ironic that the doctor himself should be wearing a medal of the Virgin around his neck and a yellow star on his jacket. SS men eventually replace the French gendarmes at the camp gates because the French are found to be somewhat "lacking in enthusiasm." Inside, however, some of the camp administration is actually in the hands of the Jews themselves. The inmates are by and large as helpful to one another as possible under the circumstances, but all of them, including Golda whom Ernie is finally able to locate after a lapse of some three months, have a look of sad indifference on their faces. She is glad to see him again, but at Drancy it is every person for himself. Her own parents had been taken from the camp some time ago. In mid-October 1500 orphans are brought in, and since they are still screaming for their parents, they are told by the other inmates that they will meet their parents again in some distant and peaceful kingdom, and this idea eventually takes on an almost mythological character among those prisoners who do not or cannot believe that they will soon be entering German gas chambers. Since some of the children are too small to know their own names, they are issued little wooden medallions with their names inscribed to wear around their necks. A few hours after these medallions have been given out, many a little boy is wearing a medallion bearing the name Estelle or Sarah. Children are children, and even at Drancy they continued to play their games.

Ernie discovers the name of Golda Engelbaum on a list of 500 adults who in addition to the children are scheduled to be shipped out of Drancy the day after next at dawn. He immediately goes to see the Jewish superintendent of documents and with some doing has his own name substituted for that of another male inmate on the list. The next morning after roll call the stars of the prospective deportees are snipped off and collected in the center of the prison courtyard "which was soon like a field carpeted with buttercups." The idyllic character of the image is momentarily shattered at Drancy station where the doors of the railway transport cars are shut on the Jews bound for their long journey to the extermination camp at Auschwitz. But Ernie tries to revive its spirit and the illusions it evokes, both on the train and in Auschwitz itself. After their arrival, the prisoners are separated into two files by an SS officer who sizes them up at a glance and directs them to the left if they are relatively healthy-looking males between the ages of twenty and forty-five. All the others including the women and children are sent off to the right. One woman, alerted by the smell in the air, screams something about people being killed here, but the guards immediately calm the prisoners, telling them that the men on the left will be called upon to build houses and roads while the others will rest up from their trip and await work assignments. When Ernie is directed to the left file, he protests that he is ill and cannot walk, for he cannot think of leaving Golda and the children who have made the trip with him. The physician in charge, the infamous Dr. Mengele, makes his only appearance in the book and grants Ernie his wish. Ernie, Golda, and the children then pass almost immediately to the gas chambers which are outfitted to look like bathing establishments in which soap is distributed and a kind of cloakroom is equipped with numbered hooks on which the victims hang their garments. To the very end Ernie tries to reassure Golda and the children, telling them they are going to a better kingdom where all will be good and beautiful. He has to protect them from a world where reality has become too horrible to accept. In such a world there is no room for truth.[20]

French Reaction Toward the Jews

Shortly after the Jews were ordered to wear the Star of David on their clothing, Jean Guéhenno wrote in his diary: "For a week now the Jews have to wear the yellow star and call upon themselves public scorn. Never have people been so friendly to them. It is no doubt because there is nothing more ignoble than to force a man at every moment to be ashamed of himself and the kind people of Paris know it."[21] It would be nice to be able to let that statement stand unqualified, but it is too frequently contradicted by the testimony of literature to be able to do so. The Poissonards in *Au bon beurre* find an apartment and a new identity card for Isaac Rappoport, it is true, but only after being assured of a rich reward in return. One of the old Jewish religious men whom Ernie Lévy visits after his return to Paris sees his concierge take all the machines that were part of his tailor's workshop from his apartment, then the furniture, then the dishes, and finally the apartment itself, but in the end at least she does not denounce him.[22]

Ernie is pleased by the gesture of a little old French woman in mourning who one day comes up to him and shakes his hand, and by that of a French workman in overalls who gets up from his seat in the Métro and offers it to Ernie, probably to compensate him in some way for the outrage of having to wear the star. But in the very next paragraph, Schwarz-Bart presents a scene in front of a synagogue in the rue Pavée in the Marais where some fashionable young lads are amusing themselves, one of them by pulling the beard of an old worshipper and screaming out the war cry of medieval French knights, "Montjoie Saint-Denis," while the others join in with "Pour Dieu et mon driot," from the motto on the British royal coat of arms.

In the next paragraph Ernie discovers Golda being abused by two laughing French men.[23]

In "La Marche à l'étoile" (1943) Vercors, whose own father was a Hungarian Jew,[24] tells the story of Thomas Muritz who as a young man comes to France from Bratislava, almost as to a utopian paradise. France is everything for him, and never will he tolerate a word spoken against her. His tears and cries when he is taken to Drancy are not provoked by the threat of immanent death but by the despair, horror, and suffering of his "assassinated" love affair with France. For Drancy was not a German creation alone, and the author-narrator reflects regretfully that henceforth he himself will no longer be able to think of France with the pure and untainted joy he once knew.[25]

In the thirties and early forties there was a staggering increase in the number of French who seemed to believe that France should be for the French and the ghetto for the Jews. The reserve lieutenant named Malinier in Marcel Aymé's *Le Chemin des écoliers*, who hated the Germans but was grateful for what he considered the benefits of the Hitler régime and ended up putting on the German uniform with the idea of somehow helping in the clean-up of France, was not alone in his way of thinking.[26] More bitter than most is the long lament of Serge Doubrovsky's *La Dispersion*. For the huge roundups that took place in Paris with increasing frequency; for the examinations in which men had to drop their trousers to show if they were circumcised; for the discrimination the narrator experienced at the hands of certain schoolmasters who asked each student in class his religion and for whom even the word Protestant struck a slightly false note in a predominantly Catholic country; for the Parisian business and professional people who remained silent before the open persecution of the Jews, satisfied that with the departure of the Jews their competition would decrease; for those who wanted "France for the French" and used this as a slogan to drive out the Jews; for those who insisted they were merely following orders in harassing the Jews and wanted to know nothing of the personal sorrows and hardships they were inflicting; for the Jews who were arrested in their homes and given instructions that looked like shopping lists informing them of what they could and must bring to the internment camps;

for the camps themselves and especially for the prison camp at Drancy that led its inmates to eventual death as surely as any fatal disease; for all these things the narrator cries out a litany of blame not only against the Germans but with equal severity against the French as well.

The first mass deportations began in France after the round-up in Paris of approximately 13,000 Jews who were herded into the Vélodrome d'Hiver on July 16, 1942.[27] At their disposition there were two toilets, and for several days the prisoners were given nothing to eat.[28] But there were roundups before that one, and a very graphic description is given in *La Dispersion* of one of the earliest roundups of foreign Jews in Paris in August 1941: "police, franco-boche, fraternally joined, arm in arm, cordons in the streets in the whole eleventh (*arrondissement*), knocks on the doors, up, faster than that, fifteen minutes to get dressed, a quarter of an hour to follow us, WHERE? we don't know, don't have to discuss orders with you . . . ."[29] All these atrocities—roundups, house arrests, discrimination, harass-ment, and the camps—existed in France. "Pas en Bochie. A Paname. Tout près. La banlieue. De vrais Parigots qui men-aient la danse." Doubrovsky's highly colloquial French can only be paraphrased: Not in Germany, but right here in Paris with real Parisians leading the dance.[30]

CHAPTER IX

The French Résistance

A Fertile Climate

In their response to the Occupation and the conditions that the Germans with collaboration from Vichy had imposed on their country, some French chose the path of active resistance. What was little more than a passive "dissidence" in 1940 became by 1942 a more active Résistance as the forces of opposition gained power, grew in size, and achieved clearer focus and better organization. But even in 1942 the spirit of resistance was not very widespread, and the majority of the French accepted the Vichy government on its own word.[1] It was 1943, in fact, before the Poissonards in *Au bon beurre* began to sense a real change in the wind. But already by mid-year 1941, acts of terrorism against the occupation authorities were on the increase. On August 21, 1941, the first German serviceman was assassinated since the armistice, a naval cadet officer by the name of Moser, shot on the platform of the Paris Métro station at Barbès-Rochechouart. On September 3 there followed the assassination of a German non-commissioned officer at the Gare de l'Est, that of an army major and a civilian official in Bordeaux on October 22, and that of the Feldkommandant of Nantes on October 20.[2] Very quickly Paris and other cities were flooded with bilingual notices in red and yellow. They were bordered in black and had black printing on them, and they bore the dual headings *Bekanntmachung* and *Avis* to notify the civilian population of the reprisals the Germans were going to exact of France for

treachery against their own. The Germans immediately connected Moser's assassination with their own execution of a
Frenchman and a Polish Jew after a communist demonstration
at the Porte de Saint-Denis and with recent arrests of Parisian
Jews. Violence was escalating; other executions followed at the
end of August, and in September the curfew was fixed at 11
PM. On October 21, the German military governor in France
posted an *Avis,* reproduced in the next day's papers, warning
that fifty hostages were to be shot in reprisal for the execution
of the Feldkommandant of Nantes and promising a reward of
15,000,000 francs to anyone who would help bring about the
arrest of those responsible. Guéhenno remarks that the newspapers printed the reward in big letters as though they were
announcing a new prize in a national lottery. On the morning
of October 22, twenty-seven inmates of the camp at Châteaubriant north of Nantes and twenty-one from Nantes prison,
making a total of forty-eight and hence two short of the promised number, were shot in a clearing in groups of three. At two
o'clock that afternoon Marshal Pétain addressed his countrymen denouncing the acts of terrorism that had taken place and
begging them, "Do not allow any longer this harm to be done
to France."[3]

The first execution by the Germans in Paris took place just
before Christmas 1940, and the victim was neither a terrorist
nor a hostage but a twenty-eight year old engineer named
Jacques Bonsergent who had dared to raise his hand against a
German Feldwebel. It was for him that the first red and black
notices appeared in Paris, and perhaps because the city did not
yet fully realize the gravity of the German threat, most of them
were slashed through on the very day they were put up. There
were also other atrocities of an unofficial nature, such as the
one that occurred outside the village of Camaret in Brittany on
June 23, 1940, in the home of Saint-Pol-Roux where the aging
poet was living with his daughter, Divine, a servant, and a dog.
As the household was preparing for bed at about ten in the
evening, a German soldier suddenly entered the door on the
pretext of looking for some English troops who were supposedly hidden there. Saint-Pol-Roux and Divine guided the German through the whole house, and when they returned to the

living room, the intruder sent the dog away and set up two revolvers and a dagger on a table in front of Saint-Pol-Roux and his daughter explaining that he was waiting for his comrades. After an hour of terrified silence Saint-Pol-Roux asked the German to leave. But instead the German ordered everyone down into the cellar, where, with a revolver in each hand, he fired at them, wounding Saint-Pol-Roux and killing the servant who tried to protect Divine. Divine tried to flee and the German fired again, hitting her in the leg. Then he carried her into the living-room and raped her. Writing about the ghastly story over a year later on September 17, 1941, Guéhenno said that by that time Saint-Pol-Roux had died of sorrow and that Divine, living with the sister of the dead servant and preferring to remember nothing of what had happened, was walking around with crutches and was mentally and emotionally shattered, unable even to read.[4] The German soldier who had done this was shot by the Germans. Divine had recognized him in a lineup, and he confessed immediately that he had seen her swimming and been attracted to her. The Germans permitted Divine and her father to attend the execution and then occupied the Saint-Pol-Roux home.

Resistance to the German presence went beyond the assassinations of the summer and fall of 1941 which Marshal Pétain's plea failed to arrest. Résistance activity consisted mainly of sabotage designed to make the Germans feel ill at ease in a country which was not theirs and to frustrate their attempts to dominate and regulate it. The railway system was especially vulnerable to acts of sabotage, and blowing up trains carrying the Germans or their supplies is a characteristic feature of the so-called *roman résistancialiste* or Résistance novel. In her short story "Le Premier Accroc coûte deux cents francs," Elsa Triolet states that by the last year of the Occupation trains were not very crowded. Ordinary people were afraid to travel, and so the only rail travelers were the Wehrmacht and the Résistance along with a few holdouts in search of provisions on the black market. The black humor of the times had it that there were only two public services still functioning well in France: the railway itself and the derailments. Triolet mentions the example of a traveler who asked a stationmaster if a particular train was going to be late. The stationmaster answered affirmatively, "my son has just left to make it derail."[5]

The courage, sacrifice, and knowledge of the trade that many railway workers brought to bear were an effective weapon in the hands of the Résistance. The pen was another. A large number of writers worked with the Résistance, especially among the poets, whose craft demanded a concision and ellipsis that were very useful to them in a time of strict censorship. They were often involved in composing, printing, and distributing Résistance tracts and articles that could only be clandestinely put together. In May 1941, Jean Paulhan was denounced for having a mimeograph machine in his home that he used to print up papers for a group of *résistants* most of whom were connected with the Musée de l'Homme. They formed one of the first cohesive resistance units and included, among others, anthropologist Germaine Tillion, who though not directly affiliated with the museum staff had maintained contacts with its members. They worked under the direction of Boris Vildé, a Russian naturalized in France, who was on the museum staff. Paulhan was visited by four men who arrived at his door one afternoon. Without any form of greeting or introduction they demanded to see the machine which Paulhan had already had the good sense to remove from the house. A thorough search revealed nothing, but Paulhan was ordered to accompany the men by car to the rue des Saussaies in the eighth *arrondissement* for interrogation. They asked him why he had visited Berlin where he had once gone to give a lecture, and why he no longer wrote for the *Nouvelle Revue Française*. He had been its editor since 1925 but had ceded that position to Drieu La Rochelle who was more willing to toe the German line. They wanted to know what his political opinions were, to which Paulhan replied that he had none; and what he thought of the Jewish question, to which he answered that he had never noticed that there were any Jews. Then the interrogator, a young student type, "genre Oxford," finally came around to questioning him about the mimeograph machine. Since he had denied ever having had one in his home, Paulhan had to stick to his line; to all accusations made by the second interrogator, a furiously barking captain, regarding the machine and the paper "Résistance" that he had printed for the group from the Musée de l'Homme, Paulhan answered negatively. With the assistance of a few friends he had broken the machine down into pieces some time ago and thrown them in the Seine, but the Germans had such good and serious proofs against him that Paulhan recalled feeling a bit stupid at denying everything. Often a person accused of a crime confessed, Paulhan decided, in order to regain an air of intelligence in his own eyes. But Paulhan swallowed his pride. Repeated questionings by the two interrogators and then a third yielded them no results, and after confining Paulhan for a week at Santé prison and then submitting him to a second interrogation, to his own amazement they released him.[6]

Most of the writing community held out against the Germans, but they did so in varying degrees and with important exceptions. In that part of his study in *The Left Bank* (1982) dealing with the Occupation, Herbert Lottman makes the point that one might conclude from the memoirs of the period, "that nearly everyone in Paris resisted the Germans during the occupation. But it is also possible to make the case that 'everybody collaborated.' "[7] Much depends, of course, on what one means by resistance and collaboration. In retrospect, once the war was over, the French public by and large wanted its writers to have resisted. Whether the public had the right to expect its writers to be more heroic than it was itself for the most part, is an open question. At any rate, the writers often wanted to oblige. They were public figures and they frequently tried to put on a good image. It is not the purpose of this study to draw up a detailed inventory. Among the most noted writers working for the Résistance, however, were communists Louis Aragon and Paul Eluard who wrote actively for it; Albert Camus who joined Combat, one of the several often rival underground Résistance movements and which gave birth to the paper *Combat;* and André Malraux who eventually became a Résistance officer, though it appears to have taken him some time to make up his mind to leave the Côte d'Azur and join the fray again. Others, not necessarily any less committed either emotionally or intellectually, deemed it wise to lie low. Out of principle Jean Guéhenno refused to publish during the Occupation, though he did write for the Résistance and had a small portion of his di-

ary of the Occupation years published clandestinely in August
1944 under the title *Dans la prison*. Sartre, too, contributed to
the underground press, but he, Simone de Beauvoir, and Jean
Anouilh continued to write: their works were published or their
plays produced. Still others like Gide and Martin du Gard, no
longer young when war was declared, while they clearly re-
sented the German presence in France, preferred not to become too involved in political thinking and retired from the
literary scene, even though Gide had allowed Drieu La Rochelle to publish some excerpts from his *Journal* in the December 1, 1940, issue of the *Nouvelle Revue Française*. Martin du
Gard went to the south of France, and Gide who was in the
south when France was invaded, stayed there until May 1942
and then went to North Africa. Henry de Montherlant remained indifferent to the Occupation, and even allowed some
of his early manuscripts and pictures, taken at different stages
in his life, to be placed on exhibit in the windows of the German bookstore, Rive Gauche, on the Boulevard Saint-Michel.
The whole display was destroyed by grenade explosions one
night in November 1941.[8] Finally there were those who openly
supported the Germans and their objectives, or at least gave
the appearance of supporting them, in part if not in full; among
these were pacifist Jean Giono, arrested for a brief period in
the fall of 1939 on grounds of spreading violent anti-war tracts
at the time of the general mobilization, and especially Céline,
whose anti-Semitic diatribes published before and during the
war verged on hysteria.

Joining the Résistance

Working for the Résistance, even if it only meant transmitting
messages, often forced people into a rather lonely life. Typically, the tasks might involve an individual's working or traveling on his own to obtain or transport secret documents, and
each individual was allowed to know only that part of a mission
that actually concerned him. He remained ignorant of the details of the larger operation with which his mission was connected. The entire organization was based on the assumption
that a person does not know what he might reveal under tor-

ture, and so it was considered best to give him as little information as possible. Résistance personnel worked under code
names. André Malraux, for example, was known as Berger, a
name he borrowed from the hero of *Les Noyers de l'Altenburg.* If
a *résistant* was captured and then released, Résistance security
regulations insisted on breaking with him.[9] And if a *résistant*
were captured and sent to Fresnes, which was to political detainees what Drancy was to the Jews, he could not be allowed to
become a source of worry and concern to the others, for the
fight had to go on. Roger Vailland's Marat, the Résistance saboteur in *Drôle de jeu,* acknowledges the isolation and solitude of
the Résistance, describing it as "une longue promenade soli-
taire."[10] But at the same time it provided a community in which
an interchange with other people and a sense of belonging were
possible. *Un Jeune Homme seul* (1951), another *roman résistancialiste* by Vailland, centers around Eugène-Marie Favart, a railway
engineer for the SNCF, the French national railroad. Despite
his work and his marriage, Favart has led a life of isolation
until one day in 1943 a Vichy-appointed inspector comes to the
town in eastern France not far south of the demarcation line
where Eugène-Marie heads a railway depot. The inspector is
on the scene to conduct an inquest into the death of a railway
mechanic, Pierre Madru, who was a friend of Eugène-Marie
and whom he knows to have been a saboteur for the Résistance. Eugène-Marie refuses to denounce his dead friend and
in so doing, for the first time in his life seems to have found a
means to integrate himself into a community. Never before has
he felt such happiness at being alive,[11] even though he eventually pays for his happiness by arrest and imprisonment.

In her "Préface à la clandestinité" introducing the collection
Le Premier Accroc coûte deux cents francs, Elsa Triolet observes
that the Résistance consisted of ordinary people: they became
heads of the *maquis* or armed Résistance units, they became liaison agents, they gave shelter to more active *résistants,* carried
packages, hid arms, took up arms, allowed themselves to be
tortured without flinching, and even went to their deaths.[12] In
"Les Amants d'Avignon" (1943) they function as "letter boxes"
(*boîtes aux lettres*), transmitting and receiving information that
the Résistance fighters had to communicate daily to one an-

other about orders, arrests, acts of sabotage past or future, about
the discovery of an informer, the activities of the Gestapo, or
even the smuggling of clandestine literature.[13] The *boîtes aux
lettres* operated all over France but particularly in Lyon which
became the capital of the Résistance and the center of its activity and where the numerous *traboules* or narrow corridors leading to inner courtyards[14] favored resistance work and provided
a measure of safety and a means of escape.

They were, it occurs to Marat one day after he comes across
a dual-language edition in French and Greek of Xenophon's
Anabasis, very much like the Ten Thousand marching to the
sea. Like Xenophon's Greeks in Persia the *résistants* were isolated in what was for all practical purposes an enemy country,
they were lacking in everything and surrounded everywhere by
an adversary who was infinitely superior to them in numbers
and arms. As with the Ten Thousand, there were all kinds in
the Résistance: heroes with integrity and those of a more mercenary nature, kind men and bitter men now working side by
side for reasons that once would have set them apart. One of
Marat's colleagues, Caracalla, for example, joins because he is
a nationalist; another, Rodrigue, because he is a communist.
But among them all "there is a common spirit: the firm will
'not to seek above all to save our lives,' not to bow before the
stronger, not to give in to a contrary destiny, not to BECOME
RESIGNED, the will TO RESIST."[15]

But it was not the will to resist that drew everyone to the
Résistance. One of the soldiers in Roger Nimier's *Le Hussard
bleu* (1950), who also appears in *Les Epées,* is the brash and cynical François Sanders who without flinching joins both the Résistance and the Milice. He gives a quick review of his pied
career. Disappointed by the French defeat in 1940, he remained in a prisoner-of-war camp until some *imbéciles* set up
clandestine radio units.

> What a bore! I escaped during the following week. Then
> through lack of imagination, I enrolled in the Résistance. One
> year later, my comrades made me join the Milice to prepare a
> political assassination. They had warned me, they had told me
> that it would be a difficult ordeal. But I found energetic guys, full
> of muscle and ideal. The English were going to win the war. Navy

blue goes well with my complexion. Traveling forms young people. Well, I stayed.

Categorically Sanders decides that the battle of France was "idiotic," the Résistance "half crazy," and the Milice "evil."[16] All of this he only alludes to in *Le Hussard bleu* but develops more fully in the earlier *Les Epées* where his is the major narrative voice. In both books that voice displays the same indifference, verging on cockiness. He joins the Milice in earnest only after putting on its snappy navy blue uniform with the large beret that gave the wearer a hard jaw and a rather dense expression. After the war someone says to him that the Milice was made up of men who were failures in life, men "who had nothing between their legs." According to Sanders himself they came mostly from the occupied zone: "young men of good families breaking their ideals, fascist tubercular workers, Bretons with a taste for insurgency and a few former offenders against the law—the salt of the earth . . . ." There were a few who defended Pétain and called him *le vieux,* while others appended the word *con.* There were those who were already dreaming of killing while others were still thinking only of repression. Sanders claims to have allied himself quickly with those who called things by their real name and recalls that during the winter of 1943 the Milice became indebted to him for a new epithet that thenceforth surrounded the name of Pétain: *le vieux cul.* After the war when an uncle insists that Sanders's father had died of sorrow upon learning that his son had joined the Milice, Sanders, always a crass realist, retorts that his father had died only after that fact became generally known and prevented him from becoming a general in the army. Around Christmas 1943, at one of the last Résistance meetings he attended before passing over to the Milice, Sanders already feels constraint. For some time he has been involved with the Milice on behalf of the Résistance plotters and his fellow *résistants* look at his blue uniform first with curiosity, then with hostility. For them he would be a hero only after his head had been separated from his body by an axe. That was what made heroes. But he held no grudges. For three months he had been considered the killer in his Résistance group and had not even soiled his hands, so he could understand the hostility of his colleagues.[17]

François Sanders is the portrait of a young man unable to decide in the end whether he was primarily a *résistant*, a *milicien*, or a *résistant* disguised as a *milicien*. He had been all three. Certainly not a very idealistic sketch for those who would seek only idealism in the ranks of the Résistance!

André Malraux wrote in his *Antimémoires* that the Résistance never really achieved a political identity. For those who joined as a sign of their active opposition to the German presence the choice lay essentially between General de Gaulle and the communists.[18] In *Drôle de jeu* Marat is attracted to the ideas of de Gaulle, while his colleague Rodrigue is taken with those of the communists.[19] It is somewhat more difficult to determine the exact orientation of Frédéric, a friend of Rodrigue's, who joins first the communists and then the Résistance in the way others might enter a cloister: to save their souls. The commitments of some of the book's characters are at times ill-defined; they play games with one another and perhaps even with themselves, but to one degree or another all are involved in the more danger-ous "game" of the Résistance and that is a serious matter how-ever one looks at it.

Some like Léon Lécuyer in *Au bon beurre* became involved in the Résistance quite by accident. Léon is asked by an acquaint-ance in Lyon if he would be willing from time to time to carry a heavy valise by train to Grenoble, Montpellier, or Toulouse. He never knows what is in those suitcases; but, dreamer that he is, he hopes they might be filled with arms.[20] Others sym-pathized with the Résistance in the abstract but did nothing to affiliate themselves with it. The thirty-three-year-old artist Al-exis Slavsky in Elsa Triolet's "La Vie privée," having fled his Paris studio after escaping from a POW camp because, though born in France, he had a Polish name and one of his grand-mothers was Jewish, is too indolent to take advantage of the coincidences and opportunities that life offers. He certainly wants the Germans to leave but does nothing to hasten their departure. Instead he and his friend Henriette remain frus-trated and complaining, first in Lyon, then in the countryside near Lyon, Alexis claiming that he does not know what to do or how to resist. That Lyon was also the center of the Résistance seems to have ecaped them.[21]

A different figure altogether, Francis de Balansun in *Les Forêts de la nuit,* takes to the Résistance quite naturally. One day by sheer chance he meets a man who identifies himself as Lorrain and who wants to cross the demarcation line. Francis knows the territory well and takes Lorrain across. By the time the Germans occupy the two zones of France after November 1942, Francis has met quite a few *résistants* in this way, and one of the local Résistance leaders, Darricade, confides to his care a number of special missions to Bordeaux, Pau, and Bayonne.[22]

One of the greatest incentives inducing young men to join the Résistance was a practical one. After having worked to death many of its laborers from Russia and Poland, Germany began by 1942 to look to the west for imported labor. In March of that year Fritz Sauckel, an early Nazi and former Gauleiter of Thuringia, was appointed to coordinate the deployment of all foreign labor in the Third Reich. In June Sauckel came to France and told Pierre Laval, who replaced Admiral Darlan on April 26 and was heading the Vichy government under Pétain, either to increase French volunteers for labor in Germany or accept a labor conscription. At this point Laval proposed what came to be known as the *relève,* a system whereby one French prisoner of war in Germany would be released for every three French workers who volunteered to go and work there. Sauckel telephoned Hitler, and the Führer accepted the proposal. Temporarily at least, Laval had won a propaganda victory, and he went in person to Compiègne on August 11 to greet the first trainload of returning prisoners of war. In practical terms the *relève* may have been doomed from the start. Laval and Sauckel agreed on June 15 that France would supply Germany with 400,000 workers of whom 150,000 would have special skills. But since the *relève* applied to skilled workers only, for the 50,000 POWs scheduled to be freed according to the system, France would, in effect, be delivering eight times as many volunteer workers. Furthermore, most of the men returning from Germany were farmers. From the long range economic point of view, the exchange of skilled laborers for farmhands was of doubtful merit.

Throughout that fall the Pétain government sought frantically to encourage volunteers for Germany by supplying names and addresses of specialists to the proper authorities, providing for the closing of shops deemed to be inefficient, and extending the work week. The *relève* started off slowly with only 19,000 skilled workers signed up by early October, but by late November the figure jumped to a total of 181,000, and of these 90,000 were specialists.

When Sauckel revised his quotas and demanded another 500,000 workers from France in January 1943, the *relève* could not handle the task. In February the notorious Service du Travail Obligatoire, the STO, was established, and it began conscripting entire age groups for forced labor in Germany.[23]

Because of the labor conscription, Alexis Slavsky, totally naïve and unsuspecting, receives a surprise visit one night when he is alone in the country home he and Henriette have rented. He is shattered at the thought that journalist Louise Delfort, a personal acquaintance, has allowed herself to be taken into custody in Lyon, and he has just finished reading some material she had once written. Suddenly it gets "like the movies": a young man, soaking wet from the rain and bleeding to boot, is standing in the doorway, begging to be let in. He has jumped from a train organized by the *relève* that would have carried him off to Germany. His name is Jean, he is from Saint-Etienne, he is twenty, and he hasn't eaten since the day before when he jumped from the train against the advice of his comrades. He has 200 francs and is determined somehow to manage. Alexis pulls together a meal, and the boy begins trying to ascertain his situation. Are there any Germans in the area? Typically, Alexis is unable to provide answers. One day he saw a boy of twenty flanked by two Germans, that is all he knows. When Jean tells him that he would like to join the *maquis* and Alexis does not know what the *maquis* is, the boy becomes suspicious. But his fears are soon allayed. Alexis doesn't know what the *maquis* is just as he doesn't know how to light the Dutch oven in the kitchen, but he can be trusted. Before the word became synonymous with the Résistance itself, the *maquis* was a relatively inaccessible place where men such as those from the *relève* went to hide. It was an island of resistance where, as if they were partisans, men went to prepare for guerilla activities. They were given officers and taught to use weapons. All of this, of course, is news to poor Alexis, and so is the fact that the local gendarmes can be quite useful in placing a young man seeking to join the Résistance, as he learns from another source the very next day. And so, even if he never finds his way into the Résistance, Alexis does well by his guest whose unexpected arrival forces him, if only for a moment, out of his lethargy.[24]

Pétain or the Résistance

The truth is that during much of the Occupation the Résistance did not stir the majority of the French. For the communists, certainly, it was a vehicle made to order for the advancement of their cause in the face of the Nazi enemy, and so they helped to form it and to influence its development. But for those who looked to de Gaulle and an Allied victory, support was often meager. Robert Paxton points out in *Vichy France* that after midsummer 1941 most Allied successes meant French losses. Even if the British abandonment of France at Dunkirk and the blowing up of the French fleet at Mers-el-Kébir could be forgiven, there was the British invasion of Syria in June 1941 and the loss of that area to French influence; the British blockade of French ports, which could be blamed in part for food shortages; after 1942 the British bombings near Paris and other northern cities with large numbers of civilian casualties. It was only after 1943 when all of France had been occupied and the STO began to function in earnest, drafting young men for work in German factories, that public opinion began to turn against the Pétain regime. To many, Vichy had implied an internal order which they wished to safeguard even at the cost of the Occupation. The Résistance, whether inspired by de Gaulle or by the communists, appeared as a threat to that order. Furthermore, writes Paxton, an "Allied victory could seem an even greater threat to social order than continued German occupation after 1942. Personal considerations aside, the promise of violent liberation at Allied hands held more risks than advantages." Allied invasion meant a return to war and perhaps to another bloodbath on French soil such as the one that had taken place during World War I. Moreover, an Allied invasion might trigger a rising of the Résistance which, thanks to its communist overtones, "could seem directed more at the French social status quo in 1942–43 than against the German Army." Most of the French may have wished to be out from under the yoke of Germany but not if they had to pay for it at the price of a revolution: "the overwhelming majority of Frenchmen, however they longed to lift the German yoke, did not want to lift it by fire and sword."[25]

Madame Loiseau, from whom Alexis Slavsky and Henriette rent their rooms in a village on the Rhône about one hour from Lyon, is fairly typical of the average well-intentioned French bourgeois. She speaks with emotion of Marshal Pétain and regards it as a crime for ordinary citizens to try to make him out to be a liar. He has accepted the conditions of the Armistice for France, and now it is up to the French to obey. People who made assaults against the Germans were revolutionaries, and one would do well to rid the country of them. As for the *relève,* she follows Laval in complete trust: the government is acting for the good of France, and since a promise had been made, France must keep her word so that a few of "our poor prisoners" will be relieved. In regard to the Germans whom she readily but harmlessly refers to as the Boches, Madame Loiseau's opinions are quite conventional, echoing what Vichy has been telling its people from the start, that this is not the time to fall out with them. France has been conquered and will do well to remain quiet and calm. In fact, France should try to get along with the Boches; in that way there will be no more war and otherwise it will never end.[26]

Probably thinking of people like Madame Loiseau in his preface to the *Journal des années noires,* Guéhenno described what he called Pétain's "crime" as having made "for a whole people a temptation out of dishonor. There is no worse crime against man than to tempt him in his baseness and his cowardice. But especially there is no worse crime against young men. I saw them struggle with themselves in the shame that was being proposed to them."[27] In a similar vein Vercors felt his heart "swell with disgust" at the thought of the men who were supposed to be leading France.[28] Yet so many people seem to have felt neither shame nor disgust before the Pétain government but rather believed that, despite all appearances, Pétain had saved France. "On est vaincu," the Marshal said, and like Madame Loiseau, Madame Poissonard in *Au bon beurre* almost takes delight in quoting him: "we are conquered." From the conquest of France, the Poissonards learn two great lessons that constitute the core of what Jean Dutourd with tongue in cheek calls the "doctrine poissonardienne": first of all, France had in some way merited its woes," and second, the time had come to pull in one's belt. People like Julie Poissonard were perhaps unaware that they had become propaganda agents for the Pétain regime, echoing in their own way the rhetoric of Vichy: the French people had lived too well in the last twenty years; to think that the wives of ordinary workers would go to market and ask for chicken, and the best pieces at that; and the Jews and freemasons had not helped matters; why didn't they stay where they belonged instead of eating our provisions and robbing our money? they didn't go off to the army! the day had come when France must pay for the errors of her ways.[29]

Men in the Résistance unit of Jacques Perret's *Bande à part* (1951) might laugh when one of their number began to hum the melody in honor of Pétain that had become popular in France, "Maréchal, nous voilà," or with a talent for mimicry, imitate the voice of Pétain introducing himself as the "old Marshal" on the radio: "Français ... c'est votre vieux Maréchal ..."[30] But people like the Poissonards did not take such matters lightly and did not joke when they spoke of the Marshal. According to Charles-Hubert Poissonard, the Marshal was the shrewdest of all parties in the war. He was allowing the Germans and the English to play out their hostilities while permitting France to stand aside and profit from their struggle. There was grumbling that the Germans had shot some people, but those people should simply have remained quiet. They deserved what they got for bringing problems on others.[31]

By the summer of 1942 the Poissonards, by supplying a nearby German *Soldatenheim* with food, have sufficiently good connections to obtain an *Ausweiss* enabling them to travel to the free zone with their two children. Since the idea of spending a whole month away from the Bon Beurre without any income is almost intolerable to Julie, she compensates by calculating that as long as they are going south, it might be in their business interest to pay a little visit to Marshal Pétain in Vichy. After all, according to the newspapers, he was welcoming everybody to come and see him. After an eighteen-hour train trip to Vichy the Poissonards are admitted to see Pétain in a general audience consisting of some boy scouts and a delegation of electricians. As it was customary to bring the old Marshal some small gift on these visits, the Poissonards have decided to bring him a dozen eggs from their dairy shop. Pétain appears delighted as he does by all the gifts of homage that are offered him, murmuring in stereotype a few verbal niceties to each group of donors. But he seems particularly pleased by the gift of particularly large French eggs laid especially for him by French chickens and brought to him by a French dairyman. The following week the Poissonards, wallowing in pride, reach the summit of their glory when in a weekly paper they read an article entitled "The Miracle of the Chickens," which Pétain's henchman, writer René Benjamin, has put together. In it he celebrates the visit of a French family and the large eggs they brought for the Marshal. Due to an error in his calculations, the visit turns out to be something of an ironic lesson for Charles-Hubert. Convinced because of his name that René Benjamin is Jewish, Charles-Hubert begins to stop making anti-Semitic observations. After all the Marshal is no fool, and if he is not too proud to have a Jew working at his side, who is Charles-Hubert to contradict him? Besides, "He writes awfully well, the Marshal's yid! . . . "[32]

As late as 1942 Count de Balansun in *Les Forêts de la nuit* still looks on Pétain as a savior, though before the end of the war he relegates a picture he owns of Pétain to the garbage heap. In the same book Madame Costellot admonishes her son Jacques, who is complaining about the sentimental tear-jerking spectacle (*comédie larmoyante*) that was unfolding around the old Marshal, that were it not for Pétain, Jacques might presently be in Hamburg or Kiel exposed to British and American bombs.[33] There were those to whom the spartan austerity of the image projected by Vichy in the slogan "Travail, Patrie, Famille," Work, Fatherland, Family, would always carry an appeal in the same way as the prohibition on *apéritif* wines that Pétain clapped on the liquor industry. As long as there were enough people sharing these opinions, people who held that France did not deserve so good a leader as Pétain and that de Gaulle was an enemy of France,[34] the Résistance could hardly be expected to get off the ground. In another of the many ironies of World War II, it was the Hitler regime itself rather than any home-grown idealism that, by instituting the STO, drove many young Frenchmen into the Résistance after 1943. Paxton provides some overall statistics. After the war, official veteran status was accorded to some 300,000 French for active service in the Résistance, of whom 130,000 had been deported and 170,000 were classified as "Resistance volunteers." With another 100,000 who had lost their lives in Résistance activity, the total active participation in the Résistance as it was officially recognized at that time, amounted at its peak to only about 2 percent of the adult population.[35] As such things go, of course, that percentage is far from negligible. The ordinary citizen is not necessarily cut out to be a hero. Perhaps one has no right to expect him to be.

But there were others like Saint-Exupéry, who fought in 1940 when it seemed useless and senseless to fight, or even like André Malraux. When Malraux was captured in 1944, attired in full dress uniform—at a time, to be sure, when the Résistance was firmly established and the tide had clearly turned against the Germans—he was interrogated by an officer of the Wehrmacht as to why he did not respect the armistice signed by Pétain. He answered bluntly: Pétain did not speak for France.

Unlike the majority of French prisoners of war, Malraux never went to Germany after the debacle in June 1940. Though still a prisoner of war by the end of September, he had remained in France and was seriously thinking about getting out from under German surveillance. In October he made good his release and left for the south where he lived at Roquebrune east of Nice in the Riviera villa belonging to Gide's British translator, Dorothy Bussy.[36] It was only in the earlier part of 1944, long after the Germans had invaded the free zone and resistance had become little by little better organized that he joined the *maquis* in earnest. The facts of his arrest and the subsequent German inquest into his Résistance activities, recorded in the

Antimémoires, can be recapitulated briefly. On July 22, 1944, a car sprouting the Cross of Lorraine pennant and carrying the uniformed Malraux entered the town of Gramat in the *département du Lot* in southwestern France. There it met tanks of the infamous SS *Das Reich* division, one of whose detachments had brutally massacred 642 people on June 10, 1944, in the town of Oradour-sur-Glane[37] near Limoges in a setup not entirely unlike that of Zuckmayer's play *Der Gesang im Feuerofen.* In the shooting that ensued, Malraux was slightly wounded in the leg, taken prisoner, and soon placed before a firing squad. The presence of the firing squad, however, was only a tactic to unnerve the prisoner. The Germans put on a mock execution, and then, identified in his papers as Berger, the name of the hero of *Les Noyers de l'Altenburg* that he adopted as an alias in the Résistance, Malraux was taken to the Hôtel de France in Gramat for interrogation. From here he was moved with stops along the way at Figeac, Villefranche-de-Rouergue, Albi, and Revel to the Gestapo prison in Toulouse and further interrogation. He remained there until mid-August when, with the departure of the Germans and the liberation of the city, he was released.

The text of the *Antimémoires* describing his ordeal is relatively straightforward and almost devoid of the metaphors, images, and other literary devices that normally enrich his text. Malraux seems really to have believed that he was going to be put to death by the Germans, even after the experience of the mock execution squad; but typically, he speaks in rather detached philosophical tones: "dying seemed banal to me. What interested me was death." Even as he stood before the firing squad he claims to have managed an existentialist sense of detachment despite what seemed like the irremediable fact that his life was soon going to be over.

In the course of describing the period of his capture and successive interrogations by Wehrmacht and Gestapo authorities, Malraux provides some of his most unflattering portraits of the Germans. He also indulges in some of the relatively few metaphors "gracing" this part of the *Antimémoires:* "The clerk, with his protruding chin and forehead, looked like a haricot bean; the interrogator like a sparrow—nose in the air, little round mouth." There are also occasional glimpses of German atrocity: the unrecognizable features of a man beaten to a pulp at Gestapo headquarters; two other men, their hands tied to their feet while they are being kicked; and still another man who in rather vague terms recounts his ordeal during the so-called bath torture when he had expected to be drowned like a rat in a tub "full of puke and all that." The reader never witnesses the torture scenes directly; they are narrated in retrospect or seen in passing and through open doorways. Malraux's almost classical restraint in speaking of Nazi torture can certainly be attributed to the limits imposed on a first-person narrator. Malraux can only describe what he himself witnessed, and he witnessed no more than he describes.[38] And yet he shows precisely the same restraint in dealing with Nazi torture in *Le Temps du mépris* where the use of an omniscient third-person narrator would have allowed him a broader field of vision. There the structure of a *récit*-like novel may have imposed certain constraints, but the argument can be made that Malraux himself chose the structure.

What clearly interested Malraux was not torture in itself nor even the state of mind of the torturer, but rather what torture could do to the spiritual state of a human being. He saw Nazism as something quite different from Italian fascism or Russian communism. Nazism attempted to rob a man of his soul.[39] The concentration and extermination camps were visible proof. Malraux arrived at this assessment long before standing in front of the Wehrmacht interrogator in Gramat or the Gestapo interrogator in Toulouse. During these interrogations he was conscious of playing a kind of game with them, the outcome of which might be his execution or deportation to Germany. But more important to him than the eventual outcome was the necessity to remain a man. In a sense that was why he and his comrades in the Résistance had chosen to fight against odds they knew in advance were overwhelming. That the Résistance was composed of all sorts of people Malraux was perfectly well aware. He could not disagree with the observation of the Wehrmacht interrogator that some young men had joined the Résistance merely to avoid labor conscription in Germany. But there was more to the Résistance than that. Those who were serving in its ranks "are only a handful compared with the Wehrmacht. It is *for that reason* that they exist. In 1940 France suffered one of the most appalling defeats in her history. Those who are fighting you are guarantors of her survival. Victors, vanquished, shot, or tortured." [40] Like Saint-Exupéry flying a perfectly useless flight to Arras and expecting possibly to die on his mission, Malraux saw the Résistance fighting in order that France might be saved. More important than the political entity was, just as it had been for Saint-Exupéry, the cluster of ideas and traditions that had gone into the making of France and the concept of man that had evolved through centuries of French civilization.

On February 4, 1944, Jean Anouilh's *Antigone* premiered in the Théâtre de l'Atelier. It presented on stage, for all of Paris to see, a resistance drama similar in its uncompromising fortitude to the heroism that Malraux and Saint-Exupéry exacted of themselves. That Anouilh cloaked his play in the guise of Greek mythology in no way hid the intimate drama involving every member of the audience, but it enabled *Antigone* to pass the German censorship. As in the Greek legend, Antigone knows that she must bury the body of her dead brother Polynices to whom their uncle Créon, now king of Thebes, has refused burial. Religious prescriptions decreed that the bodies of the dead had to be covered by earth if their souls were to be freed to find peace in the next world. But the moral obligation to fulfill the religious ritual assuring the right of passage to the dead does not appear to be a motivating force in Antigone. She does not believe in the rites any more than Créon does. In attempting to get her to drop the whole matter, Créon makes it quite clear to Antigone that her brother was not only a rebel and a traitor but a worthless good-for-nothing. She responds weakly that he is still her brother, but at last she appears quite prepared to follow Créon's advice and return to her room. Créon, however, tries to push his advantage: Antigone is young, she is engaged to his own son Hémon, they have years of happiness before them. To think that she had almost squandered that little bit of happiness by insisting on performing an inconsequential ritual and courted the death sentence that Créon would legally have had to rule if it were publicly known that she had disobeyed his ordinance. The word happiness is the drop that makes the cup overflow. For Antigone it is the principle that counts and she lashes out at Créon. In accepting the kingship, Créon had given affirmation to the state with all its laws, regulations, and obligations that now he could neither refuse nor undo. But for her, happiness could never mean daily submission to forces she could no longer control simply because she had once refused to say no, refused to obey an order or to carry out what she perceived as an obligation to herself. Rather than endure a whole life of this kind of happiness, the happiness born of compromise, she prefers death.

Hers is the spirit of the medical doctor, Bernard Rieux, in Camus's *La Peste*, working against staggering odds with untiring determination in the face of a catastrophic epidemic that has taken hold of the city of Oran in Algeria. Oran may not be Paris and the plague may not be the German occupation, but there were points of comparison, and Camus intimated in a quotation set at the head of the book's first chapter and stated more explicitly in the fourth notebook of his *Carnets*, published in 1964, that the one might be used to represent the other.[41] By casting as an historical "chronicle," furthermore, an event which did not actually take place, namely, the massive outbreak of bubonic plague in Oran in the 1940s, the narrator invites us to look for an explanation. Those quarantined in Oran could not leave the city, nor could others enter it from outside. But though they were the victims of the plague, they need not acquiesce in its power, just as France need not, body, mind, and soul, acquiesce in the power of the German occupier, or just as on the metaphysical level man cannot allow himself to acquiesce in his destiny of death.

Many of the men and women of the Résistance were quite aware of the fact that alone they could not overthrow the Germans. In numbers and *matériel* they were no match for the Germans. But by their very existence they were a symbol of France, a sign that she had survived in spirit if not in body, a sign of her will to resist.

CHAPTER X

French Prisoners of War in Germany

The Logistics

In the occupied lands of western Europe, prisoners of war were initially gathered into large camps to be screened and processed by the Germans. Officers, enlisted men considered politically unreliable, and Jews were then separated from the others and sent to special camps in the occupied areas or in Germany itself, and the remainder, after promising not to bear arms against Germany, were released and sent home with the stipulation that they were to report to local police and labor offices once they arrived. This procedure was generally adhered to in dealing with Danes, Norwegians, Dutch, and Flemish-speaking Belgians. The French-speaking Belgians and the bulk of the French Army, however, met quite a different fate. They were sent off to Germany and put to work. Between early May and late June 1940, the Germans made prisoners of some 1,850,000 French servicemen, and at first detained the great majority of them in camps set up all over France but particularly in Alsace-Lorraine. In their own economic interest they then released some of the ill and wounded as well as a certain number who were engaged in agriculture or who held positions of public service in the railroads, electricity, or the PTT which administered the postal, telephone, and telegraph systems of the country. Those released, with a few who escaped from the camps, totalled about 200,000. Approximately 80,000 prisoners, many of whom were North Africans and blacks, remained in France in what were called *Front-Stalags,* and 75,000 soldiers from Alsace and Lorraine, who had become German citizens by virtue of annexation to the Reich, were released and sent home. Occasionally someone would be released for no apparent reason but for the beauty of the gesture itself. By the end of the summer of 1940, however, almost one and a half million men made the trip across the Rhine, and by the winter of 1940–1941 the number of French POWs in Germany reached a high point of 1,580,000. On the average they were under thirty years of age; one-third of them were farmers; workers in metallurgy, construction, transportation and management, together with miners and artisans formed another third; the rest consisted of employees, professionals, career servicemen, priests, and others who defied classification.[1]

In addition to providing a source of sorely needed manpower in Germany, the French POWs could be used by the Germans as hostages in dealing with the Pétain government and as an assurance of France's future cooperation. France was being weakened economically and demographically, writes Pierre Gascar in his *Histoire de la captivité des Français en Allemagne (1939–1945).* Furthermore, any resistance would be more difficult to mount in the absence of these prisoners who constituted the younger element of the population and were already trained in the military.

Once in Germany the POWs were assigned to one of fifty-six *Stammlager* or *Stalags* if they were ordinary rank and file soldiers or to one of fourteen *Offizierlager* or *Oflags* if they were officers. All these camps, created especially for the POWs, functioned as reception centers and administrative units and were under army control. Though there was a greater concentration of camps toward the center of Germany, they were scattered throughout the whole country including what was once Austria. Two of the camps were located in Alsace-Lorraine, one in Forbach, and one, a predominantly Polish camp, in Strasbourg. Two disciplinary camps were later created outside Germany proper, one near Cracow in Poland for noncommissioned officers refusing to work, and the other in eastern Galicia which had belonged to Poland between the two world wars, was occupied by Russia in 1939 and subsequently overrun by the

Germans, for those who had made repeated attempts to escape. Most of the camps were ready for the prisoners on their arrival, though in a few cases where the housing barracks were not yet completed, the prisoners temporarily slept in tents.[2] The *Stalag* served as a kind of home base, but after initial processing most POWs were actually quartered in a sub-camp known as a *Kommando* that was generally within walking distance of their place of work.

German employers who wanted POWs submitted requests to the local labor offices or, if they were in agriculture, to the local office of the Food Ministry. These local offices then negotiated directly with the German army but, until 1942, some employers attempted to bypass local labor offices and do their own negotiating. German industrialists were obliged to pay to the army wages equivalent to those of German employees, and the army then returned a small portion of this pay to the individual POW in the amount of about one mark per day. Employers in agriculture supplied room and board and a small cash wage to their POWs. Partly because of the complications involved, more of the POWs were sent into agriculture than into industry. Furthermore, until the second half of 1941, the army followed the Geneva convention stipulations forbidding the use of POWs in war-related industries.[3]

Reactions to Life in the POW Camps

When the French POWs arrived in Germany most of them had little idea of what to expect. As Jacques Perret points out in *Le Caporal épinglé*, his *roman-souvenir* or *roman-témoignage* about the POWS, they had not been prepared for the role they were being asked to assume. They had not been raised to be soldiers for the most part, and even less to be prisoners of war. Everybody may have a picture in his head of how a horseman should look capturing an enemy standard. But what about a ragged POW pushing away with his foot the enemy's cigarette butt? This is not one of the classic images and patterns of behavior that civilization projects, and as Perret says, one cannot train a soldier with the idea that he is *a priori* going to be made captive.[4]

Perret was initially processed at Luckenwalde south of Berlin. When Daladier was premier he had prophesied that the French would march on to Berlin, but he had certainly not foreseen this manner of arrival; and when one of the soldiers, with his "here we are, boys," reminds the others that they have fulfilled Daladier's prophesy, nobody particularly appreciates the irony. After seventy-two hours of "marination" in the box-cars, most of the soldiers are too numb even to know whether they are glad the trip is over. One of the first orders to greet them upon arrival at the station is for the surrender of the wooden canes that many of them had sculpted in the form of ivy branches or serpents during leisure hours in camp. The Germans seem to fear that these canes will serve as weapons. For Perret the surrender of the canes, piled up in a heap in front of a German audience present to witness the arrival of the French prisoners, remained one of the most humiliating experiences of his captivity.

> We really seemed to be throwing down our arms. The public enjoyed the spectacle in silence and that was more painful than a snarling crowd brandishing their fists and spitting on our footsteps. Less a crowd, moreover, than an attendance; they looked at us, attentive and silent, in no way hostile, rather stupefied. Decorated veterans considered us with a sort of affectionate pity, as paternal colleagues who well understood the miseries of the trade. A disabled veteran had had himself dragged into the first row in his wheel chair; no doubt he thought he had broadly merited such a place. He was licking his lips, surely; and I understand him, but he was also shaking his head kindly to show that such delights do not exclude feelings. If he rejoiced at seeing France defeated, he was willing to pity captive Frenchmen.

Very quickly the hearts of some of the French soldiers begin to melt, and a Norman boy expresses what many of them are feeling when he observes that after all, "the old people are not mean." But another soldier, called Pater, is more critical and not so ready to be taken in. "I remind you that their children . . . are gobbling up your chickens, sleeping in your bed and doing neither more nor less than their fathers did. Can't get away from it." The impulse toward fraternization is somewhat diminished, in any case, by the German children "who took aim at us without courtesy," using the canes they had chosen from the pile. "And the parents allowed them to do it."

Next comes the forced march through the streets of town. The citizens, who have seen tens of thousands of French and Polish prisoners pass through their streets, have not yet become blasé, but are less friendly and somewhat more severe looking than those who had come to the station. Perret does not particularly feel like looking at them and so contents himself with looking at the heads of his comrades walking in front of him. By the time of the narration, just a few years later, he has gained some distance from the experience and regrets his attitude. "Obviously I was wrong, one should take advantage of every occasion to inform oneself."[5]

The lack of a precise and established code of conduct for the prisoner of war allowed each man a certain latitude and each adapted in his own way. The prisoners are put through the same shower and delousing rituals that Remarque shows the Germans imposing on their own soldiers returning from the Russian front. To Perret this cleaning up is shameful and degrading, robbing the soldier of the last vestiges of a free warrior. Little zinc plates are then distributed, each inscribed with a number, which the prisoners are to wear around their necks night and day. Perret is given the number 24772 and finds that numbers paradoxically seem to carry a stronger guarantee of existence than names. "Everybody knows that between 24771 and 24773 there is 24772; it is a comforting necessity and I carry within me a kind of eternity." Should anyone be caught without his number there are "dire sanctions not to mention the moral disgrace represented by the even temporary loss of one's personality." Any possessions the prisoners had accumulated are to be surrendered and thrown onto a community pile, and these piles often look as though they have been put together with merchandise from a Monoprix, a French version of the five-and-ten-cent store. Pockets are turned inside out and some men are ordered to strip and then frisked. Since each is allowed one pipe, Perret keeps his, hides a 100 franc note inside it, and palms off two other pipes onto his comrades. Thus purified they are admitted into the world of German discipline:

bed at 7 PM, smoking, singing, and opening windows forbidden. All of these regulations and others are written on the doors in German, Polish, and French.[6]

In Michel Tournier's *Le Roi des aulnes*, Abel Tiffauges, another French soldier become prisoner of war, welcomes his entry onto German soil and the accompanying rites of purification. Upon arrival in Schweinfurt in northern Bavaria, after having made the trip packed sixty to a car in a rail transport from France, Tiffauges experiences a feeling quite different from Perret on being stripped, showered, and disinfected. Standing naked for hours in a field encircled by barbed wire, others weep with humiliation, but Tiffauges accepts this treatment as part of a ritual, sacred in character, that will purify him of his past and prepare him for his rendezvous with destiny. Instinctively he knows he must penetrate deeper and deeper into Germany; and in a book in which symbols retain a pristine and almost medieval vigor and integrity, the trip to Germany and all the way into East Prussia is a movement toward light, the morning light of the East. He has few regrets in having left behind him the darkness of France and the West. Once out on the plain east of Berlin, Tiffauges, who knows only Paris and the gentle, more intimate countryside around it, is seized with emotion at the vastness of this new land which gives him a feeling of freedom he has never known before.[7]

Tiffauges is quartered in a camp near the small village of Moorhof in East Prussia at a point not far north of what is now Poland's northern border with Russia and somewhat east of what was then Königsberg and is now Kaliningrad in the Soviet Union. He and the other French prisoners at Moorhof are given twenty-four hours to rest from their journey and then informed that they will be spending their days constructing an immense drainage system to service the fields of the area. The insufficiency of materials would be compensated for by abundant and economical manpower. Morning begins at six, when they are given a kind of tea made from mulberry leaves, pine, birch, and alder, and which is known as *Waldtee*. This is accompanied by a slice of bread and a handful of boiled potatoes to get them through the day. Upon their return from work at night, they are fed a clear soup which at least has the merit of being hot. Most of the POWs are put to work digging trenches with spades while the construction of gutters and all technical aspects of the job are confided to German workers. The reactions of the French vary, but for the first time since his arrest at Neuilly on charges of rape just before the outbreak of the war, Abel Tiffauges feels that he belongs somewhere and enjoys the sense of security born of that feeling.

The enforced promiscuity of life in the camp barracks brought the French prisoners into close contact with people of different social, geographic, and professional backgrounds. With the customary supports of family and country removed, some experienced an unexpected freedom to be themselves and to do whatever they wanted within the limits of their situation. Others simply regressed to a state of animal-like brooding and silence. One man in *Le Roi des aulnes* named Mimile decides almost immediately to try to give full reign to his double passion for women and money. He had married too young, says author-narrator Tournier, a woman who was too virtuous, and is determined to take advantage of his stay in Germany to find a German mistress who will be a protectress for him and through whom he will one day be able to buy a house, goods, and property. Since virtually all German men had been mobilized, the French prisoners might step in and very conveniently take their place. Another prisoner named Phiphi is convinced, on the other hand, that only a French woman, and more particularly a Parisian woman, is worth his interest, and he rejects all the "Gretchens" he has thus far seen, with their plaited hair and woolen stockings. Still another man, Socrate, organizes a series of conferences on the history of literature. Soon Mimile begins putting on mysterious airs whenever the others tease him about his relations with the carpenter's wife on whose property he goes to work every day. But the day they discover Phiphi hanging from his belt on one of the fence posts of the camp, a feeling of panic spreads among them. His suicide seems to augur badly for the future.

Abel Tiffauges adapts only too well. He digs with such vigor at the Prussian soil on which the prisoners are constructing the drainage canals that his comrades begin to resent him. But Tiffauges is living more on a symbolic than on a realistic plane.

He is expecting something from this country, some sign or omen. Digging into its soil seems a way of hastening the arrival of that message. He is beginning to love this country and to learn its language, a country whose wintry landscape is dominated by the colors black and white, like a white page covered with black signs. The signs are symbols and the symbols the ultimate reality that he will have to learn to decipher and interpret. He feels himself a part of the Prussian earth and is happy now to serve it body and soul, certain that he will one day become its master.[8]

One of the stranger cases of a French POW in Germany is that of the ever naïve and bungling Léon Lécuyer in *Au bon beurre,* a young second-lieutenant who generally seems to have had more luck than intelligence. Lécuyer is quartered in an *Oflag* or officer's camp in Pomerania and with the arrival of the first spell of cold weather he begins thinking of a way to escape. He likes neither the cold nor the indignity he feels as a result of the captivity, and is further displeased when his companions start calling him Lélé after he grows a beard that does not suit him. The only captives that history, literature, and the movies bring to his mind are the likes of Napoleon on the island of Elba or the Count of Monte-Cristo, and though the situation of a French POW in Germany in 1940 had little in common with either, Léon looks to them as models. His captain, aware of Léon's romantic inability to separate life from art, reminds him that they are not in the movies and that the duty of a prisoner is to remain a prisoner. Life is good at the *Oflag,* there is time to study in peace, and everybody is getting packages from home. Furthermore, should Léon attempt to escape, his friends and comrades would be punished for a whole month and denied receipt of their packages. Léon had felt that it was a prisoner's duty to try to escape, but the words of the captain make him hesitate.

One night, however, Léon gets up around twelve, seized with the desire to walk a bit. Since the Germans permit the prisoners to come out of their barracks at night to use the toilet facilities, he runs little danger. Stumbling suddenly on some barbed wire fencing he becomes curious to know what might be enclosed behind it; and too dim-witted to realize that what is enclosed is the camp itself and he, inside it, on this side of the wire, he stretches it a bit to make an opening and passes through. After he has walked around a bit, it dawns on him that he has escaped. He is not about to go back. Within a week he manages to reach Hamburg where he dreams of strangling a German officer at night, putting on his uniform, keeping his revolver, and casting the body into the sea. As he is dreaming in this vein he perceives a rather large woman smiling at him in the street and immediately imagines himself flirting with a Valkyrie. He and the Valkyrie reach a studio apartment and finish their first kiss, before Léon decides to ask her name. The Valkyrie speaks French and guesses almost right away that Léon is an escaped prisoner, and so the surprise is entirely Léon's when she reveals herself to be Helmuth Krakenholz, first lieutenant in the Luftwaffe. Throughout this section of the novel Dutourd persists in calling Léon Lélé, and the name befits him in his predicament. Again he has not been very alert. But he is determined to make the best of a bad situation. And so, while Helmuth is preparing a tea which Lélé requests, Lélé manages to attack him, tie him up in his own sheets, and leave him moaning under the sofa. Helmuth has told Lélé of his friend in Bayonne, Major Odemar von Pabst, who every second day sends him six-page letters and a pair of silk stockings. On leaving, Léon takes along thirty pairs of stockings to exchange for money while en route, and seventy-two pages of affectionate feelings recorded in Gothic script, which may lend credence to whatever story he is called upon to fabricate on the perilous road to France. In spite of himself, Léon makes good his escape, succeeding where others, far brighter than he, fail. But his story in the novel is of secondary importance to that of the Poissonards, and in one six-line paragraph Dutourd disposes of what the reader must assume to have been an uneventful trek across Holland, Belgium, and northern France, ending with Léon's arrival at his mother's apartment in Paris in October 1940.[9]

Living with the Germans

From their initial reception center at Luckenwalde, Perret and some 900 other French POWs are transferred to a camp in the

Berlin suburb of Friedrichsfelde. Whether they spend their day working on the Reichsbahn, the German national railroad, or cutting down fir trees, or making repairs on the streets and sidewalks of Berlin, or performing unspecified jobs in local factories, they look upon their return to camp in the evening as a return to the village where each of them has his home. Here the activities of an imitation family life unfold. Family-like quarrels erupt between those who want their windows open at night and those who want them closed. Perret wants them open, and since he claims the majority of Frenchmen do not, he is out of luck. At camp the prisoners receive supplementary clothing, usually an eclectic collection of bits and pieces of uniforms taken from conquered armies in all parts of Europe. Perret, always suspicious of German intentions and suspecting that perhaps this was merely an attempt to humiliate the French army and dress them up as "soldiers of some black republic," refuses all distributions except for a shirt which might have been of Greek or Croatian origin. At camp, too, the prisoners do their wash; and in the winter they often hang out wet clothing to freeze for several days, thereby killing the lice that have taken up residence in the cloth. They leave their beds unmade if they wish or sing rounds of *Auprès de ma blonde*, at least until the Germans begin to sense sedition in their enthusiasm. There is a theater for which Perret writes a play and on Sundays the theater area substitutes as a church. Unfortunately the French priest who reads the Mass is an uninspiring preacher, and only one-seventh of the prisoners ever attend services. Prisoners were permitted to receive food packages from France both from their families and from the Vichy government which sent parcels that became known as the *colis Pétain* or Pétain packages. But if any correspondence was discovered within, the package would be confiscated, as Perret learns when a German Feldwebel spots a letter rolled up like a tube and hidden in a cake his wife had baked for him. The whole package is returned to him minus the letter about a month later. The cake had lost some of its moisture, but under a butter crock Perret finds another letter that had not been detected. In addition to packages from his wife he receives cards from his mother but apparently derives little joy from them, for they only reiterate the words of patience and confidence she had written to his father in the last war and to his older brother who had been killed on the Somme.[10]

Some POWs received letters of love and encouragement from their wives or girlfriends. Other letters, recalls Francis Ambrière in his account of the POW camps in *Les Grandes Vacances* (1956), were so graphic and crude they drew long commentaries from the German censors. Some letters simply informed a POW that a friendship or a marriage was over, and one man mentioned by Ambrière even received a letter from his wife telling him matter-of-factly that his children had adapted well to their new father.[11]

On the whole there was little fraternization with German camp personnel despite appeals for cooperation by the weekly newspaper *Trait d'Union* which was published in Berlin exclusively for the French POWs and distributed to them free of charge. But the Germans attempted to make their POWs more malleable through the use of what they thought was good psychology. Soon after their arrival in Germany Perret and his comrades are reminded of the noble traditions of the French army which are theirs to uphold. Words of this kind, however, do not seem to touch their sense of self-respect and provoke only laughter.[12] Later at Friedrichsfelde some representatives from the propaganda office come to the camp on Sunday to take pictures for the newspapers and make a filmstrip for the movie houses of Europe showing the happy, healthy, and sporty life of the camps. The prisoners are to be filmed at Sunday recreation. When the cameras are in position a sentry brings out a ball for them to play with, and an interpreter translates the order: Break ranks and play! But as Perret accurately concludes, there is no power in this world that can make children play when they don't want to. The men rush back to their barracks, and when they are ordered out to play a second time, merely stand around with their hands in their pockets showing none of the enthusiasm the photographers have come to capture. The only smile that finally appears on the pictures is that of a prisoner just emerging from the toilets with a satisfied grin on his face. For two successive Sundays the men are deprived of their ball, and henceforth all notices of sporting events at

Friedrichsfelde begin with the words "La Joie par la Force,"[13] "Joy through Force," a deliberate inversion of the famous slogan of the German *Kraft durch Freude* association that organized social, sport, and recreational activity in the Reich.

Too many of the Germans, Perret discovered, believed that it was somehow their mission to save Europe. They had to be serious because they had a job to do and their role demanded it. Sometimes they may even have envied the French who had the leisure, they believed, to indulge in liquor and women. They wrapped up this perception in the formula "Pariss-Kôniak-Madam," and in order not to disappoint one guard who offers him some bread and margarine after his return to Berlin from an aborted escape attempt, Perret spreads the tale that in civilian life he consumed a liter of alcohol per day and never spent a whole night with the same woman. This appears to coincide perfectly with the German's opinion of the average Frenchman. What a pity there is a war on![14]

When the prisoners from Perret's compound go to work in Berlin, they catch the S-Bahn, an elevated extension of the U-Bahn or subway, at the Friedrichsfelde station one kilometer from camp. There is always a compartment reserved for the POWs and clearly marked "Nur für Kriegsgefangenen." If, as happens on occasion, civilians mistakenly enter their compartment, the civilians are unceremoniously ushered out by the German sentry who has a tendency to scorn civilians to the benefit of the prisoners and is always willing to take their side if a conflict arises. The subway ride, especially in the evening when the day's work was done, reminds many of the men of the Paris Métro during rush hour, and sometimes they can almost let themselves forget that they are not at home.[15]

After February 1942, outings to Berlin are organized for the POWs on Sundays, but these treats bristle with restrictions: they are obliged to walk in the streets; sidewalks, subways, cafés, separation from the group, and conversation with people in the street are all forbidden. The French prisoners, however, are not discouraged and the first outings verge on chaos. As soon as they turn a corner, they split apart, usually in groups of two, in the quest of pleasure and adventure. Some camps had been established for French women who had been recruited to work

in the Berlin area, and these are literally "taken by assault."
The opportunity to make contact in Berlin, furthermore, could
be of inestimable value should a prisoner later wish to escape
from Friedrichsfelde.[16]

Despite warnings and threats some of the prisoners did manage to make personal contact with German civilians. Near one
work site in Berlin, German girls would throw food to the
French prisoners from the windows of their building, and on
Sundays local citizens would come to Friedrichsfelde to look at
the camp from a distance; they frequently throw cigarettes and
small food items over the fence, not to mention an occasional
billet-doux from a German girl who has taken a fancy to one
of the prisoners. These girls would wait for the prisoners every
evening at the station exit and then follow them to camp at a
discreet distance. Soon signs begin to be posted around the city
warning the Berliners that the prisoner is still an enemy whom
they are not to approach, speak to, or listen to.

The prisoners are eventually forced to sign, as an indication
they have read it, a notice informing them that any prisoner
convicted of having relations with a German woman will be
subject to the death penalty. But love proves stronger than the
threat of death, and Perret observes with delight that if the
Germans in France have seduced some French women, the
French prisoners are taking sweet revenge on their conquerors.[17]

Penalties could be and were applied on the German side also.
Ambrière reports in *Les Grandes Vacances* that many German
girls, "Gretchens," he calls them, were instrumental in securing
the escape of their French lovers from the POW camps and
suffered years of detention for their complicity. *Les Grandes
Vacances* is crammed with details gathered somewhat randomly
from the author's own experience as well as from that of other
witnesses. Unfortunately it is marred by rather frequent and
self-serving generalizations about the French and the Germans
and by the author's often moralizing stance on the events and
issues discussed. One wonders just how many German girls assisted their French lovers only in the hope of setting up house
in France after the war and living forever after "happy as God
in France" (*glücklich wie Gott in Frankreich*). That proverb, Am-

brière glibly contends, explains much in Franco-German relations over the centuries.[18] Certainly some German girls willing
to have an affair with a French prisoner may have contem-
plated marriage as the ultimate end of their relationships, but
that still does not justify Ambrière's position. Whatever were
their motives, some of these German women paid dearly for
their affections. Luise Rinser describes one such case at the
prison camp in Traunstein at some length in her *Gefängnistagebuch*. A woman, whom she identifies only as Frau H., and
who is eight months pregnant by a Frenchman named Lucien,
does nothing but sit and cry, once in a while whispering the
name of her lover.[19]

During the early part of their captivity while butter is still
included among the rations, the prisoners in *Le Caporal épinglé*
frequently make deals with civilians and sentries alike to exchange their butter for other items, especially bread. Even after
their weekly allowance of butter is replaced by margarine, Perret finds little cause to complain about the daily food rations:
at the beginning 350 grams of bread, some salami, cheese, and
jam, which each man has to divide up for himself so that it will
last the day. This diet is supplemented by an herb tea at dawn
and a mess tin in the evening.[20]

Early on these prisoners evolve the formula "nix essen, nix
arbeit," a variant of the correct German, "nicht essen, nicht ar-
beiten" ("no eat, no work".) As it was, most POWs did not kill
themselves with over-exertion. Simone de Beauvoir recalls that
Sartre had written her during his relatively brief period of captivity in Germany from September 1940 to March 1941 that
since he was not doing any work, he had plenty of time to write,
and Perret says that the prisoners on the work site look like a
group of sleepwalkers. An exception were the Bretons whom
the Germans segregated into separate barracks to encourage
the natural divisions that existed within the French population.
To their work the Bretons brought their customary zeal and
their appreciation of a job well done.[21]

Many of the German civilians with whom the POWs were put
to work, Perret recalls, were good people, cordial and generous
("de fort braves gens,") who often passed out their cigarettes
and when they felt unobserved, would speak openly, if in

hushed tones, of the scorn and disgust with which they regarded the Nazi regime. Ambrière even recollects one period
in the camp at Limburg east of Coblenz when the Germans
allowed prospective employers or their representatives to come
to the camp and bargain with the French over wages and living
conditions to get them to sign up. But certainly this was not
everywhere the case, nor did it last very long at Limburg. As
Ambrière quite correctly points out, furthermore, it must be
kept in mind in any assessment of the situation, that captivity
is more often than not a moral rather than a physical ordeal.²²

To Escape or To Remain

Despite the occasional amenities and the favors they sometimes
received, through their own resourcefulness, from the civilian
population, the French prisoners were not free, and this must
be the primary consideration in evaluating their captivity. Certainly this was what prompted some of them to try to escape.
The central character in Pierre Gascar's *Le Fugitif* (1961), a POW
named Paul, does not attempt escape until the very end of the
war. To the German girl Lena, who is hiding and sheltering
him from the authorities, and who cannot understand why he
has taken this risk just when liberation is immanent, he confides,"You hold out for five years, then suddenly you can't hold
out a month more."²³

Jacques Perret decides much earlier than Gascar's Paul that
he will have to take personal responsibility for his freedom. He
makes three escape attempts in all, and after the first two abor-
tive ventures, neither of which he has taken the time to think
through thoroughly, he realizes that it will not be an easy matter and that he will have to sharpen his calculations.

The first attempt comes during a noon break approximately
one year after his arrival at Friedrichsfelde. He manages to steal
out of the barracks and past the guards and goes off into Berlin with the vague idea of taking a train to Paris. The normal
route into town via the S-Bahn from the Friedrichsfelde station
is impossible since by now too many people know him there,
and so he is forced to spend a considerable amount of time

finding an alternate stop from which to begin his journey. Before all else, the train schedule to Paris has to be verified. On the Berlin subways, tickets had to be purchased for the length of a specific ride and one had to declare either one's destination or the fare required if one knew it in advance. Since Perret knows only that he has to get to the Schlesischer Bahnhof, which is the railway station where he is going to make his verifications, he begins tormenting himself with the pronunciation of that word whose consonant clusters are capable of tying any French tongue. It is important not to stand out too much from the local population, and even his unpolished shoes begin to cause him concern in a city where all shoes are properly shined and buffed. The subway ride takes him through the Berlin he knows, for already, like any temporary resident in a foreign city, he has his memories: in Lichtenberg he sees a detachment of prisoners working on the tracks where he himself had worked that fall. There is also a Jewish commando unit. Neither of the two groups elicit any particular sympathy from him. Then comes the Warschauer Bahnhof, and he is pleased to notice that nobody seems to be paying much attention to him, not even the Feldwebel reading the fourth page of his newspaper, bordered in black and listing the names of those who had died for the Führer. The Schlesischer Bahnhof itself is filled with officers going everywhere, from Narvick to Athens, and with gendarmes, too many for comfort. The daily train for Aachen, Brussels, and Paris will leave at 11:45 PM; he has time. Ill at ease as a foreigner without appropriate papers in a railroad station, Perret steps out into Berlin. It is a city not at all oriented toward daydreaming. The Paris *clochards* are missing and people seem to have a purpose and to know where they are going. Public benches are rare, and in his self-conscious state of anxiety, those that do exist do not strike him as being receptive to someone who simply wants to pass the time and relax. Perret has taken down the address of a French worker living in Berlin who is the father of a friend of the brother-in-law of a friend in the camp. No contact, no matter how vague and tenuous, could be ignored in these times. After having summoned the courage to ask directions of a police officer, Perret locates the house where the French worker is renting a room from a German family. Her tenant has not yet returned from work, but the landlady is cordial and hospitable, immediately takes Perret into her home and explains, very properly, that only this unfortunate war prevents her from offering him a cup of something to drink and some cookies. The tenant arrives eventually, a man in his fifties, who has come to Berlin on his own volition and seems to enjoy being there, but who is ready and happy, nonetheless, to share his bread with a fellow Frenchman. He applauds Perret's intention to get back to Paris, but to the escapee's cautious request for shelter for the night should he for some unforeseen reason be unable to depart, the man is unhesitatingly negative. It is too dangerous for him; the best is for Perret to leave that evening and good luck to him!

Perret boards his train, marveling that every night while he had been at Friedrichsfelde a train had left Berlin bound for Paris at 11:45 PM. With a few astute maneuvers such as climbing out onto the steps outside the door of the train when a ticket collector comes by, he manages to get as far as Herbesthal on the German-Belgian border where he creeps under the railway car to wait out the general examination of papers. But as he emerges from his somber nest he is spotted and taken into custody to the sound of the now all too familiar "Krieg grosses Malheur." From Herbesthal he is taken first to a *Stalag* at Düren not far from the border and then for temporary punishment to the *Straffkompagnie* in the camp at Lichterfelde in the southern suburbs of Berlin. At Lichterfelde, as in all prisons from time immemorial, there is a hierarchy among the prisoners: to have stolen from the Germans or seduced their women is considered honorable enough, but there is a question of purity of motive involved, and no escapee will tolerate being classed at this level. Among the escapees themselves there are some cases that are more interesting than others. A man named Roux, for example, had escaped from camp to take a week's vacation to explore Berlin and then returned on his own with the intention of regularly taking leave for a week or two.[24]

On his second attempt Perret decides to try a different approach, and so he buys a ticket to Mulhouse or Mülhausen as it was known in what had become German Alsace. While waiting for his train to leave Berlin, he is stopped on the street by two *Schupos,* the German municipal police or *Schutzpolizei.* A drunken woman close by creates a disturbance and this provides an opportunity to flee the policemen. But when he arrives at the railway station he finds the train to Mulhouse filled to capacity with German soldiers, and so he quickly boards the Paris train he had taken the first time. No sooner does he sit down than he finds papers are being verified, and as irony would have it, the person making the verifications is the same man, a professor of French, who had served him as an interpreter after his previous escape. Perret is removed from the train at Spandau in the western part of the city.

Upon return to Lichterfelde Perret learns that Roux has left again on one of his excursions, and that two other men who had intended like himself to return to France had gotten on the wrong train. Fourteen hours after embarking from Berlin they alighted onto a railway platform in Vienna looking too surprised to escape the notice of the local police.[25]

Perret's third try is better organized from the start. First of all he secures a pied-à-terre in Berlin provided by a French adjutant named Comminges who, without supervision, heads a small commando charged with maintaining Charlottenburg cemetery. For five weeks Perret and some other escapees circulate with relative freedom around the city, avoiding the German authorities when possible and when not, pretending to be tourists arrived that very day from Paris who have not yet had time to get their papers in order regularizing their stay in Berlin. They link up with a camp of French civilian workers in suburban Rahnsdorf. Like the fifty-year old man Perret had met just before his first departure from Berlin, these people have come to Germany voluntarily. They reproach the prisoners for their arrogance, while the prisoners expect the workers somehow to justify their presence in Berlin. A fundamental incompatibility exists between those who want to flee what the others have come to find. Some, of course, have simply come for the novelty, and Perret notes that some of them could just as easily have gone to Brazzaville as to Berlin.

Perret is quick to don the little tricolor that the French civilian workers wear on their lapels. This identification badge will assist the citizens of Berlin to classify him immediately in an

acceptable category, and he feels more at ease in his wanderings both on the street and in the subway. With obvious relish
he observes that if the Germans are vying with each other in
the Paris Métro, as he had heard, to give their seats to women,
old men, and wounded veterans, that courtesy must be due to
one of the rules in the Occupation manual. It does not extend
to Berlin. In Berlin no one gets up. Relatively free to circulate,
Perret now begins to get a real taste of the city. An encounter
with an old barber to whose shop he goes to make himself appear more presentable in the streets, helps give him a sense of
perspective. The old man, a World War I veteran who had been
a French prisoner, takes obvious delight in reminiscing about
his youth, and Perret responds to his enthusiasm.

> The day I open a barber shop, maybe I, too, will be happy to
> come upon a client to whom I can talk about Lichterfelde. My ill-
> humor at being vanquished will then be dissipated, I hope, and
> the weight of the chains forgotten; there will remain only the
> memory of the old rentier who offered me a slice of buttered
> bread in secret, of the laughs we had together in our carefree
> digs, of the Feldwebel not so bad as all that, of the girls' furtive
> winks, of the sentries' patience and the masculine friendships that
> defied all our blues.

At the end of five weeks of freedom Perret suddenly realizes
that he has done nothing about arranging his trip to Paris. He
still has no papers legitimizing his presence in Berlin or the trip
back, even though it might have been easy enough to obtain a
set of false papers through one of the French civilian workers
named Polo. He has Polo introduce him to another Frenchman
named Marcel who is leaving for Paris on a special convoy of
persons who have come to Berlin with legal permits. Their train
is to leave from Potsdam just southwest of Berlin, and they take
Perret along. As soon as Marcel and his wife are seated in a
compartment they rapidly explain his situation to the other
travelers and ask those unwilling to play the game to find places
elsewhere. Perret is quickly hidden under the seat benches and
in that uncomfortable position makes the crossing into France.
He surmounts his last hurdle upon arrival at the Gare du Nord
at four in the morning. Travelers leaving the rail platforms in

Paris had to present valid tickets to an official posted at the head of the platform, and the only thing Perret can produce is a ticket from the Berlin S-Bahn accompanied by a wink and hope the official would cooperate. "Ça ira" come the first welcoming words of home. The Berlin subway ticket will do.[26]

The punishment for attempted escape varied from one *Stalag* to another, but prisoners of war less fortunate than Perret were sometimes transferred to disciplinary camps in eastern Europe for refusing to comply with the directives of the German camp hierarchy or for repeated unsuccessful attempts at escape. Francis Ambrière wound up in one such camp in Poland and Pierre Gascar in eastern Galicia, which had belonged to Poland but which the Russians occupied in late 1939 and which subsequently became part of the Ukraine.

Le Temps des morts (1953) is a record of Gascar's experience in fictionalized form. In April, 1942, in a contingent of about 1000 French POWs, he arrives in Brodno at a camp that had been assembled out of some former Red Army barracks hastily constructed after the Russian occupation. He is assigned the job of grave digger and, with a team of other French prisoners, given the task of creating a cemetery for those of their comrades who will die during captivity. Under such circumstances, death bears no resemblance to the kind of heroism implicit in the formula, "des morts de guerre" or "war dead." From that moment, life becomes a life-in-death, for surely like a self-fulfilling prophesy, the graves will be filled. The narrator and his team of cemetery workers begin scanning the faces of their comrades trying to discern whom death will claim first. No longer do people live for life. In this "second captivity" on the fringes of European civilization with its new kind of imprisonment, a captivity different from that of the POW camps they had known, more *dépaysante,* more *romanesque,* people live in order to die. In this new world the existential dilemma between life and death is stripped of illusion. And in a way the tenders of the cemetery will be living off "their" dead.

The dead come, eventually, slowly—while the cemetery with its grass becomes ever more graceful, lovely, and "idyllic." The burials, for those who can attend them, become like little summer excursions. The narrator, however, is well aware that for

him and his team the cemetery begins, perhaps a bit too conveniently, to take first priority in their thinking. It becomes a
preoccupation and an excuse, a way to distract if not silence
their consciences. When the first Frenchman is shot and killed
trying to escape and when the first cortège of Jews from Brodno
is marched off to the train station for shipment, no doubt, to
the concentration camps and the Germans stave in the doors of
Jewish houses to "empty out" the village, the narrator and his
team become day by day more "cemetery men" (*cimetièriens*)
than ever. They return to "their" dead, that "faithful flock"
whose every name they knew.[27]

Quite a different story from either Perret's or Gascar's is that
of Abel Tiffauges in Michel Tournier's *Le Roi des aulnes*. To
Perret Germany was the country of his confinement, to Tiffauges that of his deliverance. For Perret the facts of his captivity constitute the core of the story; for Gascar they serve as a
springboard for what can be read as a meditation on death. For
Tournier, the facts are ultimately subservient to a higher level
of reality and the signs or symbols that elucidate it. Reality in
Le Roi des aulnes is apprehended by these signs, which are essentially of a non-genital sexual character, and at times they
yield unexpected results.

The book unfolds around variant adaptations of the ogre
myth, the giant of fairy tales, usually somewhat frightening in
appearance, who lives on human flesh. In Germany Tiffauges
becomes an ogre. Already as a schoolboy he suspected that destiny had singled him out when, called up on a discipline charge
by the school authorities for his involvement in a prank, a single image impresses itself persistently on his mind the night
before he is to answer the charge: his school, Saint-Christophe,
engulfed in flames. The next day when he arrives at Saint-
Christophe, he learns that his premonition has come true.

After Tiffauges is interned in the camp at Moorhof in East
Prussia, he easily gains official confidence because of the good
quality of his work. Since he had once been a garage mechanic
in Paris, he is rapidly promoted to camp chauffeur, and this
position gives him a relative freedom of movement, allowing
him to wander off into the surrounding woodlands for hours
at a time or even stay away overnight without provoking alarm.

In the woodlands he makes the acquaintance of the Oberforst-meister of the Rominter Heide, the head warden for the forest preserve at Rominten. The Oberforstmeister takes a liking to Tiffauges and has him assigned as an assistant. Since Hermann Göring has his hunting lodge nearby, Nazis of the upper echelon come there to partake of the hunt. For Göring, and for Tiffauges as well, the deer hunt has decidedly sexual overtones. The woodlands themselves are essentially phallic in nature, and the act of wearing down a deer, killing and then emasculating him, eating his flesh and cutting off his horns becomes a sacred ritual. More and more Tiffauges sees Göring in the almost mythological role of high priest of the forest preserve.[28]

After the German disaster at Stalingrad in late 1942 and early 1943, however, less and less thought can be given to the joys of the hunt and the table. The Oberforstmeister is ordered to reduce his personnel to a minimum and informs Tiffauges that he will have to return to Moorhof. But Tiffauges requests instead to be transferred to Kaltenborn. Kaltenborn is a fortress built by Kaiser Wilhelm II just before the outbreak of World War I from an existing castle that had belonged to the counts of Kaltenborn but which had fallen into disrepair. It had been meant as a sign of defiance to the Slavic enemy in the east. At the time of the novel it serves to house one of the *Nationalpolitischeerziehungsanstalten,* or *Napolas* for short, which were paramilitary schools in which to train the future elite of the Third Reich. The old Count of Kaltenborn is theoretically its head and given quarters in one of the wings of his ancestors' castle, but the operation is being run by an SS Sturmbann-führer named Stefan Raufeisen. The school is composed of a military teaching staff of thirty members, fifty additional men and non-commissioned officers who perform various functions in the running of the *Napola,* the 400 children who are its students, and Frau Netta, the *Heimmutter* or "home mother," to whom the boys can go with their problems. Tiffauges's request is granted and he is sent to Kaltenborn. The narrator has already identified Göring as the ogre of Rominten, and less than 90 kilometers from Rominten sits Adolf Hitler, the ogre of Rastenburg where he maintains his East Prussian headquarters, ex-

acting from the population, somewhat like the Cretan Mino-
taur, an annual sacrifice of young boys and girls destined for
the Hitler youth organizations. Abel Tiffauges soon becomes
the ogre of Kaltenborn.

At Kaltenborn Tiffauges comes around full cycle from his
prewar life in Paris. Here his attraction to young children can
legitimately reach its full development. While he had been arrested in France on charges of raping a little girl, his job at
Kaltenborn eventually involves rounding up young boys for the
Napola. With the blessings of his superiors he rides through the
countryside on his horse Barbe-Bleu (Blue Beard) which he has
brought along from Rominten, a horse that is also "a giant
brother which he felt alive between his thighs and which raised
him above the earth and men."

For a time Tiffauges works with an SS doctor, a Nazi race
specialist named Blättchen, who one day confers the supreme
degree of acceptance on him by declaring that the name Tiffauges is a corruption of what must have been a very ancient
Germanic name. Henceforth Blättchen always addresses his assistant as Herr von Tiefauge. Tiffauges is convinced from the
start that he will one day occupy Blättchen's place at the *Napola,*
and when Blättchen is given the task of deporting 50,000 white
Ruthenian children who were living in the occupied territories
of the east, the succession becomes a reality.

By this time the eastern front is closing in on Germany, and
even as Tiffauges witnesses what he considers to be Germany's
degradation by Allied bombs, he is certain that he personally
will emerge unharmed. Remembering the unbridgeable gap that
has always separated him from his people, he represses the mo-
mentary nostalgia he feels after encountering the first French
refugees from the German camps in the east moving westward
across Europe in a huge international exodus. Henceforth he
will belong exclusively to the Prussia that is collapsing all around
him.[29] As the signs of Germany's coming fall are made clearer,
it becomes more and more difficult to obtain recruits for the
Napola. Since the administrators want to maintain the numbers
at Kaltenborn and keep it as a *Napola* of the first category, Tiffauges is sent scouring the region in search of his prey. Like

the "Erlkönig", the "roi des aulnes," of Goethe's poem for whom
the book is named, he becomes the bane of the countryside and
the terror of local parents who are warned anonymously that if
they give up their sons they will never see them again. The
father in Goethe's poem refuses to give up his little son to the
Erlkönig, only to find the boy dead in his arms. Not unlike him
the parents of East Prussia are forced to relinquish their boys
to the ogre of Kaltenborn who rides his horse with eleven dob-
erman hounds and selects the most perfect specimens. He brings
back to the *Napola* even the most challenging and recalcitrant
cases like the red-headed twins Haio and Haro and the almost
white-blond Lothar who remain his favorites. Like Christopher
carrying the child Jesus across the waters of a raging river, Tiffauges is fulfilling his sacred mission. Not only is he the ogre,
"kidnapping" the child as it were, but he is its protector. Not
only is he the "roi des aulnes" but he has become the child-
bearer (*porte-enfant*) he has always wanted to be. At Saint-Christophe he and the other schoolboys had been exhorted in a sermon by one of the priests to pass through the evil they would
encounter in life like their patron saint, Christopher, sheltered
by the "cloak of innocence." Tiffauges had taken the message
to heart literally. And like Christopher, he is sanctified by his
task. As he writes in his "Ecrits sinistres," the series of notations
begun in Paris and continued at the *Napola*, he has metamor-
phized the deer into a child.[30]

In the course of his stay at Kaltenborn Tiffauges has several
conversations with the old Count who is as avid a reader of
symbols as he. For the Count symbols are real, and he who
scorns them had best beware. There comes a time when a symbol no longer accepts being borne by a creature; it escapes the
thing it symbolizes and takes control of it. For long hours Christ
carried his cross and then it was the cross that carried him. The
veil of the temple was rent and the sun was darkened. When
the symbol devours the thing it symbolizes, it is a sign that the
end of the world is near.[31] Tiffauges has made similar observations. War itself was a kind of game, rich in symbolism, that
men seemed to play. It allowed them as fully grown human
beings to leave their homes and their jobs to go out and play

with friends of their own age at maneuvering cannons, tanks, and planes in what was simply an enlarged version of their childish games.

Before flying to Arras Saint-Exupéry was reminded of the fact that the ruler and compass that were to chart his course over the German-held areas of northern France in 1940 were just like the tools he had used as a schoolboy to solve his math problems. But the adult no longer knew how to play the game, as Tiffauges perceives; he had become too serious. The child no longer carried his toy, instead he was carried by it, swallowed up by his tank or by his plane.[32]

As the Russian troops advance on Germany from the east and columns of refugees stream through East Prussia, Tiffauges comes upon a boy named Ephraim who had been at Auschwitz and some of the other camps. In listening to Ephraim's description of them, he is horrified. Unlike the Nazis, he personally has no grudge against the Jews. He views the Nazi attempt to eradicate the Jews and the gypsies as an eruption of the age-old hatred that exists between the sedentary and the nomadic races. The wandering sons of Abel were being trod under the heels of a booted, helmeted, and scientifically organized Cain. He applies the same analysis to the struggle between Nazism, with its insistence on race and a heredity that had put roots into the German soil, and Communism, which was a philosophy for bastards and nomads who had neither tradition nor lineage, a philosophy for rootless cosmopolitan city-dwellers.[33]

In Ephraim's tale Tiffauges recognized many similarities between the *univers concentrationnaire* and life outside the camps. This is not surprising. The camps can well be seen as a grotesque parody of human life and civilization. During her stay at Ravensbrück, Germaine Tillion discovered not only in the camp but more especially in the Nazi state as a whole "an obviously aberrant and monstrous 'civilization' which had all the physical trappings of the one I had always lived in: professors, automobiles, newspapers, cinemas, conventions... and doctors."[34] The Third Reich with its banners, its torchlight parades, and its swastikas, to name just a few, abounded in symbols. But as he listens to Ephraim, Tiffauges realizes that in the camps all the signs had been inverted, and he is particularly disturbed at the description of the shower heads which Ephraim had seen while on a work crew at Auschwitz when an SS guard had let them rest in the supposed showers. Those shower heads brought forth not the waters of cleanliness but the gas of death. The Count of Kaltenborn had told Tiffauges that the Third Reich was born of a perversion of symbols; here is confirmation.

One day when Stefan Raufeisen, the SS officer in charge of Kaltenborn, orders the ranks of boys to lie down on the frozen ground and walks not among them but literally on them, crushing the hand of one or the neck of another under his boots, Tiffauges predicts in his "Ecrits sinistres" for "Stefan of Kiel" a cruel and immanent death. Before long Stefan's sacrilege is punished in the apocalypse that befalls Nazi Germany. Raufeisen does indeed fall victim to the boots of Soviet soldiers who soon advance on Kaltenborn, and when Tiffauges sees him for the last time he is on the ground with one of his eyes rolling in a bloody liquid down his cheek. A Soviet soldier then shoots him in the neck. Haio, Haro, and Lothar are found together, broken now, each of them pierced by a sword. Like the little boy in Goethe's poem, separated in life from the Erlkönig because his father refuses to surrender him, the three children have had to die. "The stars had gone out, and the Golgotha of boys stood out against a black sky." The time has come for Abel Tiffauges to leave. Having lost his glasses in one of the explosions that rocked the *Napola* and unable to see without them, he is led out by Ephraim who explains to the Soviet soldiers that this is a Frenchman. They open a passage for the child-bearer who, in a final inversion of symbols, is now being saved by one of the children he had protected.[35]

To view Hitler and Göring on the level of the ogre is to open a new perspective on the Third Reich, and it is perhaps indicative of the times that were coming that a French prisoner of war can join them on that level. Those who were still in control were standing on the brink as much of Europe awaited a reversal of the power structure, and among those who had been conquered many waited for their turn to conquer.

CHAPTER XI

The End of the War

The Invasion in Normandy

The decisive event that marked the beginning of the end of
World War II in France was the Allied invasion of Normandy
on June 6, 1944. It was awaited by *résistants* and collaborators
alike. They did not know exactly when or where it would strike,
but by the spring of 1944 the idea of a *débarquement* was in the
air, and they knew that its consequences would be momentous.
The fever of anticipation was such that when it actually did
come there was a sense of disappointment in some Résistance
circles, says Elsa Triolet in "Le Premier Accroc coûte deux cents
francs," whose title itself was one of the prearranged signals to
the Résistance that the invasion had taken place. It seemed that
now the war should automatically come to an end.[1] But long
months of fighting still lay ahead, and they could only be anti-
climactic. For the collaborators, says Céline, on the other side
of the fence in *Féerie pour une autre fois* (1952), the invasion
presaged a "slaughterhouse."[2] They would be accused of having served too well Germany's interests.

Even though they were waiting for it, the invasion caught
most people by surprise, from the French parachustists in Joseph Kessel's *Le Bataillon du ciel* (1961), who came down in the
fields of Brittany after years of waiting and training in England
and Scotland, to the inhabitants near the coastal area who witnessed their arrival; from the local peasants and small business
people in Boris Vian's play *L'Equarissage pour tous* (1950), living

in the town of Arromanches at the center of the invasion thrust in Normandy, to the German military units assigned to defend the French coast. Despite the sense of surprise, Kessel's parachutists found in Brittany a population more prepared to assist them than they had anticipated. The surprise worked to the advantage of the Allies, and the German generals, caught off guard, like "fat rats caught in a trap," did little besides scream orders the whole day long. But the invaders, too, found surprises, and sometimes gruesome ones. One adjutant at Vannes in Brittany came across thirty FFI men, members of the Forces Françaises de l'Intérieur, who had been roasted in what must have been an oversized bread oven. Atrocity is self-propagating, and the adjutant was quick to take revenge on some German prisoners he had captured. From the very next bridge he had them hurled into the river with a stone attached to their necks. As Kessel's text moves from atrocity to reciprocal atrocity, a number of the characters can conclude that these scenes of torture and disfigurement have little to do with war, that this was not what they had trained for.[3] Like so many others in the Europe of 1939 to 1945, they were left to ponder in disgust mankind's eroded sense of humanity.

Boris Vian took a different approach entirely to present a not so different idea. He stated his aims clearly in the preface he wrote in 1952 for the second edition of *L'Equarissage pour tous:* "This text pursued one single purpose: to make people laugh with something that isn't funny, war." To those critics who attacked him for degrading the war dead and making a mockery out of the Résistance, he had already given his answer in his first preface two years earlier:

> I regret that I am among those for whom war inspires neither patriotic reflexes, nor martial movements of the chin, nor enthusiasm for killing . . . , nor poignant and emotional good-naturedness, nor sudden piety—nothing but a desperate anger, total anger, against the absurdity of battles that are battles of words but which kill men of flesh. An impotent anger unfortunately; among other alternatives, there is one possibility of escape: jesting.[4]

L'Equarissage pour tous is set on D-Day at the home of a horse butcher in Arromanches living with his wife and two daugh-

ters, all of whom are inconveniently named Marie. A son named
Jacques is serving with the American army and another daughter named Catherine is a parachutist in the Red army. Because
of the work she is doing she might as well be a boy, says her
father. Looked at in this way, the two "male" children who are
away fighting, nicely balance the two Maries who have stayed
home. When the invasion comes to disrupt the sleepy order of
things in Arromanches, the father, known simply as Père, regrets that it is a mechanized one. Once upon a time they would
have used horses instead of tanks and there would have been
work for him. As it is, Père is a bit put out to have his routine
so rudely disrupted, not to speak of the Germans who he is
certain must not have been happy to be awakened so early in
the morning!

Nothing that any of the characters says is very serious in itself. They almost all seem slightly annoyed and inconvenienced
by the trouble they are being put to, but the reader quickly
becomes aware that the text does not warrant the inclination to
deduce any profound psychological conclusions from their attitude. The play is not a realistic one. To refer again to Northrop Frye's system of classification, it is conceived in the ironic
mode, and its characters do not function on our level. We can
afford to smile at their foibles and still learn the lesson they
may have to teach us.

The citizens of Arromanches have adapted to the German
occupation by taking it in stride as they do everything else in
life, and the German presence seems no more noteworthy to
them than does the Anglo-American presence on the day of
the invasion. One of the two daughters Marie, whom Père decides in the course of the play to rechristen Cyprienne to break
the confusion and monotony of having three Maries in the
family, has been conducting an affair for four years with a German soldier named Heinz Schnittermach. Père spends much of
the day thinking about her upcoming marriage to the German.
He has no great enthusiasm for it, but then he has little enthusiasm for anything except possibly his trade. If two people love
each other they should be married, it is as simple and logical as
that and it would never occur to him to allow political considerations to spoil that dictum of human wisdom. His wife is

somewhat disturbed, however, at Père's decision to change their daughter's name just before her marriage: as it was, she would already be changing her last name. But Marie does not see this as a problem. The only thing that disturbs her is the fact that Cyprienne might not ring so harmoniously with a name like Schnittermach![5]

Into the midst of this domestic scene come two Americans who have just landed and are hoping to get a tourist's view of a French farm. It is the only farmhouse left standing. They are amazed to learn that the Germans were there before them, and only gradually does it dawn on them that they may have been sent to fight. They are indignant. Someone might at least have informed them before their departure! One of the Americans is also looking for a *marraine de guerre*, a woman who writes to a soldier and sends him little gifts and food from time to time and whom the French call a "war godmother." The second Marie, Cyprienne's sister, takes a fancy to the American and says that she will be his *marraine de guerre* if he consents to give her the metal insignia clips from his uniform. Soon Jacques and then Catherine arrive on the scene, but the household re-union provokes neither joy nor sorrow, and for a family almost indifferent to the *débarquement* if not oblivious to it, no surprise or excitement. American and German soldiers sit down to-gether in Père's house to play cards, and like little children fas-cinated by one another's clothing, they exchange uniforms and sing each other's songs, the Americans *Wenn die Soldaten* and the Germans *Happy Birthday*. Like a delinquent schoolboy, the first Marie's friend Heinz has overslept because his alarm did not go off and he bounds into this party atmosphere asking Père to give him a note of excuse for his commander, Captain Künsterlich. The captain himself finally comes to get Heinz, since out of the original 920 soldiers in his group he and Heinz are the only ones still alive. Heinz's prospective mother-in-law regrets that all those friends of his who are now no longer here will not be able to come to his wedding with her daughter Cy-prienne, and as Heinz coils himself up against Cyprienne, the captain, also with regret, explains that indeed now Heinz will not be able to get married at all. Heinz is disappointed and begins brooding. After all the Germans have done, trying for four years to improve the country! Now that the "foreigners" have landed everything the French have will go to them. Bombs continue to fly outside, destroying Arromanches, and the German captain laments like an older and already somewhat wiser child, that the Americans are breaking everything up.[6]

In this play which has so well adapted the classical structure of the three unities of time, place, and action to fit the drama of the Normandy invasion, Vian has shown a classical restraint in presenting the destruction unfolding in the town of Arromanches and the countryside around it. He was able to do this partly because the characters of the play, wrapped up in their own little world, are not classically whole human beings aware of themselves and of their place in the world. But no one escapes the brunt of Vian's satire: neither the family of the *équarisseur,* the soldiers of all the different armies on long or short-term assignment in Arromanches, two FFIs who had only joined the Résistance that morning and are attempting to learn the rules of military etiquette as rapidly as possible, nor two nuns taking up a collection amidst the battle for the poor of the parish. Like the animals of Noah's ark, as it were, the people involved in the D-day action line up in groups of two and make their appearance on the stage. And like Noah's animals, their species preserved because of the ark, so these character types with their different attitudes and actions will be preserved in the play for posterity.

In the end the sympathy of the audience and the reader comes to rest with the simple people of Arromanches, Père and his family and a neighbor man, who go quietly about their business, harming no one and giving as little thought as possible to the crisis engulfing them. The final insult against them comes with the arrival of a French captain proclaiming their liberation. Père and his neighbor know that the word liberation will not change very much for them, and so they accept the "good news" with characteristic indifference. The captain unfortunately also has some bad news to announce: according to the plans being drawn up for a new Arromanches, Père's house is not properly aligned where it is sitting. The reconstruction ministry has planned a vast prospect complete with poplar trees and fountains. Using the cliché that one has to break some eggs to make an omelette, he implies that Père's house is going to have to cede the ground on which it stands. For once Père is somewhat surprised. His neighbor seizes the captains' revolver and tries to shoot the captain but is killed himself instead. A French lieutenant shouts "Vive la France" to the accompaniment of a badly played *Marseillaise* and struts off the stage in the best German goose-stepping tradition.[7]

The Liberation of France

Once the Allied beachhead was established in Normandy, the German position in other parts of the country became critical. For a German, merely walking the streets entailed an ever greater risk. In *Le Chemin des écoliers* Marcel Aymé tells the story of a German soldier named Schulz, separated from his unit just before the liberation of Paris in August 1944. Schulz apparanently thinks he can take advantage of his freedom to go into a small café. By the time he emerges he has had too much to drink and finds himself without arms, helmet, or jacket. A crowd begins to gather around the oblivious German who goes on his way singing, and it is not long before he is knocked to the ground and literally torn to pieces. Women and children are particularly vicious, cutting off a finger, an ear, a piece of flesh. When the crowd has finished its work it disperses, leaving only a few traces of blood on the pavement.[8]

Even before the invasion in Normandy, life in Paris had become strained. In addition to the deportations that had been going on for some time, four years of submission were beginning to take their toll. Daily annoyances continued. As for the Allied invasion everybody was waiting for, rumor had it that 20,000 suspects were to be arrested in the first hours following a landing. By August 13, the Métro was shut down, and Paris began to settle in for whatever was to come. On the fourteenth Guéhenno mentions the last parades the Germans gave in the streets of Paris and on the eighteenth notes the blowing up of munitions depots around the city. Two days later:

All Paris was awaiting the arrival of the Americans the night before last. Nobody came. Yesterday was a feverish day. In every

section of town people are unaware of what is happening in other
sections. Telephone calls, uncertain and without specifics, are all
the information one can get. The Résistance has been fighting
here and there.

The morning before Guéhenno had witnessed two German
sentries on a bridge in the rue Manin in northeastern Paris,
men who seemed inoffensive enough; but by eight o'clock that
evening they were dead. They had been living among Parisians
who on the whole neither liked nor hated them, but who, nonetheless, thought only of killing them. The shooting escalated
and by the morning of August 23 had spread throughout the
city. The Résistance was occupying the Grand Palais and the
Germans set it on fire. But Paris had to have at least the illusion, wrote Guéhenno, that it was acting as its own instrument
of liberation.[9]
As Paris was preparing to deck itself out for the liberation,
nailing colored paper garlands onto apartment windows, hook-
ing flowers onto electric wires, stringing streamers and lanterns
from window to window, dying cloth at night so the women
could sew flags for the celebration, a different reality began to
dawn on those who would be excluded from the party. Jean
Genet in *Pompes funèbres* holds a matchbox in his pocket which
his imagination transforms into the coffin of his dead lover,
communist Résistance fighter Jean Décarnin, and relives the
anguish of those who were Jean's enemies in the last days before the liberation. For seven German soldiers including the
tank driver Erik Seiler and the young French *milicien* Riton,
Paris is preparing a funeral pyre even as they keep watch on a
rooftop high above the city.[10] Riton experiences a twinge of
emotion as he sees the boulevards decorated with French flags.
In his own destructive way he loves his country and now he
must bid her farewell. The Germans seem like monsters to him,
but he is proud, nevertheless, of having killed some young
Frenchmen and wounded others on the barricades that have
gone up all over the city. In his love-hate relationship with his
countrymen he would still and all like to be one of the mour-
ners for those he has killed. Since Riton is largely a creation of
Genet's fantasy, based on movie newsreel shots he had seen of

a young *milicien* in the last days of the Occupation, it is not at all surprising that his psyche should reflect that of his creator. Genet himself admired the *résistants* who seemed in general to look more noble that did the *miliciens* even if they were not always more graceful than Riton.

> Riton was struck by their beauty. The men in the underground had a finer bearing than the militiamen of the same age. Certainly they were of a nobler metal. Coming from me, this is no compliment. I mean by nobility a certain conventional combination of very beautiful lines, a certain physical and moral carriage. The noblest metal is that which goes through the fire most often: steel. One cannot regret that they were not on the German side, for the Germans were all the more handsome for having handsome enemies. Out of sadistic refinement I would have liked the men of the underground to fight for evil.

In Genet's system, where evil and solitude are synonymous, the one can be the cause but also the effect of the other. Moving in this closed circle, Genet seeks to justify the solitude he himself has experienced ever since childhood, when, because he was a bastard, he was an outcast. He does this by becoming evil, by perpetrating the evil that society expects of the person it condemns from birth to solitude, and attains moral solitude by proclaiming the opposite of what society sees as virtue.[11] Riton's solitude is not unlike Genet's, and it explains why he joined the Milice. It was out of necessity, Genet claims, out of physical and moral necessity, that the Milice fired on their fellow Frenchmen in the last days of August 1944. As an organization the Milice was the materialization of every thief's desire, enabling the outlaw and gangster to change roles with the policeman. As a *milicien* Riton could arrest without being arrested. For all the admiration he may have had for the beauty of the Résistance fighters, Genet was unable to bring them successfully into the circle of evil, and his closest attempt was to make Jean's brother Paolo do double duty in his fantasy as a *résistant* and *milicien*. In this way, even if it were only for a moment, Paolo and Riton could embrace.[12]

During the last two days described in the *Pompes funèbres* Riton lives with Erik and some other German soldiers on the rooftops of Paris. The German insignia, with which he has never before had an opportunity to become so intimate, strikes Riton as the mark of the devil, and he perceives himself to be its prey. It comes as something of a surprise to him, however, to find himself scorned not only by his countrymen but by the Germans as well, and he fears that all the Germans present on the rooftop will take it into their heads to rape him. Before the ordeal is over one German sergeant publicly and unashamedly does just that.

A "real" love exists only between Riton and Erik. Their love, involving a relationship between two people who in Genet's order of things are both dedicated to evil, is more vivid and realistic than the fantasy of love between Paolo and Riton. In the last analysis, of course, since Riton is a fantasy creation of the narrator Genet, both loves are fantasy loves. But the reader must deal with these fantasies as realities. In public even the "real" love of Erik and Riton can find expression only through the medium of language; "as their love was not recognized by the world, they could not feel its natural effects. Only language could have informed them that they actually loved each other."[13] Since theirs is a homosexual love and amorous gestures are forbidden them in public, language is the only means that enables the illicit lovers to bypass the conventions of society. It is also the only means available to Genet to make his fantasy real, to objectify it and transmit it to the reader.

In that France where for four years deceit and hypocrisy were so perfected as to give the country "the friendly look of a vicarage garden," Riton, Erik, and the other men on the roof feel pressured less by the tenants of the building where they have taken up their positions than by their own unfocused sense of fear and panic. Riton has already begun shooting at a silhouette that has appeared in a window opposite them when Erik puts his hand firmly on Riton's and orders him to stop. Laying down his own machine gun the German draws Riton to him, and in a standing position, bracing himself against a wall, takes Riton from behind, their two sets of eyes facing out over the city, "projecting the frightful ray of their love to infinity. . . . Erik and Riton were not loving one in the other, they were escaping from themselves over the world, in full view of the

world, in a gesture of victory." Thus did Genet imagine Adolf
Hitler gathering adolescents into his quarters in Berlin or near
Berchtesgaden and projecting them, as it were, over a "humil-
iated" world. Convinced that he loves Erik more than ever, Riton spends the night pressed against him. When Erik awakes
the next morning, however, his only thoughts are of Germany
and of saving his own hide. Genet records no words exchanged
between the lovers, but Riton pulls himself together, picks up
a machine gun, and shoots Erik dead. For ten seconds Riton
seems to be living in a delirium of joy and begins stomping on
his friend's corpse. All that night and the next morning he fires
away from other rooftops until he reaches a state of exhaustion,
feeling himself "abandoned by his friends, by his parents, by
his love, by France, by Germany, by the whole world . . . ." He
is killed, in turn, by a Frenchman's bullet.[14]

As the days of the German occupation began to dwindle,
France found that perhaps more than ever before, she was divided against herself. There were those like Céline who regarded the German defeat at Stalingrad as the greatest tragedy
of the times, a sign heralding the end of Europe,[15] and those
who saw it as the first ray of hope since night had fallen on
France in 1940. Some had taken to the Résistance, though not
all with noble motivation. Some had done nothing or had just
tried as hard as possible to be like everybody else. Finally at the
very end there were the arrivistes and adventurers, the "résistants de septembre," so called because they had waited until
September 1944 to make known their commitment to the Résistance, and those who were merely out to get revenge at the
last minute. There were those like the crowd of thirty people
in Pierre-Henri Simon's *Portrait d'un officier* who got their revenge by stampeding a German soldier who was wounded and
dying on a country road, spitting and screaming at him as they
danced their dance of hatred around him and then trampled
him.[16]

Not everyone necessarily looked forward to the liberation.
Many knew that they had serious accounts to settle. In Jean-
Louis Curtis's *Les Forêts de la nuit* a young man of doubtful moral
fiber, Philippe Arréguy, becomes involved in anti-Résistance
work for a German agent named Merkel, who one day gives

him the task of kidnapping his childhood friend, Francis de Balansun, then on a Résistance mission in Bordeaux. Despite the German's promise that no harm will come to Francis, Arréguy discovers the truth too late, when he sees Francis being tortured by other Frenchmen in Merkel's employ. He tries to help his former friend escape, but Francis is shot and killed in the attempt and Philippe himself forced to flee. Outlawed on all sides now and with no one to turn to, he makes off in desperation for Paris, as provincial people have done for centuries, hoping to be swallowed up in the anonymity of the big city. First he looks up an aunt to make sure he will have food until he can obtain a false identity card, and when she tries to reject him he threatens her into submission. He then bleaches his hair, calls himself Marcel Lefèvre, and becomes involved in the Paris underworld. In Saint-Clar Philippe's mother Fernande receives an anonymous package in the mail containing a piece of hemp cord and prophesying the punishment that awaits her for having slept with a German. Another local, Jacques Costellot whose mother used to receive the German commandant in Saint-Clar, has reservations of a slightly different order. If people at Saint-Clar consider him and his family collaborators, that is no irremediable evil; many can be considered collaborators. What the people will not forgive them, however, is their wealth. The Costellots have money, and to be rich and a collaborator was to transgress the limits of public tolerance.[17]

One of the Résistance leaders in Saint-Clar for whom Francis had been working was an egocentric profiteer named Darricade. After Francis's disappearance his father, old Count de Balansun, turns to Darricade for information and possible assistance in tracking down the boy. De Balansun has clung to the hope that Francis might have been taken by the Germans in one of the roundups at the Bordeaux railway station and sent off to a labor camp in Germany. At least he would be alive and might someday return. But when the Bordeaux police show him a photograph of the mutilated face of a boy they removed from the city morgue and buried four days before the Count's arrival, he begins to despair, thinking he has recognized in that face, mutilated though it is, the face of his son. Darricade's coarse, unsympathetic, and uncharitable handling of the old

ust about nothing at all for the Résistance, and for the first
time the Count begins to believe that not only is his son dead
but that he has, moreover, died in vain. As he leaves Darricade's office and emerges onto the square, he sees white-haired
old Cécile Delahaye being exposed on the pillory, half her head
already shaven, and her forehead bloodied from a stone that
someone has hurled at her. De Balansun is outraged, and with
an agility that defies his years, mounts the platform, takes Cécile by the hand and helps her down. The jeering and laughing
crowd opens a passage for them, and the narrator observes that
this scene is not very different from the pictures published in
French newspapers in 1939 and 1940 of the Nazi pogrom in
Germany. The strange old couple leaves the square.

> The derision that enfolded them was tremendous, medieval,
> apocalyptic; stupidity and hatred spread in waves through the
> smug, well-fed, contented crowd, those people of Saint-Clar who
> had never suffered, for whom the war had been a gold mine and
> the Germans a blessing.

Because of their wealth, the Costellots in the end are not subjected to the treatment meted out to others suspected of collaboration. Late in the day when a crowd arrives in front of the
Costellot house, it is immediately silenced by the sight of pale
young Jacques who goes out to meet it. Jacques is thoroughly
disgusted at the way the people have disfigured and vilified what
might have been a most noble and beautiful day. "To save these
grubs of humanity thousands of men had died, millions of men,
the finest youths of France had suffered torture . . . ," not to
mention the British, the Americans, and the Russians. Out of
the great conflict which had now passed over France and should
have purified it, the people had learned nothing!

Jacques Costellot was still young and emotions were running
high. Perhaps it required someone with the age and maturity
of Count de Balansun, comforting Cécile Delahaye after her
ordeal, to make a more objective assessment.

> France is free. She has recovered her freedom and her honor.
> Such an event cannot take place without a regrettable backwash.
> The people of France have suffered a great deal. They need to-
> ken victims. And the people choose the first victims they can lay

man in his agony prompts de Balansun to vent
men like Darricade might not be too numerous i
refers to as the "dissidence." " . . . I would pity
tomorrow."[18]

Once on its way, the France of tomorrow was s
ing. With the departure of the Germans, Darric
command of the town, and women like Fernande A
old Madame Delahaye, who was denounced by her i
for having kept company with the Germans, are
gether in the town square for a public shaving of tl
a sign of national disgrace. A similar fate befell the w
Nevers in central France in Marguerite Duras's film
roshima mon amour (1959), who recollects all these th
lying in the arms of a Japanese lover in Hiroshima y
the war. At first she simply hid in her father's cellar
fled to Paris. Perhaps she was too young and still
stricken over the death of her German lover, a youn
cut down by a sniper's bullet just before the liberatio
Saint-Clar not all the women accepted their fate as pa
she. When Fernande Arréguy is brought before Darr
some FFIs for the humiliation ceremony, her fury is t
wild animal, and since she is far too well informed al
own doings, Darricade for a moment expects the ruin
career. First she tells the leader of the FFIs that he
"screwed" (*enfoiré*), then she reveals to the public with
furious energy a whole list of Darricade's misconducts: h
self has been one of her lovers since 1941 and the only
he has been able to eat like a king for the duration of tl
is that he had charged her with establishing black marke
nections with the Germans. At Christmas in 1943 she ha
been alone in drinking with a German, Darricade had been
her then, and if they were going to shave her head today,
had better do the same to him. Some socialist and comm
colleagues try to reassure Darricade and send the still scre
ing Fernande Arréguy home.[19]

Count de Balansun is also present at the spectacle and
lows Darricade into the mayoralty. In view of Francis's acti
in the Résistance, he feels himself on equal footing with Da
cade. But Darricade informs him coldly that Francis had do

their hands on, innocent or guilty. They are not very discerning. They are almost invariably blind and stupid. We must forgive them. We must find the strength to rejoice, because this day, in spite of everything, symbolizes our honor and our liberty.

On his way home from the Delahaye residence de Balansun stops a young *résistant* in the street who reminds him of his son. What you and your comrades have done for our country is beautiful, he tells the young man, "allow me to embrace you." As he pulls the boy toward him the sobs that have for so long been repressed burst forth. The young healthy body next to his becomes for the old man the living body of Francis. One of the other *résistants* looking on at the scene explains to a colleague that the old man is probably a "patriot." "He's moved. The liberation and all that. It's the finest day of his life." [20]

The Collaborators

On the night of August 24, 1944, the first tanks of General Jacques Leclerc's French Second Armored Division began arriving before Notre-Dame cathedral in Paris, and on August 25 Leclerc himself, with his own troops and the U.S. Fourth Infantry Division, marched into the city. They found it already largely under the control of French Résistance units. [21]

In the last months before the liberation of Paris, especially after the Allied invasion of Normandy when it became evident that the end of the German occupation was at hand, life became progressively more dangerous and anxiety-ridden for those thought to have collaborated with the Germans. Among these was Louis-Ferdinand Céline, medical doctor and novelist, widely known for his *Voyage au bout de la nuit* and *Mort à crédit*, published respectively in 1932 and 1936. In 1937 Céline published an extremely virulent anti-Semitic tract, *Bagatelles pour un massacre*, and lest people believed, as did André Gide, that such venom could only be the mask of satire, Céline followed it with another ferocious blast against the Jews in 1938, *L'Ecole des cadavres*, and still another in 1941, *Les Beaux Draps*. Unlike some of his literary colleagues, such as Montherlant, who were thought to have collaborationist tendencies because of their interest in Germany and things German, Céline actually went so far as to talk about an alliance between France and Nazi Germany as a means of reducing Jewish power and influence. His reputation as a collaborator was assured even before France was defeated. In 1939 Céline tried to enlist in the French army, but he was rejected, probably for medical reasons. In any case, his wounds incurred during World War I had always convinced him that he had done his duty for France. But lest he give the impression of eagerly awaiting the German arrival in Paris in 1940, he temporarily fled the city in the general exodus, driving an ambulance to La Rochelle.[22] Whether or not Céline was a collaborator depends on what one means by collaboration. The French judicial system later attached that label to anyone who had openly fostered a climate favorable to the enemy or maintained intelligence with them in time of war with a view to favoring their undertakings against France. Céline was much too much his own man and too much of a maverick to fit conveniently into any classification, but the published and unpublished statements he made both before and during the war only helped to build the case against him.

As the Allies advanced deeper and deeper into France, many who had to fear reprisal from the liberation were granted asylum in Germany. For Marshal Pétain who was literally taken off French soil by the Germans in August 1944, it was a forced asylum. Céline was not physically forced to leave, though by June 1944 the climate in Paris had become such that he determined of his own accord to go into exile, hoping eventually to reach Denmark where he had money in a Copenhagen bank and where he hoped to wait out the end of the war and see what the liberation and the postwar period would bring.

Céline described his last months in Paris with characteristic vigor in *Féerie pour une autre fois* which he published in 1952, the year following his exoneration by a French military tribunal and his return from exile. The book opens with a visit from an old "friend" of some thirty years, Clémence Arlon and her adolescent son who, having defied all the alerts and the interruptions in the Métro service, have come to his Montmartre apartment. Throughout the first part of the book Céline wonders rhetorically why they have come, although he never really gives them a chance to explain their visit. In general in Céline's work the narration is almost totally taken over either by Céline himself or, in some cases, by the narrator Ferdinand who very much resembles him. Haranguing here, but with an energy so dauntless as to be engaging and even hypnotizing, he decides in his paranoia that Clémence and her son have come because they want to get a last look at the ogre, the "Monster of Montmartre," who will be ground into mincemeat after the liberation along with all the other traitors. In thirty-six languages, raves Céline, the radios have announced the doom of the collaborators. He claims that he himself has provoked a veritable madness in people who for some time now had been harboring sinister thoughts about him, looking at him awry, or avoiding him altogether.[23] From the Résistance he has received his share of little coffins mailed to his apartment on the rue Girardon. He particularly resents the efforts of the grotesque cripple Jules who also appears in *Normance* living on a lower floor of the same building, and who is one of the few figures in *Féerie pour une autre fois* to whom Céline devotes any real attention. Jules not only seduces his wife Arlette, referred to in some of his books as Lili, and modeled on Lucette Almanzor, who married Céline in 1943 and who shared his exile in Germany and Denmark; Jules also denounces Céline as a Boche in front of his concierge and various passers-by who can then become so many witnesses against him. As Céline sees it, Gaullism is the name of the particular hatred in vogue at the time, and if he has indeed provoked madness on the part of his contemporaries, he returns it in kind in *Féerie pour une autre fois* as well as in the three chronicle novels that describe his flight through Germany at the end of the war, *D'un château l'autre, Nord,* and *Rigodon*. World War I had been a real war with real battles and he had been wounded in that war and decorated for valor. Under no circumstances will he now allow himself to be finished off passively and without protest. "The wolf dies without screaming, not I!"[24] From his "Baltic prison" in Denmark where he spent more than a year after the end of the war waiting for the French to decide what to do with him, come screams of vengeance in the second part of *Féerie pour une autre fois*. Article 75 of the French penal code has labeled him a traitor, with the list of his treasons underlined in red: whole cities, fleets, generals, battalions, Toulon harbor, the Pas de Calais, even the Puy de Dôme, all handed over to the enemy.[25] Céline is worked up and there is no stopping him! If anything his exaggeration is his revenge for what he considered the exaggeration of the charges brought against him, and since he believed quite explicitly that the purpose of literature was to convey not ideas but emotions, the reader is made to share the emotions he experiences. In this aim Céline was as successful in his work as he apparently was in his daily life, for certainly his work has aroused emotion, though certainly not always of a sympathetic nature. Perhaps ultimately he did not care what people thought. He claimed that his only reason for writing anything at all was to make money. As is so often the case Céline is too full of contradictions to be pinned down and classified.

At any rate he never tired of venting his rage against those he felt had done him wrong and in the end ruined him. After 1944 France needed a scapegoat, but Céline was unwilling to play the role. What had he done after all, sold the Maginot Line? When the goon squads of France, which he mockingly calls a "purged and pure Vrounze," come to get him in his apartment and fail to find him there, they destroy his motorcycle as a substitute.[26] Long after the great postwar purges were over, in *D'un château l'autre* (1957), and to a lesser extent in *Nord* (1960) and *Rigodon,* which he was working on till his death and which was published in 1969, eight years later, Céline lashed out against Sartre, François Mauriac, the communist and *résistant* author and poet Louis Aragon and Aragon's wife Elsa Triolet who together had translated *Voyage au bout de la nuit* into Russian, against the particularly militant Roger Vailland who met with a Résistance group in the apartment directly above Céline's in the rue Girardon and would have been only too glad to do away with him, against Louis Noguères who presided at the trials of important collaborators after the war, and against de Gaulle. He does not hesitate when it suits him to violate family names, changing Sartre into Tartre, a word used to designate dental incrustations from food residue, calcium carbonate, and the like. Aragon becomes Harengon (or sometimes Larengon) with its obvious derivation from *hareng* or herring.

Popular parlance also has the expression "sec comme un hareng," dry as a herring, and a derivative of *hareng, harengère,* is used popularly to indicate a quarrelsome, abusive woman. Triolet is turned into Triolette, a diminutive clearly attempting to reduce Elsa in stature, and Noguères into Noguarès, which gives to the man officially appointed as the judge of what is supposedly and properly French, a name which is more Spanish in sound than French. In *Nord* Céline further attacks Sartre who had condemned his anti-Semitic tirades, for having spent the war writing plays in Paris and dismisses him as "le résistant du Châtelet."[27] Certainly Sartre had never gone out and gotten himself wounded for France! In *Rigodon* Céline accuses Vailland of having won the Prix Goncourt simply for having attacked him and spells his name Vaillant, playing mockingly on the French word for "valiant."[28] Céline's arguments *ad hominem* abound when he counterattacks his critics, and he ridicules Mauriac, whom he calls "cancerous" and "hypocritical," for his ever-present capes in the "new look."[29] He points accusingly at the relatively wealthy Paul Claudel for his membership on the board of Gnome et Rhône, one of the French armament manufacturing firms that had done work for the Germans. And neither de Gaulle nor Malraux had ever stood up to the Germans on the front lines as he, Céline, had done in World War I.[30] In the end, however, perhaps such people were no worse than his own aunt who, out of shock, almost had a stroke on seeing him alive after his return to France. Along with the French court which had fined him 50,000 francs and confiscated half his property in addition to sentencing him to a prison term, his aunt had helped herself to what she needed from his apartment and would just as soon he had not come back.[31]

These were all the "good" people of France, and by the time they got through purifying it there would be no one left to oppose the next enemy. Toward the end of Céline's life, the Chinese replaced the Jews in his mind as the greatest enemy, and they would be the ones to descend on France. But back in the summer of 1944 when all the "good" people whom Céline had alienated started coming into their own, he realized that it was time for him to leave Paris.

when the cold feet were hanging out flags... when the trem-
blers were looting, when the deserters were triumphant, when the
gollywobblers were coming up strong, when forty million yellow-
bellies were taking their vengeance, it wasn't exactly the time for
me to show my face![32]

In his last book Céline described his odyssey through Germany as a rigadoon (*rigodon*), a lively and spirited dance, that
led him to wander in crisscross fashion all up and down that
battered country. But the dance metaphor functions on another level as well, for in the end it enabled Céline to "dance"
his way out of Germany. His itinerary cannot be extracted from
the text simply by putting together in chronological order the
three books that describe it. It must be pieced together out of
the controlled and structured confusion that reigns within the
books whose seeming anarchy is a brilliant reflection of the
"apocalypse" that was descending on Germany.

Céline is not an orderly narrator, and his almost total disregard for the exigencies of time plays a definite role in his attempt not merely to tell the reader a story but to make him see
it, to *faire voir*, to make him live through it with the narrator,
not so much by means of the events themselves but through
the narrative texture and the emotions it generates. The truth
at which Céline is aiming is less a factual one than an emotional
one, and those critics who seek too literal, rational, and aca-
demic an interpretation of every statement he makes are not
reading him as he intended. Certainly he makes many outrageous statements in the course of his work. Some of these statements, however, may be less shocking and outrageous if they
are read not in isolation but rather in relation to the context in
which they occur and in relation to the whole emotional structure that the text is trying to build.

Céline left Paris in June 1944 on the pretext of going to a
medical congress, and his first stop in Germany was at the spa
Baden-Baden in the Black Forest just across the Rhine. With
his wife and a cat named Bébert he stays at a luxury hotel where
he is received by the very accommodatingly anti-Nazi Madame
von Dopf. Very rapidly, however, he decides not to place too
much trust in her under the old dictum that "tous les vaincus
sont des ordures," that the vanquished are always regarded as

just so much trash. He is angered to see the elite at Baden-Baden still savoring the joys of an haute cuisine, eating caviar while bombs are falling everywhere in their beleaguered land. From Baden-Baden Céline travels to Berlin where a well-placed friend, Doctor Harras, establishes him on an estate in Kränzlin, a small village some hundred kilometers northwest. Playing on the German word for "anger" he renames it Zornhof, and a "court of anger" it is. Zornhof and the nearby village of Moosburg house the most ill-matched group the war could have produced: Polish and Russian deportees, ferociously anti-Nazi French workers, French POWs, collaborators, radically pacifist Jehovah's Witnesses known as *Bibelforscher* and whom Céline summarily describes as "conscientious objectors," communists, Berlin prostitutes whose syphilis is far too advanced to allow them to circulate freely, and heading the whole operation, an SS man whom Céline calls the first real Nazi he has ever seen, an individual who looks as stubborn and fierce as one might imagine a real Nazi to be and whom Céline, drawing from *Madame Bovary*, describes as an "Homais Nazi." This form of Prussian "quarantine" in Zornhof where Céline seems to fall somewhere between the Nazis and the anti-Nazis and thus appropriately incurs the hatred and hostility of everybody, is originally intended as a reprieve. But as time goes on at Zornhof he can only content himself with the knowledge that things would have been no better for him in Paris. Zornhof reinforces Céline's conclusion that his greatest success in life has been to set everyone from all the ranks and persuasions of global society against him.[33] Certainly this idea coincides with what Erika Ostrovsky has called Céline's need to "blacken" himself and play the victim.[34] But he plays that role well. In his fiction, the role, if it is a role, and the reality merge to the point where in certain passages, especially in *Féerie pour une autre fois*, *D'un château l'autre*, and *Rigodon*, Céline becomes what is almost an archetypal victim.

At the beginning of *Rigodon* with his destination at Copenhagen still in mind, Céline is finally able to leave Zornhof on a train bound for Rostock and Warnemünde, once considered among the most fashionable of the beaches on the north German coast. But the war raging in Germany prevents his crossing over to Denmark just then and he soon finds himself back at the station in Moosburg. By this time Pétain had been moved to Sigmaringen, a little town in southwestern Germany just east of where the Danube emerges from the Black Forest and where there stood an old castle that had once belonged to the royal Hohenzollerns. In Sigmaringen the Germans were attempting to set up a French government in exile, and though Pétain was not particularly cooperative, Sigmaringen became the gathering place for a "who's who" of Vichy officialdom. And so Céline, his wife, his cat, and the actor Le Vigan with whom he had left Paris, head south for Sigmaringen where Céline functions as medical doctor to the community. The Sigmaringen period, which began in November 1944, takes up almost the whole of *D'un château l'autre.* At the end of the book Céline briefly interrupts his stay at Sigmaringen to travel again, this time as part of a delegation to Hohenlychen, north of Berlin, where funeral services are held for Jean Bichelonne, the Vichy cabinet minister of commerce and industry who died under suspicious circumstances in a German hospital at the hands of an SS doctor. After the funeral he returns for a short time to Sigmaringen and in *Rigodon* relates his last desperate attempts to reach Denmark in a spell-binding trip through the demolished German Reich.

The Sigmaringen exile laid out in *D'un château l'autre* is certainly one of the strangest episodes in Céline's chronicle. Violating the details of historic chronology, Céline begins the book in Paris after the 1940 exodus and then suddenly shifts focus to Sigmaringen, ignoring the earlier stop-offs at Baden-Baden and Zornhof. The text starts with a long introduction that takes up almost a quarter of the book and consists of a series of harangues directed against Céline's enemies. It is a static narration in that there is no horizontal movement to advance the plot. But it does build an emotional climate verging on hysteria against which to view the Sigmaringen period and the end of the Vichy regime. The narration begins to move forward when Céline describes a visit to one of his patients, a Madame Niçois, who lives near the Seine in the Paris suburbs and can see the river from her windows. She has a form of cancer, and Céline reckons she has another five or six weeks to live. He treats her and then she begins to doze. He claims to see an old boat called *La Publique* moored at the quai but then questions whether he is not dreaming or hallucinating. He tries to draw Madame Niçois into a conversation about the boat, in part simply to have confirmation that what he is seeing is indeed real, but she is not interested and dozes off again. Céline is intrigued, nonetheless, and goes down to the quai. There he meets his friend from the exodus days, Robert Le Vigan, and together they embark on the boat. Its captain has the ominous name of Charon and he demands gold coins in payment for a ride. Charon, it turns out, is a monster who customarily bashes in the heads of his passengers with his oars, whether they have paid or not, and then fumbles around in their brains. When Céline emerges from his vision, he attributes it to some sort of attack he has had. But whether the vision was hallucinatory or not is not critical. The fact is that it has occurred and that it exists at least as an image. In its otherworldliness it will combine toward the end of the novel with the anachronistic elegance of the funeral train to Hohenlychen, a train especially outfitted by Wilhelm II for a visit by the Shah of Persia in August 1914, as this train with all its fine tapestries and curtains and Oriental rugs, but no glass panes in its windows, races through the ruins of Germany. Together the two images will describe a circle of death, timeless, eerie, and somewhat grotesque, around the Sigmaringen episode.

Sigmaringen itself is variously depicted by Céline as a ghetto and an escape from destiny for the French collaborators, a place that looked like an opera setting, "baroque boche," with its wedding-cake castle where fantasy and reality could come together. From here the doomed of Vichy watched Allied "flying fortesses" loaded with bombs move eastward across the sky toward the heart of Germany. Like Bayonne in 1940 Sigmaringen became a haven for those who were considered the derelicts of Europe. Ironically the derelicts of 1944 and 1945 had been the masters in 1940! Into the exotic and fantastic atmosphere of Céline's Sigmaringen in which everybody hates everybody else and in which Céline as victim concludes that the real hatred of the Germans had been for the collaborators and not for the Jews, there strut some of the strangest characters of literature: the lunatic doctor whose mania for cutting people up has earned him a reputation worse than that of the notorious "chop chop" Senegalese troops making swift purges after the liberation in Strasbourg; a man who claims to be a Catharist bishop with title to the see of Albi in southwestern France; Raoul Orphize who had gone to film the ashes of Dresden and now wants to make a movie in Sigmaringen; and finally, the appropriately named Frau Frucht who manages an establishment called the "Löwen" where Céline and his wife are staying, who hates the French but does not hesitate to sleep with them and who even attempts to get Céline to "set up" his wife for her. Into this "idyllic" atmosphere where people can still be concerned with collecting stamps and smoking cigarettes while the whole country around them is being pulverized into ashes, all kinds are seeking entrance. For a bored continent war is a holiday, intones Céline in a mood more reminiscent of 1914 than of World War II. But now the game is coming to an end and all the leftovers from the collaboration are arriving in Sigmaringen. Two hundred thousand female French workers encamp there in their flight from the east and regard it as another "Lourdes" where Pétain will still save them. Again and again Céline's narrative returns to the toilets to which Sigmaringen's standard fare (*Stammgericht*) seems to be confining people for life: kohlrabi, red cabbage, and sour beer. The *miliciens* who found their way to Sigmaringen have to be barred from the hospitals for defecating into the bathtubs. The BBC from London regularly warns the local Germans that what they are harboring is a particularly detestable group of French who are abusing their kindness and will end up betraying them even as they have betrayed France. From Sigmaringen with its maudlin ironies and paradoxes and its still relatively carefree idleness, despite Céline's own personal harried existence as medical doctor to the colony in exile, he takes off on the senseless mission to Bichelonne's funeral in Prussia. The elegant train which the Shah ironically never got to use because it wasn't delivered in time for his visit, has no windows and no heat, and so the French delegation use whatever they can find among the furnishings to keep warm. Fortunately there is no lack of Bukhara rugs and endless yards of drapery material covering the glassless window frames, and they dismantle the car with a vengeance. The blinding snow prevents them from seeing much of the outside world. Magdeburg goes by unnoticed and detours are made around Berlin. Upon arrival at Hohenlychen they are appropriately geeted with the *Horst Wessel Lied* and the *Marseillaise*. It is not until the return trip to Sigmaringen that Céline and his company begin to get a true picture of what is going on in Germany that last winter of the war.[35]

The Collapse of Germany

On the way back to Sigmaringen Céline's train is made a Red Cross train after Berlin, and some forty or fifty children who have been evacuated from Königsberg in East Prussia are put on board along with some pregnant women from Danzig to be transported to Constance on the Swiss border. Though the children are provided with their own food and supplies, they try to get additional blankets from the French, and though this inconvenience is not to Céline's liking, he is grateful to be traveling under the auspices of the Red Cross.[36] There is less likelihood that the train will be bombed. By the time they get to Ulm he is fully aware of just how precarious a position they might otherwise have been in. All the glass panes in the station at Berlin-Anhalt have been shattered, and Ulm is virtually wiped out.

> we were in the station... except there wasn't any station... we stop... here we are!... this is it, a sign... but no more Ulm!... the sign says Ulm... and that's all!... gutted sheds all around us... twisted scrap... the houses are nothing but grimaces... big chunks of wall... enormously off balance, waiting for you to pass underneath... the R.A.F. had come back... while we were up there... they'd wrecked the wreckage...

There is only one heartening note. ". . . Ulm is completely razed, they won't come back right away!... I hope!... there's a slight chance that they'll miss us! No more Ulm!... "[37]

Céline left Sigmaringen for good in March 1945, and took up his subsequent meanderings through Germany in *Rigodon*. Actually *Rigodon* creates its own chronology, skipping the Sigmaringen period entirely. It takes off directly from Zornhof, allowing Céline to speed through his itinerary in northern Germany and finally reach Denmark without the confusion of having to dwell on two additional trips to the south. Céline deliberately chose to alter the chronological facts of his stay in Germany, and this certainly was not, as has been suggested,[38] because he was unable to finish *Rigodon*. Though Céline may only have stopped working on *Rigodon* the day before he died,[39] the structure of the book was already far too advanced to allow him to return to Sigmaringen and since he had already described the Sigmaringen period at length in *D'un château l'autre,* there was really no need to return to it. Céline quite simply freed himself from having to write a text that would have been too cumbersome and confusing in its detail to handle artistically.

Céline's odyssey through Germany is a massive and powerful tableau of cities liquefied into "marmelade"[40] and, as he had already said in *D'un château l'autre,* of simple people, fires, tanks, and bombs being turned into "bouillabaisses."[41] Metaphors of destruction stand out in his text. In *Nord* he describes a bombed eight-story Berlin department store where he is trying to buy a walking stick. The bombs have made a "salad" of it.

> no more shelves... or stairs... or showcases... or elevators... all jummixed, toppling down in the basement... ah, the staff is still there!... salesmen, old fossils... oh, very friendly... all smiles... two three to a counter... counters full of nothing under signs... "Silks"... "China"... "Men's Suits"... but what about canes?... or crutches?

Informed that there are canes on the third floor Céline begins his climb.

> No more stairs... we climbed up on stepladders... the "Notions" counter... *"Leider! leider!* We'll have them soon! *Bald!"*
> Still smiling, the old gentlemen send us away... canes are on fourth floor... more little ladders... They've got some!... heavens above! the only counter with goods! all the canes you could wish for! and people!... the only busy counter! soldiers and civilians!... and kids!... here the salesmen aren't old, they're all cripples!... one leg, no legs!... as bad off as the customers... the up-and-coming department... the "Court of Miracles!"[42]

Railway stations all over Germany are filled with sleeping soldiers and wounded people with nowhere to go. At one point in *Rigodon* Céline witnesses a complete breakdown of discipline when a group of Finns, Estonians, Latvians, and Danes from Zornhof, which he has just left, see a train enter the station at Berlin-Anhalt bound for Ulm. This is the train that is to take Céline on his first trip to the south. Without scruple or hesitation the refugees from Zornhof break into a car that is clearly marked reserved for the Wehrmacht, rousing the sleeping Wehrmacht personnel and forcing them out of their couchettes in every stage of undress. All the refugees want is to get out of Berlin, to go south, and they succeed.[43] What can the Wehrmacht do at this point? A short time earlier such disorder would have been unthinkable, but Germany was a roller coaster heading for collapse. Céline, Lili, Bébert, and Le Vigan arrive in Ulm just in time for Field Marshal Rommel's funeral and even gain access to Field Marshal von Rundstedt, the commander-in-chief of the German armies in France who was historically present at Ulm to deliver his colleague's funeral oration. Probably not knowing what to say to this little group from Paris he evinces a special interest in the cat Bébert and wishes them luck on their upcoming trip to Sigmaringen.[44] In *Rigodon* Céline remains in Sigmaringen only long enough to establish the fact of his arrival and then almost immediately heads north toward Denmark with his first major urban stopover being Hanover.

He arrives there at night somewhere near what apparently was once a big railway station at Hanover-South. There are only three or four platforms left of the whole complex. His next task is to cross the city to Hanover-North where there are still rumored to be trains going to Hamburg. The dominant image of Hanover is one of fire, no true Biblical fire of purge and punishment, to be sure, for even though Céline speaks of an apocalypse he in no way sustains its imagery, but a simply dazzling fire of destruction. Even as his train approaches the remains of the city he can see the flames.

> I can see there aren't many houses standing... more? or less than in Berlin? the same, I'd say, but hotter, more flames, whirls of flame, higher... dancing... green... pink... between the walls... I'd never seen flames like that... they must be using a different

kind of incendiary gook... the funny part of it was that on top of every caved-in building, every rubble heap, these green and pink flames were dancing around... and around... and shooting up at the sky!... those streets of green... pink... and red rubble... you-can't deny it... looked a lot more cheerful... a carnival of flames... than in their normal condition... gloomy sourpuss bricks... it took chaos to liven them up... an earthquake... a conflagration with the Apocalypse coming out of it!

Day begins to break and confirms the horror of the night. "... there really wasn't a thing standing... nothing but fires and scraps of wall... all the ex-buildings were still full of soot and flames... and little explosions... " By now the smells are familiar to him, "charred beams, roasted meat..." The whole group from the train that has brought Céline to Hanover seems destined for Hamburg and they all walk together arm in arm down the middle of the street, headed for the northern railway terminal.

the day was breaking... lucky there were no houses left... I mean nothing left to clobber... the swirls of flame were like pink and violet ghosts... on top of every house... thousands of houses!... it was getting lighter... I've told you: not a single inhabitable house!... wrong again! over there!... no! people standing stiff against the walls!... there! now we can really see them... a man!... we stop we go over, we touch him... he's a soldier!... and another one... a whole string!... leaning against the wall... stiff!... killed right there! by the blast!... we'd seen it in Berlin... instant mummies!... they've got their hand grenades on them, in their belts... they're still dangerous! if they're armed... *bam*!... if they collapse on those grenades! *Vorsicht*! careful!... we take our hands away... the other side of the street, another patch of wall... more of them... more frozen soldiers... one thing's sure, they didn't have time to let out a peep... caught right there... bomb blast!... I'd forgotten one detail, now that I get a good look at them, they're all in "chameleon" camouflage!... stone dead!...

The translator has added several metaphors which do not occur in the original text. The idea of the dead men being "frozen" and not having had time to let out a bird's "peep" are not without interest, but they are superfluous and possibly even inappropriate to describe supposedly toughened soldiers who were killed ultimately, despite the cold weather, by fire and not by ice. It is, of course, ironic, nonetheless, that there are people, including Céline's wife Lili, on what was left of the platforms of Hanover-South shivering with cold in a city that has become a barnfire. The very irony of the situation provides a base for one more description of the burning city.

it's the cold... of course... all these people on the platforms around us, they know how to talk, but none of them thinks of making a fire... God knows there's plenty of that... a hundred yards away, all the streets on the right and left, all Hanover, I think... tail ends of houses burning... you had to see it... every single house... in the middle... in between the ex-walls a flame... yellow... violet... spinning... whirling... and flying away!... up to the sky!... dancing... disappearing... starting up again... the soul of the house... a farandole of colors from the first rubble heaps as far as you could see... the whole city... red... blue... and violet... and smoke...

There are some English people on the station, owners of a large horse farm left relatively undisturbed by the Nazis, a paralyzed man in the company of three women who were running all over the platforms and trying without success to find other English people. The women are concerned about how they are going to transport the paralytic to Hanover-North. At Zornhof Céline had seen a cripple chucked into liquid manure, and here there are flames everywhere! The devoted English women would have every opportunity and there would be no one to raise a voice against them. "... there's a time for everything!... when the 'anything goes' hour strikes, you will keep your trap carefully shut... " Perhaps the war itself more than Céline is responsible for the suggested breakdown of the moral code.

Céline and his family have in their possession a number of provisions including dishes, cups, knives, rice, and flour, and he reckons that these can be transported more easily to Hanover-North on one of the little station platform luggage carts standing idly by. He slips one of the station employees one 100 mark note and then a second one to appease him for the loss of the cart since there will be no one to return it. Then they take off, Céline, Lili, the cat Bébert, an Italian brick worker whose acquaintance they had made, and the English people who insist on accompanying them and load their own baggage onto the cart even before they are invited to. On top of the cart they hoist the cripple. They dash through the crater-filled streets of Hanover, a motley group resembling some crude and grotesque circus act, pursued by a whole mob of other travelers who have sprung to life, appropriating the remaining luggage carts once the initiative had been given. Just as Céline thinks they are gaining on their pursuers they are stopped by a portion of a large balcony that has fallen from one of the buildings into the street. To make matters worse more bombs start falling nearby. "... you'd think they were finished around here, they've wrecked the whole place!..." Céline is hit by a brick between his head and his neck and tries to remain lucid. The bombing continues, mostly in the southern part of town. More of the same flames, green and red. The Allies must have more money than they know what to do with to bomb Hanover again at this stage of her destruction! Maybe they are just doing it for amusement? By this time night is approaching, and the full moon lends an operatic setting to the scene. Céline had witnessed the bombing of the Renault plant outside of Paris earlier in the war, but it was no match for Hanover. Not even Hollywood could duplicate it.[45]

Céline manages to get out of Hanover on what supposedly is the last train for Hamburg. He has heard that for strategic reasons the rails are going to be ripped up in its wake. En route the train stops at one point and a mountain of scrap metal is revealed ahead, with a locomotive perched upside down on top of it. The passengers debate how the locomotive might have gotten there, but no explanation seems adequate and one seems as reasonable as the other.[46]

On the train Céline and Lili meet another French woman making the trip to Hamburg, Odile Pomaré who has a degree in German from the Sorbonne and had been teaching at the University of Breslau in Silesia. She is accompanying about a dozen children fleeing to the west before the Russian advance. They, too, are hoping that Hamburg will be their exit from the German inferno. But if Céline had thought that Hanover represented the pinnacle of destruction, Hamburg is even worse. Hamburg is totally destroyed. As they approach:

> plenty to see!... there in the distance... say, it's a port!... and
> there's the basin... enormous... all full ships... but all these ships
> are ass up, propellers out of the water... bows in the muck... I'm
> not drunk, but it's comical! grotesque!... at least ten ships, and
> good-sized ones, at least fifteen thousand tons... there must be
> some little ones too... I couldn't see them... the big ones I was
> sure... not hard to understand... we'd seen the finish of Berlin...
> Ulm... Rostock... but Hamburg was really finished... not just the
> city... the docks and the population... what about the cranes?... not
> a trace!... they'd knocked everything flat!...

Beginning to wonder whether he is hallucinating, what with
locomotives turned upside down in the air and boats standing
in what once was a harbor with their sterns reaching toward
the sky, Céline cuts short his own revery. The ships are there
in front of him and like Christ to the doubting Thomas who
refused to believe in his resurrection, so Céline takes the reader
by the hand quoting the Latin text of the Scriptures: "vide
Thomas! vide latus!" The platforms at the railway terminal are
of wood, indicating a kind of provisional station rapidly gotten
together.[47]

It is somewhat incredible and yet not unlike Céline that in
the middle of his text on the destruction of Hamburg he should
turn his attention away from that unhappy city to new attacks
against his enemies, Sartre, Roger Vailland, Mauriac, and others. But the digressions are not accidental, he is perfectly well
aware of what he is doing and even makes a mild apology to
the reader for them. In fact, they often provide relief from the
horrors of the bombings. They serve, too, as occasions for Céline to establish a discourse with the reader, sometimes to insult, more often to pacify or cajole, and certainly to manipulate.
As always, furthermore, in *Rigodon* Céline is striving for the
right notes for his composition, the appropriate musical setting,
and to find it he uses the digressions as counterpoint. Céline
thrives on the hostility he can generate against his enemies, and
the digressions seem actually to help him summon up the energy he needs to finish the Promethean task of describing
Hamburg in March 1945. Other writers have tried to describe
the fiery collapse of Germany, like Kurt Vonnegut with the fire-
bombing of Dresden in *Slaughterhouse-Five* (1969), or Bruno

Werner describing the same city in *Die Galeere* (1949), or Guy
Sajer witnessing the end in the city of Memel in East Prussia in
Le Soldat oublié (1967), as German soldiers sought to evacuate it
under a Russian bombardment. After trying his best, Sajer con-
cedes that the task is beyond him. No one could describe the
fall of Memel.[48] And yet Céline has described the virtual ob-
literation of Hamburg, Hanover, and other German cities, and
his descriptions are without equal. It is only by comparison with
narrators less powerful than he that one can appreciate the
magnitude of the accomplishment.

When he returns to his portrait of Hamburg, Céline takes
the reader right into the ruins, with seagulls flying overhead,
searching out the dead and dying so that they can pluck their
eyes out and gulp them down. Céline's customary three dots,
his run-on sentences and sentence fragments are particularly
appropriate here. They help maintain the rapid pace of the
narration, as a whole new world of sights and smells impinges
on the narrator's senses. The destruction of the internal order
of the sentence mirrors the chaos being described. Hamburg
now consists only of bricks and dead people and the charred
smell that can be found everywhere in Germany. But here there
is in addition the smell of burnt asphalt. Metaphor helps Céline
describe to his readers what they do not know in terms of
something they do: it was like the old days when there was no
war and workers made the pavement run as they repaired the
streets. The streets are no longer burning but they are still hot
enough to leave footprints. Céline was becoming accustomed to
cities that looked like "stewed fruit," (*des villes en compote*), but in
Hamburg absolutely everything had gone into the "sauce."
"Hamburg had been destroyed with liquid phosphorous... the
Pompeii deal... the whole place had caught fire, houses, streets,
asphalt, and the people running in all directions... even the
gulls on the roofs... the R.A.F. wasn't picky and choosy... they
just unloaded!..." As Céline, his wife, cat, and acquaintances go
off prospecting in the ruins accompanied, too, by the children
Mademoiselle Odile Pomaré had brought from the east, they
begin to see first limbs and then whole bodies stuck dead in the
sticky, melted asphalt. At one point they come upon a family:
"a man, a woman, a child!... the child in the middle... they're
still holding each other by the hand... and a little dog right next

to them... a lesson... people trying to get away, the phosphorous set fire to the asphalt... I heard about it later, thousands and thousands..." The pavement gets softer as they proceed on into the city, and Céline compares the feeling of instability underfoot with that generated by the moving sands of the Bay of Mont Saint-Michel on the English channel where Normandy and Brittany meet. He is reaching for a means to describe the indescribable.

Climbing among the ruins that from time to time still emit explosions, Céline and his party come upon what was once a grocery store that seems to have suffered a direct hit from an aerial bomb. The merchant is still sitting at his cash desk, dead, his guts exposed, the drawer of the desk open and full of paper mark notes. The grocery store and the city at large have begun to smell of dead flesh, but the cold impedes the process of decay and the odors of fire and death are not yet intolerable.

The children in Céline's entourage play fearlessly in the craters that have been torn open in the ruins and which seem especially made for them. Whether or not they were oblivious to what surrounded them, they were still young enough to be able to transcend it. These children would make their lives in the Europe of tomorrow, and already they were adapting to it as children will, making the most of an unusual opportunity. For them the ashes of Hamburg had become a playground. They were like the little children one sees today on summer afternoons on the hills above the beaches of Normandy, clambering about without awe or apprehension, in, out, and on top of the massive German concrete bunkers that once formed part of the Atlantic Wall. The children appear fragile only because they are still so small.

Hamburg had all but vanished, and Céline cannot tire of repeating it, for his repetitions are calculated to make the reader see and feel the enormity of the city's end. Among his last views of the once great port that Charlemagne himself had built, he hears the alert sounded at the railway station warning the would-be passengers, already living in a "bacchanal of rails, flatcars, shocks, and chains," of yet another bombing.[49]

Céline wrote that he did not intend to make his reader feel pity for him amid the difficulties surrounding his exit from Germany; he was merely indicating what was. What he said of his own plight he might have said of Germany's plight in 1945. Céline has shown as few others have what human beings at war can accomplish: "... Racine, Aeschylus, even Sophocles could keep you panting for three or four tragic acts with next to nothing . . . today, I ask you: a continent needs to be wiped out? nothing to it, two three minutes... at the most!..."[50]

Among the countless atrocities committed during World War II—which must not be forgotten if we are to profit from the experience of the past—the bombing of German cities must remain in human memory. Céline made that point unequivocally in *D'un château l'autre,* published the year following the Hungarian revolution of 1956. He was evoking the fire-bombing of Dresden of which the last Vichy government consul in that city had given him an eye-witness account while they were both at Sigmaringen.

> They talk about fires in mines... illustrations and interviews!... they weep, they jerk off about the poor miners... those treacherous fires and explosions!... shit!... and poor Budapest, the ferocity of the Russian tanks!... they never say a word... and they're wrong!... about how their brethren were roasted alive in Germany beneath the spreading wings of democracy... one doesn't speak of such things, it's embarrassing!... the victims?... they shouldn't have been there, that's all!...[51]

Céline is finally able to leave Hamburg accompanied by Mademoiselle Pomaré's children. At Flensburg before the Danish border they manage to get on a Swedish Red Cross train headed for the safety of neutral Sweden. There are, of course, plenty of other people who would like to board that train, clutching at the doors and couplings in a futile effort to get on. Lili throws herself under the train and screams loudly enough to enable Céline to attract the attention of a Swedish medical doctor to her predicament. Céline assures the Swede that he himself is a French Red Cross doctor who had served as a prisoner in one of the camps, that his wife is a Red Cross nurse, and that the children are all Swedish, their papers unfortunately destroyed in the cataclysm of Hamburg. Their passage is settled. Under no circumstances will Céline be allowed to go on to Sweden but he is welcome aboard for the trip to Denmark. This is what he had wanted all along.

The stay in Denmark, however, was not a happy one, for the Danes cooperated with French judicial officials who were pursuing Céline. Until the end of his life he would evoke with bitterness the fourteen months he spent in his "Baltic prison," sometimes exaggerating the length of the term to two years. And even after the prison term was over he was not free for another several years to return to France.

As Céline was fleeing north, Germans from the east, military personnel and civilians alike, were fleeing west in the hopes of escaping the Russian advance. Among them was Guy Sajer, an Alsatian recruited into the German army after the debacle in France. He spent almost all of his combat experience in Russia, and the German retreat at the end of the war brought him to Memel on the Baltic Sea in East Prussia. Though he had taken part in the French exodus of 1940, fleeing the German troops he would later join, the mass attempt to escape from East Prussia and West Prussia was of a different order entirely. In France the exodus had taken place in late spring and the weather was beautiful. "In Prussia," he recalls in *Le Soldat oublié,* "it was snowing and everything had been destroyed all around us. Refugees were dying by the thousands, and no one was able to help them. The Russians, when they were not fighting our troops, pushed the tide of civilians along in front of them, firing at them and driving tanks through the terrified mob." In a world turned upside down people and things no longer perform their customary functions: trucks are being pulled by men and tanks serve as locomotives to trains of endless length. Food rations are reduced to such a point that five people have to make do with what in normal times would scarcely have been considered adequate for a child's lunch. Ships are still leaving Memel, and long files of refugees jam the docks defying the efforts of the local authorities to register them. The crowds are visible targets for the Russian planes whose bombs open appalling gaps in their screaming midst, but still the crowds remain, hoping to get on the next ship. Heroism and despair are intermingled as old people simply kill themselves and mothers hand over their children to other women, begging them to feed the children with the ration cards the mother herself is sacrificing. "Capitulation would at least have put an end to this hideous nightmare. But Russia inspired such terror and had demonstrated such cruelty that no one even considered the idea. We had to hold or die." The West has never really understood, Sajer observed after his repatriation to France, what the specter of Russia had meant to the Germans in 1945.

When the snow stops and the skies clear, the appearance of the sun brings with it no joy. All it can mean is more Russian planes. Like many others Sajer finally manages to board a ship that takes him to Danzig which provisionally became the terminal point of the East Prussian exodus. He welcomes the return to military discipline because it signals a return to the world of the living. The demands it imposes are demands that can legitimately be made of human beings. But like Céline in the far worse cataclysm that had befallen some of the cities in the west such as Hamburg where one could no longer even talk of evacuating refugees, Sajer feared that the nightmare of human misery and destruction that had visited the German people was being lost on the world. They were the enemy of virtually all of Europe and of America, and these countries needed revenge for all the barbaric horrors that the Germans themselves had perpetrated. ". . . the spectacle of Memel will not even be helped by the last judgment. It is growing dim and vanishing without ever having been seen."[52]

Sajer was happy to have made it to Danzig, but even from Danzig people who were able to were fleeing to the west, to relatives in the Rhineland if they were lucky enough to have any relatives still living there. For in Danzig, too, Günter Grass recalls in *Die Blechtrommel,* everything was "washed up and finished."[53] In *Hundejahre* he elaborates:

> . . . everybody who has a nose to smell with runs, swims, drags himself away: away from the Eastenemy toward the Westenemy; civilians on foot, on horseback, packed into former cruise steamers, hobble in stocking feet, drown wrapped in paper money, crawl with too little gas and too much baggage; behold the miller with his twenty-pound sack of flour, the carpenter, laden with doorframes and bone glue, relatives and in-laws, Party members, active and passive, children with dolls and grandmothers with photograph albums, the imaginary and the real, all all all see the sun rising in the west . . . .[54]

From Grass's perspective the refugees were doing no more or less than the Führer's dog Prinz who also happened to come from Danzig. One day Prinz decides he has had enough of the Führer's expeditions all over Europe, living always under some kind of restriction and never knowing where he really belongs. So he heads for freedom toward the Elbe. The people from the eastern portions of the Reich were simply taking their cue from him, running from the "Eastenemy" to the "Westenemy." Grass draws up the balance sheet. For some the chance to escape would be a chance to forget or to be forgotten.

> Left behind: mounds of bones, mass graves, card files, flag-poles, party books, love letters, homes, church pews, and pianos difficult to transport.
> Unpaid: taxes, mortgage payments, back rent, bills, debts, and guilt.
> All are eager to start out fresh with living, saving, letter writing, in church pews, at pianos, in card files and homes of their own.
> All are eager to forget the mounds of bones and the mass graves, the flagpoles and party books, the debts and the guilt.

In the early morning of May 8, 1945, the dog Prinz swims across the Elbe above Magdeburg almost unseen, and he goes to look for a new master on the western side of the river.[55]

In Berlin people were scampering to flee the Russians and go over to the Americans. The Russians were rumored to have raped and beaten people; and the experiences of numerous women raped by the Russians at the end of the war in Berlin, Vienna, and other cities and villages in the areas they occupied later confirmed the rumor.

Those who did not flee, whether they were from the east or the west, had to make some other kind of adaptation. Hildegard Knef describes some of the Berliners during the final shooting, sitting in their cellars as tanks rolled through the streets outside and waiting for the end like sheep in a slaughterhouse. On occasion German soldiers tried to hide with the civilians in their cellars and sometimes they were asked to leave as it became clear from sounds echoing through the walls that the Russians had entered a neighboring cellar. The civilians feared the Russians would demolish their house if they found soldiers harbored within.[56] One remembers the French family in Sartre's *La Mort dans l'âme* who chase Brunet from their house in 1940 out of fear that the Germans will find him there and take revenge! The war was closing a full circle.

Nazi Party members or soldiers who stayed in the cellars of Berlin and other German cities did well to destroy any vestige of their affiliations. In Swiss writer Max Frisch's play *Als der Krieg zu Ende war* (1949), Horst Anders, a German army officer just returned from Poland and Russia, waits in the cellar of his Berlin home for his wife, Agnes, to bring him suitable civilian attire. Unhappily some Russians arrive, demand to be billeted in Agnes's house, and Anders is trapped, unable to emerge from his hideout until some three weeks later at the end of the play. When he does emerge, he finds that his wife has been carrying on an affair with one of the Russians. Agnes is a noble soul, torn initially between her duty to her husband and her instinct for survival. The audience has witnessed her struggle. It cannot now condemn her. Anders, too, furthermore, had seen things in the east, perhaps even been a party to some of them, about which he might now prefer to pass over in silence. In a moral sense the play is a microcosm of the war. When it ended, who was innocent enough to cast the first stone? In a highly dramatic final scene the Russian leaves the embarrassed German couple to confront each other and their past.

Told in a much lower emotional key is the story of the end of Nazi Party member Alfred Matzerath, Oskar's father in *Die Blechtrommel*. In Danzig Matzerath is also awaiting the arrival of the Russians in his cellar, his Party pin inadvertently still attached to his lapel. His neighbor, the widow Greff, advises him to remove it, but he does not know where to hide it. Fearing to go upstairs lest the Russians should come and surprise him in the act, he throws the pin to the ground intending to grind it into dust on the concrete floor. Before Matzerath can destroy it, however, the little boy Kurt grabs the badge from him. Kurt is the son he has sired in a marriage contracted after Oskar's mother's death, and Oskar disputes him the child's paternity to the end. Oskar, of course, does not wish to have "his" son caught with the deadly thing and so snatches it away from Kurt just as three Russian soldiers poke their heads into the cellar opening.

Women's screams coming from other cellars have alerted everybody that the Russians have penetrated the neighborhood. Their arrival does not disturb the life of the ants, which continue to go back and forth between provisions of potatoes and sugar. Nor does it seem to disturb the widow Greff who has to "spread her legs" for all of them and appears rather delighted after ten years of widowhood to be the object of so much attention. All this while Oskar is still holding onto the Nazi badge. One after the other the Russians pick him up, with his drum, faithfully upholding the dictum that Russians liked children. Oskar still resembles a child. Then he holds out his hand to Matzerath, and since the Russian who is holding him already has enough medals not to need any more, he deposits the badge into his father's confidently extended palm. To those who might question the intent and morality of Oskar's gesture he replies evasively and with typical bravado that Matzerath shouldn't have grasped at his hand. In desperation Matzerath shoves the pin into his mouth hoping to swallow it, but the movement of his hand to his mouth attracts the Russians' attention. Unfortunately in his anxiety Matzerath has forgotten to close the pin. When the Russians demand to see his hands he is literally choking and this makes it impossible for him to oblige. So they empty a whole magazine of bullets into his body. True to form, Grass relies on irony to squelch the potential for emotion before it can mature. The scene ends when Oskar squashes a louse pulled off the Russian who is holding him as his father is dying. Matzerath's dead body now lies squarely across the ant trail, but the little creatures are undaunted and soon build a new path around it.[57]

Another person who decides to remain at home is the one-time communist Ilse Kremer living in Cologne in Heinrich Böll's *Gruppenbild mit Dame*. After debating whether she should flee to the east or go still farther west, she decides to settle in. Her experiences are no less hair-raising. On March 2, 1945, according to Frau Kremer, many people went either totally or partially beserk during one of the worst air raids to hit the city. She herself had gone across the street into the cellar of a brewery with three men and another woman who had a boy of three. One of the men was still wearing a Nazi "brownshirt" uniform

which she claims was incredible at that late date. The Brownshirt was so terrified that he simply released all his functions
into his pants and fled into the street where later, not so much
as a collar button was to be found on him. The other two men
were younger, and she suspected them of being deserters
dressed in civvies who had been lurking in the ruins. Fright
had driven them inside. The young woman with the boy was
trembling so much that she bit through her lips until they were
bleeding. To prevent her from doing further damage to herself the others inserted a smooth little piece of wood between
her lips. At the time of the narrator's investigations Frau Kremer is sixty-eight years of age, but she still recalls vividly that
fateful March 2, twenty-five years earlier, when she was forty-
three years old, and the two young fellows no more than twenty-
two or twenty-three. They

> . . . suddenly started—how shall I put it, getting randy, pester-
> ing us, no that's all wrong, and after all, for three years, ever since
> they tortured my husband to death in the concentration camp, I
> hadn't looked at another man—well the two of them, you can't
> exactly say they fell on us and we didn't put up much of a fight
> either, they didn't rape us—anyway: one of them came over to
> me, grabbed me by the breast and pulled down my underpants,
> the other one went over to the young woman, took the piece of
> wood out from between her teeth and kissed her, and suddenly
> there we were, going at it together, or however you want to call
> it, with the little boy sleeping right there in the middle, and I
> know it must sound terrible to you, but you simply can't imagine
> what it's like when for six and a half hours the planes come over
> and drop bombs, aerial mines and nearly six thousand bombs—
> we simply closed in together, the four of us, the little boy in the
> middle . . . .[58]

The narrator in French Huguenot-descended Gertrud von le
Fort's *Am Tor des Himmels* (1954), also describes what it was like
to experience this kind of bombing while hiding in a cellar. It
is a time that no clock can measure. It is a time that somehow
falls outside the human sphere, a time spent "in the hand of
Satanic forces." One can only breathe again after the realization sinks in that one has not been hit.[59]

The confusion reigning in Germany in 1945 is well illustrated in the person of Liane Hölthohne, again in *Gruppenbild mit Dame*. She is part Jewish, has been an advocate of separation for Germany's "far west," the areas west of the Rhine, and at times she has used the alias of Elli Marx from Saarlouis. Not knowing which is the safest identity to assume as the Allies are poised to take possession of the country, she decides to remain Liane Hölthohne. ". . . toward the end you really never knew what was the safest thing to be—a Jewish woman in hiding, a Separatist in hiding, a German soldier who had not deserted or who had, a convict who had escaped or who had not, and of course the city was swarming with deserters, and with them around it was anything but pleasant, all of them trigger-happy, both sides."[60] Perhaps as never before, Kafka's world had become reality!

Many Germans tried to forget issues and labels, or at any rate, to overlook them. Other needs, the need to find food and shelter, the simple need to survive, had become too pressing. For Leni Pfeiffer's boss in *Gruppenbild mit Dame,* at the establishment where at the end of the war she is employed making wreathes and flower arrangements for the city's large cemeteries, that notorious second of March 1945 brings home some realizations. Walter Pelzer goes into the cemetery vaults to seek refuge with some of his work crew and acquaintances consisting of Nazis, anti-Nazis, communists, and indifferents.

> . . . we spent almost seven hours cooped up together on "the Second," clinging to one another, our teeth chattering, and believe me, even that atheist Lotte was murmuring her Our Father after Boris as he recited it for us, even the Hoyser brats were quiet, scared and awed, Margret was crying, we had our arms around one another like brothers and sisters as we crouched there thinking our last moment had come. I tell you, it was as if the world were coming to an end. It didn't matter any more whether one person had once been a Nazi or a Communist, the other a Russian soldier, and Margret an all-too-merciful sister of mercy, only one thing mattered: life or death.[61]

But in some sectors atrocities continued to the very end. After Russian tanks appeared in Berlin, Hildegard Knef finally decided to leave the city and escape into the countryside where she hoped to find Americans. Before leaving she witnessed some

German tanks heading for the Gedächtniskirche on the Kur-
fürstendamm and from a nearby tree trunk saw a pair of legs
dangling in front of her at eye level. A boy, his face blue and
his tongue sticking out of his mouth, was hanging from the tree
with a cardboard sign attached to his chest: "I AM A COW-
ARD I WAS TOO AFRAID TO FIGHT FOR MY FATHER-
LAND." Later, fearing to approach any of the local farmhouses
for food, she and a companion ate their last crusts of bread
and then relied on grass and the barks of trees to satisfy their
hunger. Soon they met up with a column of refugees carrying
French and Dutch flags hastily sewn together from rags. The
refugees were laughing and singing, and as they passed, shouted
"German swine,"[62] just as Germans had once called Jews swine
and were now calling the Russians swine.[63]

Like the French in 1940, the Germans in 1945 were wondering what their fate would be. Just as it has been claimed that
many in the Soviet Union would have welcomed the Germans
earlier in the war had they not been so brutal and vicious, so it
was claimed that all Berlin would willingly have gone over to
the Russians had they not been so vengeful. In addition the
Russians seemed totally uncivilized to the Germans: they would
flush their potatoes down the toilet to wash them, scream "sabotage" when the potatoes disappeared, and begin firing their
weapons. Civilization, of course, is a relative term. What was
left of Berlin and of Germany, at any rate, was divided like a
"birthday cake" among the Allies.[64] The war was over in Europe. The postwar era had begun.

Epilogue

Unlike the wars of antiquity, the Napoleonic wars, the American Revolutionary and Civil wars, Crimea, and even World War I, World War II never gave birth to a mythos in any true sense of the word. Hollywood, to be sure, with its unending sequence of war films succeeded in creating a feeble and superficial mythology of "blood, guts, and action" in which two-dimensional characters are supposed to seem heroic. But in France and Germany not even the ideal of manly comradeship, which had been so strongly reflected, especially in Germany, in the literature of World War I, seemed able to take hold. The French Résistance alone was an exception. France needed an idea capable of raising her above the ignominy of defeat and occupation, and the Résistance responded to that need. It was a movement in which by the end of the war almost all the French could unite, whether they were gaullists, communists, aligned to one politically aspiring faction or another, or totally unaligned. No doubt the *roman résistancialiste* helped to create and then perpetuate the legend that emerged from the Résistance, though that legend is today undergoing increasingly sober scrutiny from historians. Even in the late nineteen-forties Jean-Paul Sartre's Brunet in *La Mort dans l'âme* and Jean-Louis Curtis's Darricade in *Les Forêts de la nuit* were not without their failings; they were no *héros sans tache*.

At the end of the war France experienced a terrible need for revenge. Unquestionably she also suffered a strong feeling of guilt operating below the surface in the national consciousness, and that feeling of guilt, in turn, contributed to her need for revenge. Collectively and individually the nation and its citizens needed to find scapegoats for the more than four years of humiliation that they had endured. Marcel Aymé's *Uranus* (1948) and Jean-Louis Curtis's *Les Justes Causes* (1954) are piercing indictments of the mentality that set the French one against the other in an often noble yet pitiful refusal to bind up the country's wounds before what they thought was the presence of infection had been removed. Ironically most of the characters in these books, both those who were exalted after the war and those relegated to disgrace, had sought only to do well by themselves and by France. But both sides could not triumph, and unfortunately for themselves and for France some had made the wrong choice.

In Germany, too, there were people who sought revenge. Günter Grass's Walter Matern in *Hundejahre* roams all about the country in a personal vendetta directed against people who had wronged him during the Hitler years. Perhaps more poignant, however, than the desire for revenge was the feeling of guilt and the need for atonement. Frantz von Gerlach in Sartre's play *Les Séquestrés d'Altona* (1959) locks himself up for thirteen years after the end of the war in the family home on the edge of Hamburg, refusing to go out and witness the recovery city and his country. His reaction is obviously extreme, as is that of Rudolf Höller, a presiding judge close to retirement and a former SS officer in Thomas Bernhard's *Vor dem Ruhestand* (1979). Not unlike Frantz and his family, he lives with his two sisters but dreams of a Nazi return to power and every year on Himmler's birthday puts on his SS uniform. More characteristic are the heroes of Gertrud von le Fort's tales such as "Die Unschuldigen" published in *Gelöschte Kerzen* (1960) or *Das fremde Kind* (1961) whose memories of the Third Reich prevent them from living a normally unfolding life in the present. Or Siegfried Lenz's *Deutschstunde* (1968) or the heroes of Böll's novels of the postwar period such as *Billiard um halb zehn* (1959) and *Ansichten eines Clowns* (1963), where guilt, memory, the desire to learn from as well as the desire to forget the experience of the Nazi past are ever ready to come to the surface. Of course, many people had little time to spend reflecting or feeling guilty. Personal survival amid the economic shortages that plagued the country had to take precedence, and together with their own personal survival came the task of rebuilding Germany.

For the Alsatian Guy Sajer, central character, author, and narrator of *Le Soldat oublié,* the problems of the postwar period were compounded. At different times he had belonged to both France and Germany, but in a sense he belonged to neither. Repatriated to France once the war was over, he was advised by the military clearing officer to volunteer for a stint in the French army to give proof of his good will. But as he marched in a parade in Paris in 1946 to honor France's dead, he could not help but remember his dead German comrades and silently intoned their names during the long commemorative silence that was part of the ceremony. They were men with whom he had fought on the Russian front, whom he had loved as brothers, and who were now also gone from the earth.[1]

In France as well as in Germany the literature that has evolved from the war has shown a more marked tendency toward experimentation in theme and in formal structure as distance in time from the experience increases. To some extent this is a reflection of the highly experimental current that has swept through literature in the last three decades. But the very fact that the themes of World War II should have lent themselves to that kind of experimentation is significant. Günter Grass's tin-drummer Oskar, whimsically anti-heroic in his person and in his style of narration, would have been difficult to imagine right after the war, as would Michel Tournier's Abel Tiffauges, accused in France in 1939 of sexually criminal behavior and ending in 1944 as a French POW in East Prussia with the leadership of a Nazi *Napola* virtually in his hands. Claude Simon's preoccupations with the structural development of his text in *La Route des Flandres* are part of the general revitalization of the French novel undertaken by the *nouveaux romanciers* in the 1950s and the 1960s. The preoccupations of his principal narrator, Georges, trying to reconstruct the life, marriage, and death of his captain who died during the battle of France are probably not those to which the public of 1945 would have been most receptive. Both the subject and the form that shaped it clearly required time to mature. With the advent of writers like Grass, Tournier, and Claude Simon perhaps the time has come when it can be said with accuracy that sufficient distance from World War II has been obtained to treat it artistically in all the varied manifestations of its theme, when the theme of World War II has truly become "matter" for literature.

Notes

Preface

1. Antoine de Saint-Exupéry, *Pilote de guerre* (Paris: Gallimard, 1967), p. 130 (orig. ed., 1942). Lewis Galantière, trans., *Flight to Arras* (New York: Harcourt, Brace & World, 1969), p. 81. All published translations into English of works cited will be fully documented the first time they are mentioned. All succeeding references will include the page number of the English version in parentheses following the page number of the original.

CHAPTER I: *Technological War and the Fall of France*

1. William L. Shirer, *The Collapse of the Third Republic* (New York: Pocket Books, 1971), pp. 165–66. Orig. ed., 1969.
2. Simone de Beauvoir, *La Force de l'âge* (Paris: Gallimard, 1980), II, 438, 440–42, 446. Orig. ed., 1960.
3. Jean Dutourd, *Les Taxis de la Marne* (Paris: Gallimard, 1965), p. 19 (orig. ed., 1956). Harold King, trans., *The Taxis of the Marne* (New York: Simon & Schuster, 1957), pp. 13–14. Dutourd uses the words "parties de belote," *belote* being a game of cards. The original Siegfried Line was actually a fortified line occupied by German troops in France in World War I, which the Allies had called the Hindenburg Line.
4. Shirer, *The Collapse of the Third Republic,* p. 613.
5. Saint-Exupéry, *Pilote de guerre,* p. 13 (p. 7).
6. *Ibid.,* p. 40 (p. 25).
7. *Ibid.,* p. 78 (p. 47).
8. *Ibid.,* pp. 8–9 (pp. 3–4).
9. Shirer, *The Collapse of the Third Republic,* p. 3.

10. Saint-Exupéry, *Pilote de guerre*, p. 93 (p. 57).
11. *Ibid.*, pp. 129–30 (p. 81).
12. *Ibid.*, p. 12 (p. 6).
13. *Ibid.*, p. 49 (pp. 29–30).
14. *Ibid.*, p. 118 (p. 73).
15. *Ibid.*, p. 121.
16. *Ibid.*, p. 123 (p. 76).
17. *Ibid.*, p. 193 (p. 120).
18. *Ibid.*, p. 73 (p. 44).
19. *Ibid.*, pp. 99–100 (pp. 60–61).
20. *Ibid.*, p. 10 (p. 5).
21. *Ibid.*, pp. 5–6 (p. 1).
22. *Ibid.*, p. 27 (p. 17).
23. Albert Camus, *Le Mythe de Sisyphe* (Paris: Gallimard, 1968), p. 165. Orig. ed., 1942.
24. Saint Exupéry, *Pilote de guerre*, p. 76 (p. 46).
25. *Ibid.*, p. 17.
26. *Ibid.*, p. 27.
27. *Ibid.*, p. 90 (p. 55).
28. *Ibid.*, p. 176 (p. 110).
29. *Ibid.*, p. 203.
30. *Ibid.*, p. 105 (p. 64).
31. Orconte is a village on the outskirts of Saint-Dizier in northeastern France where Saint-Exupéry's unit was stationed in the winter of 1939.
32. Saint-Exupéry, *Pilote de guerre*, pp. 106–7 (p. 65).
33. *Ibid.*, p. 221.
34. *Ibid.*, p. 209 (p. 131).
35. Saint-Exupéry, *Oeuvres* (Paris: Gallimard, 1959), pp. xxix–xxx. Herbert R. Lottman, *The Left Bank* (Boston: Houghton Mifflin, 1982), pp. 156, 177, 207.
36. Jean Lacouture, *André Malraux* (New York: Pantheon, 1975), p. 290. Orig. published in French in Paris by Seuil in 1973.
37. André Malraux, *Les Noyers de l'Altenburg* (Paris: Gallimard, 1948), pp. 252–53 (orig. ed., 1943). Terence Kilmartin trans., *Anti-Memoirs* (New York: Holt, Rinehart and Winston, 1968), p. 206 (orig. French ed., 1967).
38. *Ibid.*, p. 265 (p. 206).
39. Saint-Exupéry, pp. 5–6.
40. Malraux, *Les Noyers de l'Altenburg*, p. 273 (p. 210).
41. Saint-Exupéry, p. 73.
42. Malraux, *Les Noyers de l'Altenburg*, p. 267 (p. 207).
43. *Ibid.*, pp. 268–69 (p. 208).

44. *Ibid.*, p. 271. The text does not occur in the *Antimémoires*.
45. *Ibid.*, pp. 273–74 (pp. 210–11).
46. *Ibid.*, p. 275.
47. *Ibid.*, pp. 282–84 (pp. 214–15).
48. *Ibid.*, p. 277.
49. *Ibid.*, p. 284 (p. 215).
50. *Ibid.*, p. 287.
51. *Ibid.*, pp. 288, 291 (p. 217).
52. Ernst Jünger, "Gärten und Strassen," in *Ernst Jünger: Werke* (Stuttgart: Ernst Klett, 1960–65), II, 150–51, 160–68. Orig. ed. 1942.
53. Malraux, *Les Noyers de l'Altenburg*, pp. 288, 291.
54. Malraux, *Antimémoires* (Paris: Gallimard, 1972), p. 300 (orig. ed., 1967). Kilmartin trans., p. 199.
55. Malraux, *Les Noyers de l'Altenburg*, p. 251 (p. 200).
56. Wilbur M. Frohock, *André Malraux and the Tragic Imagination* (Stanford, Calif.: Stanford University Press, 1952), p. 127.
57. Wilbur M. Frohock, *Style and Temper* (Cambridge, Mass.: Harvard University Press, 1967), pp. 62–63, 74.
58. Malraux, *Les Noyers de l'Altenburg*, pp. 17–18, 23.
59. *Ibid.*, pp. 14, 19–20.
60. *Ibid.*, pp. 16–17. This episode does not occur in the *Antimémoires*.
61. *Ibid.*, pp. 16, 20, 22.
62. *Ibid.*, p. 158.
63. *Ibid.*, p. 191.
64. *Ibid.*, p. 15.
65. Lothar-Günther Buchheim, *Das Boot* (München: R. Piper, 1973), p. 217. Denver and Helen Lindley, trans., *The Boat* (New York: Alfred Knopf, 1975), pp. 158–59.
66. *Ibid.*, p. 129 (p. 102).
67. *Ibid.*, p. 103 (p. 84).
68. *Ibid.*, p. 154.
69. Erich Maria Remarque, *Im Westen nichts Neues* (Berlin: Propyläen, 1929), pp. 219–25.
70. Buchheim, *Das Boot*, p. 25 (p. 19).
71. *Ibid.*, p. 33 (pp. 25–26).
72. *Ibid.*, p. 331 (p. 249).
73. *Ibid.*, pp. 123, 129, 132 (pp. 102, 104–5).
74. *Ibid.*, p. 29 (p. 22).
75. *Ibid.*, p. 13 (p. 8).
76. *Ibid.*, p. 327 (p. 245–46).
77. *Ibid.*, p. 13 (p. 9).
78. *Ibid.*, p. 9.
79. *Ibid.*, pp. 27–28 (p. 21).

80. *Ibid.,* pp. 139–40.
81. *Ibid.,* p. 10 (p. 6).
82. Remarque, *Im Westen nichts Neues,* p. 166.
83. Henri Barbusse, *Le Feu* (Paris: Flammarion, 1945), pp. 173–74. Orig. ed., 1917.
84. Buchheim, *Das Boot,* pp. 110, 96 (p. 88).
85. *Ibid.,* p. 121 (p. 96).
86. *Ibid.,* pp. 71, 338, 468 (pp. 57, 256, 369).
87. *Ibid.,* p. 51 (p. 40).
88. *Ibid.,* p. 396 (pp. 308–9).
89. *Ibid.,* pp. 52–53 (p. 41).
90. Zuydcoote is a coastal village in the *département du Nord* belonging to the Dunkirk *arrondissement.*
91. Robert Merle, *Week-end à Zuydcoote* (Paris: Gallimard, 1972), pp. 26–27. Orig. ed., 1949.
92. *Ibid.,* p. 69.
93. *Ibid.,* pp. 108, 106, 26.
94. *Ibid.,* pp. 212, 181.
95. Shirer, *The Collapse of the Third Republic,* p. 756.
96. *Ibid.,* pp. 779, 781.
97. Jean Guéhenno, *Journal des années noires* (Paris: Gallimard, 1973), p. 15. Orig. ed., 1947.
98. Jean-Paul Sartre, *La Mort dans l'âme* (Paris: Gallimard, 1972), pp. 235–45. Orig. ed., 1949.
99. Pierre Seghers, *La Résistance et ses poètes* (Paris: Seghers, 1974), p. 55.
100. Shirer, *The Collapse of the Third Republic,* pp. 919–26.
101. When *La Résistance et ses poètes* was published in 1974, it was the first full anthology and *vue d'ensemble* of the Résistance poets to be published in France.
102. Pierre Seghers, p. 57.
103. Claude Simon, *La Route des Flandres* (Paris: Union Générale d'Editions, 1963), pp. 13, 243 (orig. ed., 1960). Leon Roudiez, *French Fiction Today* (New Brunswick, N.J.: Rutgers University Press, 1972), p. 167.
104. *Ibid.,* pp. 93, 85.
105. *Ibid.,* p. 140.
106. *Ibid.,* p. 109.
107. *Ibid.,* p. 156.
108. *Ibid.,* p. 270.

CHAPTER II: *The French Army*

1. Shirer, *The Collapse of the Third Republic*, p. 890.
2. Georges Bernanos, *Les Enfants humiliés* (Paris: Gallimard, 1973), p. 7. Orig. ed. 1949.
3. Michel Tournier, *Le Roi des aulnes* (Paris: Gallimard, 1975), p. 206 (orig. ed., 1970). Barbara Bray, trans., *The Ogre* (Garden City, N.Y.: Doubleday, 1972), p. 128.
4. Dutourd, *Les Taxis de la Marne*, pp. 223, 124.
5. *Ibid.*, p. 10 (p. 4).
6. Pierre-Henri Simon, *Portrait d'un officier* (Paris: Seuil, 1971), p. 16. Orig. ed., 1958.
7. *Ibid.*, p. 17.
8. *Ibid.*, pp. 153, 157.
9. Jacques Perret, *Le Caporal épinglé* (Paris: Gallimard, 1972), p. 8. Orig. ed., 1947.
10. Dutourd, *Les Taxis de la Marne*, pp. 168–69, 131.
11. *Ibid.*, p. 116 (p. 112).
12. *Ibid.*, p. 145.
13. *Ibid.*, p. 144 (p. 140).
14. Dutourd, *Au bon beurre* (Paris: Gallimard, 1972), p. 19. Orig. ed., 1952.
15. Dutourd, *Les Taxis de la Marne*, p. 86.
16. Perret, pp. 20–21.
17. Sartre, *La Mort dans l'âme*, p. 95. Gerald Hopkins, trans., *Troubled Sleep* (New York: Random House, 1973), p. 96.
18. *Ibid.*, pp. 244–45.
19. Bertolt Brecht, *Die Geschichte der Simone Machard* (Frankfurt/Main: Suhrkamp, 1970), p. 18. Written in 1942–43; copyright 1957.
20. Perret, p. 91.
21. Pierre-Henri Simon, p. 9.
22. Sartre, pp. 145–46.
23. *Ibid.*, pp. 266, 268 (p. 280).
24. Dutourd, *Les Taxis de la Marne*, p. 176 (p. 170).
25. Sartre, p. 84.
26. Tournier, p. 205.
27. *Ibid.*, p. 241.
28. Sartre, p. 271 (p. 286).
29. *Ibid.*, p. 353.
30. Perret, p. 54; Sartre, p. 226.
31. Perret, p. 54.
32. Sartre, pp. 25, 255, 203.
33. Perret, p. 101.

34. Sartre, pp. 88, 179.
35. Perret, pp. 14, 19.
36. Sartre, p. 260.
37. Perret, pp. 54, 98.
38. Sartre, pp. 130, 53–54, 205.
39. Dutourd, *Les Taxis de la Marne,* p. 146.
40. *Ibid.,* pp. 127–28 (pp. 123–24).
41. *Ibid.,* p. 169.
42. Perret, pp. 50–51.
43. Sartre, p. 273.
44. *Ibid.,* pp. 353–54 (p. 389).
45. Perret, p. 39.
46. Dutourd, *Les Taxis de la Marne,* pp. 142–43 (pp. 138–39).
47. Sartre, pp. 235–36, 230.
48. *Ibid.,* p. 194.
49. *Ibid.,* p. 259.
50. Dutourd, *Les Taxis de la Marne,* pp. 211–14 (pp. 206, 208).
51. Perret, pp. 34–35, 46–47.
52. Sartre, p. 258 (p. 271).
53. *Ibid.,* p. 318.
54. *Ibid.,* pp. 353–354 (pp. 388–90).
55. Perret, p. 25.
56. Sartre, p. 213 (p. 222).
57. Perret, p. 77.
58. Sartre, p. 260. The translation here is my own. The Hopkins translation does not accurately render Sartre's text.
59. Sartre, p. 260 (p. 273).
60. *Ibid.,* p. 261 (p. 274).
61. *Ibid.,* p. 286 (p. 306).
62. Perret, p. 34.
63. *Ibid.,* p. 65.
64. Sartre, p. 252 (p. 263).
65. Perret, p. 78.
66. Dutourd, *Les Taxis de la Marne,* pp. 166, 144.
67. Sartre, pp. 344–45 (pp. 377–78).
68. Perret, pp. 85, 95.
69. Sartre, p. 301.
70. Perret, pp. 74, 85.
71. Beauvoir, *La Force de l'âge,* II, 473–74.
72. Sartre, p. 334 (p. 364).
73. Perret, pp. 36, 27.
74. Sartre, pp. 301–302 (p. 325).
75. *Ibid.,* pp. 326, 329.

76. Perret, pp. 93–94.
77. *Ibid.*, pp. 51–52.
78. Sartre, pp. 351–52 (p. 385).
79. Perret, p. 99.
80. *Ibid.*, pp. 14, 86–87.
81. Pierre Gascar, *Histoire de la captivité des Français en Allemagne (1939–1945)* (Paris: Gallimard, 1967), p. 35.
82. Perret, p. 103.
83. *Ibid.*, p. 105.
84. *Ibid.*, pp. 106–9.
85. Sartre, p. 375.
86. *Ibid.*, pp. 376–77.

CHAPTER III: *Civilian France in the Defeat*

1. Jean Guéhenno, *Journal des années noires*, p. 43.
2. Robert Brasillach, *Notre Avant-guerre* (Paris: Plon, 1973), p. 133. Orig. ed. 1941.
3. *Ibid.*, p. 341.
4. Franz Werfel, *Jacobowsky und der Oberst* (Frankfurt/Main: Fischer, 1976), p. 127 (orig. ed. 1944). Gustave O. Arlt trans., *Jacobowsky and the Colonel* (New York: The Viking Press, 1944), p. 96.
5. Jean-Paul Sartre, *La Mort dans l'âme*, pp. 182–83 (pp. 189–90).
6. Beauvoir, *La Force de l'âge*, II, 509.
7. Saint-Exupéry, *Pilote de guerre*, pp. 109, 111 (67–68).
8. Sartre, p. 24 (p. 19).
9. Jean Dutourd, *Au bon beurre*, p. 16.
10. Michel Tournier, *Le Roi des aulnes*, p. 235.
11. Sartre, pp. 18–21, 27 (pp. 16–19, 22–23).
12. Saint-Exupéry, pp. 111, 114–16 (pp. 70–71).
13. Dutourd, *Au bon beurre*, pp. 15–16.
14. Werfel, pp. 18–19.
15. *Ibid.*, pp. 42–44 (pp. 30–31).
16. *Ibid.*, p. 90. The translation is mine. The Arlt translation is inappropriate to the context in which the quotation is used here as well as to the character of Stjerbinsky who speaks these lines.
17. Jacques Perret, *Le Caporal épinglé*, pp. 69–70.
18. Werfel, p. 79 (p. 58).
19. *Ibid.*, pp. 131–32.
20. Bertolt Brecht, *Die Geschicte der Simone Machard*, pp. 6, 10–11. Ralph Manheim, trans., "The Visions of Simone Machard," in *Bertolt Brecht, Collected Plays* (New York: Random House, 1974), VII, 5.
21. *Ibid.*, p. 16.

22. Sartre, pp. 249–51 (pp. 259–62).
23. Tournier, pp. 239–40.
24. Sartre, p. 257 (pp. 269–70).
25. *Ibid.*, p. 360 (p. 397).
26. Tournier, pp. 244–45.
27. Sartre, pp. 267–68 (pp. 281–82).
28. *Ibid.*, pp. 121–22 (pp. 124–25).
29. Brecht, p. 9 (p. 4).
30. *Ibid.*, pp. 25, 28 (p. 15).
31. *Ibid.* pp. 40, 42 (pp. 24, 26).
32. *Ibid.*, pp. 62–63 (p. 39).
33. Werfel, p. 125.
34. Dutourd, *Au bon beurre,* pp. 16–18. Robin Chancellor, trans., *The Best Butter* (New York: Greenwood Press, 1955), pp. 4–5.
35. Sartre, p. 98 (p. 100).
36. *Ibid.*, pp. 145–46 (pp. 150–51).
37. *Ibid.*, pp. 101–3 (pp. 103–6).
38. *Ibid.*, pp. 147, 158.
39. Serge Doubrovsky, *La Dispersion* (Paris: Mercure de France, 1969), pp. 114–16.
40. Guéhenno, p. 44.
41. *Ibid.*, p. 13.
42. Dutourd, *Les Taxis de la Marne,* p. 111.
43. *Ibid.*, pp. 110, 112–13, 123. See also footnote, p. 113 (p. 108).
44. *Ibid.*, p. 146.
45. Werfel, p. 123 (p. 93).
46. Perret, p. 30.
47. Sartre, pp. 305–7 (p. 330).
48. Michael R. Marrus and Robert O. Paxton, *Vichy France and the Jews* (New York: Basic Books, 1981), p. 198. Orig. published in France by Calmann-Lévy as *Vichy France et les juifs,* 1981.
49. Perret, pp. 99–100.
50. Brecht, pp. 58–59, 65, 68–69, 91–94 (pp. 41, 43, 58–60).
51. Werfel, p. 61.
52. *Ibid.*, p. 115.
53. Dutourd, *Les Taxis de la Marne,* p. 156.
54. William Shirer, *The Collapse of the Third Republic,* p. 889.
55. Werfel, pp. 151, 159–160.
56. *Ibid.*, p. 154.

CHAPTER IV: *Germany—Life under the Nazis*

1. William L. Shirer, *The Rise and Fall of the Third Reich* (New York: Simon and Schuster, 1960), pp. 226, 241, 253–54.

1. *Ibid.*, pp. 244–45.
3. *Ibid.*, pp. 203, 233.
4. *Ibid.* pp. 234–40.
5. *Ibid.*, p. 239.
6. *Ibid.*, pp. 270–72.
7. Stefan Zweig, *Die Welt von Gestern* (Frankfurt/Main: Fischer, 1975), pp. 260–61 (orig. German ed., 1944). E. and C. Paul, trans., *The World of Yesterday* (New York: The Viking Press, 1943), pp. 361–62, 439 (orig. English ed., 1943).
8. *Ibid.*, pp. 273–90.
9. Albrecht Goes, *Das Brandopfer* (Frankfurt/Main: Fischer, 1968), pp. 10–11. Orig. ed., 1954.
10. Günter Grass, *Die Blechtrommel* (Darmstadt: Luchterhand, 1979), pp. 92–93, 140–41 (orig. ed., 1959). Ralph Manheim, trans., *The Tin Drum* (New York: Random House, 1964), pp. 115–16.
11. *Ibid.*, p. 162 (p. 20l). Grass erroneously lists the date of the Kristallnacht as November 8. It actually occurred on the night of November 9.
12. Shirer, *The Rise and Fall of the Third Reich*, p. 430.
13. Grass, *Die Blechtrommel*, p. 162 (p. 201).
14. Erich Maria Remarque, *Zeit zu leben und Zeit zu sterben* (Frankfurt/Main:Ullstein, 1974), pp. 76–77 (orig. ed., 1954). Denver Lindley, trans., *A Time To Love and a Time To Die* (New York: Harcourt, Brace, 1954), p. 117.
15. *Ibid.*, pp. 105–7.
16. Carl Zuchmayer, *Des Teufels General* (Frankfurt/Main: Fischer, 1974), p. 100. Orig. ed., 1946.
17. Heinrich Böll, *Gruppenbild mit Dame* (München: DTV, 1978), p. 192 (orig. ed., 1971). Leila Vennewitz, trans., *Group Portrait with Lady* (New York: Avon, 1974), p. 224.
18. Remarque, *Zeit zu leben und Zeit zu sterben*, pp. 36, 40 (p. 54).
19. *Shirer, The Rise and Fall of the Third Reich*, p. 934.
20. Remarque, *Zeit zu leben und Zeit zu sterben*, pp. 44–47, 64 (pp. 59, 70, 72, 97). The geographical location of the actual Werden on the Ruhr just south of Essen does not fit Remarque's description.
21. Richard Meran Barsam, *Filmguide to "Triumph of the Will"* (Bloomington, Ind.: Indiana University Press, 1975), pp. 14–15.
22. Klaus Mann, *Mephisto* (Reinbek bei Hamburg: Rowohlt, 1980), pp. viii, 344. Orig. ed., 1936.
23. Ernst Wiechert, *Der Totenwald* (Frankfurt/Main: Ullstein, 1972), pp. 13, 16–18, 20. Orig. ed., 1946.
24. Goes, pp. 15–16.
25. *Ibid.*, pp. 52–53, 57–58, 60–61.
26. *Ibid.*, p. 70.

27. Böll, *Ansichten eines Clowns* (München: DTV, 1980), pp. 25–26. Orig. ed., 1963.
28. Luise Rinser, "Weihnacht hinterm Totenholz" in *Weihnachts-Triptykon* (Zürich: Peter Schifferli Verlags AG Die Arche, 1963), pp. 40–41.
29. Remarque, *Zeit zu leben und Zeit zu sterben,* pp. 66, 85–86, 91.
30. Günter Grass, *Hundejahre* (Darmstadt: Luchterhand, 1978), pp. 232–38, 27l. Orig. ed., 1963. Remarque, *Zeit zu leben und Zeit zu sterben,* pp. 204–6.
31. Remarque, *Zeit zu leben und Zeit zu sterben,* pp. 50–51 (p. 77).
32. *Ibid.,* 84–85.
33. *Ibid.,* p. 146.
34. *Ibid.,* pp. 79, 88 (p. 136).
35. *Ibid.,* p. 64 (pp. 97–98).
36. Hildegard Knef, *Der geschenkte Gaul* (Frankfurt/Main: Ullstein, 1975), p. 42. Orig. ed., 1970.
37. Zuckmayer, p. 91.
38. *Ibid.,* p. 17.
39. *Ibid.,* pp. 119, 45.
40. *Ibid.,* pp. 139–40.
41. *Ibid.,* pp. 154–56.
42. *Ibid.,* pp. 149–54.
43. Heinrich Böll, "Die Postkarte" in *Als der Krieg ausbrach* (München, DTV, 1968), pp. 78–83. Orig ed. of this collection, 1965. Dates when the individual stories from the collection were written appear in the bibliography.
44. Böll, "Als der Krieg ausbrach," in *Als der Krieg ausbrach,* p. 23.
45. Böll, *Wo warst du, Adam?* (München, DTV, 1975), pp. 57–58. Orig. ed., 1951.
46. Böll, *Gruppenbild mit Dame,* pp. 37–42.
47. Scherwin is located in Mecklenburg east of Hamburg in what is now East Germany,
48. Grass, *Hundejahre,* pp. 159–60, 200, 206–10, 129–30. Ralph Manheim, trans., *Dog Years* (Greenwich, Conn.: Fawcett, 1965), pp. 251, 159.
49. *Ibid.,* p. 163 (p. 199).
50. Grass, *Die Blechtrommel,* pp. 128–30.
51. *Ibid.,* pp. 174, 200–201.
52. *Ibid.,* pp. 10–11.
53. Grass, *Hundejahre,* p. 301.
54. Grass, *Die Blechtrommel,* p. 9.
55. Northrop Frye, *Anatomy of Criticism* (Princeton, N.J.: Princeton University Press, 1971), p. 34. Orig. ed., 1957.

56. Remarque, *Zeit zu leben und Zeit zu sterben*, p. 218.
57. *Ibid.*, p. 194.
58. Böll, "Die blasse Anna," in *Als der Krieg ausbrach*, p. 138.
59. Grass, *Hundejahre*, p. 218.
60. Böll, *Gruppenbild mit Dame*, pp. 67–68, 217.
61. Remarque, *Zeit zu leben und Zeit zu sterben*, p. 127.
62. Bertolt Brecht, "Und was bekam des Soldaten Weib," in *Gedichte und Lieder aus Stücken* (Frankfurt/Main: Suhrkamp, 1976), pp. 128–29. This *Lied* is taken from the play *Schweyk im zweiten Weltkrieg* which was written in 1943 and copyrighted in 1957.
63. Zweig, pp. 169–70.
64. Robert Merle, *La Mort est mon métier* (Paris: Gallimard, 1968), p. 399. Orig. ed., 1952.
65. Grass, *Die Blechtrommel*, pp. 245–46.
66. Knef, p. 8. David Anthony Palastanga, trans., *The Gift Horse* (New York: Dell, 1972), p. 8.
67. Merle, *La Mort est mon métier*, pp. 18–20.
68. Böll, *Gruppenbild mit Dame*, p. 108.
69. *Ibid.*, pp. 54–74 (pp. 89–90). Langemarck is located in Belgium, just northeast of Ypres.
70. *Ibid.*, p. 117.
71. Böll, "Entfernung von der Truppe" in *Als der Krieg ausbrach*, p. 240.
72. Alfred Andersch, *Die Kirschen der Freiheit* (Zürich: Diogenes, 1968), pp. 89–90. Orig. ed., 1952.
73. Böll, *Der Zug war pünktlich* (München: DTV, 1975), pp. 38–40. Orig. ed., 1949.
74. Zweig, pp. 99–100.
75. Rolf Hochhuth, *Der Stellvertreter* (Reinbek bei Hamburg: Rowohlt, 1975), p. 40. Orig. ed., 1963.
76. Remarque, *Zeit zu leben und Zeit zu sterben*, p. 131.
77. *Ibid.*, pp. 130–31 (p. 204).
78. *Ibid.*, pp. 17–18 (p. 24).
79. Grass, *Die Blechtrommel*, pp. 270–71.
80. *Ibid.*, p. 97.
81. *Ibid.*, p. 273 (p. 332).

CHAPTER V: *Roundheads and Peakheads*

1. Bertolt Brecht, "Die Rundköpfe und die Spitzköpfe oder Reich und Reich gesellt sich gern" in *Gesammelte Werke* (Frankfurt/Main: Suhrkamp, 1967), III. N. Goold-Verschoyle, trans., "Roundheads and Peakheads" in *"Jungle of Cities" and Other Plays* (New York:

Grove, 1966), p. 177. The play was first published in an abridged version in English in 1935. The complete German version was first published in 1938 by the Malik Verlag with an address in London and a publishing house in Prague.

2. Zweig, p. 304.
3. Hochhuth, *Der Stellvertreter,* pp. 62, 66, 231.
4. *Ibid.,* pp. 65–66. Richard and Clara Winston, trans., *The Deputy* (New York: Grove, 1964), p. 80.
5. *Ibid.,* pp. 66–67 (pp. 80–81).
6. *Ibid.,* p. 16.
7. *Ibid.,* p. 233 (p. 294).
8. *Ibid.,* p. 16.
9. Grass, *Hundejahre,* pp. 237–38 (p. 288).
10. Remarque, *Zeit zu leben und Zeit zu sterben,* pp. 166–68.
11. Inge Scholl, *Die Weisse Rose* (Frankfurt/Main: Fischer Taschenbuchverlag, 1981), pp. 103–34. Orig. ed., 1953.
12. Grass, *Hundejahre,* p. 228 (p. 277).
13. *Ibid.,* pp. 252–61 (pp. 312–13).
14. *Ibid.,* p. 228 (pp. 277–78).
15. Hochhuth, p. 47.
16. Knef, p. 16.
17. A more complete commentary on the background for Nazi racial theory is provided by Karl Schleunes, *The Twisted Road to Auschwitz* (Urbana: University of Illinois Press, 1970), pp. 3–35; Carl Schorske, *Fin-de-Siècle Vienna* (New York: Alfred A. Knopf, 1980), pp. 116–46; William Shirer, *The Rise and Fall of the Third Reich,* pp. 21–28.
18. Knef, pp. 53–54.
19. Böll, *Gruppenbild mit Dame,* pp. 21, 171–74.
20. *Ibid.,* p. 241.
21. Sartre, *La Mort dans l'âme,* p. 354.
22. Grass, *Hundejahre,* pp. 220–21.
23. See footnote 1 above for date and place of publication.
24. Remarque, *Zeit zu leben und Zeit zu sterben,* pp. 40–42.
25. Marc Hillel and Clarissa Henry, *Of Pure Blood* (New York: McGraw-Hill, 1976), p. 137. Orig. pub. as *Au nom de la race* by Librairie Fayard in 1975.
26. Böll, *Gruppenbild mit Dame,* pp. 25–26.
27. *Ibid.,* pp. 47–48 (p. 60).
28. A more complete commentary on Nazi efforts directed against the Jews from 1933 until the beginning of the war is provided by Karl Schleunes, *The Twisted Road to Auschwitz,* pp. 62–168, 248.
29. *Ibid.,* p. 82.
30. Goes, p. 13.

31. *Ibid.*, p. 43.
32. Knef, p. 14.
33. Ilse Aichinger, *Die grössere Hoffnung* (Frankfurt/Main: Fischer, 1975), pp. 22–25. Orig. ed., 1948.
34. *Ibid.*, pp. 70–74.
35. *Ibid.*, pp. 79–83.
36. *Ibid.*, pp. 52–54, 77.
37. *Ibid.*, pp. 114–25.
38. Grass, *Die Blechtrommel*, pp. 134, 163–64.
39. André Schwarz-Bart, *Le Dernier des justes* (Paris: Seuil, 1959), pp. 81–82.
40. *Ibid.*, pp. 127–31. Stephen Becker, trans., *The Last of the Just* (New York: Bantam, 1973), p. 155.
41. *Ibid.*, pp. 148–55.
42. *Ibid.*, pp. 166–71.
43. *Ibid.*, pp. 192–93, 196–220, 251.
44. Schleunes, pp. 199–200.
45. *Ibid.*, pp. 185–86.
46. The trip of the *Saint-Louis* is the subject of Gordon Thomas's and Max Morgan Witts's *Voyage of the Damned* (New York: Stein & Day, 1974). Schwarz-Bart also speaks of it, pp. 251–52.
47. Zweig, p. 305.
48. Horst Krüger, "Nachwort" in Elisabeth Langgässer, *Ausgewählte Erzählungen* (Frankfurt/Main: Ullstein, 1980), p. 350. Orig. ed., 1979.
49. Elisabeth Langgässer, "An der Nähmaschine," in *Ausgewählte Erzählungen*, pp. 275–81. Orig. ed. of this story, 1956.
50. Langgässer, "Untergetaucht" in *Ausgewählte Erzählungen*, pp. 206–11. Orig. ed. of this story, 1948.
51. Schwarz-Bart, pp. 237–40.
52. Grass, *Die Blechtrommel*, pp. 254–61.
53. Aichinger, pp. 142, 62.
54. Remarque, *Zeit zu leben und Zeit zu sterben*, p. 207.
55. Knef, pp. 24–25.
56. Remarque, *Zeit zu leben und Zeit zu sterben*, p. 53.
57. Knef, p. 42.
58. Remarque, *Zeit zu leben und Zeit zu sterben*, p. 173.
59. *Ibid.*, p. 233.

CHAPTER VI: *The World of the Camps*

1. Anna Seghers, *Das siebte Kreuz* (Darmstadt: Luchterhand, 1976), p. 288 (orig. German ed. 1943). James A. Galston, trans., *The Seventh Cross* (Boston: Little, Brown, 1942). Orig. Eng. ed., 1942.

2. Wiechert, p. 153.
3. *Ibid.*, pp. 95, 83–84, 26.
4. *Ibid.*, pp. 80–81.
5. *Ibid.* See also Erich Maria Remarque, *Der Funke Leben* (Frankfurt/Main: Ullstein, 1975), pp. 7, 95. Orig. ed., 1952.
6. Wiechert, pp. 77, 80.
7. Jean Lacouture, *André Malraux* (New York: Pantheon Books, 1975), p. 165. Orig. ed. (Paris: Seuil), 1973.
8. "Les Cahiers de la Petite Dame," in *Cahiers André Gide* (Paris: Gallimard, 1974), V, 367. André Gide, *Littérature engagée* (Paris: Gallimard, 1950), pp. 41–42.
9. *Ceux qui ont choisi* (Paris: Association des Ecrivains et Artistes Révolutionnaires, 1933), p. 8.
10. André Malraux, *Le Temps du mépris* (Paris: Gallimard, 1935), p. 8.
11. Lacouture, p. 184.
12. Malraux, *Le Temps du mépris*, pp. 11–13. Haaken M. Chevalier, trans., *Days of Wrath* (New York: Random House, 1936), pp. 6–8.
13. *Ibid.*, pp. 53–55, 102, 111, 114, 147, 164 (pp. 91–92).
14. Thomas J. Kline, *André Malraux and the Metamorphosis of Death* (New York: Columbia University Press, 1973), p. 91.
15. Gaston Bachelard, *L'Eau et les rêves* (Paris: José Corti, 1942), p. 9.
16. Malraux, *Le Temps du mépris*, p. 8 (p. 4).
17. Wiechert, pp. 29, 71.
18. Remarque, *Der Funke Leben*, p. 5. James Stern, trans., *Spark of Life* (New York: Appleton-Century Crofts, 1952), p. 1.
19. Stefan Lorant, *Sieg Heil* (New York: W.W. Norton, 1974), p. 246.
20. Remarque, *Der Funke Leben*, pp. 222–25.
21. Wiechert, pp. 66, 76. Germaine Tillion, *Ravensbrück* (Garden City, N.Y.: Anchor Press/Doubleday, 1975), pp. 14–15, 23. Original French edition published as *Ravensbrück* (Paris: Editions du Seuil), 1973.
22. Steinbrenner is a name whose hardness in sound and meaning probably appealed to Remarque for depicting a particularly fanatical Nazi, since he used it again two years later in *Zeit zu leben und Zeit zu sterben*.
23. Remarque, *Der Funke Leben*, pp. 105–7.
24. Robert Merle, *La Mort est mon métier*, pp. 331, 349.
25. Remarque, *Der Funke Leben*, p. 13.
26. *Ibid.*, p. 6.
27. Wiechert, pp. 87, 101–2, 107.
28. Luise Rinser, *Gefängnistagebuch* (Frankfurt/Main: Fischer Taschenbuch Verlag, 1979), p. 47. Orig. ed., 1946.
29. Remarque, *Der Funke Leben*, p. 108.

30. *Ibid.*, p. 58.
31. Merle, *La Mort est mon métier*, pp. 295–98, 277.
32. Wiechert, p. 125.
33. Remarque, *Der Funke Leben*, pp. 17, 40, 46, 75–76. Tillion, pp. 18–19, 40.
34. *Ibid.*, pp. 121–22, 168, 184.
35. *Ibid.*, pp. 62–63.
36. Wiechert, p. 143.
37. Remarque, *Der Funke Leben*, p. 175.
38. Merle, *La Mort est mon métier*, p. 305.
39. Wiechert, pp. 141–42, 136, 139.
40. Anna Seghers, p. 115. Anna Seghers emigrated to France in 1933 and later to Mexico.
41. Remarque, *Der Funke Leben*, pp. 35–36, 140.
42. Merle, *La Mort est mon métier*, p. 293–94. The term *Nacht und Nebel* actually refers to an incantation in *Das Rheingold* by which Alberich was able to make himself disappear (Tillion, p. 91).
43. Remarque, *Der Funke Leben*, pp. 188, 204–5.
44. *Ibid.*, pp. 57, 207.
45. Jean Genet, *Journal du voleur* (Paris: Gallimard, 1963), pp. 130–31. Orig. ed., 1949.
46. Remarque, *Der Funke Leben*, pp. 217–18.
47. *Ibid.*, pp. 24–25, 28, 86, 158–61, 191–93, 209–11.
48. Anna Seghers, p. 288.
49. Merle, *La Mort est mon métier*, pp. 202–5, 282, 284, 415.
50. Jean Genet, "Pompes funèbres" in *Œuvres complètes* (Paris: Gallimard, 1976), III, 95. Orig. ed., 1947.
51. Merle, *La Mort est mon métier*, pp. 397–98.
52. Remarque, *Der Funke Leben*, p. 98.
53. *Ibid.*, pp. 10–11.
54. Anna Seghers, p. 25, 61.
55. *Ibid.*, pp. 63–67, 88–92, 94, 102, 112, 171–72, 180–83.
56. *Ibid.*, p. 151.
57. *Ibid.*, pp. 209, 213.
58. Remarque, *Der Funke Leben*, pp. 43–44.
59. *Ibid.*, pp. 149–55.
60. Rinser, *Gefängnistagebuch*, pp. 13, 64, 103, 117.
61. Wiechert, p. 39. Tillion, p. 16.
62. Remarque, *Der Funke Leben*, pp. 207–8.
63. Wiechert, p. 73.
64. Remarque, *Der Funke Leben*, pp. 83, 251.
65. *Ibid.*, pp. 233, 235–36.
66. *Ibid.*, pp. 97, 229, 243–47.

67. Merle, *La Mort est mon métier,* pp. 417–35.
68. Malraux, *Antimémoires,* p. 599.

CHAPTER VII: *The German Occupation of France*

1. Guéhenno, *Journal des années noires,* p. 138.
2. Elsa Triolet, "La Vie privée" in *Le Premier Accroc coûte deux cents francs* (Paris: Denoël, 1973), pp. 168–69. Orig. ed., 1945.
3. Jean-Paul Sartre, "Paris sous l'occupation" in *Situations III* (Paris: Gallimard, 1949), p. 24. Orig. ed., 1945.
4. Guéhenno, p. 325.
5. Jean-Louis Curtis, *Les Forêts de la nuit* (Paris: René Julliard, 1973), p. 28. Orig. ed., 1947.
6. *Ibid.,* p. 306.
7. Roger Vailland, *Drôle de jeu* (Paris: Buchet-Chastel, 1973), p. 212. Orig. ed., 1945.
8. Curtis, *Les Forêts de la nuit,* p. 66.
9. Sartre, "Qu'est-ce qu'un collaborateur?," in *Situations III,* p. 45. Orig. ed., 1945.
10. Marcel Aymé, *Le Chemin des écoliers* (Paris: Gallimard, 1972), pp. 162, 15. Orig. ed., 1946.
11. Werner Rings, *Leben mit dem Feind* (München: Kindler Verlag, 1979). J. Maxwell Brownjohn, trans., *Life with the Enemy* (Garden City, N.Y.: Doubleday, 1981), p. 77.
12. Vercors, "Le Silence de la mer," in *Le Silence de la mer* (Paris: Albin Michel, 1971), pp. 26–33. Orig. ed. of the collection, 1951; orig. ed. of the story, 1942.
13. *Ibid.,* p. 30.
14. *Ibid.,* pp. 31–32, 34, 40–41, 45, 54–55.
15. Sartre, "Paris sous l'occupation," pp. 20–21; Beauvoir, *La Force de l'âge,* II, 548–49. Sartre had been interned in a POW camp in Germany near the border with Luxemburg. The Germans had decided to release as civilians a certain number of prisoners who could claim physical disability. Sartre pointed to his bad eye and claimed to have problems of balance.
16. Guéhenno, p. 44.
17. Sartre, "Paris sous l'occupation," pp. 24–27.
18. Guéhenno, p. 328.
19. Roger Nimier, *Les Epées* (Paris: Gallimard, 1967), p. 151. Orig. ed., 1948.
20. Pierre Seghers, p. 77.
21. Triolet, "La Vie privée," pp. 222, 285.
22. Guéhenno, p. 135.

23. Jean Dutourd, *Au bon beurre*, p. 118.
24. Guéhenno, p. 89.
25. Vailland, *Drôle de jeu*, pp. 365–66.
26. *Ibid.*, pp. 122, 65. According to statistics of the Federal Reserve Bank of New York, the average annual value of the French franc in 1940 until June 15, 1940, which was the last day on which an official listing was made in New York was 2.0827 cents. The first official listing of the Federal Reserve in New York after the war was made in August 1945, when the value of the franc stood at 2.0189 cents.
27. Guéhenno, p. 428.
28. Vailland, *Drôle de jeu*, p. 105.
29. *Ibid.*, pp. 425–26, 185.
30. *Ibid.*, p. 315.
31. Curtis, *Les Forêts de la nuit*, p. 434.
32. Dutourd, *Au bon beurre*, pp. 22, 42–44, 46–47, 53, 60, 79, 159, 267–68 (p. 28).
33. Curtis, *Les Forêts de la nuit*, pp. 239–40. Nora Wydenbruck, trans., *The Forests of the Night* (New York: G.P. Putnam's Sons, 1951), pp. 152–53.
34. Dutourd, *Au bon beurre*, pp. 171.
35. Guéhenno, p. 431.
36. Dutourd, *Au bon beurre*, pp. 171–72.
37. Beauvoir, *La Force de l'âge*, II, 675–76; Sartre, "Paris sous l'occupation," pp. 32–33; Triolet, "Les Amants d'Avignon," in *Le Premier Accroc coûte deux cents francs*, pp. 86–87 (orig. ed., 1943); Vailland, *Drôle de jeu*, pp. 203–4.
38. Pierre Seghers, p. 145.
39. Guéhenno, pp. 217–22, 224.
40. Vailland, *Drôle de jeu*, p. 82.
41. Guéhenno, p. 244.
42. *Ibid.*, p. 333. Winston S. Churchill, *The Hinge of Fate* (Boston: Houghton Mifflin, 1950), p. 756 (the fourth volume of the series *The Second World War*). Louis-Ferdinand Céline, *Rigodon* (Paris: Gallimard, 1973), p. 172 (orig. ed., 1969).
43. Louis-Ferdinand Céline, *Féerie pour une autre fois, II. Normance* (Paris: Gallimard, 1954), pp. 18, 20, 22–25, 39, 67. Albert Speer, *Inside the Third Reich* (New York: Macmillan, 1970), p. 288. Orig. published in German as *Erinnerungen* (Frankfurt/Main: Ullstein, 1969).
44. Vailland, *Drôle de jeu*, pp. 410–11.
45. Curtis, *Les Forêts de la nuit*, p. 236.
46. *Ibid.*, p. 180.

47. Guéhenno, pp. 80, 101, 231; David Pryce-Jones, *Paris in the Third Reich* (New York: Holt, Rinehart and Winston, 1981), pp. 208–9. Photographs.

48. Dutourd, *Au bon beurre*, pp. 65–102, 211, 213–14, 375–76.

49. Guéhenno, p. 104.

50. Dutourd, *Au bon beurre*, p. 180 (p. 114).

51. Guéhenno, pp. 107–8.

52. Pierre Seghers, pp. 257, 77.

53. Guéhenno, pp. 104, 145, 174–75, 272.

54. Curtis, *Les Forêts de la nuit*, p. 69.

55. Jean-Louis Bory, *Mon Village à l'heure allemande* (New York: Editions de la Maison Française, 1945), pp. 69, 205, 228–30, 234–35, 252.

56. Vailland, *Drôle de jeu*, p. 180.

57. Curtis, *Les Forêts de la nuit*, pp. 110–11.

58. Guéhenno, pp. 243, 273, 59.

59. Beauvoir, *La Force de l'âge*, II, 523–25, 537, 543.

60. Guéhenno, pp. 150–51.

61. Sartre, "Les Mouches," in *Huis clos* suivi de *Les Mouches* (Paris: Gallimard, 1968), p. 88. Orig. ed., 1947. First performed in 1943.

62. Guéhenno, pp. 10, 66, 165–67, 374–75. Nimier, *Les Epées*, p. 104.

63. Guéhenno, pp. 136–37. Jünger develops a picture of his life in Paris in his diaries, "Das erste Pariser Tagebuch," covering the period from spring 1941 through October 1942, and "Das zweite Pariser Tagebuch," spanning February 1943 through August 1944. Both are contained in *Ernst Jünger: Werke*, vols. II and III, published in 1949.

64. Vercors, "Le Silence de la mer," pp. 67–77.

65. Bachelard, *L'Eau et les rêves*, pp. 20, 178.

66. Aymé, *Le Chemin des écoliers*, pp. 101, 143, 176–77.

67. Dutourd, *Au bon beurre*, pp. 157, 242–43.

68. Guéhenno, p. 321.

69. Dutourd, *Au bon beurre*, pp. 304–13 (p. 203). Chancellor translates Poissonard's remark in more colloquial and less literal fashion: "France . . . doesn't give a good God damn for you." (p. 202).

70. *Ibid.*, pp. 350–51.

71. Sartre, "Morts sans sépulture" in *La P... respectueuse* suivi de *Morts sans sépulture* (Paris: Gallimard, 1967), p. 161 (orig. ed., 1947). First performed in 1946.

72. Pierre Seghers, p. 230.

73. Jean Genet, *Pompes funèbres*, pp. 13, 17. Bernard Frechtman trans., *Funeral Rites* (New York: Grove, 1970), pp. 17, 22.

74. *Ibid.*, pp. 41–42 (p. 54).

75. *Ibid.*, pp. 64–70, 58–59, 71.

76. *Ibid.*, pp. 133, 142–45.
77. *Ibid.*, p. 59 (p. 78).
78. Carl Zuckmayer, *Der Gesang im Feuerofen* (Frankfurt/Main: Fischer, 1960), pp. 134–35, 140, 143–44. Orig. ed., 1950.
79. Curtis, *Les Forêts de la nuit*, pp. 246–47, 197–200, 266 (p. 126).
80. Wolfgang Borchert, "Marguerite" in *Die traurigen Geranien* (Reinbek bei Hamburg: Rowohlt, 1975), pp. 93–94. Orig. ed. of this collection 1962. The stories contained in the collection already appeared in Borchert's *Gesamtwerk* in 1949.

CHAPTER VIII: *The Jews in Occupied France*

1. Robert O. Paxton, *Vichy France* (New York: Norton, 1975), p. 371. Orig. ed., 1972.
2. Schwarz-Bart, *Le Dernier des justes*, pp. 254–58, 263 (pp. 313, 315).
3. Paxton, p. 181. Marrus and Paxton, *Vichy France and the Jews*, pp. 226–27.
4. Doubrovsky, *La Dispersion*, pp. 146–47, 151, 154, 198.
5. Paxton, pp. 170–71, 174–76. Marrus and Paxton, *Vichy France and the Jews*, p. 3.
6. Doubrovsky, p. 144.
7. Paxton, p. 177. Two agencies appear to be confused in Doubrovsky's text, the Commissariat-Général aux Questions Juives and the Direction Générale de l'Enrequistrement des Domains et du Timbre.
8. Doubrovsky, pp. 193–95.
9. *Ibid.*, pp. 136, 149–51, 154.
10. Guéhenno, p. 238.
11. Doubrovsky, pp. 210, 226, 190.
12. Paxton, p. 184.
13. Doubrovsky, p. 210.
14. Beauvoir, *La Force de l'âge*, II, 587. Vercors, "L'Imprimerie de Verdun" in *Le Silence de la mer*, pp. 143–82 (orig. ed., 1951).
15. After his internment in a French camp for enemy aliens, Lion Feuchtwanger parodied the idea of the proverb in the title of his *Der Teufel in Frankreich*, published in 1941.
16. Dutourd, *Au bon beurre*, pp. 325–26, 328, 335 (pp. 212–14). The Chancellor translation insists much more strongly on a foreign word order in Rappoport's speech than does the original French.
17. Schwarz-Bart, *Le Dernier des justes*, p. 281 (p. 343).
18. *Ibid.*, p. 296 (p. 362).
19. *Ibid.*, pp. 305–11 (pp. 372–73).
20. *Ibid.*, pp. 326–30, 332–34 (p. 406).
21. Guéhenno, p. 266.

22. Schwarz-Bart, p. 288.
23. *Ibid.*, pp. 289–90.
24. Lottman, *The Left Bank*, p. 183.
25. Vercors, "La Marche à l'étoile," in *Les Animaux dénaturés* suivi de *La Marche à l'étoile* (Paris: Albin Michel, 1971), pp. 425–29. Orig. ed. of the collection 1952. *La Marche à l'étoile* was first published separately in 1943.
26. Aymé, *Le Chemin des écoliers*, pp. 103–4, 176–77; Marrus and Paxton, *Vichy France and the Jews*, pp. 34–71.
27. Paxton, *Vichy France*, p. 181.
28. Pierre Seghers, pp. 196–97.
29. Doubrovsky, p. 180.
30. *Ibid.*, p. 292.

CHAPTER IX. *The French Résistance*

1. Dutourd, *Au bon beurre*, p. 244.
2. Paxton, *Vichy France*, p. 223.
3. Doubrovsky, p. 305. Guéhenno, p. 200. Pierre Seghers, p. 146.
4. Guéhenno, pp. 185–86. Pierre Seghers, p. 50.
5. Triolet, "Le Premier Accroc coûte deux cents francs," p. 440.
6. Pierre Seghers, pp. 121–25. The text by Paulhan himself describing his ordeal is taken from Gabriel Audisio, *Ecrivains en prison* (Paris: Seghers, 1945), and reprinted here. See also Martin Blumenson, *The Vildé Affair* (Boston: Houghton Mifflin, 1977), pp. 11, 180–84; David Schoenbrun, *Soldiers of the Night* (New York: E.P. Dutton, 1980), p. 70; Lottman, *The Left Bank*, pp. 144, 176. Lottman claims Paulhan was denounced by an NRF writer's wife; and Mavis Gallant's review of *The Left Bank* in the *New York Times*, April 4, 1982, mentions Elise Jouhandeau, wife of Marcel Jouhandeau. Lottman attributes Paulhan's release to intervention by Gerhard Heller, an aide in the German Propaganda Department.
7. Lottman, p. 165.
8. Guéhenno, pp. 212–13.
9. Vailland, *Un Jeune Homme seul* (Paris: Buchet-Chastel, 1970), p. 238. Orig. ed., 1951.
10. Vailland, *Drôle de jeu*, p. 66.
11. Vailland, *Un Jeune Homme seul*, p. 252.
12. Triolet, "Préface à la clandestinité," in *Le Premier Accroc coûte deux cents francs*, p. 13. The author copyrighted this preface in her own name in 1965.
13. Triolet, "Les Amants d'Avignon," p. 96.
14. Triolet, "La Vie privée," p. 140.

15. Vailland, *Drôle de jeu,* p. 430–31.
16. Roger Nimier, *Le Hussard bleu* (Paris: Gallimard, 1967), p. 12. Orig. ed., 1950.
17. Nimier, *Les Epées,* pp. 68–69, 126, 185.
18. Malraux, *Antimémoires,* p. 117. (1967 ed.)
19. Vailland, *Drôle de jeu,* pp. 430–31.
20. Dutourd, *Au bon beurre,* pp. 179–90.
21. Triolet, "La Vie privée," p. 118.
22. Curtis, *Les Forêts de la nuit,* p. 247.
23. Paxton, pp. 311, 367–69; Edward L. Homze, *Foreign Labor in Nazi Germany* (Princeton, N.J.: Princeton University Press, 1967), p. 187.
24. Triolet, "La Vie privée," pp. 276–86.
25. Paxton, pp. 239–41, 286–87, 294–95.
26. Triolet, "La Vie privée," pp. 243–44.
27. Guéhenno, p. 13.
28. Vercors, "Désespoir est mort," p. 14.
29. Dutourd, *Au bon beurre,* pp. 40–42.
30. Jacques Perret, *Bande à part* (Paris: Gallimard, 1965), p. 20. Orig. ed., 1951.
31. Dutourd, *Au bon beurre,* pp. 61–62.
32. *Ibid.,* pp. 168–70, 217–30.
33. Curtis, *Les Forêts de la nuit,* pp. 12, 52–53, 267.
34. Dutourd, *Au bon beurre,* pp. 92, 95.
35. Paxton, pp. 294–95.
36. Lottman, p. 135.
37. Shirer, *The Rise and Fall of the Third Reich,* p. 993.
38. Malraux, *Antimémoires,* pp. 234, 222, 224, 246–47 (pp. 155, 147–48, 163).
39. *Ibid.,* p. 623.
40. *Ibid.,* pp. 238–39 (p. 158).
41. Albert Camus, *Carnets, janvier 1942–mars 1951* (Paris: Gallimard, 1964), pp. 50, 72.

CHAPTER X. *French Prisoners of War in Germany*

1. Pierre Gascar, *Histoire de la captivité des Français en Allemagne (1939–1945),* pp. 25–27, 35–37.
2. *Ibid.,* pp. 40–41. Two hard-discipline camps were also created within Germany for officer POWs, as were a few small special camps, including one for aviators.
3. Homze, *Foreign Labor in Nazi Germany,* pp. 46–48.
4. Perret, *Le Caporal épinglé,* p. 180.
5. *Ibid.,* pp. 114–15.

6. *Ibid.*, pp. 122–23, 136.
7. Tournier, *Le Roi des aulnes*, pp. 249–53.
8. *Ibid.*, pp. 256–63, 272.
9. Dutourd, *Au bon beurre*, pp. 25–32.
10. Perret, pp. 213, 222–23, 235, 260–61, 269, 550, 586.
11. Francis Ambrière, *Les Grandes Vacances* (Paris: Seuil, 1968), pp. 107–11. Orig. ed. 1956.
12. Perret, p. 124.
13. *Ibid.*, p. 283.
14. *Ibid.*, pp. 458, 455.
15. *Ibid.*, pp. 193–94.
16. *Ibid.*, pp. 615–16.
17. *Ibid.*, pp. 283–85, 361.
18. Ambrière, p. 241.
19. Rinser, *Gefängnistagebuch*, p. 22.
20. Perret, pp. 156, 200.
21. *Ibid.*, pp. 151–52, 167; Beauvoir, *La Force de l'âge*, II, 535.
22. Perret, pp. 300–301; Ambrière, pp. 329–37, 366.
23. Gascar, *Le Fugitif* (Paris: Gallimard, 1961), p. 18. Merloyd Lawrence trans., *The Fugitive* (Boston: Little Brown, 1964), p. 17.
24. Perret, pp. 388–423, 461, 476, 484. A strikingly similar description of wartime Berlin is given by Guy Sajer, an Alsatian serving in the German army, in *Le Soldat oublié* (Paris: Robert Laffont, 1967), p. 162.
25. *Ibid.*, pp. 517–29, 533.
26. *Ibid.*, pp. 623, 642, 644, 651, 662, 664–85.
27. Gascar, "Le Temps des morts," in *Les Bêtes* (Paris: Gallimard, 1953), pp. 210–13, 229, 265–73.
28. Tournier, *Le Roi des aulnes*, pp. 87–91, 100–103, 331.
29. *Ibid.*, pp. 307–9, 385, 363–70, 355, 531.
30. *Ibid.*, p. 470.
31. *Ibid.*, p. 473.
32. *Ibid.*, pp. 455–56.
33. *Ibid.*, pp. 431, 460.
34. Tillion, p. 89.
35. Tournier, pp. 578–79 (p. 368).

CHAPTER XI. *The End of the War*

1. Triolet, "Le Premier Accroc coûte deux cents francs," pp. 409–10.
2. Céline, *Féerie pour une autre fois* (Paris: Gallimard, 1977), pp. 18–19.

3. Joseph Kessel, *Le Bataillon du ciel* (Paris: Gallimard, 1974), pp. 130, 132, 152–53.

4. Boris Vian, "L'Equarrissage pour tous" in *Théâtre I* (Paris: Union Générale d'Editions, 1974), pp. 49, 46. Orig. ed. of this play, 1950.

5. *Ibid.*, pp. 111–14.

6. *Ibid.*, pp. 147–48.

7. *Ibid.*, pp. 178–84.

8. Aymé, *Le Chemin des écoliers*, p. 16.

9. Guéhenno, pp. 407, 431–34, 436.

10. Genet, *Pompes funèbres*, p. 115.

11. *Ibid.*, pp. 173–75, 156–57, 128 (pp. 208–9).

12. *Ibid.*, pp. 120–21, 128, 152–55, 169, 183.

13. *Ibid.*, pp. 190–91 (p. 254).

14. *Ibid.*, pp. 133, 187, 191, 189. (pp. 177, 249, 255).

15. Céline, interview with Claude Sarraute in *Castle to Castle* (New York: Dell, 1968), p. 5. Orig. interview, 1960.

16. Pierre-Henri Simon, *Portrait d'un officier*, p. 30.

17. Curtis, *Les Forêts de la nuit*, pp. 373, 381, 406–7, 428.

18. *Ibid.*, pp. 392–96.

19. *Ibid.*, pp. 462–64.

20. *Ibid.*, pp. 466–69, 470–71, 475, 479, 484–85 (pp. 293, 299, 302).

21. Guéhenno, pp. 437–38. Shirer, *The Rise and Fall of the Third Reich*, p. 1085.

22. Allen Thiher, *Céline: The Novel as Delirium* (New Brunswick, N.J.: Rutgers University Press, 1972), pp. 135, 232–33.

23. Céline, *Féerie pour une autre fois*, pp. 12–14, 18–19.

24. *Ibid.*, p. 38.

25. *Ibid.*, p. 134. The Pas de Calais is a *département* in northern France located on the English Channel. The Puy-de-Dôme is a *département* in the Massif Central. Clermont-Ferrand is located in the Puy-de-Dôme.

26. Céline, *D'un château l'autre* (Paris: Gallimard, 1973), pp. 31–51. Orig. ed., 1957.

27. Céline, *Nord* (Paris: Gallimard, 1971), p. 299 (orig. ed., 1960). Patrick Mc Carthy, *Céline* (New York: Penguin, 1977), p. 192 (orig. ed., 1975).

28. Céline, *Rigodon*, pp. 203–4.

29. *Ibid.*, p. 214.

30. Céline, *D'un château l'autre*, pp. 20, 408.

31. *Ibid.*, pp. 73–74.

32. *Ibid.*, p. 64. Ralph Manheim, trans., *Castle to Castle* (New York: Dell, 1968), p. 64.

33. Céline, *Nord*, pp. 20, 13, 118–19, 153, 425.

34. Erika Ostrovsky, *Céline and His Vision* (New York: New York University Press, 1967), p. 61.
35. Céline, *D'un château l'autre,* pp. 156, 165, 169, 183, 189, 206, 245–46, 382–85, 398–407. Though Céline claims to have traveled still farther east after Berlin to get to Hohenlychen, Hohenlychen is actually north of Berlin. It was the site of a Red Cross hospital run by SS doctor Karl Gebhardt. At the Nürnberg trials after the war it was revealed publicly that Gebhardt had performed experiments on concentration camp prisoners. Céline refers to Charon as Caron, a less common French variant.
36. *Ibid.,* pp. 416–17.
37. *Ibid.,* p. 421 (pp. 324–25).
38. Thiher, p. 170.
39. Bettina L. Knapp, *Céline: Man of Hate* (University, Alabama: University of Alabama Press, 1974), p. 232.
40. Céline, *Rigodon,* p. 123.
41. Céline, *D'un château l'autre,* p. 13.
42. Céline, *Nord,* pp. 50–51. Ralph Manheim, trans., *North* (New York: Penguin, 1976), p. 35.
43. Céline, *Rigodon,* pp. 86–90.
44. *Ibid.,* pp. 131–33.
45. *Ibid.,* pp. 161–62, 165, 166, 170–72, 175. Ralph Manheim, trans., *Rigadoon* (New York: Penguin, 1975), pp. 130–31, 133–34, 135, 140.
46. Céline, *Rigodon,* pp. 179, 184–85.
47. *Ibid.,* pp. 200–202 (p. 167).
48. Sajer, pp. 487–88.
49. Céline, *Rigodon,* pp. 174–75, 208, 211, 215, 223–25, 228, 230, 238–45 (pp. 187, 191, 202).
50. *Ibid.,* pp. 253, 273 (pp. 229–30).
51. Céline, *D'un château l'autre,* p. 313 (p. 247).
52. Sajer, pp. 487–89, 499, 516. Lily Emmet trans., *The Forgotten Soldier* (New York: Harper & Row, 1971), pp. 415–16, 426.
53. Grass, *Die Blechtrommel,* p. 345 (p. 417).
54. Grass, *Hundejahre,* p. 297 (p. 360).
55. *Ibid.,* pp. 295, 297–98 (p. 360).
56. Knef, pp. 62–63, 73, 76.
57. Grass, *Die Blechtrommel,* pp. 323–26.
58. Böll, *Gruppenbild mit Dame,* pp. 231–33 (p. 272).
59. Gertrud von le Fort, *Am Tor des Himmels* (Wiesbaden: Insel-Verlag, 1954), p. 76.
60. Böll, *Gruppenbild mit Dame,* pp. 247–48 (pp. 288–89).

61. *Ibid.*, p. 263 (p. 306).
62. Knef, pp. 76, 79–82 (p. 85). The quote is incomplete in the original text.
63. Max Frisch, "Als der Krieg zu Ende war" in *Stücke I* (Frankfurt/Main: Suhrkamp, 1974), p. 218. Orig. ed. of collection, 1962. Orig. ed. of play, 1949.
64. Knef, pp. 92–93, 98.

Epilogue

1. Sajer, p. 545.

Selected Bibliography

Aichinger, Ilse, *Die grössere Hoffnung.* Frankfurt/Main: Fischer, 1975. Orig. ed., 1948.

Ambrière, Francis, *Les Grandes Vacances.* Paris: Seuil, 1968. Orig. ed., 1956.

Amouroux, Henri, *La Grande Histoire des Français sous l'occupation.* Paris: Robert Laffont, 1976-present. Ongoing series of volumes.

Andersch, Alfred, *Efraim.* Zürich: Diogenes Verlag AG, 1967.

————, *Die Kirschen der Freiheit.* Zürich: Diogenes Verlag AG, 1952.

Anouilh, Jean, *Antigone.* Paris: La Table Ronde, 1947. First performed in 1944.

Apitz, Bruno, *Nackt unter Wölfen.* Leipzig: Reclam, 1980. Orig. ed. 1958.

Aymé, Marcel, *Le Chemin des écoliers.* Paris: Gallimard, 1972. Orig. ed., 1946.

————, *Uranus.* Paris: Gallimard, 1948.

Bachelard, Gaston, *L'Eau et les rêves.* Paris: José Corti, 1942.

Barbusse, Henri, *Le Feu.* Paris: Flammarion, 1945. Orig. ed., 1917.

Barsam, Richard Meran, *Filmguide to "Triumph of the Will."* Bloomington, Ind.: Indiana University Press, 1975.

Beauvoir, Simone de, *La Force de l'âge.* Paris: Gallimard, 1960. Vols. I and II.

————, *Le Sang des autres.* Paris: Gallimard, 1945.

Bernanos, Georges, *Les Enfants humiliés.* Paris: Gallimard, 1973. Orig. ed., 1949.

Bernhard, Thomas, *Vor dem Rubestand.* Frankfurt/Main: Suhrkamp, 1981. Orig. ed. 1979.

Bloch, Marc, *Strange Defeat.* London: Oxford University Press, 1949. Written in 1940. Orig. published as *L'Etrange Défaite.* Paris: Société des Editions Franc-Tireur, 1946.

Blumenson, Martin, *The Vildé Affair.* Boston: Houghton Mifflin, 1977.

Boisdeffre, Pierre de, *Les Fins dernières.* Paris: La Table Ronde, 1952.

Böll, Heinrich, *Als der Krieg ausbrach.* München, DTV, 1968. Orig. ed. of this collection, 1965. The stories most relevant to this study in the order of their appearance in the collection are:
"Als der Krieg ausbrach," 1961, pp. 7–26;
"Als der Krieg zu Ende war," 1962, pp. 27–47;
"Die Postkarte," 1952, pp. 78–85;
"Die blasse Anna," 1953, pp. 134–39;
"Kümmelblättchen, Spritzenland, Kampfkommandantur," 1965, pp. 191–98;
"Entfernung von der Truppe," 1963–1964, pp. 199–261.

———, *Ansichten eines Clowns.* Müchen: DTV, 1980. Orig. ed., 1963.

———, *Billard um halb zehn.* Köln: Kiepenheuer & Witsch, 1959.

———, *Gruppenbild mit Dame.* Müchen: DTV, 1978. Orig. ed., 1971.

———, *Haus ohne Hüter.* Köln: Kiepenheuer & Witsch, 1954.

———, *Wo warst du, Adam?* München: DTV, 1975. Orig. ed., 1951.

———, *Der Zug war pünktlich.* München: DTV, 1975. Orig. ed., 1949.

Borchert, Wolfgang, *Draussen vor der Tür.* Reinbek bei Hamburg: Rowohlt, 1947.

———, *Die traurigen Geranien.* Reinbek bei Hamburg: Rowohlt, 1975. Orig. ed. of this collection, 1962. All the stories contained in the collection appeared in Borchert's *Gesamtwerk* in 1949. The most relevant to the theme of this study are:
"Die Mauer," pp. 44–47;
"Ein Sonntagmorgen," pp. 68–76;
"Maria, alles Maria," pp. 82–89;
"Marguerite," pp. 90–95.

Bory, Jean-Louis, *Mon Village à l'heure allemande.* New York: Editions de la Maison Française, 1945.

Bosmajian, Hamida, *Metaphors of Evil.* Iowa City: University of Iowa Press, 1979.

Brasillach, Robert, *Notre Avant-guerre.* Paris: Plon, 1973. Orig. ed., 1941.

Brecht, Bertolt, "Furcht und Elend des Dritten Reiches" in *Gesammelte Werke,* vol. 3, pp. 1073–1193. Frankfurt/Main: Suhrkamp, 1967. Orig. ed., 1945. First performed in Paris in 1938.

———, *Die Gesichte der Simone Machard.* Frankfurt/Main: Suhrkamp, 1970. Written in 1942–1943; copyright 1957.

———, "Die Rundköpfe und die Spitzköpfe oder Reich und Reich gesellt sich gern" in *Gesammelte Werke,* vol. 3, pp. 907–1040. Orig. ed., 1938. First performed in Copenhagen in 1936.

———, *Schweyk im zweiten Weltkrieg.* Frankfurt/Main: Suhrkamp, 1957. Written in 1943.

Bredel, Willi, *Die Prüfung.* Dortmund: Weltkreis-Verlag, 1981. Orig. ed. 1935.

Brée, Germaine, and Margaret Buiton, *An Age of Fiction*. New Brunswick, N.J.: Rutgers University Press, 1957.

Brée, Germaine, *Camus*. New Brunswick, N.J.: Rutgers University Press, 1972. Orig. ed., 1959.

——, *Camus and Sartre, Crisis and Commitment*. New York: Dell, 1972.

Brée, Germaine, and G. Brenauer, *Defeat and Beyond*. New York: Pantheon Books, 1970.

Buchheim, Lothar-Günther, *Das Boot*. München: R. Piper, 1973.

"Les Cahiers de la Petite Dame" in *Cahiers André Gide*. Paris: Gallimard, 1974, vol. V.

Camus, Albert, *Carnets, mai 1935–février 1942*. Paris: Gallimard, 1962.

——, *Carnets, janvier 1942–mars 1951*. Paris: Gallimard, 1964.

——, "Lettre à l'Allemand," *Cahiers de la Libération*, III, February 1944. Pages unnumbered. See also "Letters to a German Friend" in *Resistance, Rebellion, and Death*. New York: Random House, 1974. Some of Camus's letters remained unpublished in French.

——, *Le Mythe de Sisyphe*. Paris: Gallimard, 1942.

——, *La Peste*. Paris: Gallimard, 1947.

Céline, Louis-Ferdinand, *D'un château l'autre*. Paris: Gallimard, 1973. Orig. ed., 1957.

——, *Féerie pour une autre fois*. Paris: Gallimard, 1977. Orig. ed., 1952.

——, *Féerie pour une autre fois, II. Normance*. Paris: Gallimard, 1954.

——, Interview with Claude Sarraute in *Castle to Castle*. New York: Dell, 1968. Orig. interview, 1960.

——, *Nord*. Paris: Gallimard, 1971. Orig. ed., 1960.

——, *Rigodon*. Paris: Gallimard, 1973. Orig. ed., 1969.

Ceux qui ont choisi. Paris: Association des Ecrivains et Artistes Révolutionnaires, 1933.

Chabrol, Jean-Pierre, *Un Homme de trop*. Paris: Gallimard, 1976. Orig. ed., 1958.

Chamson, André, *Suite guerrière*. Paris: Plon, 1975. Included in this collection: "Ecrit en 1940," pp. 21–32 (1944); "Le Dernier Village," pp. 35–94 (1946); "Le Puits des miracles," pp. 97–268 (1945).

Churchill, Winston S., *The Hinge of Fate*. Boston: Houghton Mifflin, 1950. This is the fourth volume in the series *The Second World War*.

Craig, Gordon, *The Germans*. New York: G. P. Putnam's Sons, 1982.

——, *Germany 1866–1945*. New York: Oxford University Press, 1978.

Curtis, Jean-Louis, *Les Forêts de la nuit*. Paris: Julliard, 1973. Orig. ed., 1947.

——, *Les Justes Causes*. Paris: Julliard, 1954.

Des Pres, Terrence, *The Survivor*. New York: Oxford University Press, 1976.

Doubrovsky, Serge, *La Dispersion*. Paris: Mercure de France, 1969.

Druon, Maurice, *La Dernière Brigade*. Paris: Plon, 1970. Orig. ed., 1946.

Duras, Marguerite, *Hiroshima mon amour*. Paris: Gallimard, 1973. Orig. ed., 1960.

Dutourd, Jean, *Au bon beurre*. Paris: Gallimard, 1972. Orig. ed., 1952.

————, *Les Taxis de la Marne*. Paris: Gallimard, 1965. Orig. ed., 1956.

Esslin, Martin, *Brecht: The Man and his Work*. Garden City, N.Y.: Doubleday, 1971. Orig. ed., 1959.

Frisch, Max, "Als der Krieg zu Ende war" in *Stücke 1*. Frankfurt/Main: Suhrkamp, 1974. Orig. ed. of this collection, 1962. Orig. ed. of this play, 1949.

Frohock, Wilbur M., *André Malraux and the Tragic Imagination*. Stanford, Calif.: Stanford University Press, 1952.

Frohock, W. M., *Style and Temper*. Cambridge: Harvard University Press, 1967.

Frye, Northrop, *Anatomy of Criticism*. Princeton: Princeton University Press, 1971.

Fussel, Paul, *The Great War and Modern Memory*. New York: Oxford University Press, 1975.

Gascar, Pierre, *Le Fugitif*. Paris: Gallimard, 1961.

————, *Histoire de la captivité des Français en Allemagne (1939–1945)*. Paris: Gallimard, 1967.

————, *Les Bêtes*. Paris: Gallimard, 1953.

————, "Le Temps des morts," in *Les Bêtes*. Paris: Gallimard, 1953.

Genet, Jean, *Journal du voleur*. Paris: Gallimard, 1963. Orig. ed., 1949.

————, "Pompes funèbres" in *Œuvres complètes*. Paris: Gallimard, 1976. Volume 3. Orig. ed., 1947.

Gide, André, *Littérature engagée*. Paris: Gallimard, 1950.

Goes, Albrecht, *Das Brandopfer*. Frankfurt/Main: Fischer, 1968. Orig. ed., 1954.

Grass, Günter, *Die Blechtrommel*. Darmstadt: Luchterhand, 1979. Orig. ed., 1959.

————, *Hundejahre*. Darmstadt: Luchterhand, 1978. Orig. ed., 1963.

————, *Katz und Maus*. Neuwied am Rhein: Luchterhand, 1961.

Guéhenno, Jean, *Dans la prison*. Paris: Editions de Minuit, 1944. Published under the code name Cévennes.

————, *Journal des années noires*. Paris: Gallimard, 1973, Orig. ed., 1947.

Guiral, Pierre and Emile Temime, *La Société française 1914–1970 à travers la littérature*. Paris: Armand Colin, 1972.

Hartman, Geoffrey H., *André Malraux*. New York: Hillary House, 1960.

Hastings, Max, *Das Reich*. New York: Holt, Rinehart and Winston, 1981.

Hillel, Marc and Clarissa Henry, *Of Pure Blood*. New York: McGraw-Hill, 1976. Orig. published as *Au nom de la race* by Librairie Fayard in 1975.

Hochhuth, Rolf, "Die Berliner Antigone" in *Die Berliner Antigone.*
Reinbek bei Hamburg: Rowohlt, 1975. Orig. ed. 1971.
————, *Soldaten.* Reinbek bei Hamburg: Rowohlt, 1967.
————, *Der Stellvertreter.* Reinbek bei Hamburg: Rowohlt, 1975. Orig.
ed. 1963.
Homze, Edward L., *Foreign Labor in Nazi Germany.* Princeton, N.J.:
Princeton University Press, 1967.
Horvath, Violet M., *André Malraux: The Human Adventure.* New York:
New York University Press, 1969.
Jünger, Ernst, *Werke.* Stuttgart: Ernst Klett, 1960–65. Vols. 2 and 3.
Included in this collection are: "Gärten und Strassen," II, 27–230
(1942); "Das erste Pariser Tagebuch," II, 233–426 (1949); "Das
zweite Pariser Tagebuch," III, 11–304 (1949); "Kirchhorster Blät-
ter," III, 307–415 (1949).
Kessel, Joseph, *L'Armée des ombres.* Paris: Plon, 1963.
————, *Le Bataillon du ciel.* Paris: Gallimard, 1974. Orig. ed., 1961.
Koestler, Arthur, *Scum of the Earth.* New York: Macmillan, 1968. Orig.
ed., 1941.
Knapp, Bettina L., *Céline: Man of Hate.* University, Alabama: Univer-
sity of Alabama Press, 1974.
Knef, Hildegard, *Der geschenkte Gaul.* Frankfurt/Main: Ullstein, 1975.
Orig. ed., 1970.
Lacouture, Jean, *André Malraux.* New York: Pantheon, 1975. Orig.
published in French in Paris by Seuil in 1973.
Langer, Lawrence L., *The Holocaust and the Literary Imagination.* New
Haven: Yale University Press, 1975.
Langgässer, Elizabeth, *Ausgewählte Erzählungen.* Frankfurt/Main: Ull-
stein, 1980. Orig. ed. 1979. Included in this collection are: "Un-
tergetaucht," pp. 206–10 (1948); "Lydia," pp. 211–14 (1948);
"Glück haben," pp. 230–36 (1948); "An der Nähmaschine," pp.
274–81 (1956).
————, *Märkische Argonautenfahrt.* Reinbek bei Hamburg: Rowohlt,
1966. Orig. ed., 1950.
Léautaud, Paul, *Journal littéraire.* Paris: Mercure de France, 1962–64,
vols. 12–16.
le Fort, Gertrud von, *Am Tor des Himmels.* Wiesbaden: Insel-Verlag,
1954.
————, *Das fremde Kind.* Frankfurt/Main: Insel-Verlag, 1961.
————, *Gelöschte Kerzen.* München: Ehrenwirth Verlag, 1960. In this
collection: "Die Unschuldigen," pp. 51–111.
Lenz, Siegfried, *Deutschstunde.* München, DTV, 1978. Orig. ed., 1968.
Lorant, Stefan, *Sieg Heil.* New York: W. W. Norton, 1974.
Lottman, Herbert. R., *The Left Bank.* Boston: Houghton Mifflin, 1982.

Malraux, André, *Antimémoires*. Paris: Gallimard, 1972. Orig. ed. 1967.
————, *Les Noyers de l'Altenburg*. Paris: Gallimard, 1948.
————, *Le Temps du mépris*. Paris: Gallimard, 1935.
Mann, Klaus, *Mephisto*. Reinbek bei Hamburg: Rowohlt Taschenbuch Verlag, 1980. Orig. ed., 1936.
Marrus, Michael R., and Robert O. Paxton, *Vichy France and the Jews*. New York: Basic Books, 1981. Orig. published as *Vichy et les juifs* (Paris: Calmann-Lévy), 1981.
McCarthy, Patrick, *Céline*. New York: Penguin, 1977. Orig. ed., 1975.
Memmi, Albert, *La Statue de sel*. Paris: Gallimard, 1966.
Mercier, Vivian, *The New Novel*. New York: Farrar, Straus and Giroux, 1971. Orig. ed., 1966.
Merle, Robert, *La Mort est mon métier*. Paris: Gallimard, 1968. Orig. ed., 1952.
————, *Week-end à Zuydcoote*. Paris: Gallimard, 1972. Orig. ed., 1949.
Modiano, Patrick, *La Place de l'étoile*. Paris: Gallimard, 1976. Orig. ed., 1968.
Nimier, Roger, *Les Epées*. Paris: Gallimard, 1967. Orig. ed., 1948.
————, *Le Hussard bleu*. Paris: Gallimard, 1967. Orig. ed., 1950.
Novick, Peter, *The Resistance versus Vichy*. New York: Columbia University Press, 1968.
O'Brien, Justin, *The French Literary Horizon*. New Brunswick, N.J.: Rutgers University Press, 1967. In the order of their appearance in the collection the following essays are of relevance to this study:
"Was Gide a Collaborationist?" pp. 87–90 (orig. ed., 1951);
"The Plague," pp. 147–49 (orig. ed., 1949);
"French Literature and the War," pp. 277–82 (orig. ed., 1940);
"Writers at Midnight," pp. 293–98 (orig. ed., 1945);
"Vercors," pp. 303–5 (orig. ed., 1947);
"Sartre: *Roads to Freedom*," pp. 313–16 (orig. ed., 1947).
O'Flaherty, Kathleen, *The Novel in France*. Cork: Cork University Press, 1973. Particularly relevant is Chapter 4, "War and the Novel," pp. 55–70.
Ostrovsky, Erica, *Céline and His Vision*. New York: New York University Press, 1967.
————, *Voyeur Voyant*. New York: Random House, 1971.
Paxton, Robert O., *Parades and Politics at Vichy*. Princeton: Princeton University Press, 1966.
————, *Vichy France*. New York: W. W. Norton, 1975. Orig. ed., 1972.
————, *Vichy France and the Jews*. See Marrus, Michael R.
Perret, Jacques, *Bande à part*. Paris: Gallimard, 1965. Orig. ed., 1951.
————, *Le Caporal épinglé*. Paris: Gallimard, 1972. Orig. ed., 1947.
Peyrefitte, Roger, *La Fin des ambassades*. Paris: Flammarion, 1953.

Pryce-Jones, David, *Paris in the Third Reich*. New York: Holt, Rinehart and Winston, 1981.

Queffelec, Henri, *Journal d'un salaud*. Paris: Stock, 1972. Orig. ed., 1944.

Queneau, Raymond, *Le Dimanche de la vie*. Paris: Gallimard, 1951.

Rebatet, Lucien, "Les Décombres," in *Mémoires d'un fasciste*. Paris: Pauvert, 1976, vol. I. Originally published (Paris: Denoël), 1942.

Reck, Rima Drell, "Malraux's Transitional Novel: 'Les Noyers de l'Altenburg.' " *The French Review*, XXXIV (May 1961), 537–44.

Reddick, John, *The "Danzig Trilogy" of Günter Grass*. New York: Harcourt, Brace Jovanovich, 1974.

Reid, James Henderson, *Heinrich Böll*. London: Oswald Wolff, 1973.

Remarque, Erich Maria, *Arc de Triomphe*. Frankfurt/Main: Ullstein, 1978. Orig. ed., 1947.

———, *Der Funke Leben*. Frankfurt/Main: Ullstein, 1975. Orig. ed., 1952.

———, *Die letzte Station*. Peter Stone, trans., *Full Circle*. New York: Harcourt Brace Jovanovich, 1974. Orig. German ed., 1956.

———, *Im Westen nichts Neues*. Berlin: Propyläen, 1929.

———, *Zeit zu leben und Zeit zu sterben*. Frankfurt/Main: Ullstein, 1974. Orig. ed., 1954.

Rémy, *Compagnons de l'honneur*. Paris: Editions France-Empire, 1970. Orig. ed., 1966.

Rings, Werner, *Life with the Enemy*. Garden City, N.Y.: Doubleday, 1981. Orig. published as *Leben mit dem Feind* (München: Kindler Verlag), 1979.

Rinser, Luise. *Gefängnistagebuch*. Frankfurt/Main: Fischer Taschenbuch Verlag, 1979. Orig. ed., 1946.

———, *Weihnachts-Triptychon*. Zürich: Peter Schifferli Verlags AG Die Arche, 1963.

Roudiez, Leon, *French Fiction Today*. New Brunswick, N.J.: Rutgers University Press, 1972.

Rousset, David, *L'Univers concentrationnaire*. Paris: Editions du Pavois, 1946.

Roy, Jules, *La Vallée heureuse*. Paris: Charlot, 1946.

Saint-Exupéry, Antoine de, *Pilote de guerre*. Paris: Gallimard, 1967. Orig. ed., 1942.

Sajer, Guy, *Le Soldat oublié*. Paris: Robert Laffont, 1967.

Sartre, Jean-Paul, *La Mort dans l'âme*. Paris: Gallimard, 1972. Orig. ed., 1949.

———, "Morts sans sépulture" in *La P... respectueuse* suivi de *Morts sans sépulture*. Paris: Gallimard, 1967. Orig. ed., 1947. First performed in 1946.

————, "Les Mouches" in *Huis clos* suivi de *Les Mouches*. Paris: Gallimard, 1968. Orig. ed., 1947. First performed in 1943.

————, *Les Séquestrés d'Altona*. Paris: Gallimard, 1965. Orig. ed., 1960. First performed in 1959.

————, *Situations III*. Paris: Gallimard, 1949. Orig. ed., 1945. Essays in this collection particularly relevant to the present study in the order of their appearance in the collection are:
"La République de silence," pp. 11–14 (orig. ed., 1944);
"Paris sous l'occupation," pp. 15–42 (orig. ed., 1945);
"Qu'est-ce qu'un collaborateur?" pp. 43–61 (orig. ed., 1945);
"La Fin de la guerre," pp. 63–71 (orig. ed., 1945).

Schleunes, Karl, *The Twisted Road to Auschwitz*. Urbana: University of Illinois Press, 1970.

Schoenbrun, David, *Soldiers of the Night*. New York: E. P. Dutton, 1980.

Scholl, Inge, *Die weisse Rose*. Frankfurt/Main: Fischer, 1973. Orig. ed., 1953.

Schorske, Carl E., *Fin-de-Siècle Vienna*. New York: Alfred A. Knopf, 1980.

Schwarz-Bart, André, *Le Dernier des justes*. Paris: Seuil, 1959.

Seghers, Anna, *Das siebte Kreuz*. Darmstadt: Luchterhand, 1976. Orig. ed. in English trans., 1942. Orig. German ed., 1943.

Seghers, Pierre, *La Résistance et ses poètes*. Paris: Seghers, 1974.

Semprun, Jorge, *Le Grand Voyage*. Paris: Gallimard, 1972. Orig. ed., 1963.

Shactman, Tom, *The Phony War 1939–1940*. New York: Harper & Row, 1982.

Shirer, William L., *Berlin Diary*. New York: Alfred A. Knopf, 1941.

————, *The Collapse of the Third Republic*. New York: Pocket Books, 1971. Orig. ed., 1969.

————, *The Rise and Fall of the Third Reich*. New York: Simon and Schuster, 1960.

Simon, Claude, *La Route des Flandres*. Paris: Union Générale d'Editions, 1963. Orig. ed., 1960.

Simon, Pierre-Henri, *Portrait d'un officier*. Paris: Seuil, 1971. Orig. ed., 1958.

Sonnenfeld, Albert, "Malraux and the Tyranny of Time." *Romanic Review*, LIV (October 1963), 198–212.

Sontag, Susan, "Fascinating Fascism" in *Under the Sign of Saturn*. New York: Farrar Straus & Giroux, 1980, pp. 78–105. Orig. ed. of this essay, 1974.

Speer, Albert, *Inside the Third Reich*. New York: Macmillan, 1970. Orig. published as *Erinnerungen*. Frankfurt/Main: Ullstein, 1969.

Steiner, Jean-François, *Treblinka*. Helen Weaver, trans., *Treblinka*. New

York: New American Library, 1979. Orig. French ed., 1966.

Thiher, Allen, *Céline: The Novel as Delirium.* New Brunswick, N.J.: Rutgers University Press, 1972.

Thomas, Gordon, and Max Morgan Witts, *Voyage of the Damned.* New York: Stein & Day, 1974.

Tournier, Michel, *Le Roi des aulnes.* Paris: Gallimard, 1975. Orig. ed., 1970.

Triolet, Elsa, *Le Premier Accroc coûte deux cents francs.* Paris: Denoël, 1973. Orig. ed. of the collection excluding the preface, 1945. Included in the order of their appearance in this collection are:
"Préface à la clandestinité," pp. 9–46 (Elsa Triolet copyrighted this preface in her own name in 1965);
"Les Amants d'Avignon," pp. 29–116 (orig. ed., 1943);
"La Vie privée," pp. 117–290;
"Cahiers enterrés sous un pêcher," pp. 291–406;
"Le Premier Accroc cofe deux cents francs," pp. 407–42.

Vailland, Roger, *Drôle de jeu.* Paris: Buchet-Chastel, 1973. Orig. ed., 1945.

————, *Un Jeune Homme seul.* Paris: Buchet-Chastel, 1970. Orig. ed., 1951.

Vercors, "Les Armes de la nuit," in *Les Armes de la nuit* et *La Puissance du jour.* Paris: Albin Michel, 1951, pp. 9–90.

————, "La Marche à l'étoile" in *Les Animaux dénaturés* suivi de *La Marche à l'étoile.* Paris: Albin Michel, 1971. Orig. ed. of the collection, 1952. *La Marche à l'étoile* was first published separately in 1943.

————, *Le Silence de la mer.* Paris: Albin Michel, 1971. Orig. ed. of the collection 1951. Included in the order of their appearance in this collection are:
"Désespoir est mort," pp. 7–20;
"Le Silence de la mer," pp. 21–78 (orig. ed., 1942);
"Ce Jour-là," pp. 79–92;
"Le Songe," pp. 93–112;
"L'Impuissance," pp. 113–130;
"Le Cheval et la mort," pp. 131–40;
"L'Imprimerie de Verdun," pp. 141–82.

Vian, Boris, "L'Equarrissage pour tous" in *Théâtre I.* Paris: Union Générale d'Editions, 1974. Orig. ed. of this play, 1950.

Werfel, Franz, *Jacobowsky und der Oberst.* Frankfurt/Main: Fischer, 1976. Orig. ed., 1944.

Werner, Bruno, *Die Galeere.* Frankfurt/Main: Suhrkamp vorm. S. Fischer Verlag, 1949.

Wiechert, Ernst, *Der Totenwald*. Frankfurt/Main: Ullstein, 1972. Orig. ed., 1946.

Zuckmayer, Carl, *Der Gesang im Feuerofen*. Frankfurt/Main: Fischer, 1960. Orig. ed., 1950.

——, *Des Teufels General*. Frankfurt/Main: Fischer, 1974. Orig. ed., 1946.

Zweig, Stefan, *Die Welt von Gestern*. Frankfurt/Main: Fischer, 1975. Orig. ed. in English trans., 1943. Orig. German ed., 1944.

Available English
Translations
of Selected Works Discussed

Anouilh, Jean, "Antigone" in *Jean Anouilh*. New York: Hill & Wang, 1958. Volume 1. Lewis Galantière, trans.

Böll, Heinrich, *Group Portrait with Lady*. New York: Avon, 1974. Leila Vennewitz, trans.

Brecht, Bertolt, "The Visions of Simone Machard" in *Bertolt Brecht, Collected Plays*. New York: Random House, 1974. Volume 7. Ralph Manheim, trans.

Buchheim, Lothar-Günther, *The Boat*. New York: Alfred A. Knopf, 1975. Denver and Helen Lindley, trans.

Camus, Albert, *The Plague*. New York: Alfred A. Knopf, 1969. Stuart Gilbert, trans.

Céline, Louis-Ferdinand, *Castle to Castle*. New York: Dell, 1968. Ralph Manheim, trans.

———, *North*. New York: Penguin, 1976. Ralph Manheim, trans.

———, *Rigadoon*. New York: Penguin, 1975. Ralph Manheim, trans.

Curtis, Jean-Louis, *The Forests of the Night*. New York: G. P. Putnam's Sons, 1951. Nora Wydenbruck, trans.

Dutourd, Jean, *The Best Butter*. New York: Greenwood Press, 1955. Robin Chancellor, trans.

———, *The Taxis of the Marne*. New York: Simon & Schuster, 1957. Harold King, trans.

Genet, Jean, *Funeral Rites*. New York: Grove, 1970. Bernard Frechtman, trans.

Grass, Günter, *Dog Years*. Greenwich, Conn.: Fawcett, 1965. Ralph Manheim, trans.

———, *The Tin Drum*. New York: Random House, 1964. Ralph Manheim, trans.

Hochhuth, Rolf, *The Deputy*. New York: Grove, 1964. Richard and Clara Winston, trans.

Knef, Hildegard, *The Gift Horse.* New York: Dell, 1972. David Anthony Palastanga, trans.

Malraux André, *Anti-Memoirs.* New York: Holt, Rinehart and Winston, 1968. Terence Kilmartin, trans.

———, *Days of Wrath.* New York: Random House, 1936. Haaken M. Chevalier, trans.

Remarque, Erich Maria, *Spark of Life.* New York: Appleton-Century Crofts, 1952. James Stern, trans.

———, *A Time To Love and a Time To Die.* New York: Harcourt, Brace, 1954. Denver Lindley, trans.

Saint Exupéry, Antoine de, *Flight to Arras.* New York: Harcourt, Brace & World, 1969. Lewis Galantière, trans.

Sajer, Guy, *The Forgotten Soldier.* New York: Harper & Row, 1971. Lily Emmet, trans.

Sartre, Jean-Paul, *Troubled Sleep.* New York: Random House, 1973. Gerald Hopkins, trans.

Schwarz-Bart, André, *The Last of the Just.* New York: Bantam, 1973. Stephen Becker, trans.

Seghers, Anna, *The Seventh Cross.* Boston: Little, Brown, 1942. James A. Galston, trans.

Simon, Claude, *The Flanders Road.* New York: Braziller, 1961. Richard Howard, trans.

Tournier, Michel, *The Ogre.* Garden City, N.Y.: Doubleday, 1972. Barbara Bray, trans.

Werfel, Franz, *Jacobowsky and the Colonel.* New York: The Viking Press, 1944. Gustave O. Arlt, trans.

Zweig, Stefan, *The World of Yesterday.* New York: The Viking Press, 1943. E. and C. Paul, trans.

Index